BEST OF RAMPSTYLE | BY MICHAEL KÖCKRITZ

men's style manual

a ramp book

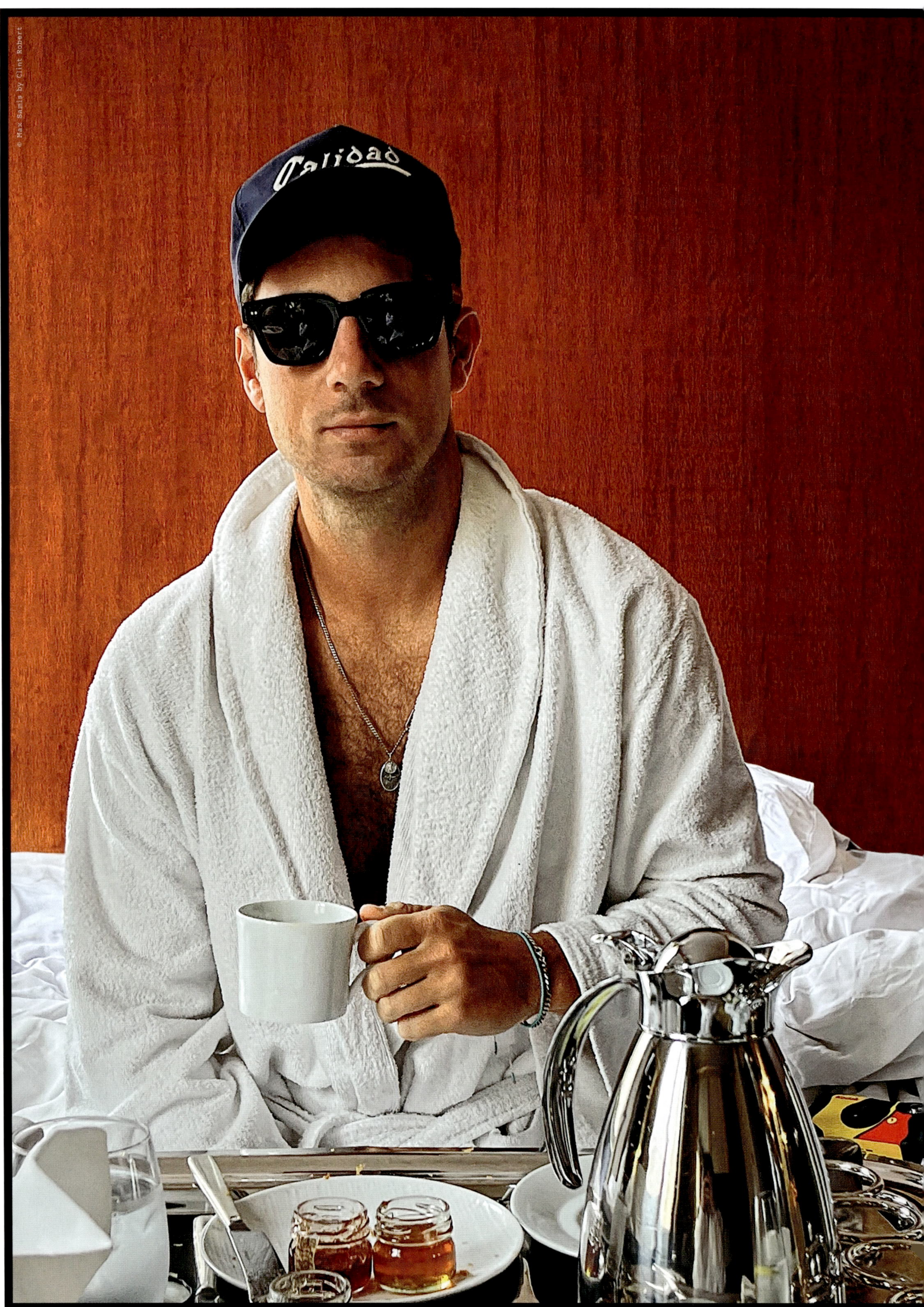
Calidad

preface

So you've bought this book. Or someone gave it to you. Or you borrowed it. Either way, here it is, right in front of you. A good start.

Even better if you approach it as something to enjoy at your own pace – a book you pick up again and again, leaf through, dip into. A book to live with. No big plan. Something that will leave you entertained and feeling pleasantly surprised. Again and again.

That, in turn, was our plan.

Surprise, after all, is what it's all about.

English has the perfect term for it: serendipity. The happy, unexpected discovery of something valuable, meaningful or simply surprising – something you weren't really expecting or actively searching for. That coincidental coming together of chance, attention and openness. A moment when the unforeseen suddenly makes sense, or at least delights and inspires.

And so here it is: *Men's Style Manual No. 2*. Once again the very best of *rampstyle*. A fresh, up-to-date collage of topics, stories and things for men who don't need anything explained to them. For real men, wild guys and cool boys. Remixed with pleasure and newly expanded. Easy-going, playful, in good spirits, not always politically correct, but always bold and intense, adventurous and, yes, delightfully surprising. Exactly how we like to imagine a charismatic man.

Rough edges included.

Simply masculine.

Yours,

Michael Köckritz,
Publisher & Editor-in-Chief

contents

water melon sugar 1

crack another egg on it 2

3 the cool elegance of freedom

4 play it as it was

contributors

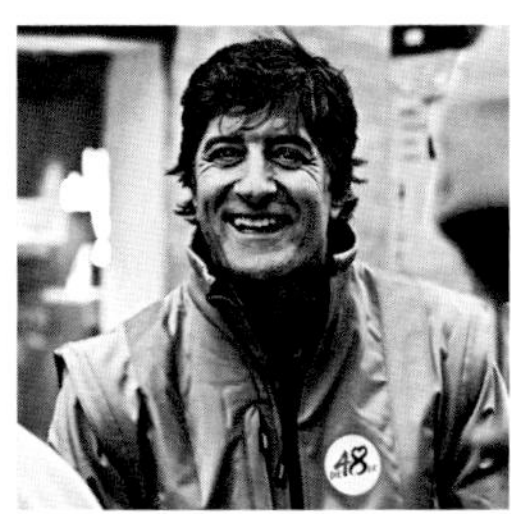

KURT MOLZER

AUTHOR

In his former life as a journalist, the Vienna native once drove a Ferrari 575 Modificata Maranello from Munich to Hamburg - in, allegedly, three hours and fourteen minutes. What we're saying is: this is exactly the right person to tell the story of the Ferrari 355.

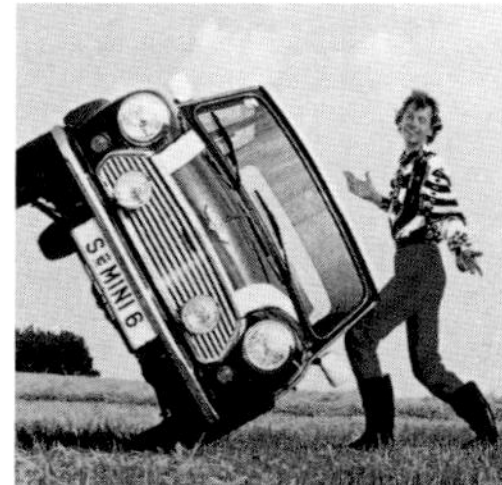

DAVID STARETZ

AUTHOR

When you've got nothing left to prove, what do you do? You get together with like-minded souls. In David Staretz's case, those happened to be a Porsche 911 Turbo S and a Lamborghini Gallardo LP560-4.

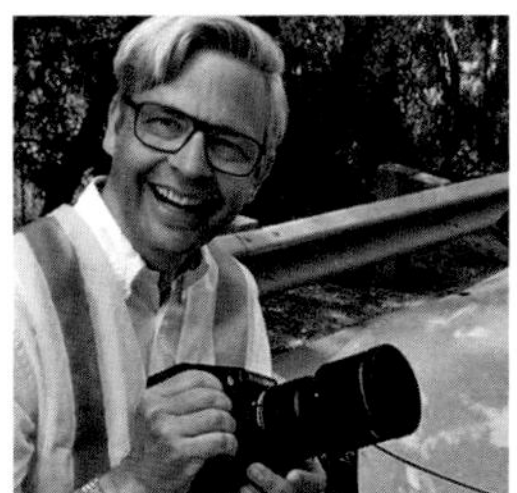

STEFFEN JAHN

PHOTOGRAPHER

We don't break with tradition - especially not with ones that produce such beautiful results as Steffen Jahn's watch features. So once again, our advice: take a moment, stop time, and enjoy the photos.

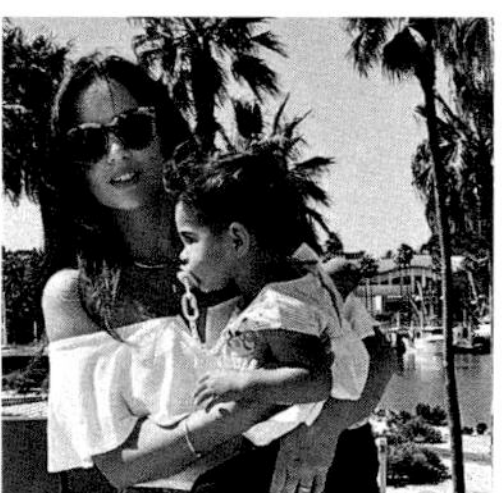

ANTONIETTA PROCOPIO

ART BUYER & PICTURE EDITOR

Her network stretches from Cape Town to Oslo and from Tokyo to Los Angeles, where she lived for several years. Since becoming the mother of two adorable children, there's not a single creative mood swing on set that can throw her off balance anymore.

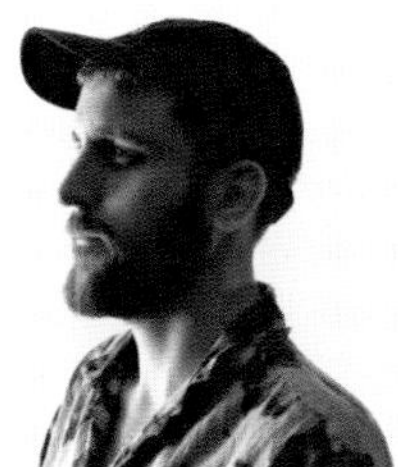

PHILIPP GENTNER

DEPUTY CREATIVE DIRECTOR

Watching him work, you might be reminded of a concert pianist: sometimes virtuoso, always finely attuned to harmony and rhythm. Which makes sense, since music quite literally runs in his veins.

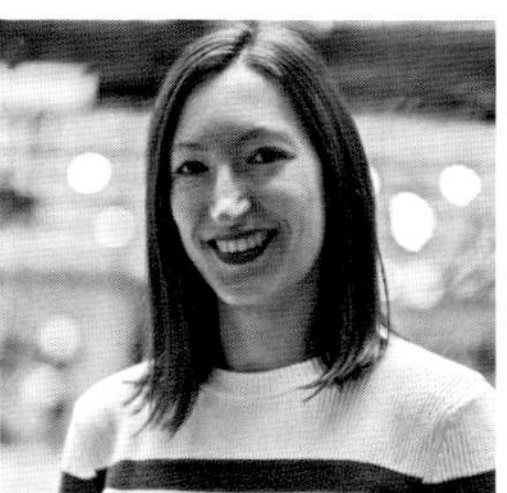

JULIA KAMM

PROJECT MANAGER

Okay, so the book says *Men's Style* on the cover. And yes, plenty of guys did work on this publication. But without Julia's oversight and persistence, those guys would probably still be arguing about who's got the best style instead of getting down to work.

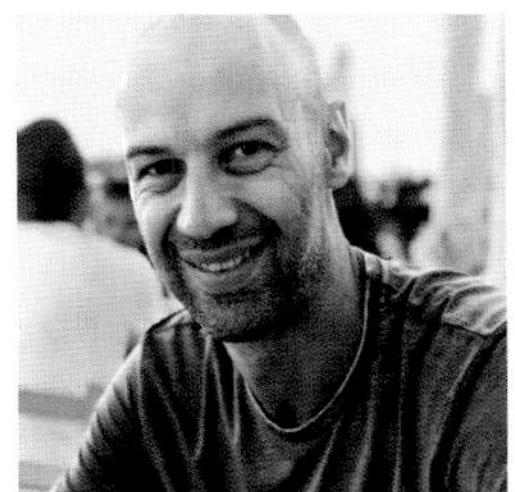

MARTIN TROCKNER

AUTHOR

Life in Berlin in the late 2000s taught our author one thing: that he's much happier in his hometown of Munich. Which doesn't stop him from writing for us about anywhere in the world – and, when necessary, even travelling through time. As he did for his story on the cruiser scene along L.A.'s Van Nuys Boulevard in the 1970s.

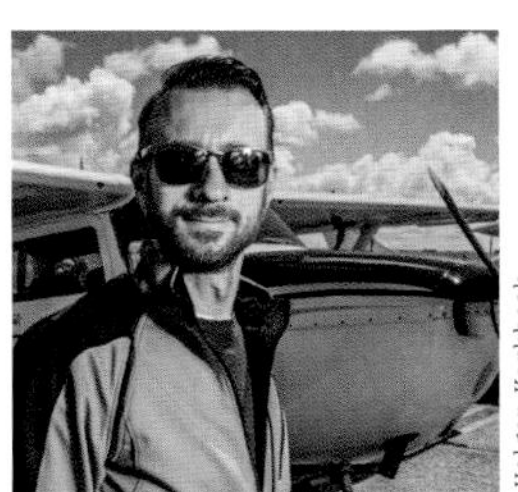

© Holger Karkheck

MARIO PUKSEC

MANAGING EDITOR

Men's Style, part two: naturally, for a book with that title, you need someone with petrol in his veins. The Hamburg native certainly fits the bill – and knows just how to light a fire under the team, in the most collegial way possible, of course.

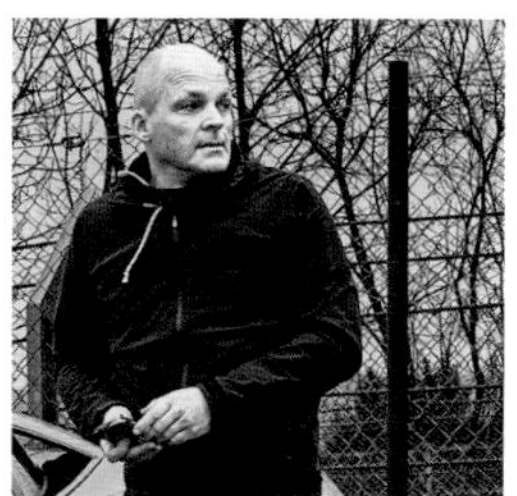

LUTZ FÜGENER

AUTHOR

As a professor of Advanced Mobility Design at Hof University of Applied Sciences, he sometimes explores the future of mobility by pondering the point of rain dances. Sounds absurd? Read for yourself.

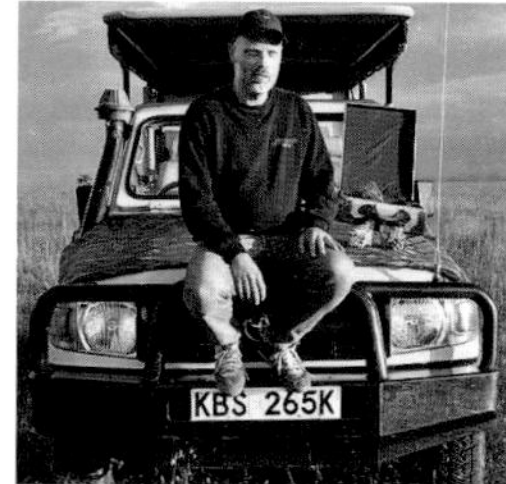

ULF LIPPITZ

AUTHOR

If anyone can capture both disappointment and admiration in a single text about Giorgio Armani, it's our Berlin-based author.

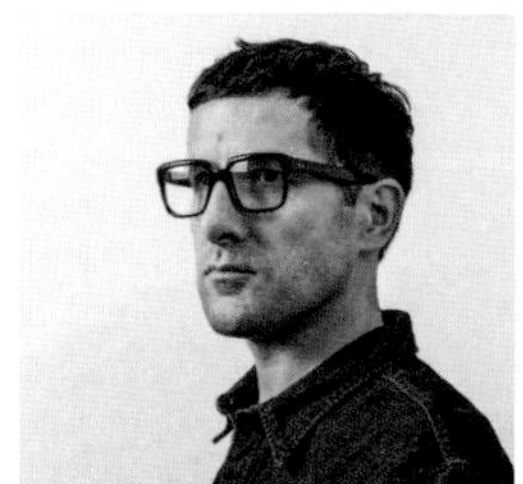

GREGORY GILBERT-LODGE

ILLUSTRATOR

Should the award-winning illustrator ever lose touch with the ground, a single episode of *The Jetsons* or *The Flintstones* will bring him right back down. Not that we'd mind if he stayed above it all - as long as his linework remains as inspired as in the illustrations accompanying Philipp Tingler's essays.

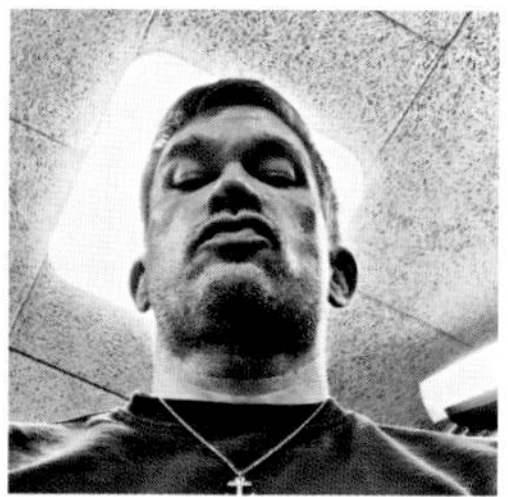

PHILIPP TINGLER

AUTHOR

Our man for detail - for nuance and the hidden logic of society. For instance, when it comes to the joy of doing nothing in particular - and why we need that joy now more than ever. Not just on Sundays.

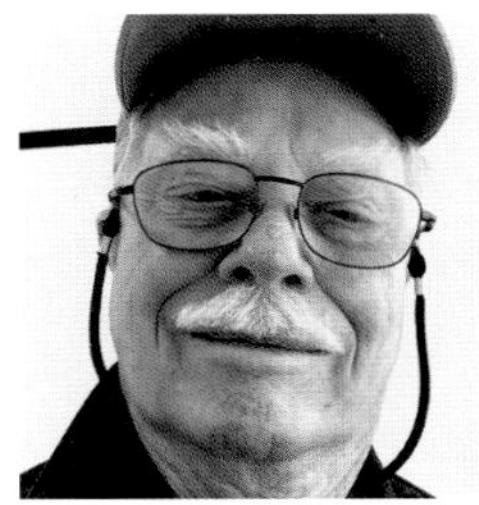

RICK MCCLOSKEY

PHOTOGRAPHER

When he set out in 1972, fresh out of college, to document the cruising scene on Van Nuys Boulevard in Los Angeles, he could not have known it would soon vanish forever. That his photos became a time capsule of the American dream on four wheels is hardly surprising – he grew up just a few blocks away from where it all happened.

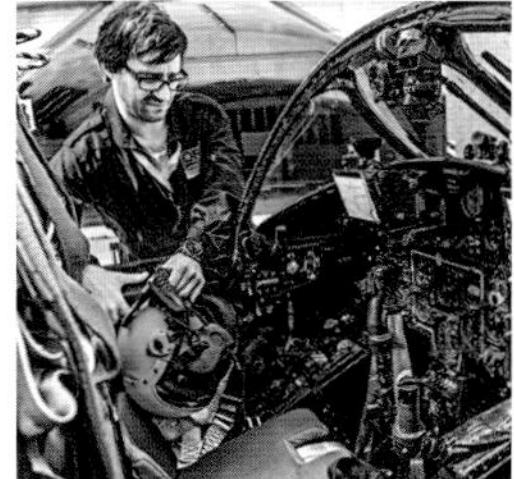

MATTHIAS MEDERER

PHOTOGRAPHER & AUTHOR

A rare double talent. Trained as a journalist, he's built a reputation as an automotive and reportage photographer – and as a gifted storyteller. No wonder that his writing, too, is rich in imagery.

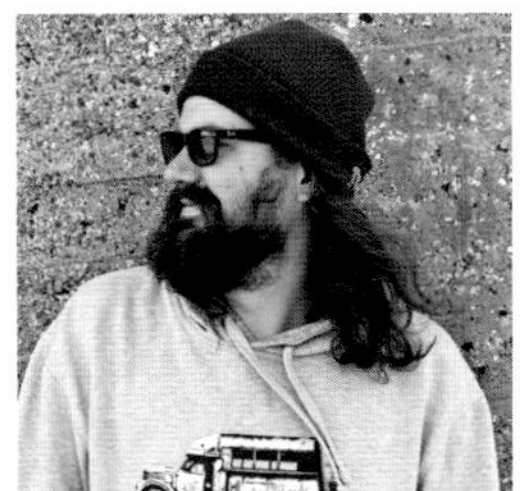

MICHAEL NEHRMANN

PHOTOGRAPHER

There are few things our Hamburg-based photographer loves more than travelling, though this time he didn't have to go quite so far. Our story took him to visit Luciano Favaron, who works on Ferraris (among other brands) right in his own hometown.

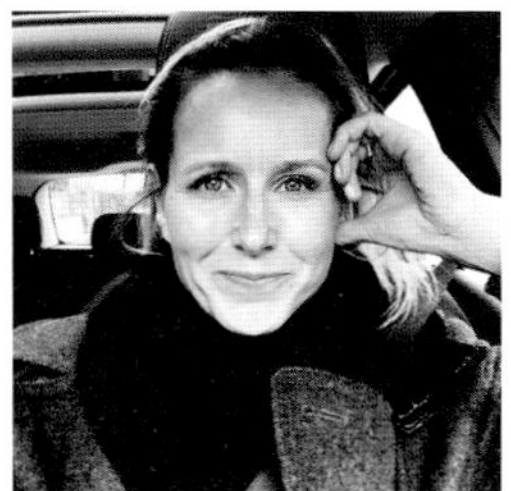

WIEBKE BRAUER

CHIEF COPY EDITOR

The Hamburg native not only ensures every word lands in the right place, she can also explain beautifully why black is never just black – here with the words of Yohji Yamamoto.

water 1 melon sugar

In June 1966 the crew members of Apollo 1, NASA's first manned mission of the Apollo program, practiced water egress procedures in a swimming pool at Ellington Air Force Base in Houston. The following January, Edward White, Roger Chaffee and Virgil "Gus" Grissom were killed during a launch simulation.

In a speech a few years earlier, Grissom had said: "We are in a risky business, and we hope that if anything happens to us, it will not delay the program. The conquest of space is worth the risk of life."

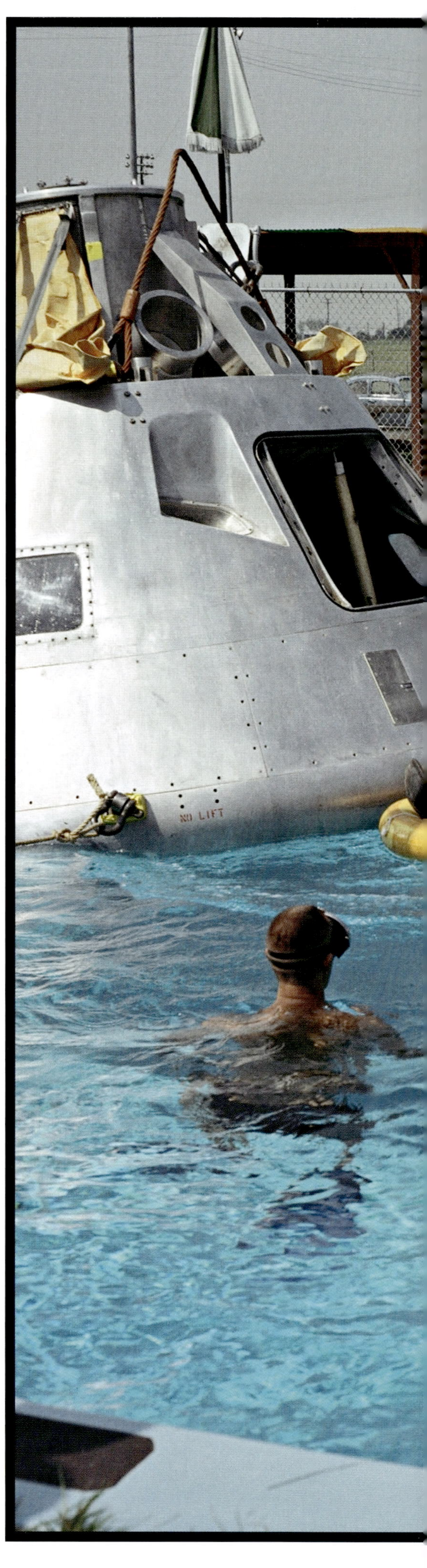

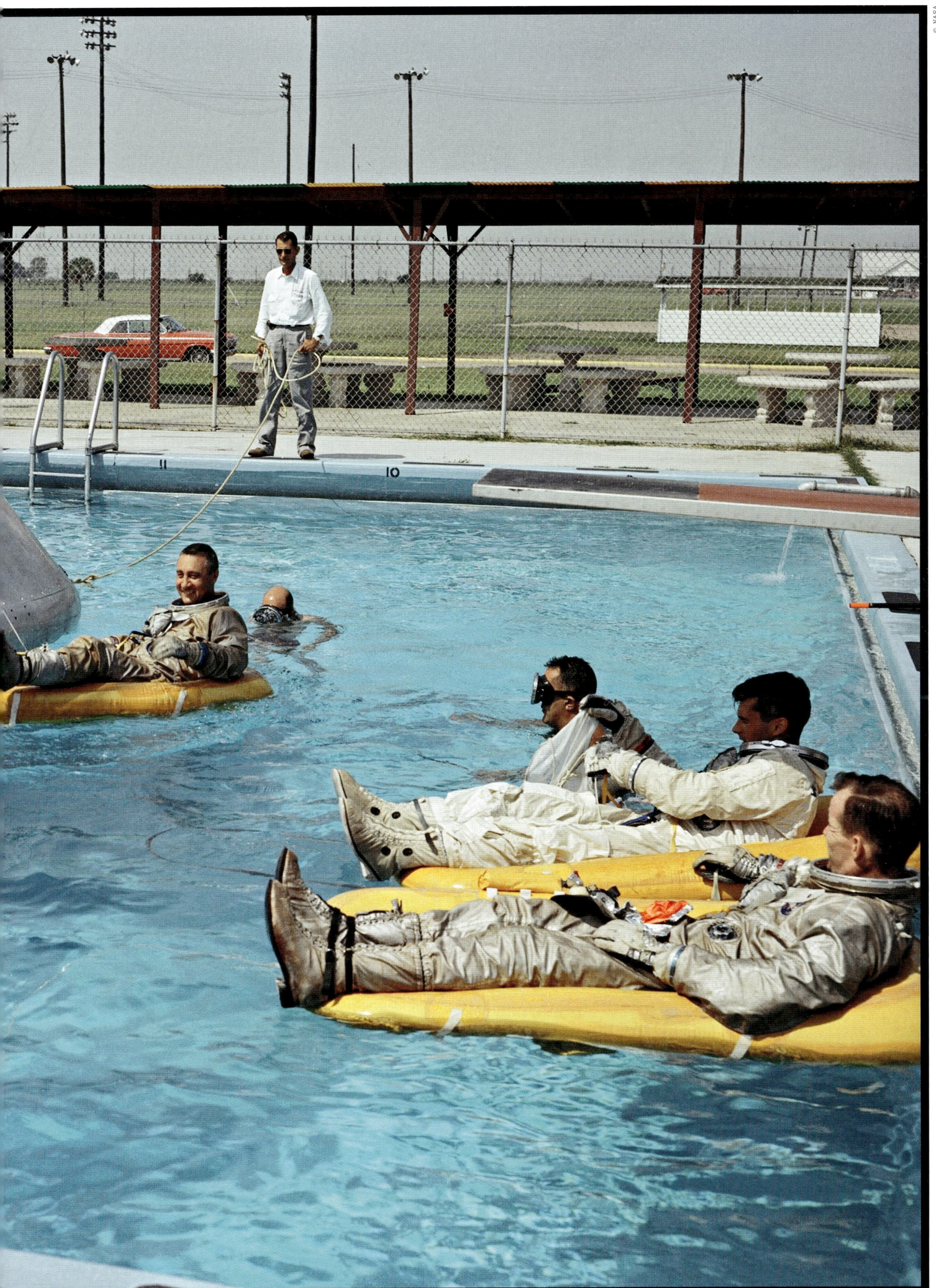
11
10

cool stuff

1.01

TEXT *Wiebke Brauer / Martin Trockner*

ROCKY SPEAKS

"The world ain't all sunshine and rainbows. It's a very mean and nasty place and I don't care how tough you are it will beat you to your knees and keep you there permanently if you let it. You, me, or nobody is gonna hit as hard as life. But it ain't about how hard ya hit. It's about how hard you can get it and keep moving forward."

→ desede.ch

INCENTIVE

File under *Women who stand their ground*: “Riding a bike around the world was probably an extreme reaction to heartbreak,” architect Elspeth Beard said about her 1982 trip on a BMW R60/6. If that has piqued your interest, you should read her memoir, *Lone Rider: The First British Woman to Motorcycle Around the World* – and order the matching helmet and goggles from the collaboration between Brett and Hedon.

→ brett-eyewear.com

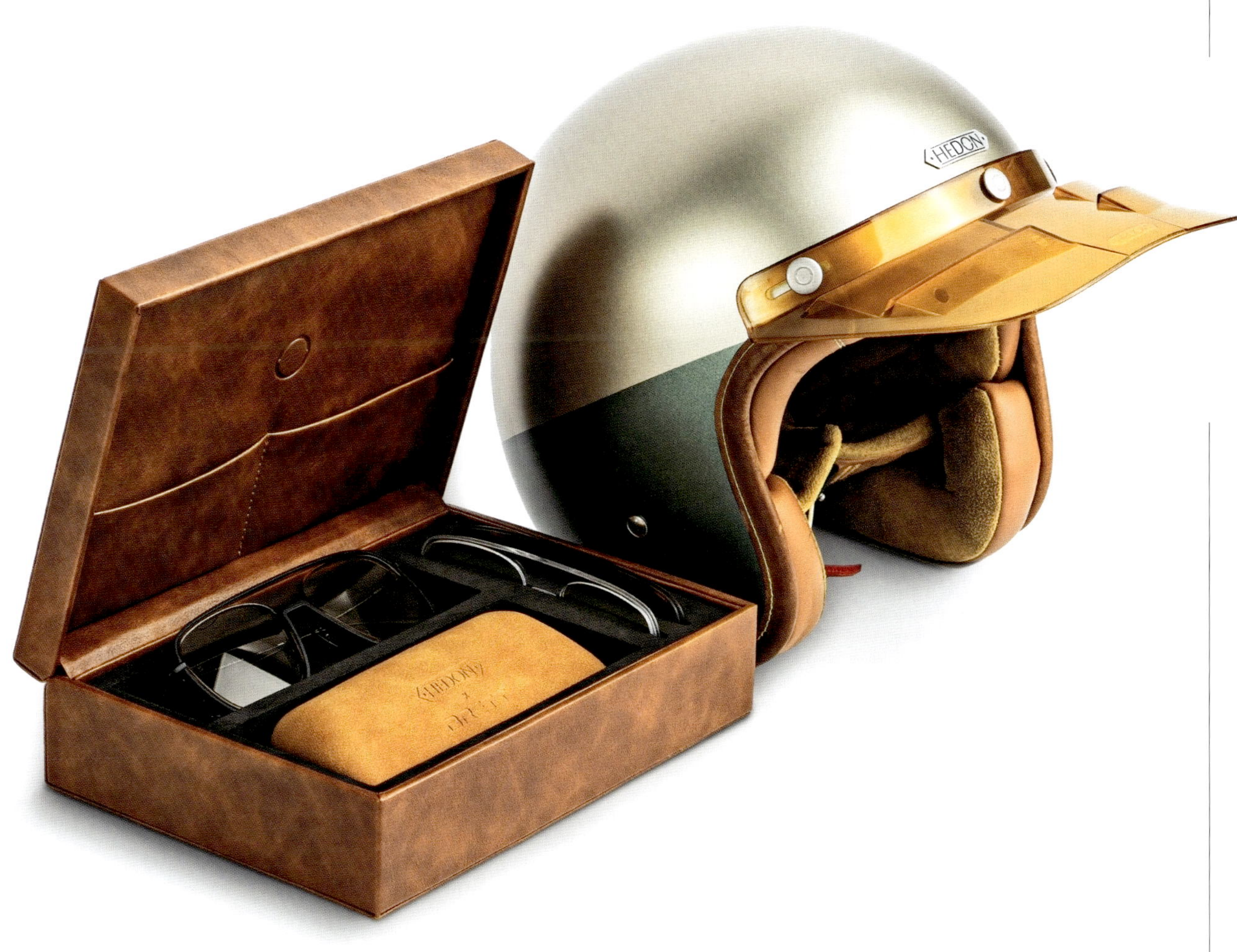

RECORD-BREAKING

First the bad news: production of the 2021 KTM RC 8C track bike was limited to just 100 units; and as a racetrack-only model, it's obviously not street legal. But now the good news: it set a new speed record. Precisely four minutes and thirty-two seconds is all it took for buyers to snatch up every single one of the one hundred bikes in the series. And even more good news: revised versions were released in 2023 and 2024 - again in strictly limited quantities. Which means that a sequel is not out of the question.

→ ktm.com

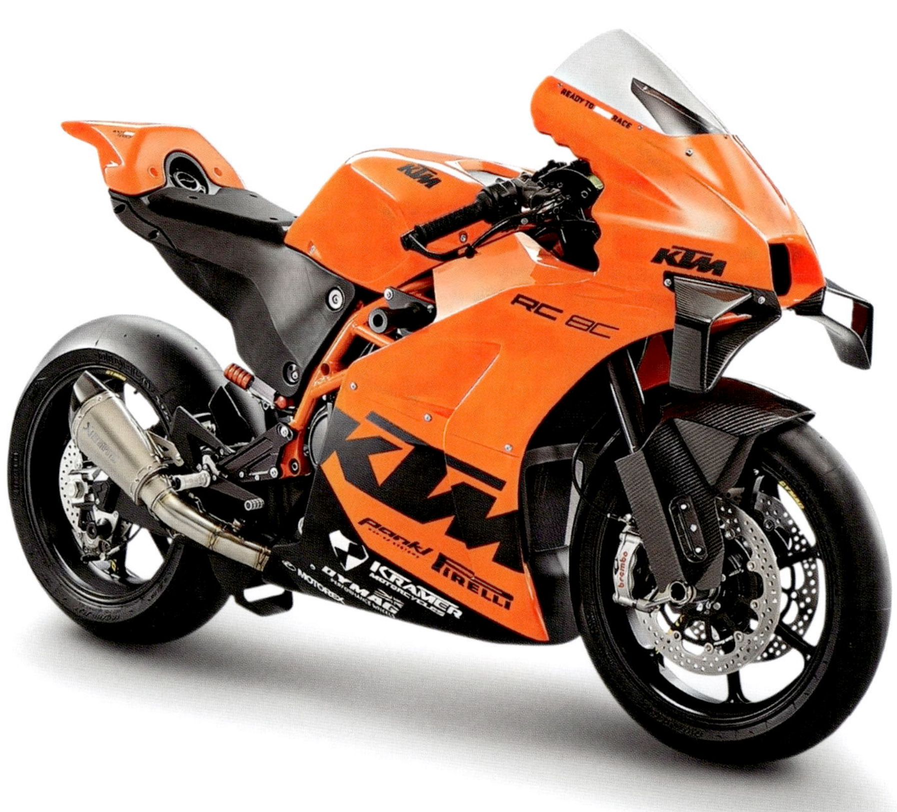

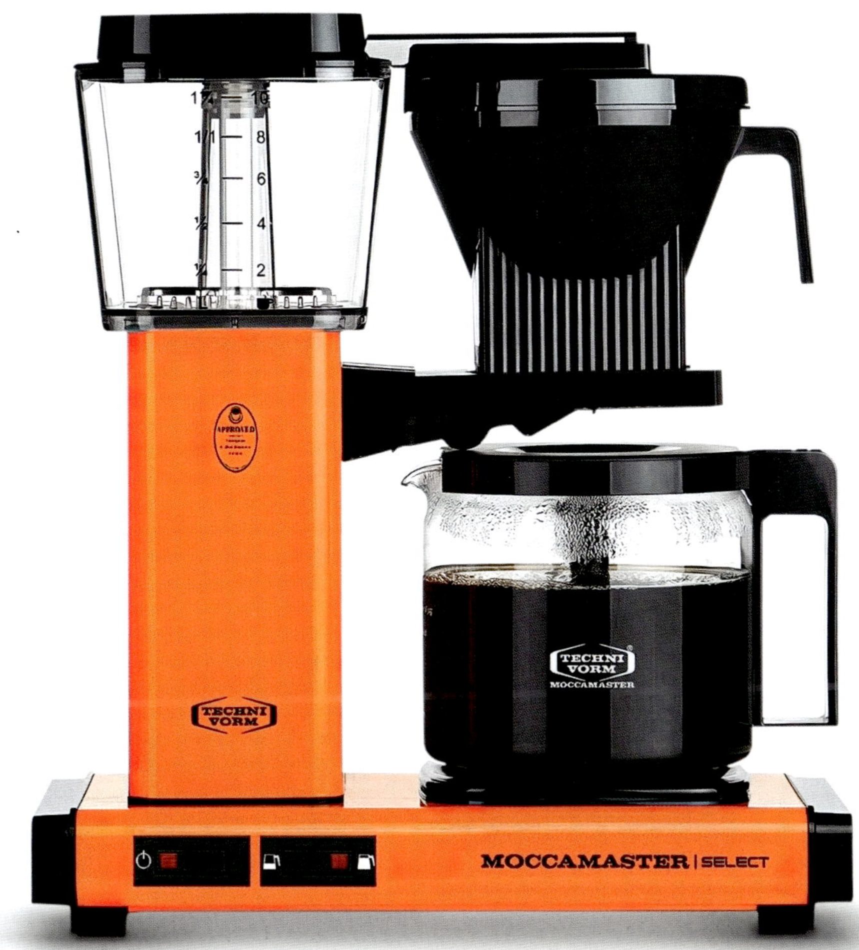

THE BEST PART OF WAKING UP

The filter coffee machines from Moccamaster have been handmade in the Netherlands since 1968. And the design classic you see here can be almost fully disassembled so you can replace any defective parts yourself. But let's talk about the coffee. The water from the tank is heated to around 93 °C and rains down, like a hot shower, over the coffee grounds for a truly excellent flavor experience.

→ moccamaster.com

SURFIN' U.S.A.

If the term "Surfing Cowboys" has got you scratching your head - we didn't make it up: there's been a store with that name in California since 1995, currently located in Malibu. Among other things, they sell vintage boards like the one that had previously belonged to David Nuuhiwa. The Hawaiian surfer was one of the first real stars on the waves. The board, by the way, dates back to around 1970.

→ surfingcowboys.com

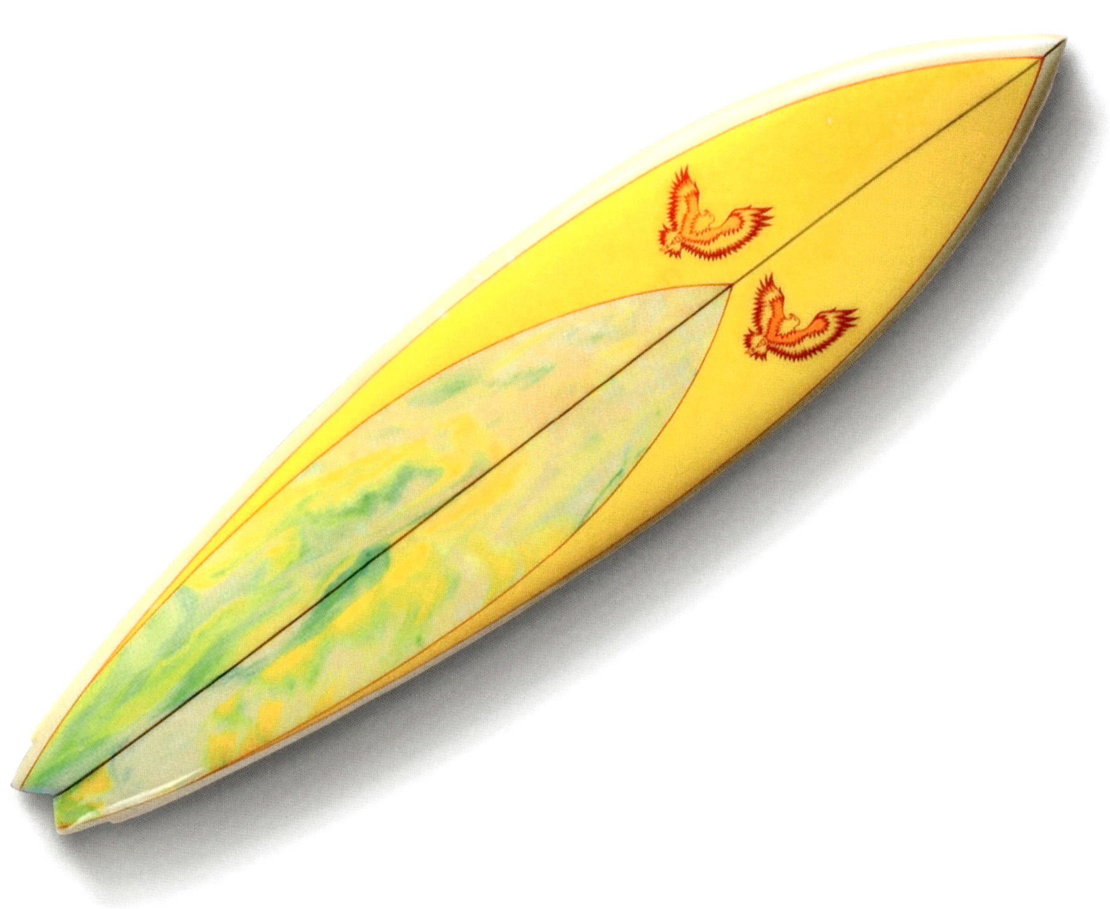

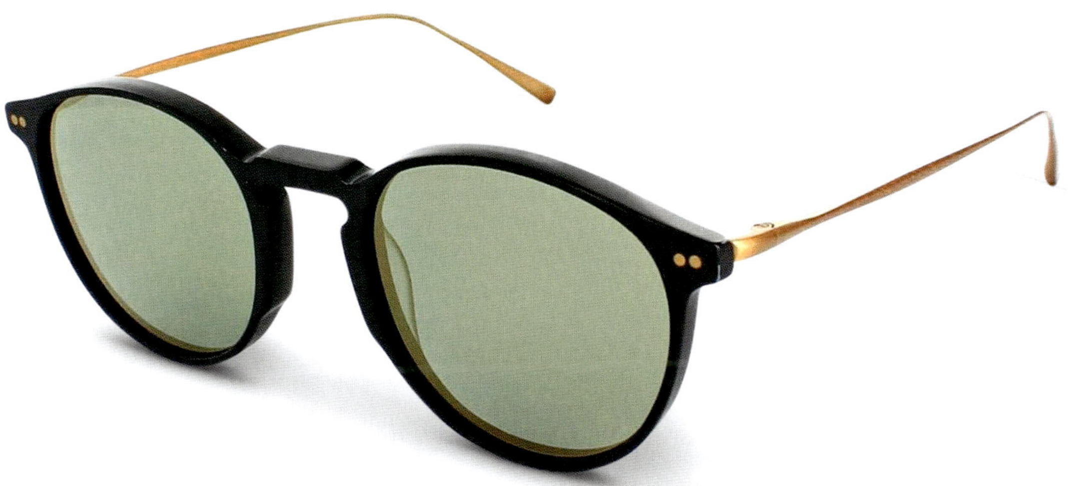

BLACK HOLE SUN

We would like to take a moment to remember Stephen Hawking – because the world is not the same without him. And because of his humor. He once said: “I can’t disguise myself with a wig and dark glasses – the wheelchair gives me away.” Still, we think the Miles Sun model from Brett would definitely have looked good on him.

→ brett-eyewear.com

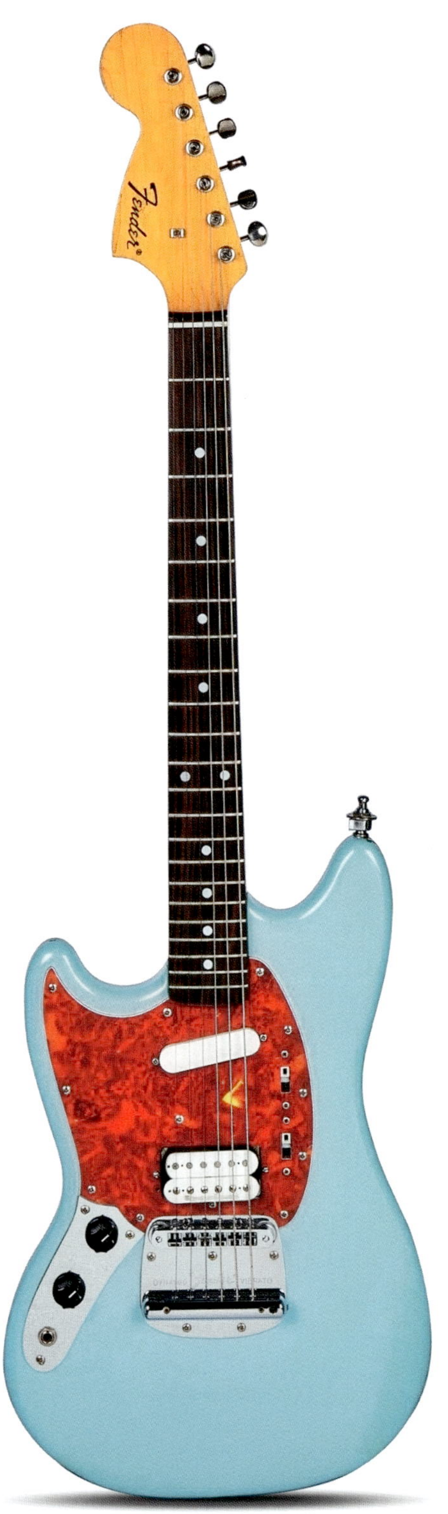

NEVERMIND

According to Nirvana frontman Kurt Cobain, music gets commercial the moment you go out onto the street with your guitar and you want people to listen to you. He'd probably still find it amusing that his Fender Mustang Skystang I, which he played on Nirvana's *In Utero* arena tour, sold for $1,587,500 at an auction in November 2023.

→ julienslive.com

FRIENDLY REMINDER

This friendly-looking Bluetooth speaker remembers everything it's heard for the past two hours. That could be a radio broadcast of a hard rock classic, for example, which the OB-4 could then theoretically play over and over again at full volume for eight hours. Cool!

→ teenage.engineering

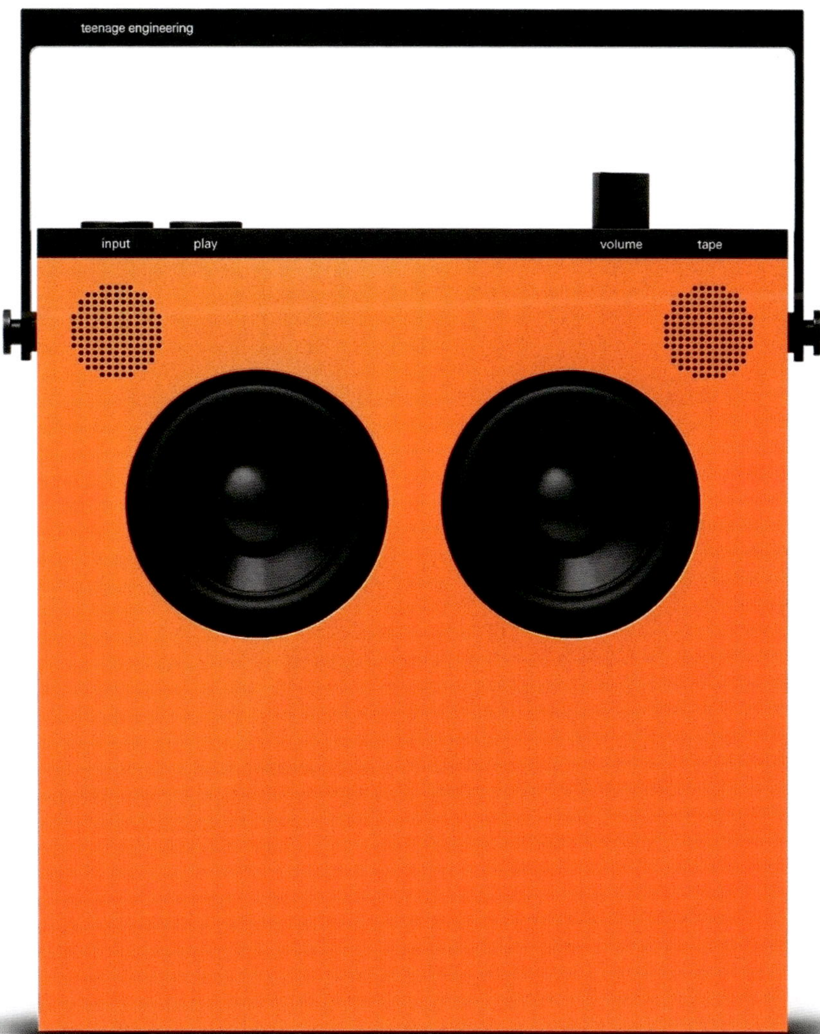

future to go

1.02

THE WORLD WANTS TO REINVENT ITSELF.

FOR THE FUTURE AND IN GENERAL. OVER AND OVER AGAIN. BECAUSE NEW IS THE BETTER DIFFERENT ANYWAY.

OR SO YOU MIGHT THINK.

COME WALK WITH US AS WE EXPLORE THE MATTER A BIT FURTHER . . .

TEXT *Michael Köckritz*

Reinvention is one of those things. Just because something has been reinvented, it doesn't mean that it will work right away or that it will keep on working in the long run. There's also no guarantee that the thing is truly new or forward-looking in the most innovative sense. The next good question to ask is just how recognizable and plannable such a future actually wants to be.

So what now?

Let's see who has a plan and where some suggestions might be lurking.

*

In retrospect, the third of July 1886 was not a good day for the horse-drawn carriage industry. In fact, it was a pretty bad day for them, and all because the engineer Carl Benz went proudly rattling through Mannheim that day with his Benz Patent-Motorwagen, officially introducing the internal combustion automobile to the world – and with this revolutionary technology ushering in the imminent demise of their entire industry. But that's just how it goes with ideas that change the world.

"Disruption" is the technical term for such game-changing inventions that displace or even pulverize established, traditional business models, products, technologies or services, and it's no wonder that the start-up scene in particular has elevated this term to a buzzword that they happily exhale any time they can. With a fundamental prospect of success. Because disruption is not just a concept, but a principle. Every business idea and every service provider, no matter how successful, sees such disruptions as a threat to their very existence, especially if they are focused more on their customers' current instead of future needs. It is virtually impossible for established companies to change their business model so easily from the ground up. Start-ups are more flexible. They have little to lose and much to gain, as Harvard professor Clayton Christensen, who developed the theory of disruptive innovation in 1997, explains. Moreover, new markets usually emerge unexpectedly for established companies. Due to their initially small volume and limited customer segment, emerging markets are not very appealing to them. This makes disruption the "innovator's dilemma".

"Disruption" is the technical term for such game-changing inventions that displace or even pulverize established, traditional business models, products, technologies or services.

The options and excitation patterns of the digital age in an already overexcited and overagitated world, the pressing necessities that demand an awareness for limited resources and systematic sustainability thinking, plus a succession of disruptive start-up eruptions – everything may, will, must reinvent itself right now and without delay. For a future that no one knows, except perhaps a number of experts who don't even know that they are experts for the future – which is a good thing, because the moment they think they are experts or want to be experts, they will very likely end up splendidly off the mark with their forecasts, which may, when expressed in such pointed terms, sound a bit confusing now but can be summed up quite simply in one statement: when it comes to the future, today's experts are, unfortunately, not very accurate.

"The average expert is roughly as accurate with his predictions as a dart-throwing chimpanzee," is how psychologist and forecasting researcher Philip Tetlock summed it up a few years ago. In a long-term study conducted over twenty years, Tetlock had tracked and evaluated more than 80,000 forecasts from 284 analysts from television, government agencies and institutions. Tetlock also provides an explanation for this sobering conclusion: experts, who tend to have a fairly strong ego, usually rely on knowledge in areas of their own expertise and on the explanatory patterns they have learned over the years. Now couple that with a receptive audience that loves to hear confidently presented, simple truths. Everyone loves certainty, after all. These experts rarely have to be measured against reality. Incidentally, experts whose reputation is at stake are particularly prone to overestimating themselves.

Superforecasters are curious and open-minded, willing to learn and creative, they aggregate information from a variety of different sources.

But Tetlock also proposed a solution. Working together with the U.S. intelligence community, he spent more than four years investigating how to improve predictions of political and economic developments. The first results are contained in his book *Superforecasting: The Art and Science of Prediction*, which Tetlock co-wrote with journalist Dan Gardner. Tetlock researched more than 28,000 forecasts on current world events, made by people as diverse as a retired computer programmer from California, a military historian from New York and a secretary from Alaska. He then calculated the accuracy of each forecaster and discovered that some of them were actually significantly better than others at predicting the future. How come?

The authors argue that the main contributor to the forecasting success of these "superforecasters" is not their (usually somewhat higher) intelligence or that they possess some special prior knowledge, but the fact that they think and work in a way that anyone can adopt and train. Superforecasters are curious and open-minded, willing to learn and creative, they aggregate information from a variety of different sources. They like to read books and prefer quality news outlets, are modest, work well in teams and are willing to question their own views and correct them based on new findings. "For superforecasters, beliefs are hypotheses to be tested, not treasures to be guarded."

Unfortunately, even superforecasters are not immune to the black swan phenomenon. The black swan theory, developed by risk analyst Nassim Nicholas Taleb, refers to unexpected events whose occurrence had been considered impossible. For a long time, people were certain that there was no such thing as a black swan – until some specimens were actually discovered in Australia. In a highly regarded essay published in German newspaper *Frankfurter Allgemeine Zeitung* a few years ago, Nikolaus von Bomhard, the CEO of Munich Reinsurance Company, observed a "fatal readiness to be surprised" in both politics and business. His argument: the supposed unpredictability of events is often used as an excuse for a lack of risk management. Management deficits are justified by force majeure, bad luck or fate. Bomhard argues that the aim should not be to not take risks, but to take them with awareness. "If you are prepared for what is essentially predictable, you have your hands free for what is truly unpredictable." So when you realize that the car that had once

Innovation and progress with-out creativity? Unthinkable. But creativity doesn't just mean invent-ing something, discovering some-thing or designing something new.

been derided as a black swan might now have become a fat Christmas goose for hungry disruptors, you're already navigating the journey a little more mindfully than before.

Speaking of books and literature and black swans: if you're interested in getting to the bottom of what is basically predictable, you should talk to Thomas Le Blanc from the Phantastische Bibliothek Wetzlar, one of the largest public libraries for fantasy literature and utopian novels worldwide. In the past, the Phantastische Bibliothek served mainly as a reference library for students conducting research for their academic papers. Recently, however, more and more banks and insurance firms, energy and communications companies, and automobile and chemical corporations have been clamoring for literary experts to evaluate and assess for them the possible future scenarios that can be gleaned from science fiction novels and films. "We don't make futurological predictions," says Le Blanc, "we show possibilities."

The trend of having literary experts prepare you for the future comes from the U.S. Authors and creative people are increasingly being asked to help companies spark their imaginations. A few years ago, Microsoft invited a group of award-winning sci-fi writers and a comic artist to its research lab. The idea was to see how the company's current innovations would inspire the authors in their writing. They were given almost complete freedom, with access to more than fifty-five research areas, and were allowed to talk to the researchers. The result was an anthology of short stories called *Future Visions: Original Science Fiction Inspired by Microsoft* (Melcher Media, 2015). The critics were impressed.

Creativity is another buzzword. Innovation and progress without creativity? Unthinkable. But creativity doesn't just mean inventing something, discovering something or designing something new. That is actually rarely the case. Creativity thrives above all on being able to open oneself up with both curiosity and an open mind, to see things differently, fresh, in a new way, to connect these things in new contexts and so open up a different dimension for them.

The ability to change one's point of view, to think outside the box. Then, as Paul Klee once so imaginatively realized, a line suddenly becomes a dot that went for a walk.

But how do you come up with an idea like that? And how do we actually arrive at new ideas, thoughts and solutions? How do we see things in a new way? Where do new things come from?

After all, the future is open precisely because not everything is possible all the time. Instead, new things always emerge from whatever happens to be at the moment. We need to be inspired, eager, open to what is possible, seeing all that is already there. And it is completely irrelevant if the possible becomes possible through mere coincidence or as the result of a historically evolved idea. Innovations and novelties develop from the interaction of man and the environment, from the combination of self-creation and inspiration. All you have to do is to creatively mix together what you have available, anticipate coincidence, and trust in the art of combination and improvisation. Mindful action, not mindless activism. As in improv theater, what counts is the willingness to take up opportunities and ideas thrown at you by the other participants on the stage or from the audience and to perform them at the right moment. The ability to anticipate, the instinct for good timing. Along with intuition, it's the moment that matters.

If you love surprises, you've got an advantage. What makes our lives and our world so exciting and vibrant are precisely those things and experiences that we didn't expect. Like a gift that the person who receives knows nothing about. Our life and our world as a wonderful surprise present. That's a beautiful way of looking at it. Above all, it is a fantastic attitude. We know who we are and what is important to us. So bring it on. Come what may, we are looking forward to it.

Or we think of it ourselves. Then it's our turn to surprise.

With an attitude like that, unforeseen events and situations suddenly become ingenious possibilities. In special moments, we may even experience a eureka effect. These moments not only make us suddenly alert and attentive, but also positively impact our mood and stimulate our thinking. Psychologists call this "high processing fluency". We're in flow. With the nice side effect that a person who experiences a sudden insight intuitively evaluates the correctness of the solution with a higher degree of accuracy. So inspiration and flashes of insight are usually not only surprising, but also surprisingly accurate. What's more, they're fun. Brilliant!

Of course, it's not as if flashes of inspiration simply shoot merrily and wildly about the place. In truth, they don't come as sudden flashes, but rather are the result of prolonged engagement with a task or problem. Surprising moments act as the catalyst. They cause "happy accidents".

Creativity at the push of a button? Difficult. We have the economic theorist Joseph Schumpeter to thank for the notion that creativity, usually referred to as innovation in the business world, is rarely economically motivated or that it can be called up on demand. It is the joy of creating that drives us. If you believe that your ideas can make the world a better place, then you will also work harder than someone who only wants to be better placed in the ego and profit rankings. The right environment and atmosphere, a positive outlook and a sense of humor also contribute to accelerating this process.

When you realize that the car that had once been derided as a black swan might now have become a fat Christmas goose for hungry disruptors, you're already navigating the journey a little more mindfully than before.

For good reason, therefore, wise CEOs make sure to recruit not only intelligent and well-educated employees, but also those with soft skill creativity. How about a quota for art school graduates to complement the business admin staff? In the U.S. this has already become a successful trend.

In 2016 the exhibition *Human Factor – endless prototyping* curated by Ars Electronica Linz at DRIVE Volkswagen Group Forum in Berlin showed just how inspiring the interface between art, society and industry can be. The event focused on prototype artworks from around the world that address central questions and challenges of the digital age and reflect on the human factor in its increasingly technologized environment. With their works, artists collaborating with engineers and scientists presented their strategies for confronting the uncertainties and imponderables of our contemporary world. All concepts and projects that are not yet finished, not yet matured, not yet tested. Their outcome or progress? Uncertain. The smallest common denominator? The human factor. Trial and error – and man in the middle of it all, in this case sensitized to a possible way of dealing with the merry unpredictability of an increasingly technologized world and the realization: if you can confidently improvise, you're clearly at an advantage.

Martin Honzik, artist, curator of the *Human Factor* exhibition and one of the defining personalities behind Ars Electronica Linz, once said, "The world doesn't function because it is perfect, but because it is not."

And that's a good thing.

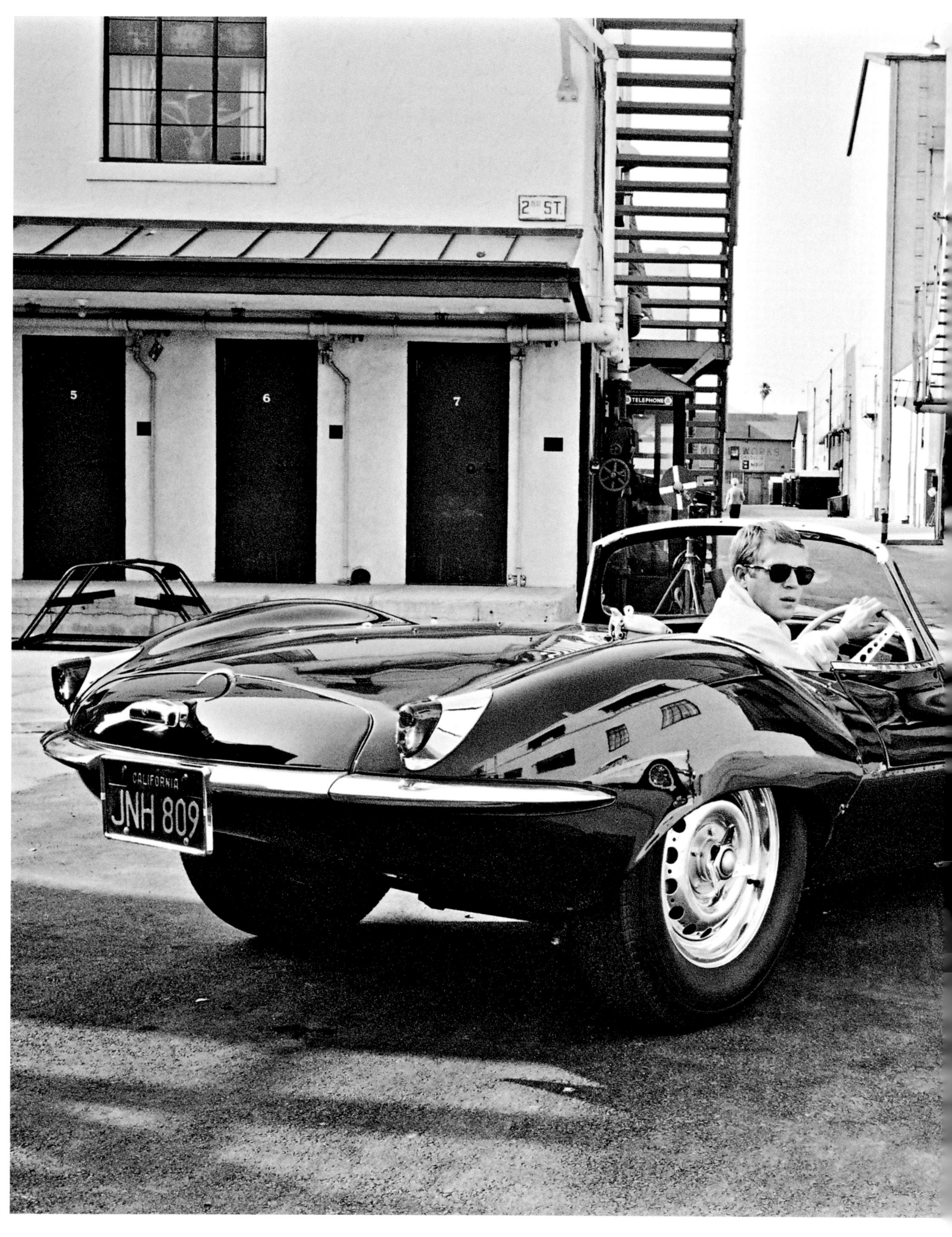
2ND ST.
5
6
7
TELEPHONE
CALIFORNIA
JNH 809

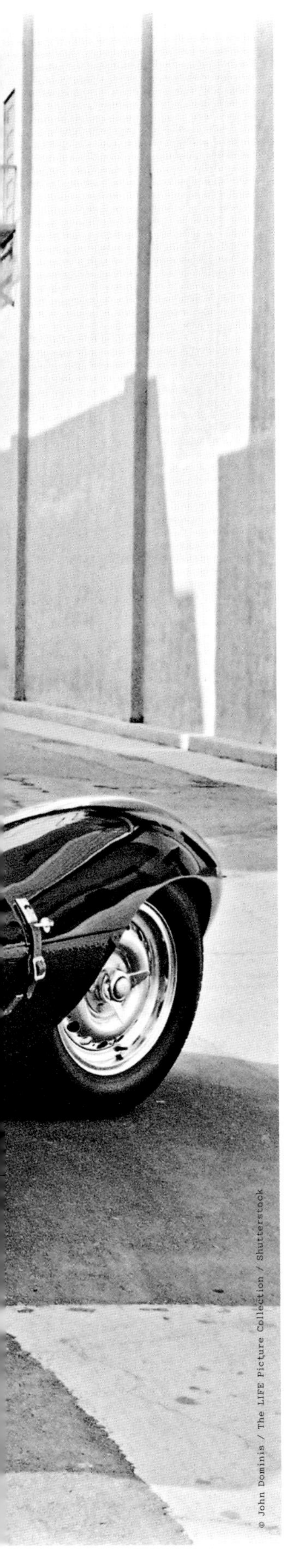

IN THE SIXTIES, STEVE MCQUEEN WAS THE COOLEST ACTOR IN HOLLYWOOD.

TODAY, HE IS CONSIDERED THE COOLEST PERSON IN THE WHOLE WORLD.

IF NOT THE UNIVERSE.

BUT THAT'S THE WAY IT GOES WHEN A MAN'S PERSONALITY, SOME INTERESTING STORIES AND LOTS OF GREAT IMAGES COME TOGETHER TO FORM AN IDEAL OF COOL THAT IS AS AUTHENTIC AS IT IS ICONIC AND ABSTRACT.

TEXT *Michael Köckritz*

king of cool

1.03

Steve McQueen was an actor, racing driver, style icon and the biggest movie star of his generation. A charismatic darling of women and the public, he shaped pop culture like no other Hollywood star before or since.

Especially because Steve McQueen was real, because he was experienced as real. That's how he was, and that's how he wanted to be. Just himself. He was aware of this authenticity, he lived it and knew how to give it the proper amount of attention. McQueen loved what he did – and he was damn good at it. He couldn't be average. He wanted to be a star. *The* star.

His characters' passion for motorsports, speed and extreme situations was his own. A car guy who was as talented as he was experienced, he took part in several top-level car and motorcycle racing events – as a serious competitor, not just for fun. In 1964 he was part of the U.S. team that traveled to what was then East Germany for the International Six Days Trial, an off-road motorcycle event, in Erfurt; he finished second in the 1970 12 Hours of Sebring in a Porsche 908/02; and if his insurance company hadn't protested so strongly, he would have been right there on the starting line that same year in the 24-hour classic of Le Mans together with reigning Formula 1 world champion Jackie Stewart.

It goes without saying how difficult it was to keep him from doing his own stunts. The famous motorcycle chase scene in *The Great Escape* was added specifically for McQueen. After reviewing the script, he had threatened to pull out of the production because he didn't think his role was credible enough. When the stuntmen who had actually been scheduled realized how dangerous the renegotiated shoot would be for them, they refused completely. So McQueen, as Captain Virgil Hilts, was not only allowed to jump over a barbed wire fence in his legendary Stalag sweater, but also took over the stunts for his adversary in these new scenes. Wearing different uniforms for each shot, McQueen then ended up pursuing himself.

McQueen was only slowed down by the insurance agents for the production companies. As happened on the set of the classic *Bullitt*. The underwriters were unwilling to insure Hollywood's most valuable star during the most dangerous seconds of his high-speed chase through the streets of San Francisco. In order not to challenge McQueen's commitment too much, the crew sometimes shot secretly before work actually started or long after hours. In many of the less risky scenes for the 1968 blockbuster, however, McQueen was able to chase after the Dodge Charger driving the dark green Ford Mustang himself. The window was always open, as he had insisted.

With McQueen wearing a turtleneck sweater beneath his tweed blazer.

In several close-ups during one of the most important and intense car chases in film history, McQueen's turtleneck focuses the viewer's attention in the middle of all the high-speed action – and in the process becomes a defining style element. When McQueen was asked how he pictured his character, the hard-boiled cop Frank Bullitt, he immediately knew he would be wearing a turtleneck. Only beatniks and jocks wore turtlenecks back then. In *Bullitt*, it gave the tough-as-nails big-city cop a mysterious, serene elegance in the extremely suspenseful action scenes. In combination with the raw power of the Mustang, McQueen's outfit, above

Steve McQueen was real, because he was experienced as real. That's how he was, and that's how he wanted to be. Just himself. He was aware of this authenticity, he lived it and knew how to give it the proper amount of attention. McQueen loved what he did – and he was damn good at it.

all the dark Pierre Cardin turtleneck sweater, gave the film the appropriate poise. The actual plot becomes secondary; all of a sudden, it's clear what this picture is really about: attitude.

Attitude and authenticity were always matters of style for Steve McQueen, and his best films were always perfect stylistic exercises. In any situation, his typical sixties style is timeless. Simple, but always tasteful. Steve McQueen knew exactly what his impact was in every film he made. Other actors would fight for every extra line; McQueen, in contrast, had every unnecessary bit of dialogue removed from the script of *Bullitt*. Instead, his long, penetrating stares burned themselves into the history of action cinema. His clothes, his attitude, his movements with that bouncy, confident gait, the character portrayed in the film – they all still resonate today. Since *Bullitt*, all big-screen cops dream of being as stylish and tough. An authentic, imperfect anti-hero. McQueen the leading man, the star. "He created the movie archetype of today's modern action hero," as biographer Marshall Terrill sums it up.

From the very beginning, he left nothing to chance. Already in the late fifties, he had himself photographed like James Dean, with a keen sense for how he would come across. In *The Getaway* and *The Thomas Crown Affair*, he wore glasses specially made to his specifications, which immediately became legendary accessories. No matter if he was splattered with dirt, wearing leather boots and riding a motorcycle, or dressed in a tailor-made three-piece suit with Persol sunglasses, as in *Thomas Crown* – McQueen always cut a handsome figure.

"In the movies, style is content," explained Norman Jewison, the director of *The Thomas Crown Affair*. The brilliantly shot, intelligently ironic heist film shows how you can develop an exciting story with a subdued narrative and almost no suspense – as long as you have Steve McQueen on your side. Thomas Crown remains a mystery to the viewer throughout the entire film. McQueen plays the character with incredible composure, exuding absolute coolness at every moment. Only in the last scene do we understand what drives him and what he's all about when he so unnecessarily puts himself in danger. It's the thrill, that adrenaline rush that you get as a reward for taking risks and crossing boundaries. The excitement of the forbidden. For Crown, and for McQueen, it's a way of life. The combination of skill and passion.

Steve McQueen's life was as if made for the movies: Born into a dysfunctional family in Indiana in 1930, his father was a gambler and stuntman who left when young Steve was

Since *Bullitt*, all big-screen cops dream of being as stylish and tough. An authentic, imperfect anti-hero. McQueen the leading man, the star.

just six months old. His mother was a nightclub dancer and alcoholic, with changing male acquaintances and little interest in raising a child. He spent parts of his youth with a great-uncle and, after a bad-boy excursion into gangland, was remanded to a reformatory school for incorrigible youth. McQueen remained gratefully indebted to the California Junior Boys Republic for the rest of his life and supported the institution financially. This was probably the foundation for the melancholy that accompanied him throughout his life. He would later recall, "When a kid doesn't have any love when he's small, he begins to wonder if he's good enough. My mother didn't love me, and I didn't have a father. I thought, 'Well, I must not be very good.'"

Somehow, at age seventeen, he found his way into the military. He served in the Marines as a mechanic and tank driver. Because of an unauthorized absence to visit a girlfriend, he spent thirty days in the brig, the first twenty-one on bread and water. After that, he was more disciplined.

But when push came to shove, he rose to the occasion – and became a hero. During an

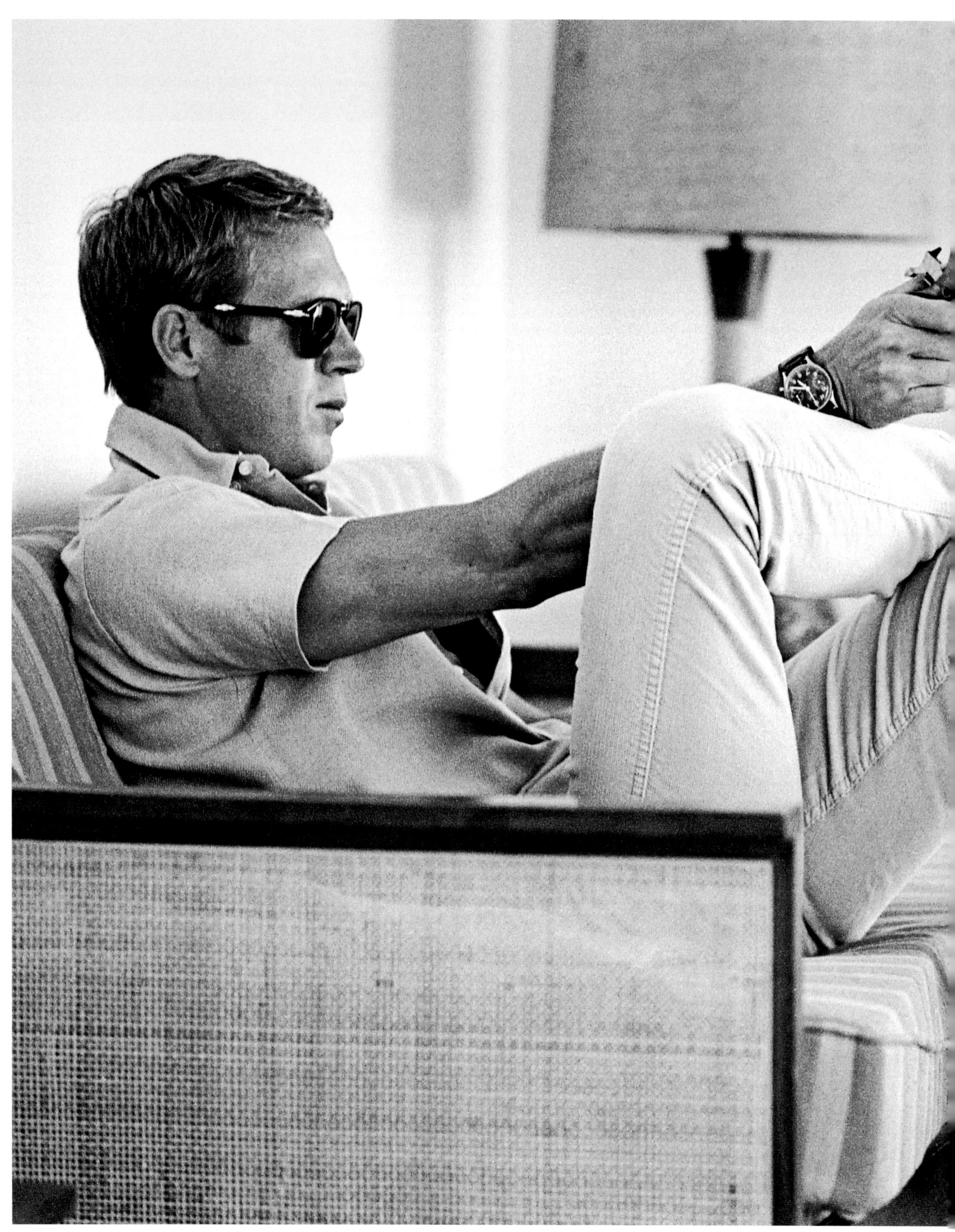

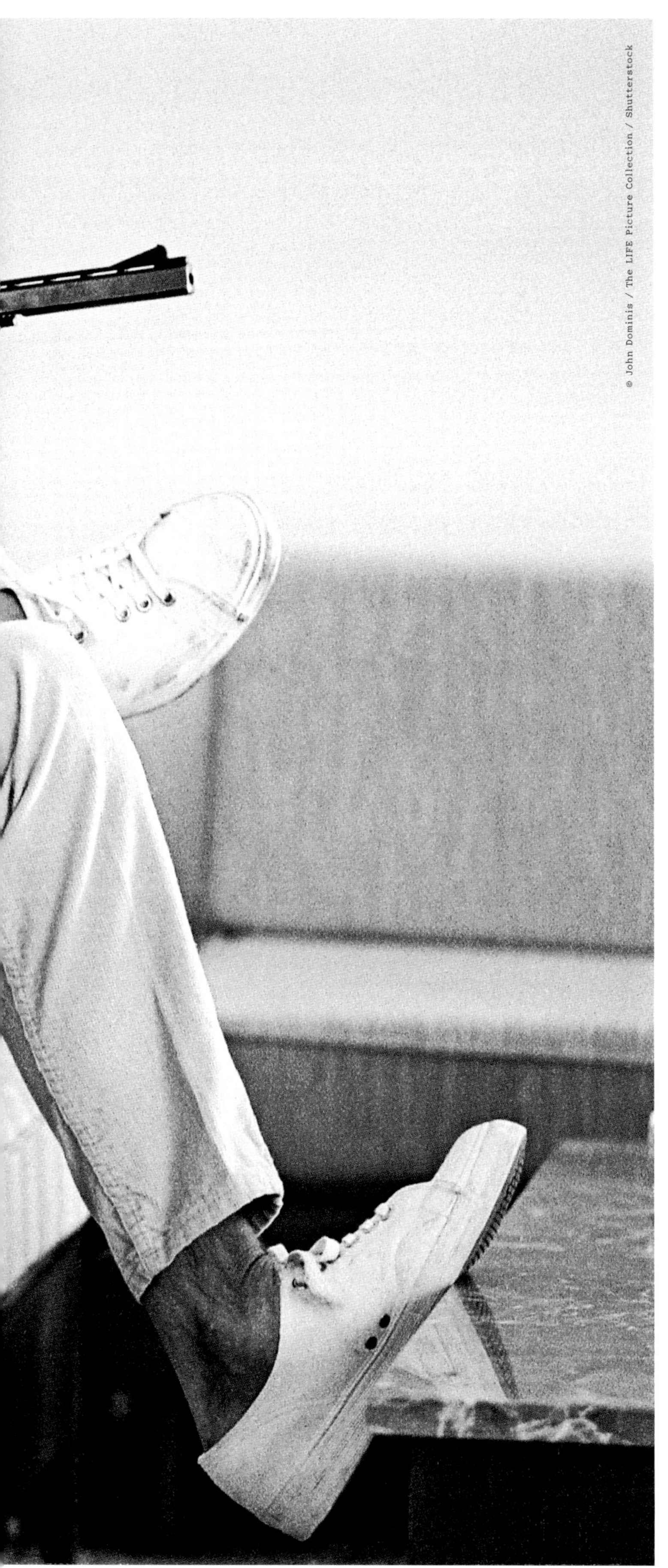
© John Dominis / The LIFE Picture Collection / Shutterstock

exercise in the Arctic, his landing craft ran aground on a sandbar, and several tanks with their crews slid overboard onto the ice. McQueen saved five comrades from drowning before the tank broke through. As a reward, he was assigned to the honor guard responsible for guarding President Harry S. Truman's presidential yacht. McQueen enjoyed his time in the Marines. It was his therapy, he once said.

Following an honorable discharge, he decided to take up acting. Despite the fact that he had no acting background and lacked the financial means, McQueen eventually made it to the most famous of all acting schools, Lee Strasberg's Actor's Studio in New York. Marlon Brando, James Dean and Paul Newman had already trained here. He had to hitchhike to get there because he didn't have enough money. Later, he never spoke much about this time.

McQueen's first breakout role was in 1958 in the American Western television series *Wanted Dead or Alive*, where he portrayed the gentleman bounty hunter Josh Randall, a man who dutifully and silently does his job and who can shoot faster than his opponents with a shortened Winchester 92. Not particularly profound, but extremely popular. The show made McQueen famous with a broad audience. And it established the personality traits for which he would be known. The reserved straight-talker, honest and straightforward, who diligently pursues his goal – it's all there, successfully rehearsed over the course of three seasons before being perfected in the sixties and seventies.

In 1960 McQueen then landed his first international hit on the big screen with *The Magnificent Seven*. For his role as gunslinger Vin Tanner, he cleverly incorporated several small, crowd-pleasing touches of his own into the scenes that were not part of the original script. Star Yul Brynner was furious, protesting that, with his antics, supporting actor McQueen was trying to steal the show. The gamble paid off. Lead roles and important supporting parts in blockbusters followed.

McQueen became a superstar in 1963 with his role in *The Great Escape*. "When I did *The Great Escape*," he would later recount, "I kept thinking, 'If they were making a movie of my life, that's what they'd call it: *The Great Escape*.'"

Cinema audiences and the media adored him, and he was celebrated as the best actor in Hollywood. At the time, he was also the world's highest-paid film star. Movie journalists today still rave about his achievements during those years: "When

Steve McQueen finds himself in a hopeless situation in his films, he pits hope against hopelessness and passes this feeling on to the viewer," the *Neue Zürcher Zeitung* wrote in 2020 on the occasion of the fortieth anniversary of his death.

"If they were making a movie of my life, that's what they'd call it: *The Great Escape*."

Men loved his indomitable, courageous and genuine demeanor, a guy who does his own thing without any self-conceit. For women, he was a handsome and likeable conqueror that they simply couldn't resist. The real reason McQueen wanted to become an actor was to "meet chicks", as one of his biographers later wrote. Worked out pretty well.

McQueen became the perfect sex symbol. A cool guy with turquoise eyes and a penetrating gaze who could be charming or boyish, a rebel with a charismatic, dangerous aura, a nonchalant, laconic manner and a melancholic elegance. The seductive power of the man adored as the "manliest of men" was not just a role in a script, it was who he was.

He had affairs with Barbara Leigh, Jacqueline Bisset and Lauren Hutton and was married three times: to actresses Neile Adams and Ali MacGraw and to fashion model Barbara Minty. He was never able to remain truly faithful. He admitted that he was a chauvinist – but also said that it didn't bother him.

His true love was for cars and motorcycles – and *Le Mans* was a project of passion for him. Not only did he have special camera equipment designed for the film, he even risked his marriage to Neile Adams to finish it.

Le Mans was supposed to be the ultimate film about motor racing. The shooting turned into a nightmare, and the finished film flopped both with the critics and at the box office. The disaster nearly ruined McQueen financially and marked the end of his marriage. "Racing is life. Anything before or after is just waiting," he says in the film. A line that fits his cinematic persona and his real life in equal measure.

Steve McQueen died much too early, aged fifty, on November 7, 1980, following two heart attacks as a result of his battle with lung cancer. His heart stopped beating after surgery at a hospital in Ciudad Juarez, Mexico, where he had checked in to remove several metastatic tumors in his neck and abdomen. Either in the army or while wearing the fireproof protective suits used in motor racing, he had clearly inhaled too much asbestos. He also was a heavy smoker.

Of all the dead actors from the Dream Factory, he remains the most alive – thanks in no small part to his incredible coolness. Perhaps also because McQueen's anti-hero personality always had such an undertone of intensity and rage, melancholy and rebellion. Beneath his controlled surface as a style icon, you can see just how sensitive and restless and full of contradictions he was. Throughout it all, he remained eternally true to himself. In life and on the screen.

For actor and director Gary Oldman, however, the common appreciation of Steve McQueen as the "King of Cool" doesn't go far enough. In the very watchable documentary *I Am Steve McQueen*, he explains: "He predated cool. There's Steve McQueen, and then there's cool."

Beneath his controlled surface as a style icon, you can see just how sensitive and restless and full of contradictions he was. Throughout it all, he remained eternally true to himself. In life and on the screen.

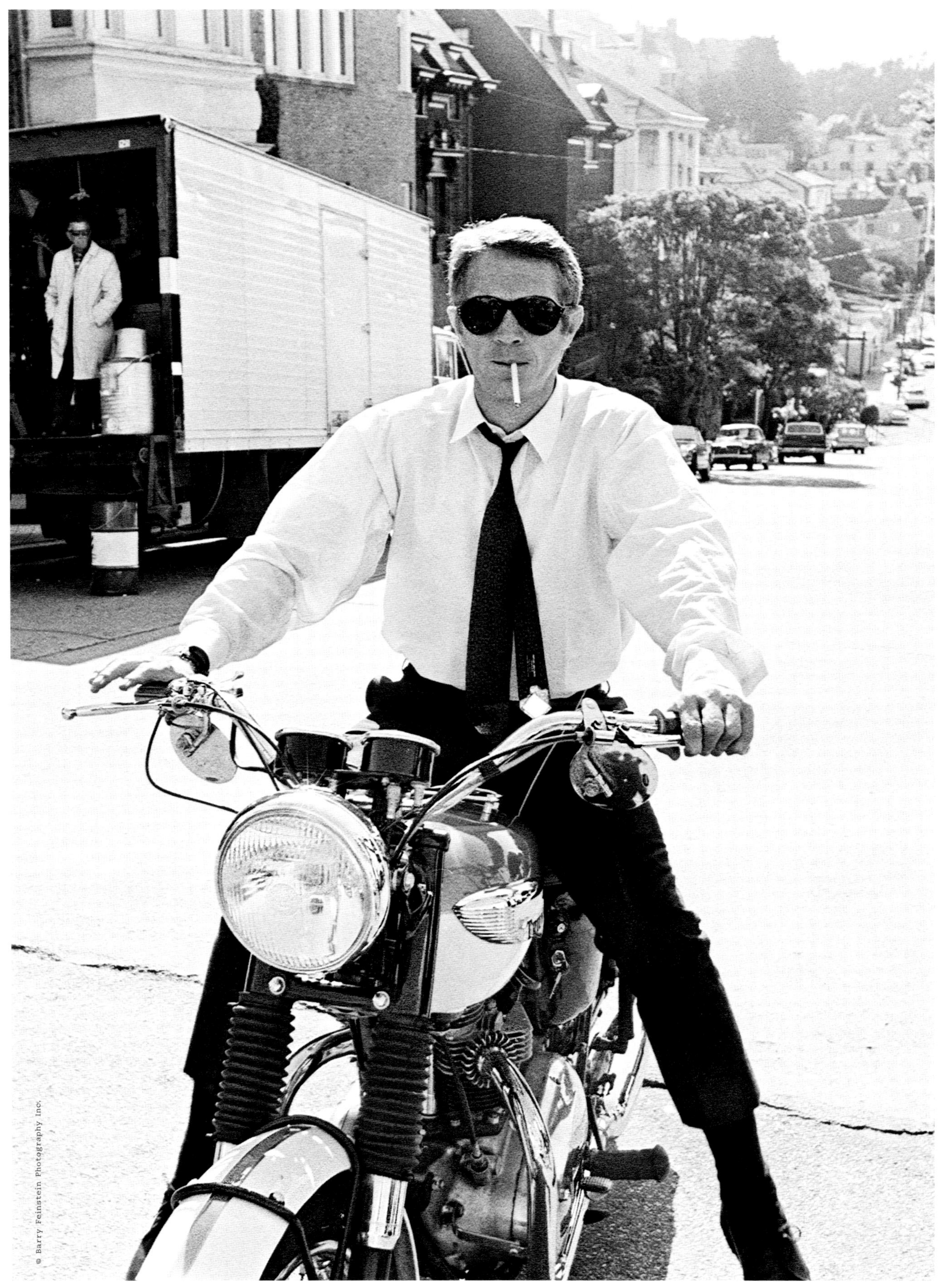

1.04

the simulation of sover-eignty

THE MORE WE KNOW ABOUT THE WORLD, THE LESS WE FEEL WE CAN CONTROL IT. FORTUNATELY, TECHNOLOGY IS THERE TO STEP IN AND TAKE OVER. WELL, MOST OF THE TIME ANYWAY. AMONG OTHER THINGS.

A FEW THOUGHTS ON SELF-PERCEPTION AND RISK ASSESSMENT.

TEXT *Lutz Fügener*

On January 28, 1938, Rudolf Caracciola drove his Mercedes over a stretch of the autobahn between Frankfurt and Darmstadt at a record-breaking speed of almost 432 km/h. A short time later Bernd Rosemeyer attempted to push the envelope even further, but lost control of his Auto Union car and suffered a fatal crash.

At 4:50 a.m. on a Sunday morning in July 2021, Radim Passer, the Czech owner of a Bugatti Chiron, took his foot off the gas on the autobahn between Berlin and Hanover after reaching a speed of 417 km/h as measured by GPS. Driver and co-driver cheered into one of the onboard cameras after successfully hitting the magic four hundred mark.

The two events are over eighty-three years apart, and the locations and protagonists have little in common, yet the story is essentially the same. Not to mention the fact that it is difficult to overstate the lack of complexity in the underlying concept: humans trying to drive as fast as they can without losing control of the vehicle.

A note on the margins, yet important enough not to let go by the wayside, is that Mr. Passer has done a disservice to the illustrious community of hypercar owners by making his private record-setting drive public, although we are used to all of the chest-thumping on social media after supposed driving exploits. In this specific case we are dealing with circles that adhere to the code of Hanseatic restraint: a certain reluctance to play to an audience when performing minor escapades on the margins of social acceptance. A gentleman doesn't kiss (or race?) and tell. Just knowing how exclusive such a feat is should be enough. It is likely in the interest of marketing such unicorns for us to probably leave to the imagination how many of these dynamic driving experiments actually take place on lazy summer mornings. After all, such a secretive approach fuels the myths that enshroud them far more than any pornographic close-up of their excess might.

Philosopher Peter Sloterdijk, one of the most important intellectuals in the German-speaking world, acknowledges our human ability to use our senses to perceive danger but denies us the ability to perceive risks in the same intuitive way. We simply lack the necessary organ for detecting risk. His favorite example is the shark versus the tropical mosquito: we perceive sharks as extremely dangerous, while mosquitos – measured solely by quantitative "success" – actually are. We depend on two tools to assess risks: information and the ability to process it. Most of the time, we lack both. Thinking is exhausting and takes time, and it is often a

We depend on two tools to assess risks: information and the ability to process it. Most of the time, we lack both.

scarce commodity given the speed with which problems sometimes come at us, or with which we come at them. Sloterdijk has also developed a disturbing hypothesis on our ability to assess risks and come to terms with the complexity of our world, flanked nevertheless by a perspective-based guide for action, presumably motivated by the fact that at the time he held a professorship at the Karlsruhe University of Arts and Design and the responsibility he feels for shaping young designers that that entails. Sloterdijk describes the dilemma between increasing complexity and the concomitant rise in demands placed on individuals as a paradox of competence. As our knowledge of the world grows, so does the certainty that we are unable to master it. We can excel in our specialized fields, but overall control has slipped from our grasp. We are all familiar with these feelings of powerlessness; the list of subjects we no longer master is long and seemingly unending and applies differently to each individual. This could include setting up or operating technically complex devices and computer technology, wrestling with the sea of red tape involved in tax returns and insurance matters, handling complex planning processes, using communication technology, coping with tricky situations behind the wheel, making health-related decisions, evaluating political processes, navigating safely in unfamiliar areas and, of course, every conceivable combination of these and other subject matters.

The smartphones in our pockets must devote a significant portion of their superpowers to adapting to our limited information processing capabilities.

It seems as if we were moving on an upward spiral that generates so-called black boxes with increasing frequency. Under pressure from the conflict arising from the parallel phenomena of growing complexity and an increased need for simplification, this spiral winds ever upwards to a level matching our capabilities by spitting out ever new, ever more helpful black boxes. The smartphones in our pockets must devote a significant portion of their superpowers to adapting to our limited information processing capabilities, a computational effort that is remarkably elaborate in its dimensions. For comparison's sake, Boeing has been using supercomputers to develop its airplanes since 1980. This is when the Boeing 767, still in use worldwide, was developed. The computing power of the supercomputers available back then was roughly on a par with that of an iPhone 4 today, which means that today's airline passengers enjoy more computing power while scrolling on their smartphones than was available at the time to build the aircraft they are sitting in. Objects that previously seemed completely harmless are increasingly getting caught up in the gravitational field of this upward spiral. Until now, the good old bicycle was considered an ideal antagonist to the black box: its structure and technology are completely visible, nothing hidden from our gaze. The use of electronic circuits and electric powertrains means that it is now on a par with other motorized vehicles, rendering it opaque and gradually excluding its now evolved interior processes from our influence. Et tu, Brute?

Even before the dawn of the computer era, when the first paying passengers set foot on the brand-new Concorde supersonic aircraft in 1976, the airlines and their employees understandably and justifiably took a great deal of pride in their futuristic aircraft, granting a VIP or two a look inside the cockpit. However, these backstage glimpses left a rather ambivalent impression on those chosen few. On the one hand, the cockpit was brimming with an unmanageable abundance of switches, display instruments and, for the layman, unidentifiable equipment at the three pilot and flight engineer workstations. It was a testament to the impressive degree of technological progress; on the other hand, the visitors were left puzzled as to how the pilots could maintain control of such a system. Rumor has it that they decided to hold off with the cockpit tour until after the plane was again firmly on the ground. Incidentally, all of the Concorde's crews always landed safely at their destination; the tragic accident of the Air France plane in 2000 was not caused by a crew overwhelmed by all the bells and whistles, but by a collision with an engine part lying on the runway, a legacy of a plane that had taken off shortly before. The obstacle suddenly materializing on the runway was a "little reminder" of the diabolical forces of entropy.

In order to deprive the experience of powerlessness of its depressing one-two punch, Sloterdijk proposed a strategy in his 2006 lecture "Das Zeug zur Macht" (roughly: "The Things of Power"), which he sums up as a "simulation of sovereignty". In his strategy, designers, who function as the protagonists in the lecture, are tasked with ensuring that their work gives users the illusion that they alone have sovereignty over their possessions. Sloterdijk leaves no doubt that this certainty about their sovereignty is an illusion, and that this illusion – as if things were not difficult enough – is very unstable. For comparison, he refers to indigenous peoples whose ways of life seem primitive from our point of view, but who have come up with an instruction manual on what to do or rituals for all situations that arise. Consequently, they face the world with more robust certainty than we are able to muster under the influence of our partial knowledge. He recommends trying an experiment: If you want it to rain, start doing a rain dance. You'll see that it works. You just have to keep at it long enough.

Sloterdijk's hypothesis about the purpose of design has frequently been confirmed over the past eighteen years. It has proven apt as a generally valid and meaningful conceptual approach to the currently fastest-growing specialization in design known as UX design (UX = user experience). The design of graphical interfaces alone, which allow us to use the aforementioned supercomputers in our pockets so they seem like playthings, justifies this area's growing self-confidence. The younger generation, justifiably referred to today as digital natives, use these products excessively and have indeed become virtuosos, but they are seldom in a position to dig down and tackle problems at the ground floor level of the programming. They, too, are dependent on having information translated into an intuitive language. The principle of the simulation of sovereignty is no longer limited to the task of design. Examples can be found almost everywhere. No motorcycle in the 200 hp class comes out onto the market today without assistance systems that young and moneyed

If you want it to rain, start doing a rain dance. You'll see that it works. You just have to keep at it long enough.

PETER SLOTERDIJK

Sloterdijk speaks of the "skillful handling of the skill-less". As far as the simulation of sovereignty is concerned, one problem unfortunately remains unresolved: the more skillfully the simulation succeeds, the more problematic the side effects are.

customers, still in the trial-and-error phase of driving, simply cannot do without. A lack of such systems might cause them to do harm to themselves or to others, making them an unwilling object of media attention. These devices – or things, as Sloterdijk calls them, borrowing from Heidegger – come in quite handy when zipping around bends, ironing out a carelessly induced amplitude or two while alternating between the gas and the brake, without alerting these supposed driving aces too nakedly to their incompetence. Sloterdijk calls this the "skillful handling of the skill-less". As far as the simulation of sovereignty is concerned, one problem unfortunately remains unresolved: the more skillfully the simulation succeeds, the more problematic the side effects are. Self-perception and risk assessment become difficult when the line between your own actions and the influence of an invisible helping hand becomes blurred.

Passer was successful in his private attempt at setting a new record; Rosemeyer was not. The question of probability remains. Is it a simple case of good luck versus bad luck? And how does Caracciola factor in? The Auto Union and the Mercedes on the one hand and Passer's Chiron on the other are eight decades apart, eight decades of technical development in vehicle engineering, road construction, communications technology and weather forecasting. The Chiron, with nearly three times the engine power, is far superior to the cars of the past in terms of chassis, passive safety, reliability and comfort. But Passer, unlike Caracciola and Rosemeyer driving on a closed section of highway, accepted his inability to factor in uninvolved traffic participants, and in the worst case, their risk of potential harm. Targeted by criticism after his private record-setting feat had gone public, he defended himself citing the extraordinary technical prowess of his vehicle. The manufacturer of the Chiron, certainly not unreservedly happy at its customer's hyperactive guerrilla-style marketing moves, issued a muted statement in defense of Passer: "No road-legal vehicle drives more safely at high speed than the Chiron." And after all, the experiment gave us a new record. All's well that ends well.

Passer was successful, Rosemeyer was not. The question of probability remains.

Self-perception and risk assessment become difficult when the line between your own actions and the influence of an invisible helping hand becomes blurred.

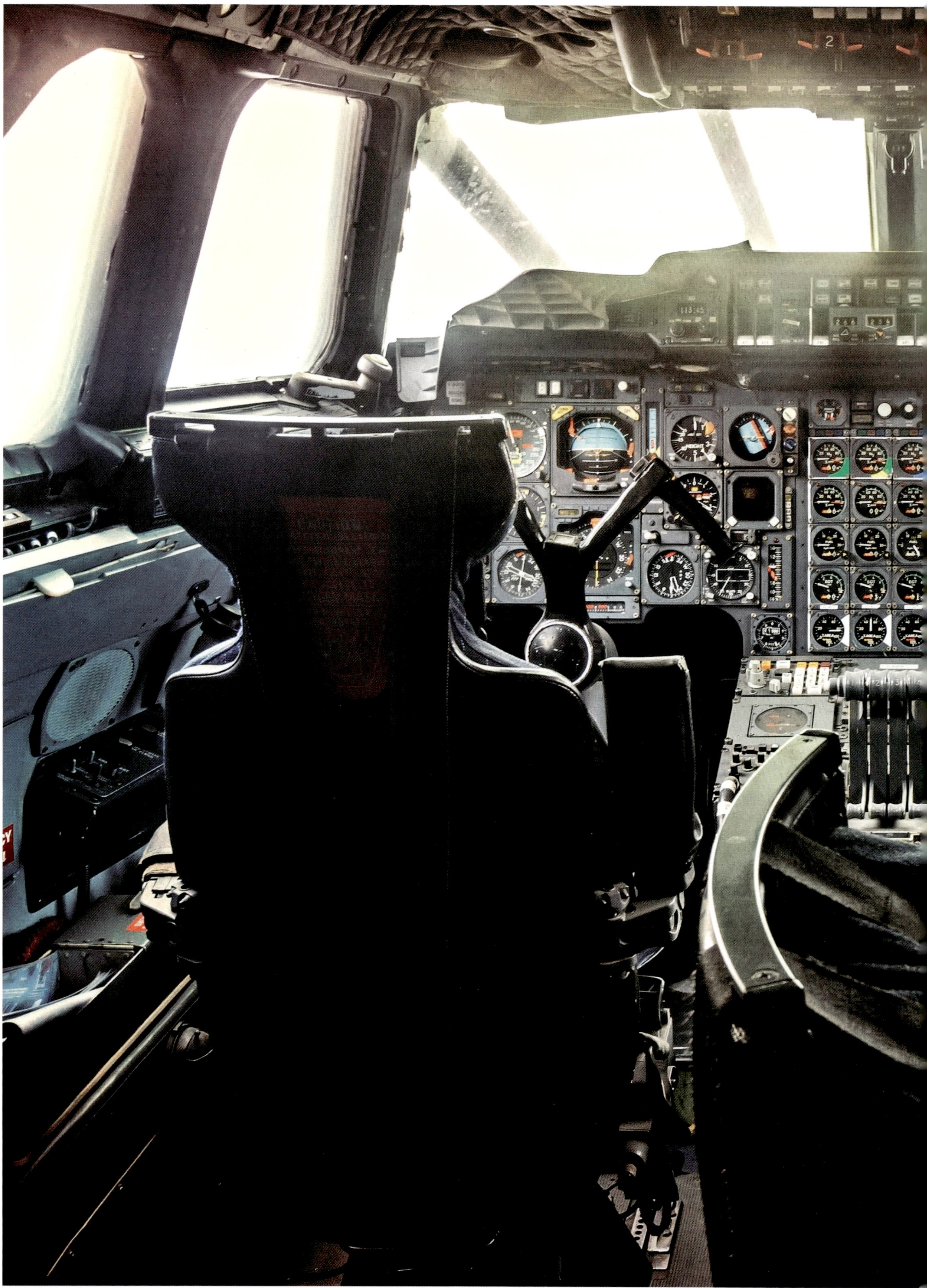

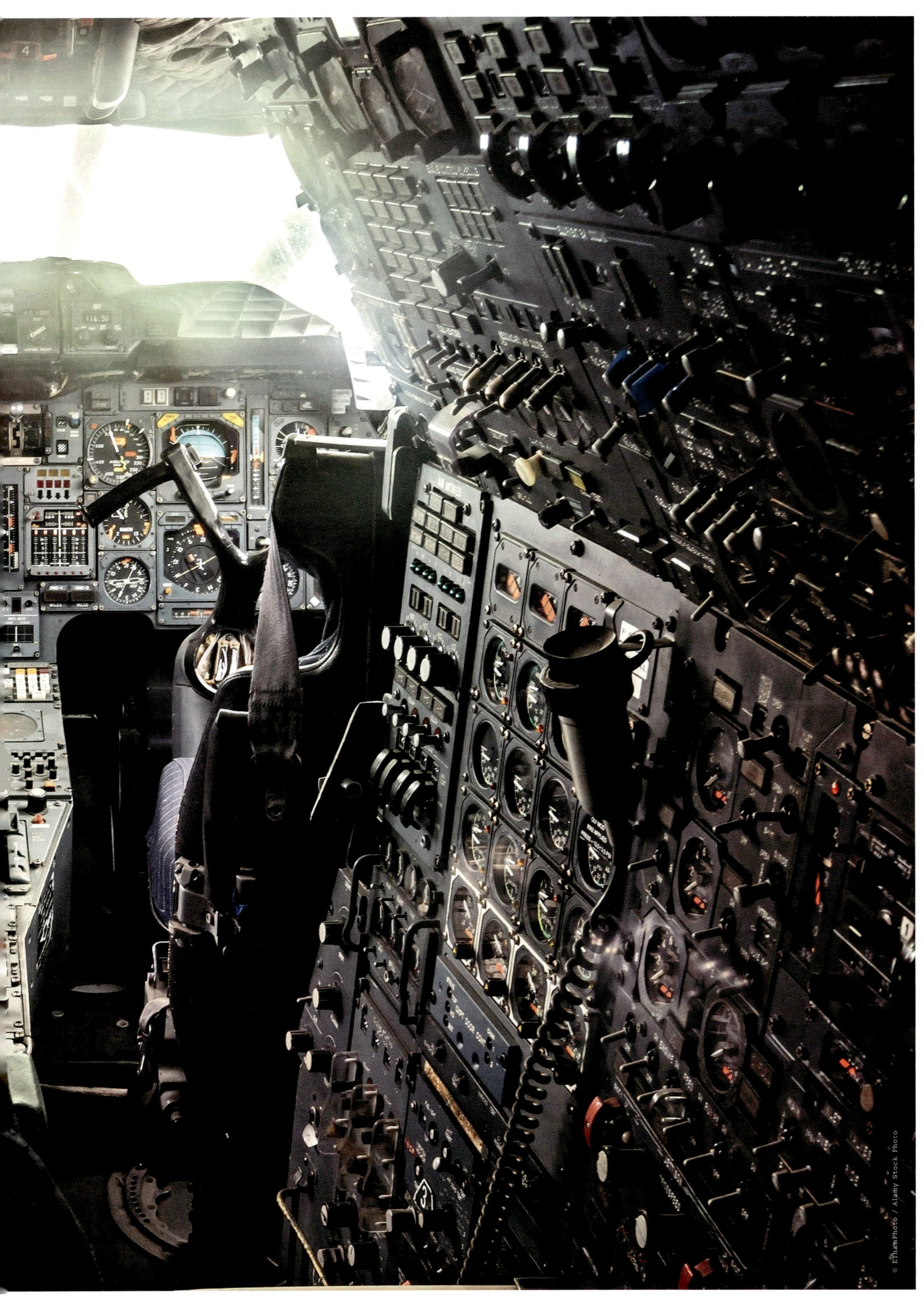

NO MATTER HOW OLD YOU ARE, A SHINY BROWN CHESTNUT THAT HAS JUST FALLEN FROM THE TREE IS A TREASURE TO BE CHERISHED.

Me: "I'd like to buy a pair of jeans."
Saleswoman:
"Skinny, slim fit, extra slim, straight, tapered or regular?"
Me: "Blue."

Ever since I asked her for her ring size, my girlfriend has been in a really good mood.
She probably already suspects that I'm getting her a bowling ball for her birthday.

"The dog is doing great without a leash!"
"Cool, where is he now?"
"No idea."

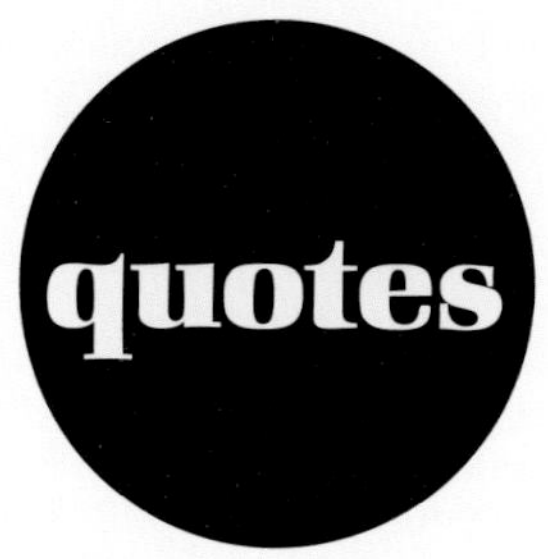

I'M NEVER IN A BAD MOOD WHEN I'M ALONE, SO IT'S NOT MY FAULT.

My husband positions the garden sprinkler and shouts:
"Okay, turn on the water – but wait until I'm gone!"

You would have done it too.

BETTER A HEALTHY BIT OF MISCHIEF THAN A SICKLY SENSE OF VIRTUE.

A new study has found that women who carry a few extra pounds tend to live longer than the men who mention that fact.

I'm constantly being forced to do things I'm not good at. Like being nice to stupid people.

The look on the face of the person sitting next to you on the flight to Barcelona when you ask them what they're planning to do in London – priceless.

YOU KNOW HOW SOME ATHLETES THROW A BALL TO THE CROWD AFTER A GAME? NOT SUCH A GOOD IDEA IN BOWLING, AS I FOUND OUT YESTERDAY . . .

This morning I printed out a photo of my wife and put it in a frame in the kitchen.

Text: "Employee of the Month"
A word of advice: Don't do it!

"YOU LOOK BETTER WHEN YOU'RE NOT WEARING GLASSES."

"THANKS! YOU ALSO LOOK BETTER WHEN I'M NOT WEARING GLASSES."

I REALLY KNOW HOW TO FLIRT.

My grandfather doesn't use his turn signal because it's "nobody's business where I'm going".

My girlfriend: "One day the two of us will go to the hospital and three of us will come back home."

I'm still wondering why she would want to kidnap a doctor.

You can tell a lot about a woman's mood by looking at her hands.

If she's holding a weapon, for example, she's probably angry.

SUNDAYS MY CAT GETS REALLY ANNOYED WITH ME BECAUSE I'M IN HER APARTMENT ALL DAY.

IN THE EARLY SEVENTIES, VAN NUYS BOULEVARD IN THE SAN FERNANDO VALLEY OF LOS ANGELES WAS THE CENTER OF A YOUTH PHENOMENON THAT CELEBRATED A CAREFREE AUTOMOTIVE LIFESTYLE: CRUISING. PHOTOGRAPHER RICK MCCLOSKEY HAD A UNIQUE EYE FOR CAPTURING THE SPIRIT OF CRUISE NIGHT.

PERHAPS BECAUSE HE WAS A CRUISER HIMSELF.

TEXT *Martin Trockner*
PHOTOS *Rick McCloskey · rickmackvannuys.com*

1.06

once upon a time. in america

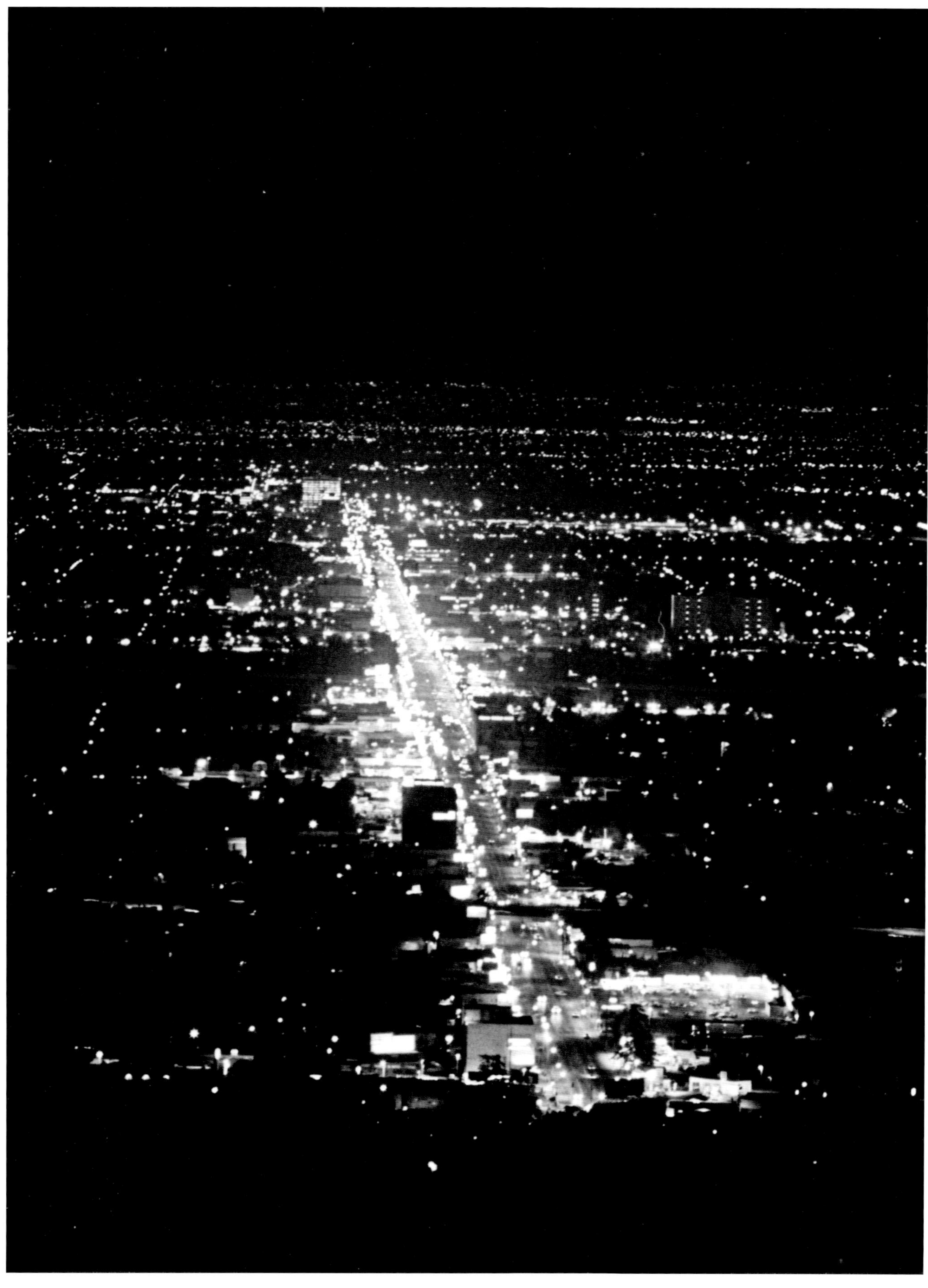

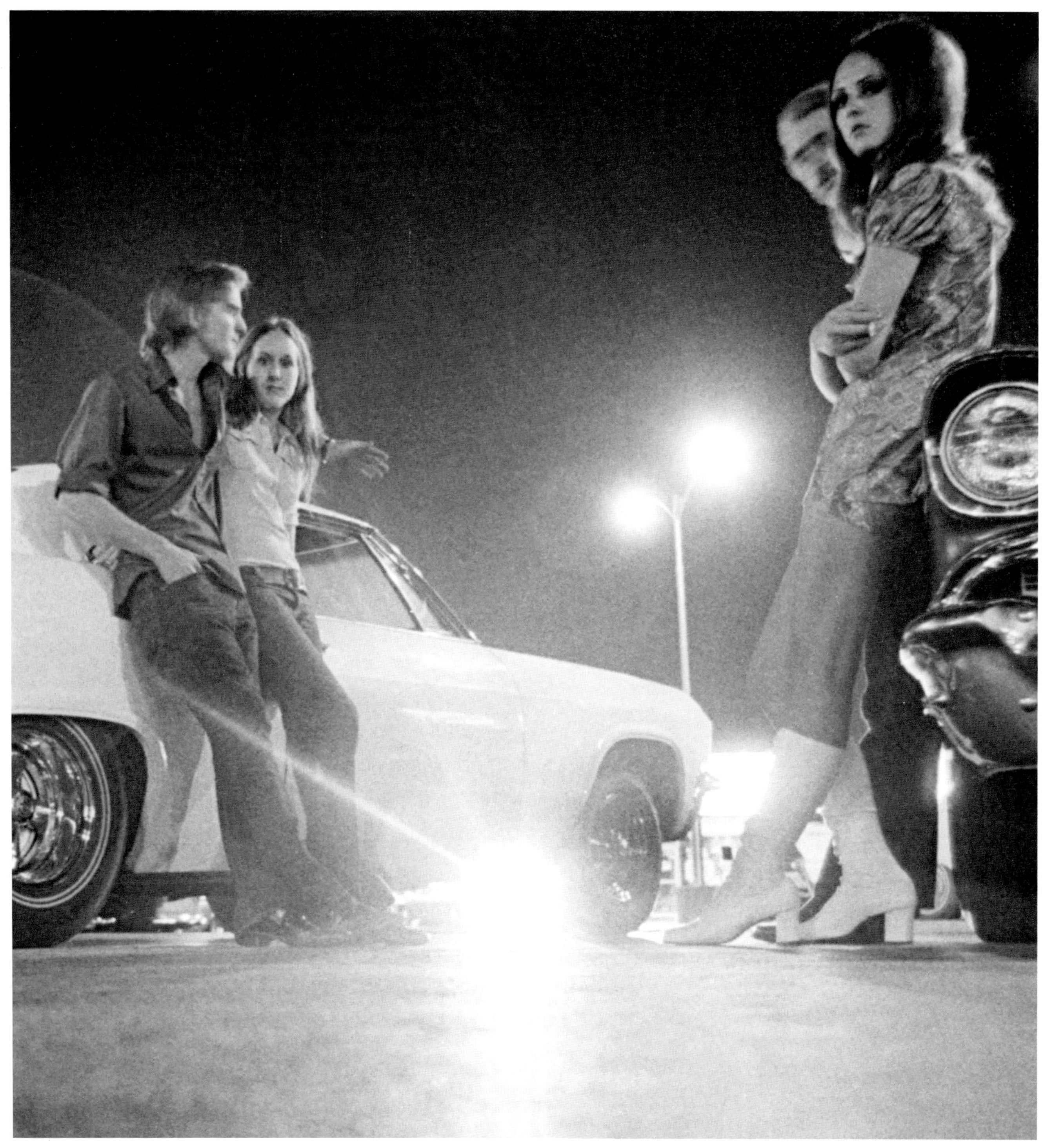

Van Nuys Boulevard was more than just a street. It was like a lifeline connecting people to their dreams.

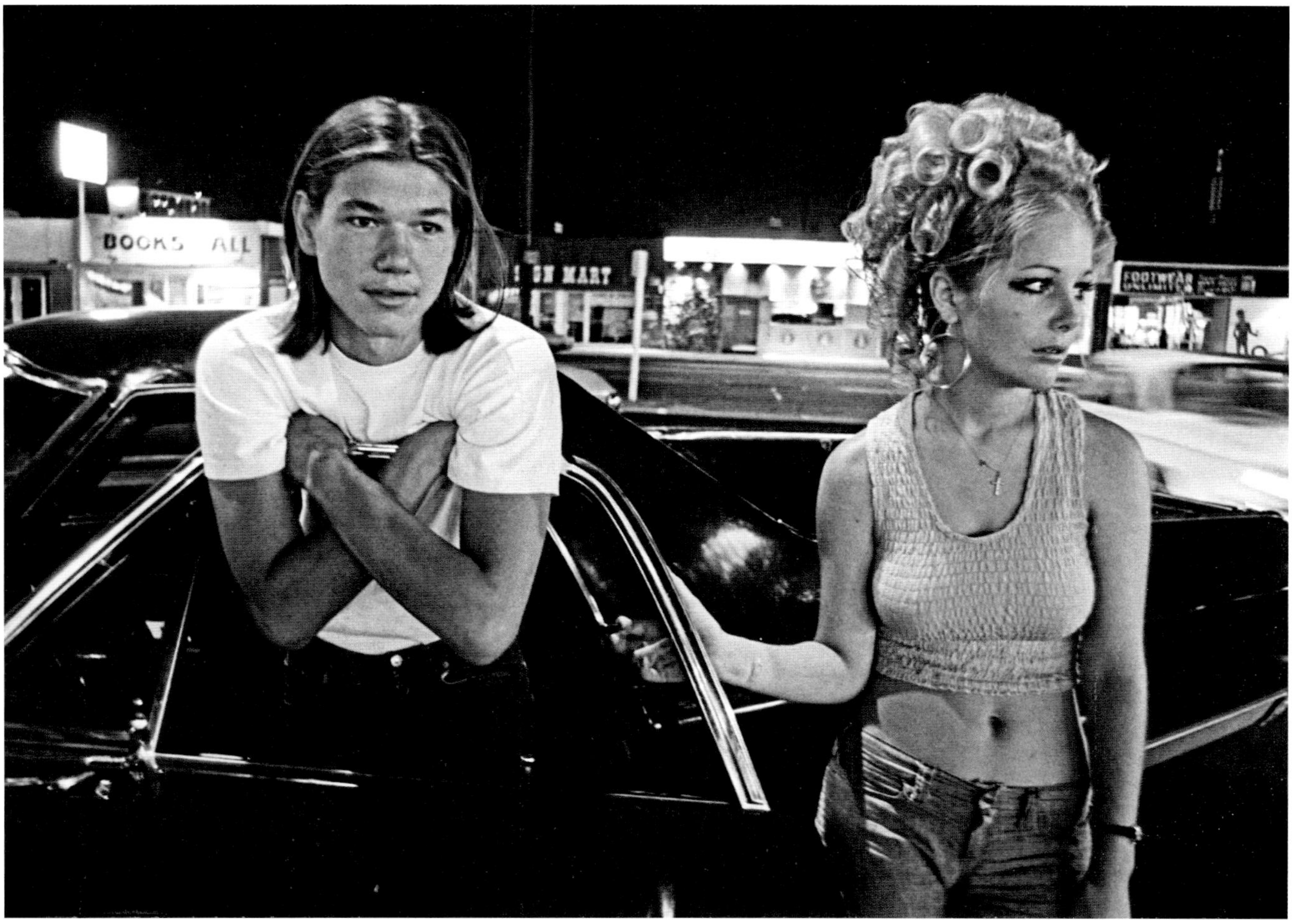

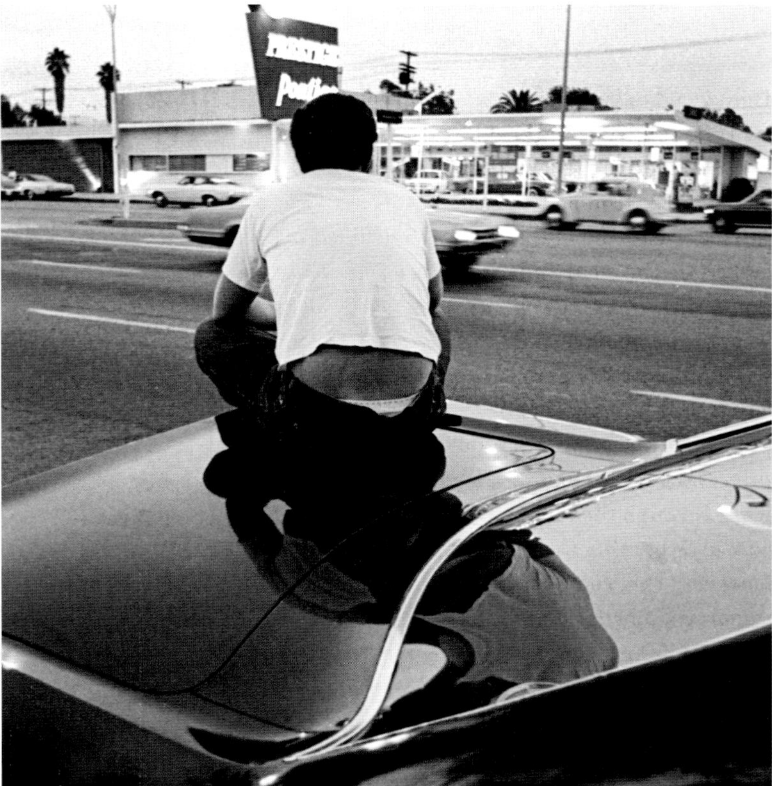

The photographs show young people who have not yet been affected by the burdens of life or who, behind the wheel or at the side of the road, are able to forget their everyday lives for a few hours.

Van Nuys Boulevard was the number one place to see and be seen, a stage for the San Fernando Valley's social life.

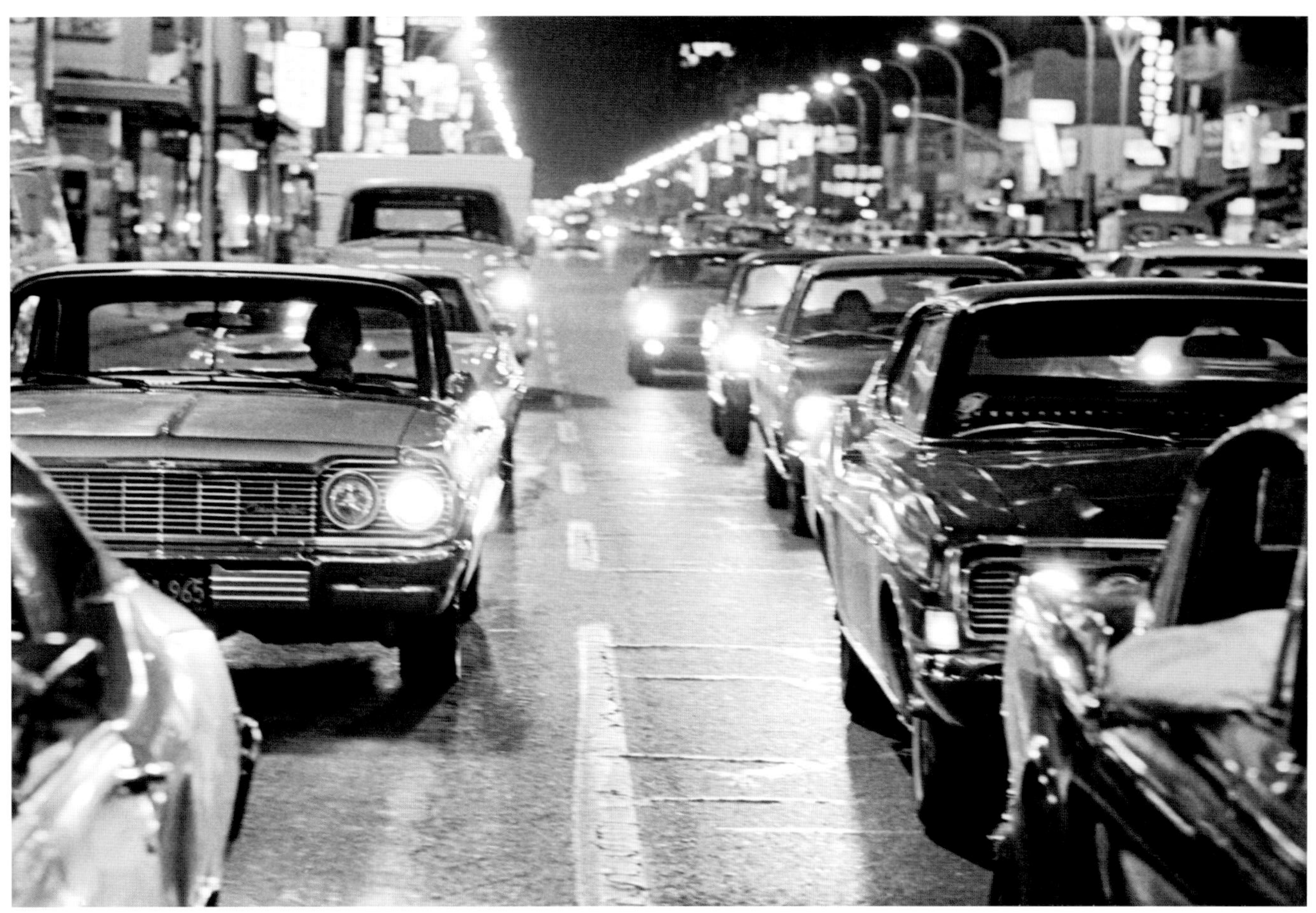

When people talk about the American dream, it's all about achievement and wealth. It's about moving up the socioeconomic ladder from one class to the next – or, ideally, about particularly clever people skipping the intermediate steps and going straight to being a millionaire. Americans love these kinds of stories. They have exported them all over the world and still tell them in thousands of variations at home.

Yet there was also a time when the American dream wasn't just told differently, but also lived differently. This dream was also about big emotions: about freedom, about carefree living, about being young, about the feeling that the future still lay ahead and everything was possible, about being part of a movement that would later become known as cruising culture.

Rick McCloskey was at the heart of the action. In 1957 his family moved from West Hollywood to Van Nuys, a neighborhood in the central San Fernando Valley region of Los Angeles that is today considered one of the city's most troubled areas. McCloskey was thirteen years old at the time, and he lived not far from the cruising epicenter: Van Nuys Boulevard. "Our new house was just a block west of the boulevard; I could see it from my window, not two hundred feet away," McCloskey recalls.

Starting at Ventura Boulevard in Sherman Oaks, Van Nuys Boulevard runs northward through the San Fernando Valley all the way to Panorama City and beyond. Back then, however, the road was more than just an important north-south thoroughfare. It was like a lifeline connecting people to their dreams.

Of course, the cruising phenomenon had been around long before McCloskey was even born. Already in the forties and fifties people

McCloskey didn't want to take pictures from a distance, didn't want to look at the scene from the outside. Getting in wasn't difficult, as he was still in the boulevard demographic.

would meet on the streets at night. The times were more carefree, and America had yet to experience the dark days of Vietnam. The peak of the early cruising era is often considered to be the late fifties. A decade later, in part because of the Vietnam War, the craze subsided – until there was a visible resurgence in the early seventies. The draft numbers were going down, people were once again gathering on the streets at night, and Van Nuys Boulevard emerged as the number one place to see and be seen, a stage for the valley's social life. The first cruise nights started on Wednesdays. There was no real reason why this day was chosen instead of another – except, perhaps, to celebrate the fact that the week was halfway over. In 1972 McCloskey was out with his camera in hand, capturing the essence of the boulevard scene. What remains is a document of contemporary history, like the photos from Woodstock that went around the world a few years earlier.

In 2020 McCloskey published his pictures in the coffee table book *Van Nuys Blvd 1972*. The photographs show young people who have not yet been affected by the burdens of life or who, behind the wheel or at the side of the road, are able to forget their everyday lives for a few hours.

McCloskey was studying photography in the Art Department of California State University at Northridge when he took his camera to the legendary cruising mile as part of an art project. He knew the area, the scene, the diners and gas stations, knew exactly where the cruisers met. McCloskey didn't want to take pictures from a distance, didn't want to look at the scene from the outside. Getting in wasn't difficult, as he was still in the boulevard demographic. "Being in my mid-twenties with long hair facilitated my easy acceptance by those on the street, allowing me to closely approach my subjects," he says. "Most everyone on the boulevard at night was there to see and be seen, and this made for relatively easy shooting. Indeed, many of my subjects would play for my camera; they very much wanted to be on stage, to perform and to be photographed. This allowed me to take my time and concentrate on composition and timing. I deliberately worked at getting people to look directly at my camera before I took the shot. I concentrated as much, or more, on making images of the people than their cars." Many of the images were taken in a parking lot at the south end of Van Nuys Boulevard. It was a good place to park, show off your car and just hang out with friends.

What McCloskey didn't realize at the time was that the black-and-white photos he shot over several nights in 1972 document some of the last cruise nights in the San Fernando Valley. "I had no idea at the time that cruising nights would come to an end a short time later." That happened the next year. Slowly at first. Then the oil crisis caused gasoline prices to go through the roof, and hardly anyone wanted or could afford to cruise up and down the boulevard anymore. In addition, the police increasingly issued tickets for loitering and in some places even issued curfews for young people. Slowly but surely, cruise nights became a thing of the past, like a river that had gradually but finally dried up. While McCloskey isn't exactly sad about it, he does feel a certain nostalgia looking back: "Cruising of this type does not happen anymore. It is gone, probably forever. These photos and fine memories are what are left. Enjoy."

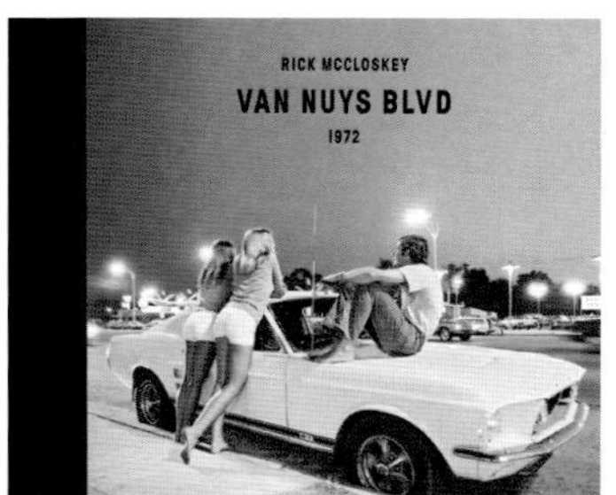

The coffee table book *Van Nuys Blvd 1972* with photos by Rick McCloskey was published by Sturm & Drang Publishers (hello@sturmanddrang.net).

"Many of my subjects would play for my camera; they very much wanted to be on stage, to perform and to be photographed."

RICK MCCLOSKEY

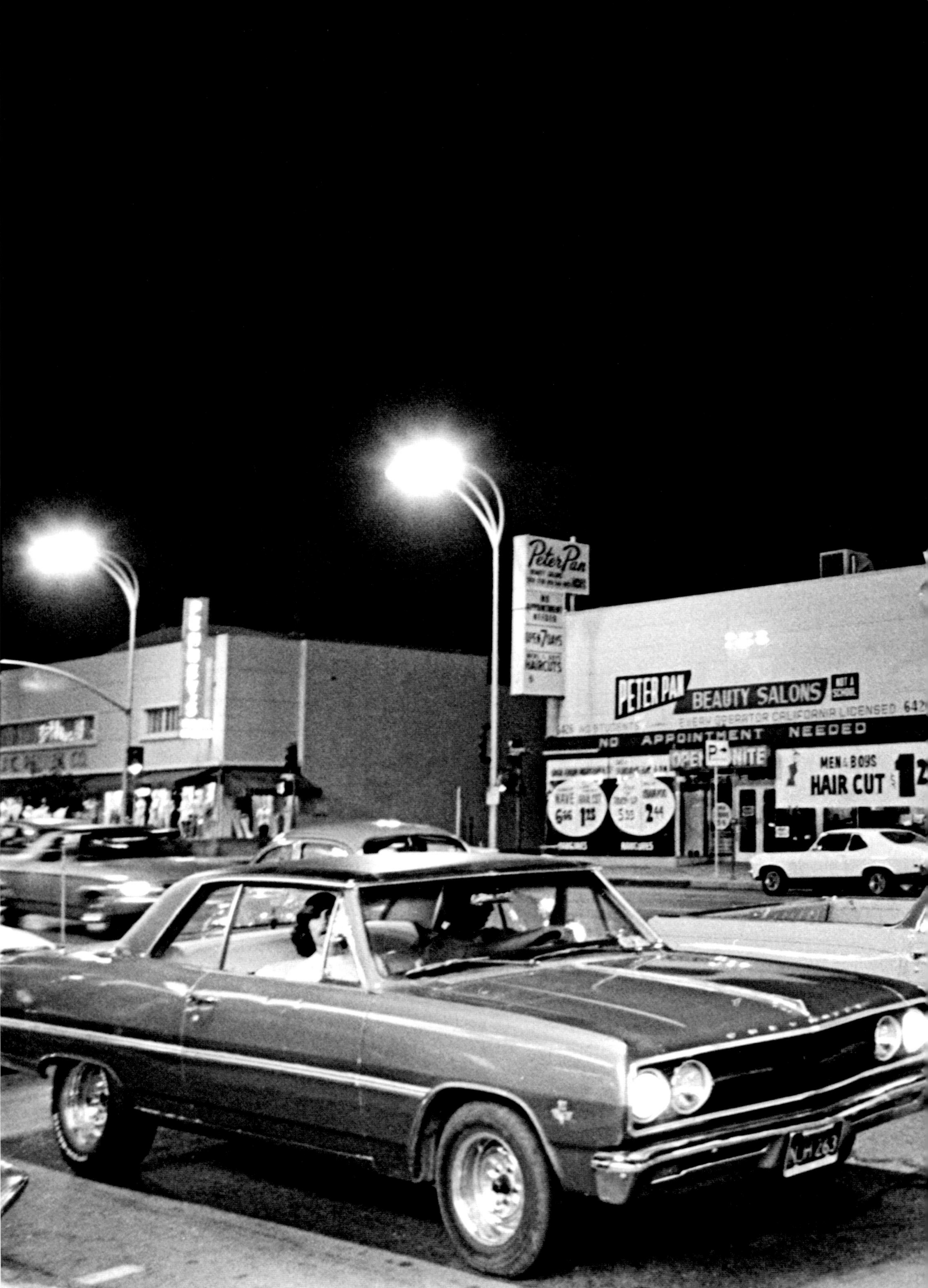

Peter Pan
PETER PAN
BEAUTY SALONS
NOT A SCHOOL
EVERY OPERATOR CALIFORNIA LICENSED
NO APPOINTMENT NEEDED
MEN & BOYS
HAIR CUT

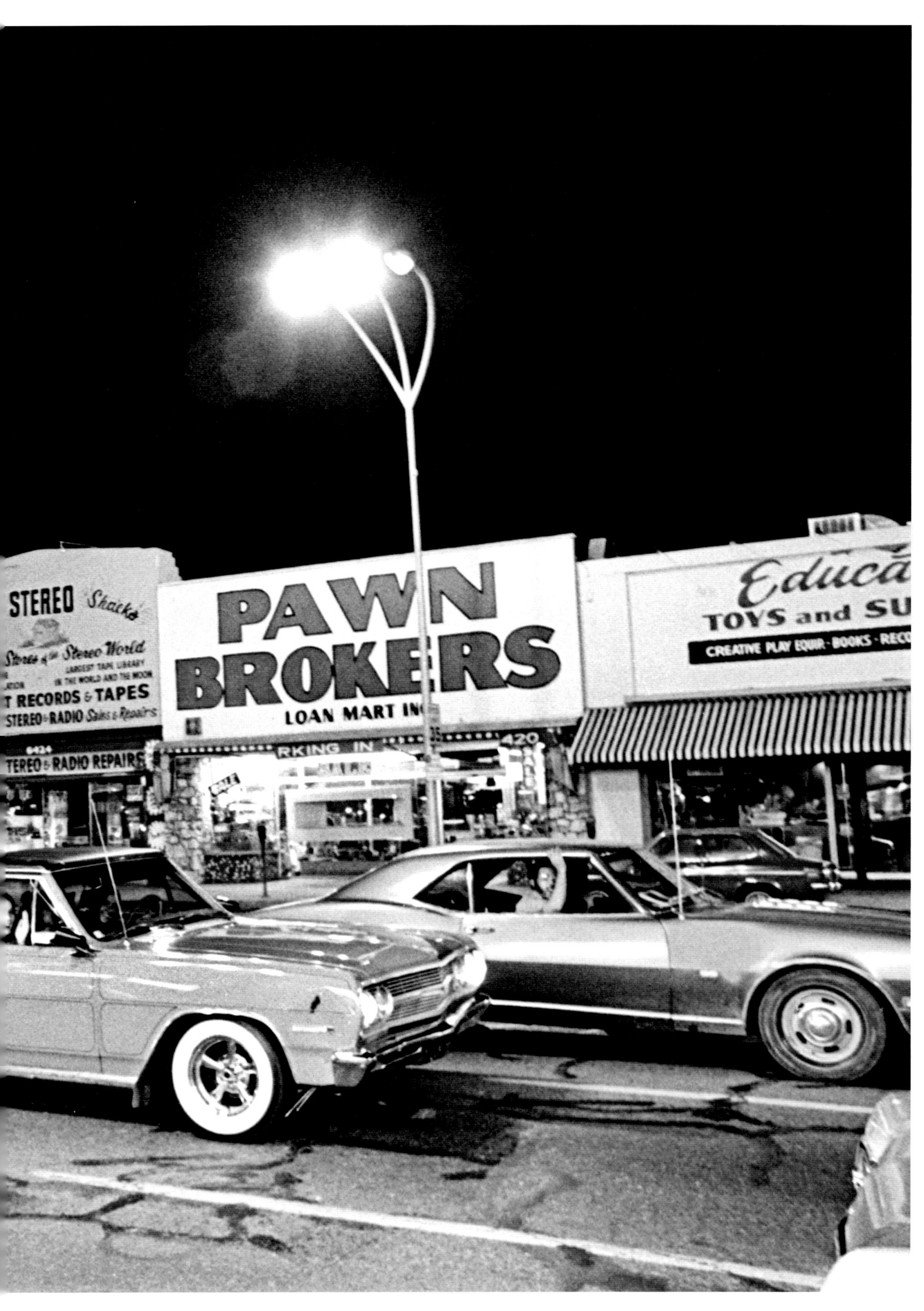

STEREO Shacks
Stores of the Stereo World
LARGEST TAPE LIBRARY
IN THE WORLD AND THE MOON
RECORDS & TAPES
STEREO & RADIO Sales & Repairs
6424
RADIO REPAIRS
PAWN
BROKERS
LOAN MART INC
420
TOYS and
CREATIVE PLAY EQUIP. · BOOKS ·

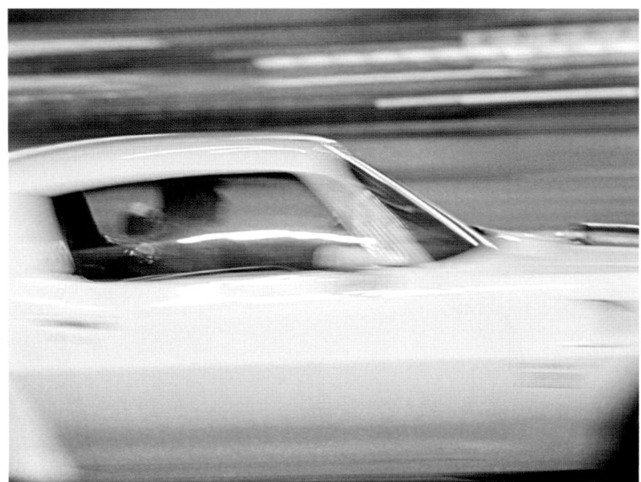

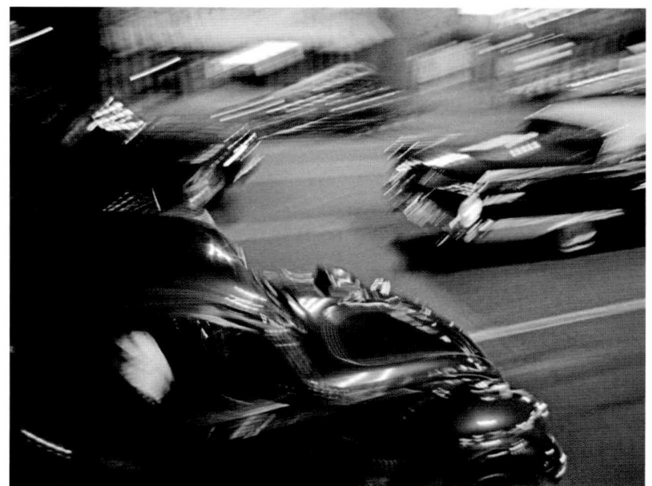

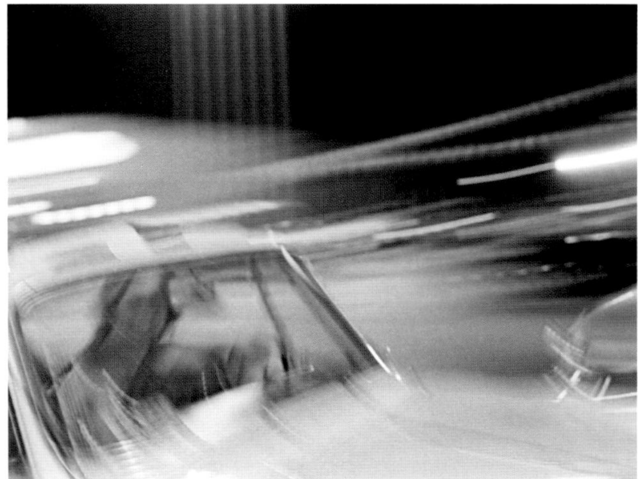

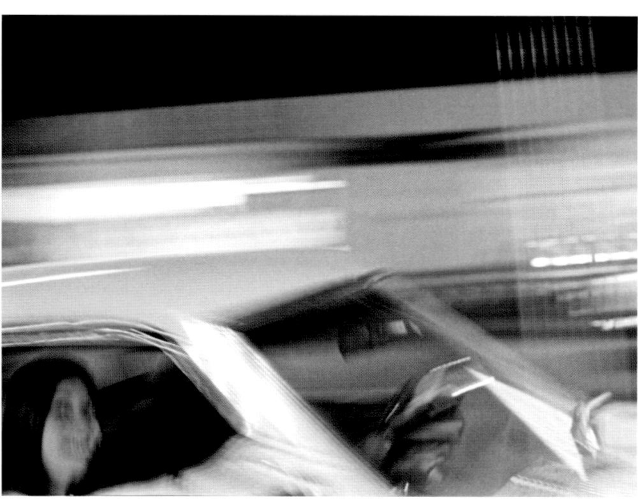

"I deliberately worked at getting people to look directly at my camera before I took the shot. I concentrated as much, or more, on making images of the people than their cars."

Many of the images were taken in a parking lot at the south end of Van Nuys Boulevard. It was a good place to park, show off your car and just hang out with friends.

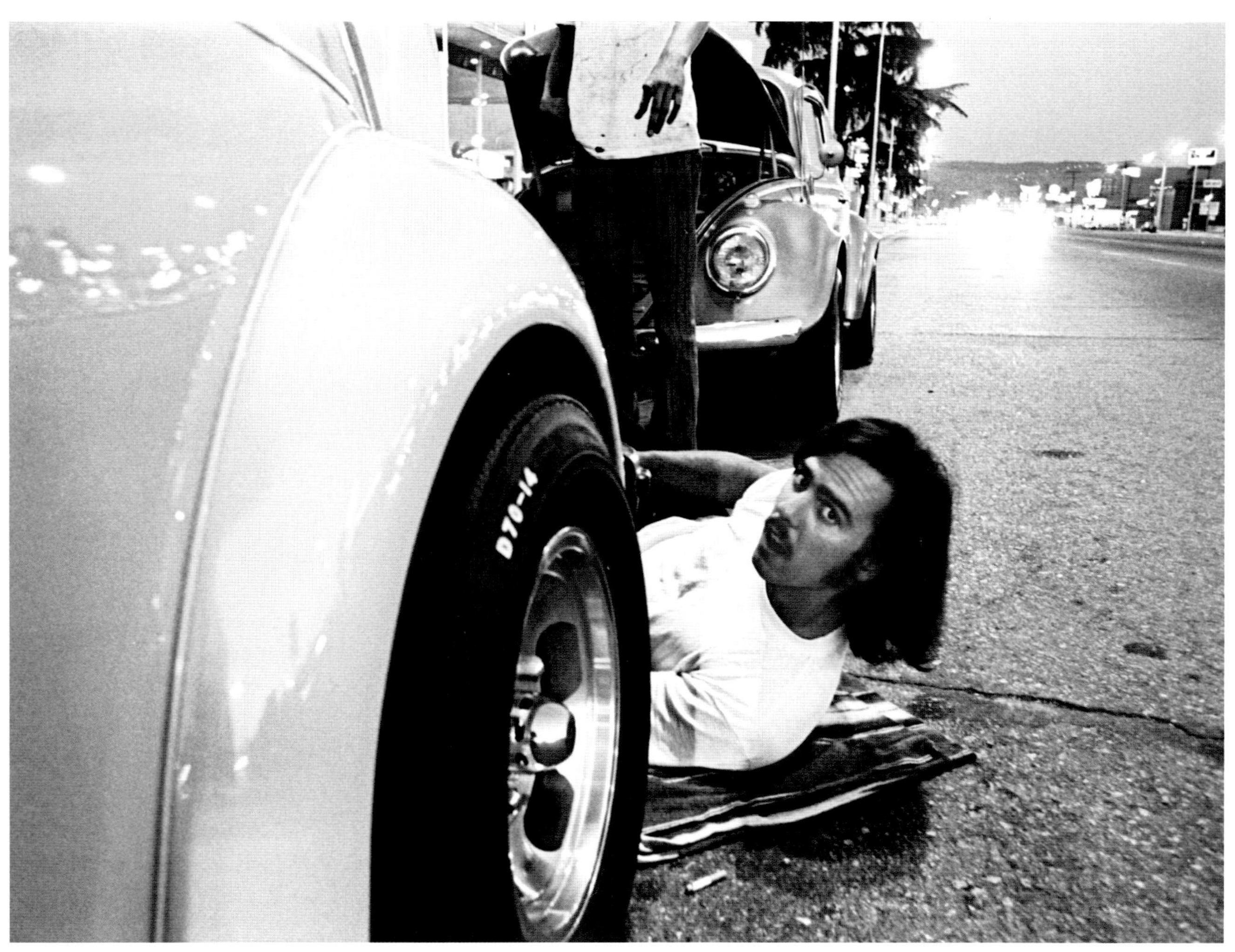

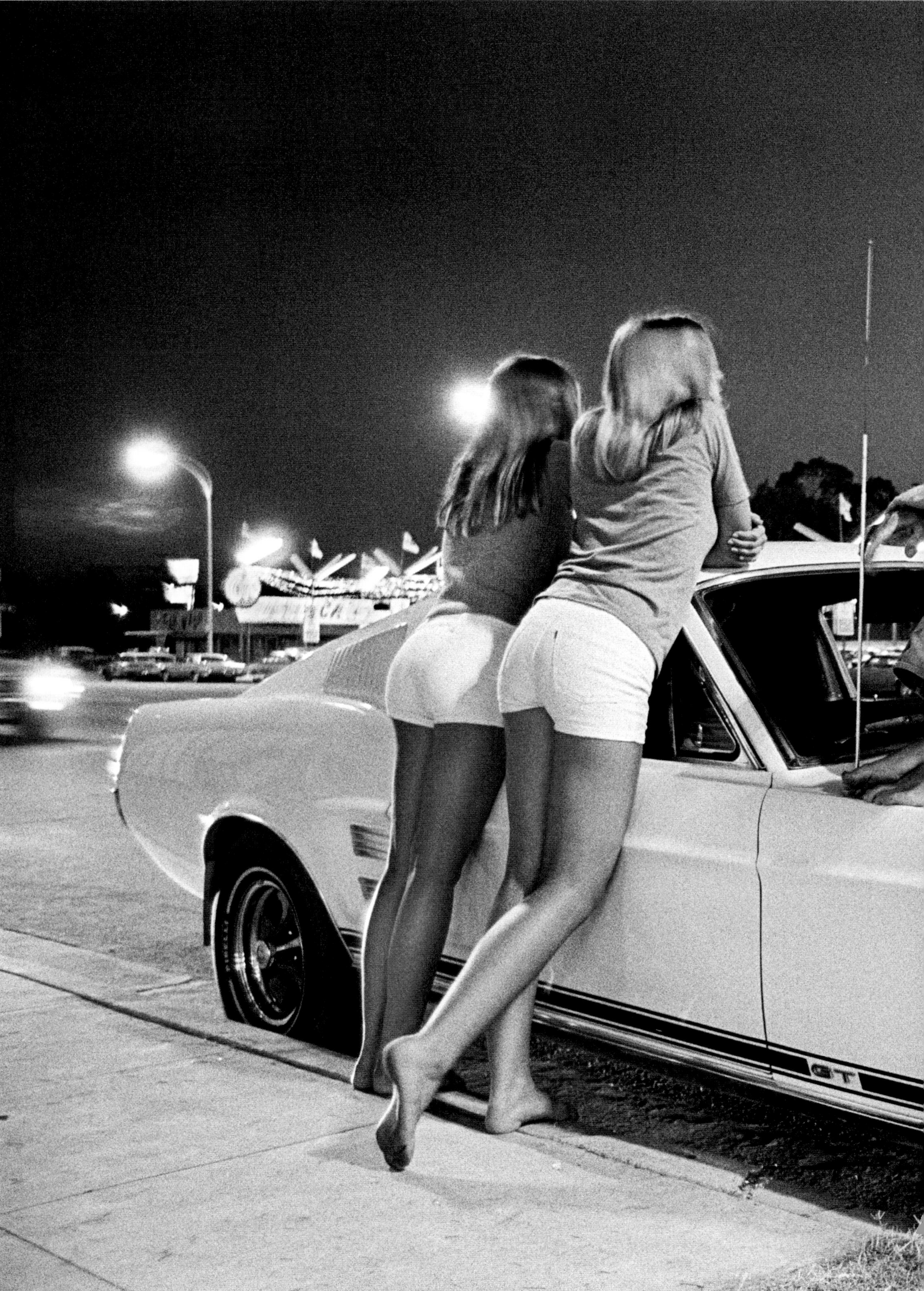
GT

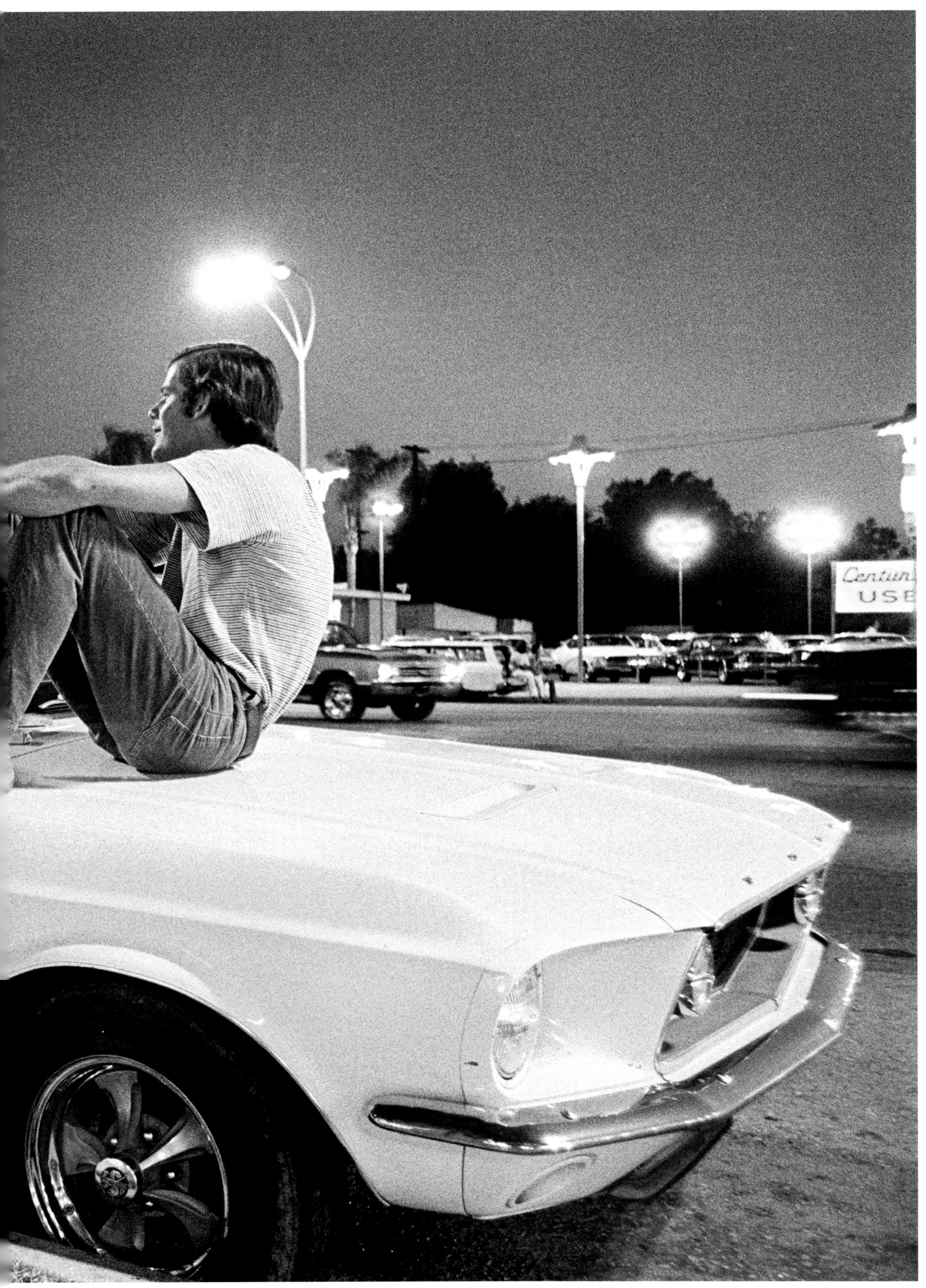

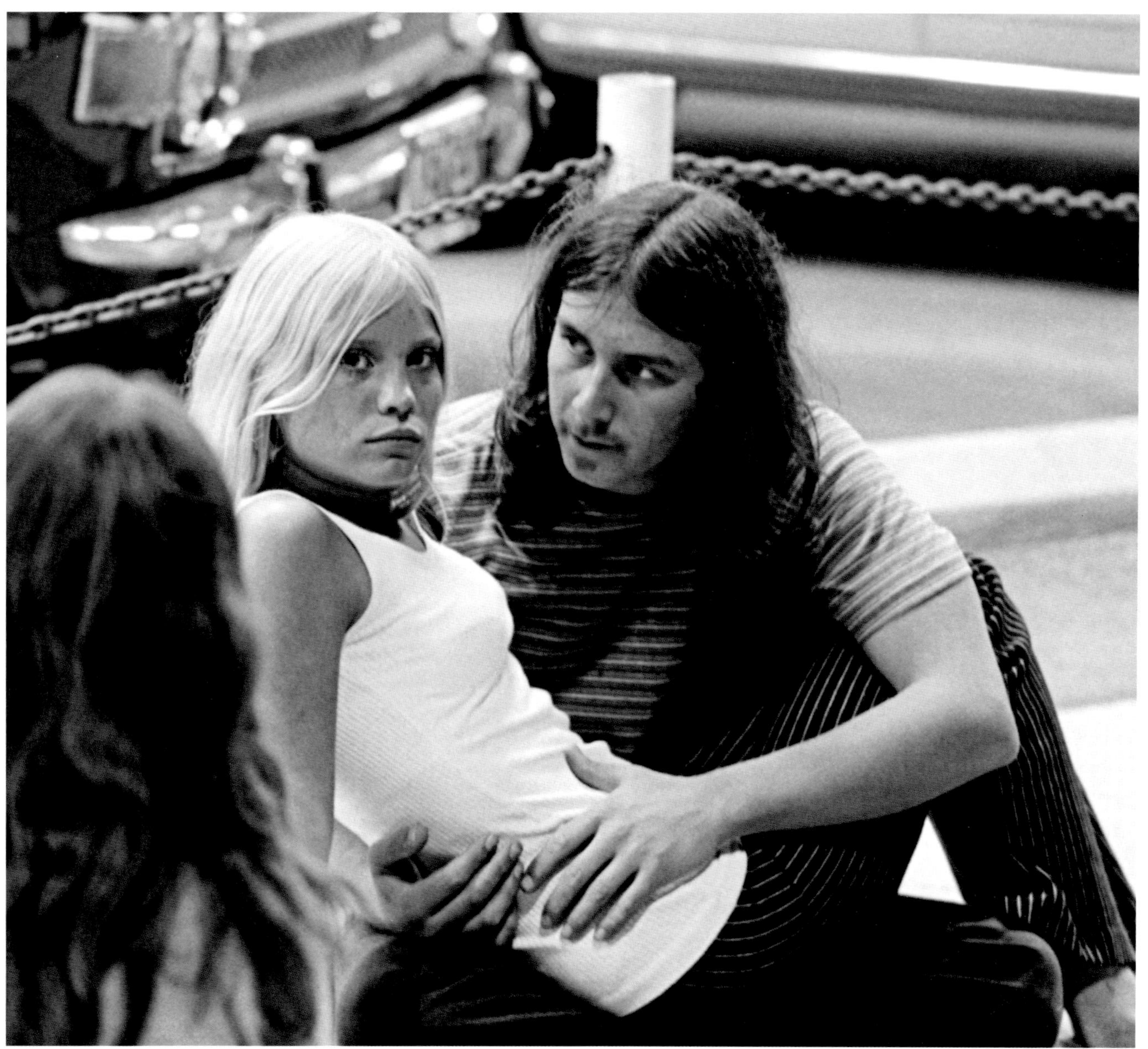

The draft numbers were going down, and people were once again gathering on the streets at night.

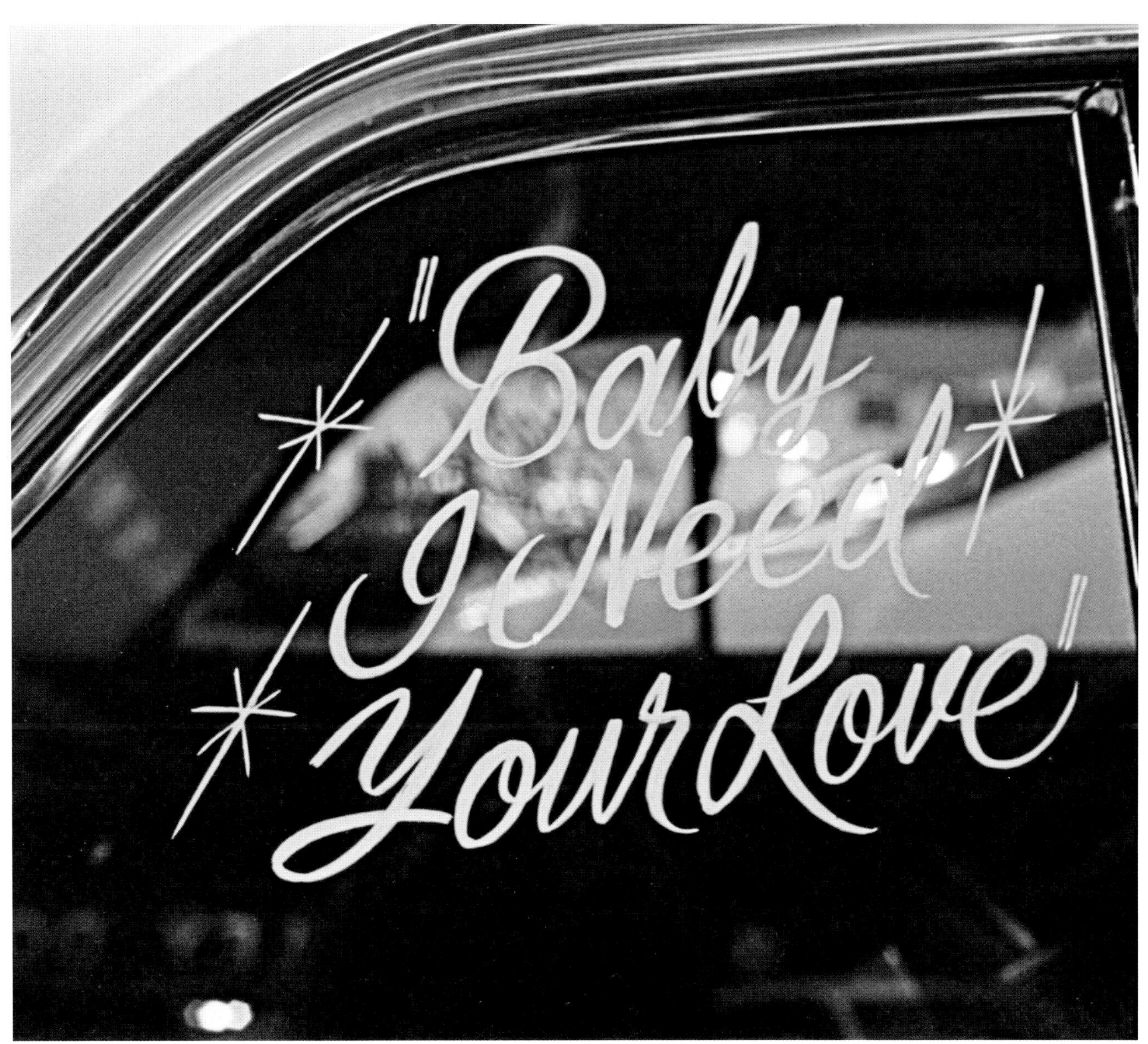

1972 was the last big year for the cruise nights on Van Nuys Boulevard. Then came the oil crisis, gasoline prices went through the roof, and the police increasingly issued tickets for loitering.

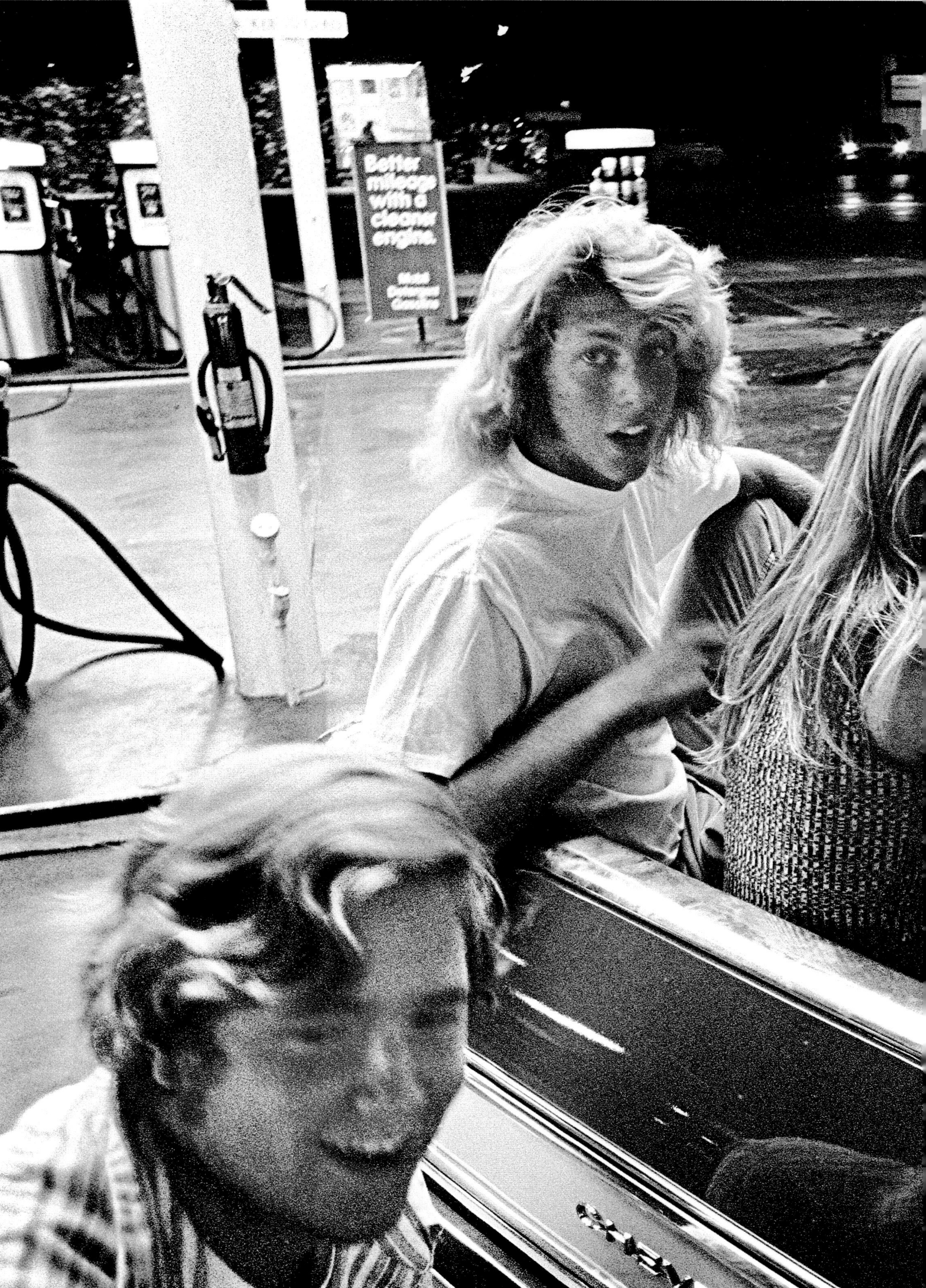
Better mileage with a cleaner engine.

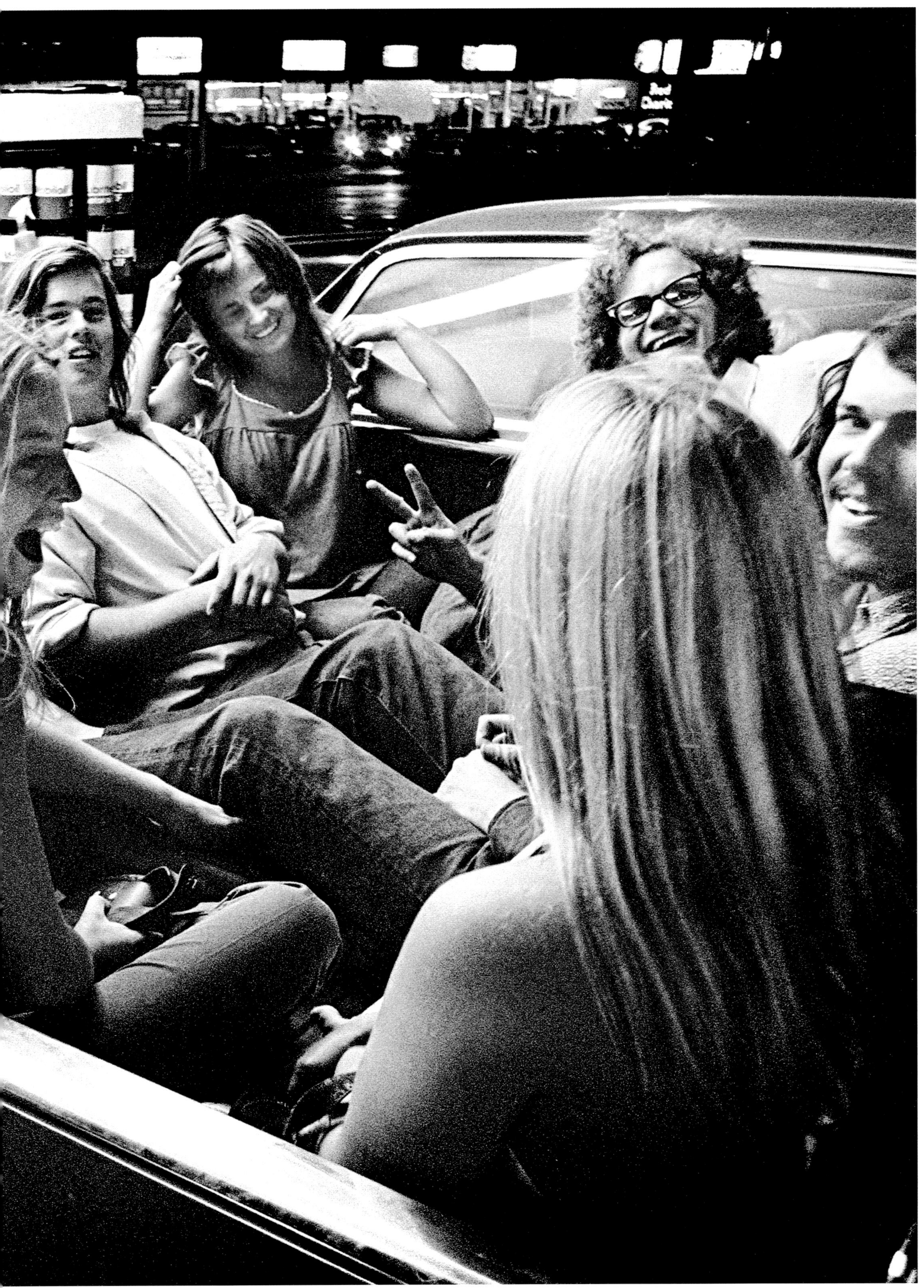

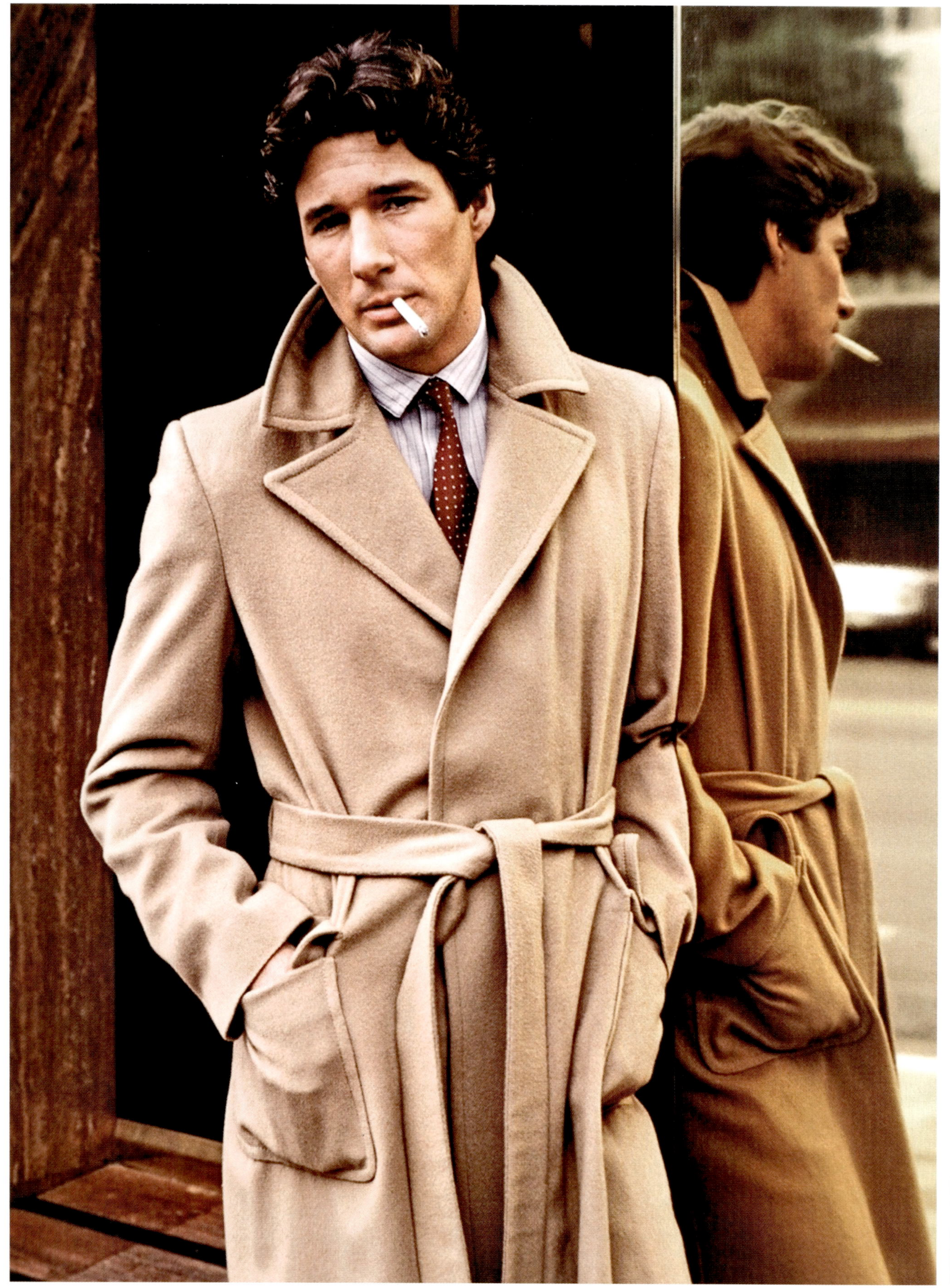

GIORGIO ARMANI'S BIG BREAKTHROUGH CAME WITH RICHARD GERE IN *AMERICAN GIGOLO.*

1.07

the armani code

TEXT *Ulf Lippitz*

AND IF THERE'S ONE THING WE SHOULD THANK THE ITALIAN DESIGNER FOR, IT'S FOR SAVING MAN-KIND FROM THE BOXY SUIT JACKET.

It all started with a pair of scissors. A small tool with an enormous impact. Giorgio Armani used these scissors to cut the inner lining out of a suit, thus changing men's silhouettes, and even their gait. As if he had taken a weight off their shoulders, allowing golfers, musicians and bankers to stroll along leisurely – just like the character played by Richard Gere in the 1980's movie *American Gigolo*, a guy who will only let water and Armani touch his skin.

The movie was a breakthrough: for its leading actor, for Giorgio Armani, and for Italian fashion at large. Even years later, Giorgio Armani would say that he had been amazed when he had understood that the movie was in effect advertising his look all around the world: "I would never have been able to afford advertising like that back then."

The scene in which Richard Gere gently touches an Armani jacket and opens drawers containing carefully folded shirts and well-sorted ties marks the turning point in the fashion designer's career. If you want to understand why his reserved look of plain shirts, cotton trousers and casual jackets became such a huge success, you have to think of the era in which this movie came to the theaters.

The 1970s, an extravagant era that British magazine *The Face* described as "the decade that taste forgot" had just ended. The seventies were the time when stars like Elton John, Mick Jagger or David Bowie were always dressed like circus clowns. And all of a sudden, this Italian fashion designer came along who no longer stood for fringes, feathers and gender fluidity but for a clear-cut style that emphasized male silhouettes. Where disco propagated glamour, Armani demanded class.

Armani also discovered a new target group which had been largely neglected up to that time. While Paris fashion shows focused on women, designers in Milan experimented with men's fashion. Male consumers soon adopted the diligent way in which Richard Gere treated his clothes in *American Gigolo*. For the first time, men consciously chose a style. After the movie's success, American journalists traveled to Italy and sent home enthusiastic reports of new fashion designers whose names they had to form in their mouths like arancini balls: Gianfranco Ferré, Gianni Versace and, of course, Giorgio Armani.

Armani's fashion became a trademark of casual elegance for modern men firmly anchored in their lives. Wearing Armani meant that you were dancing on the bright side of life. In 1986 the Pet Shop Boys' Milan hymn "Paninaro" included the reference "Armani, Armani, A-A-Armani". Bret Easton Ellis's bestseller *American Psycho* describes over several pages the making of an Armani suit. The Italian's name experienced a change in meaning: from a relatively common northern Italian family name to a synonym for fashion know-it-alls.

There's this scene in the 1993 thriller *Rising Sun* describing a phenomenon that manifested itself across various classes. Sean Connery plays a policeman with impeccable manners who encounters a group of gangsters. When they see the policeman's fancy suit, one of the bad guys asks, "Emporio or Giorgio?" Sean Connery answers: "Giorgio". The criminals nod their heads, the ice is broken: this cop is cool. Rumor has it, by the way, that Sean Connery "forgot" to return his suits after the shooting had been completed.

You practically can't overestimate Gior-

Armani changed men's silhouettes, and even their gait. As if he had taken a weight off their shoulders.

The Italian designer stood for a clear-cut style that empha-sized male silhou-ettes. Where disco propa-gated glamour, Armani demanded class.

gio Armani's life-time achievements. He outfitted men and, later on, also women, with a style reminiscent of Japanese minimalism, using mostly subtle colors, always classy. Cate Blanchett and Julia Roberts called him a friend. Suzy Menkes, the world's most influential fashion critic, frankly admitted that she was a fan of his work, abandoning her usual professional distance. Even at the age of ninety-one, Giorgio Armani still designed fashion himself, receiving the audience's kudos after fashion shows. With an estimated fortune of €8.5 billion, he would have been perfectly able to do nothing but enjoy the *dolce vita*. But that wasn't an option for him: Giorgio Armani didn't go voluntarily; he kept working up until the very end.

Giorgio Armani was born in Piacenza in northern Italy. Actually he (and his parents) had planned for him to study medicine in Milan. Young Giorgio, however, felt a different calling. He dropped out of university and started working as a window dresser at La Rinascente, a luxury department store in Milan. Armani later became head buyer at the store and head of the men's fashion boutique. In 1961 he started to design suits for Nino Cerruti. Armani's partner, the architect Sergio Galeotti, finally persuaded him to produce his first own men's collection.

When Giorgio Armani became a brand, Giorgio Armani the person increasingly disappeared in the background. Over the years, he perfected his ability of cooling down rooms with his glance, becoming unapproachable, walling himself off. If you look at interviews from the 1980s, it'll break your heart to see him answering questions on Italian TV with a charming smile on his lips. Twenty-five years later, Giorgio Armani the person hardly had anything to do with the man he used to be back then.

He often sat in his office at his Teatro Armani, where he regularly celebrated his fashion shows (some say that there were paid claqueurs among the audience). If you had seen him there, sitting enthroned in his chair behind his desk, surrounded by two bodyguards and two assistants, you would have been forced to acknowledge: Giorgio Armani was as cold as a fish. Maybe it was the wounds inflicted on him by life and the side-effects of success that made him become like that.

Armani would never have said anything that could have damaged his reputation. He didn't allow himself any weaknesses, not even mourning the love of his life, Sergio Galeotti, who passed away in 1985. At his fashion week parties, everyone knew that the two were a couple, but everyone abided by the unspoken rule of "Don't ask, don't tell." It seemed as if Giorgio Armani had taken the old platitude of "What doesn't kill you only makes you stronger" to heart. Discipline always was very important to him. "My private life only comes second to my business life." Just another cool manager statement.

Up to his death, he allowed himself hardly any breaks when he was at work. "I abide by strict rules", he explained. He expected absolute commitment from his staff. If one of them left the company to work for another fashion house, the master would withdraw his favor. "That's cheating on me – as if a married woman leaves her husband to live with her lover." They would receive the harshest punishment in the Armani universe: they were forgotten. In the good Italian tradition, trust was only placed in "la famiglia". Armani installed two of his nieces and one of his nephews in leading positions. "My family will always stand by me – no matter what," he said.

Without any doubt, his determination was part of his success – in addition to his talent of identifying the signs of the times early on. At the beginning of the new millennium, Suzy Menkes proclaimed the new brand trend for the twenty-first century: "To BE or not to BE", with BE standing for brand extension, i.e., extending a brand to other areas.

Giorgio Armani had already paved the way for this strategy in his own business. He was the first luxury designer to combine the worlds of fashion and home decoration for downmarket products. After the Hollywood movies of the 1980s, wardrobe contents had been thoroughly Armanized, although the wardrobes themselves were still from IKEA. So the master of good taste went on to design wardrobes – and aesthetic interior designs to surround them. In his department store in Milan at the Montenapoleone metro station, he started selling furniture and home textiles, chocolates and flowers, perfumes and glasses. He also opened a restaurant and a club there. And just a stone's throw away, the brand even opened up a new spa. Armani even furnished an entire hotel in Dubai.

Anyone who has seen *Halston*, the Netflix series about the eponymous designer, was able to witness how marketing too many products can result in a dilution of a brand if there's no one supervising these developments and if customers grow tired of it. Giorgio Armani always remained in charge of his licensing; his products still have the typical minimalistic Armani touch. Or can anyone remember an Armani suit with flower prints, silk cords and glitter appliques?

After the success of *American Gigolo,* American journalists traveled to Italy and sent home enthusiastic reports of new fashion designers whose names they had to form in their mouths like arancini balls.

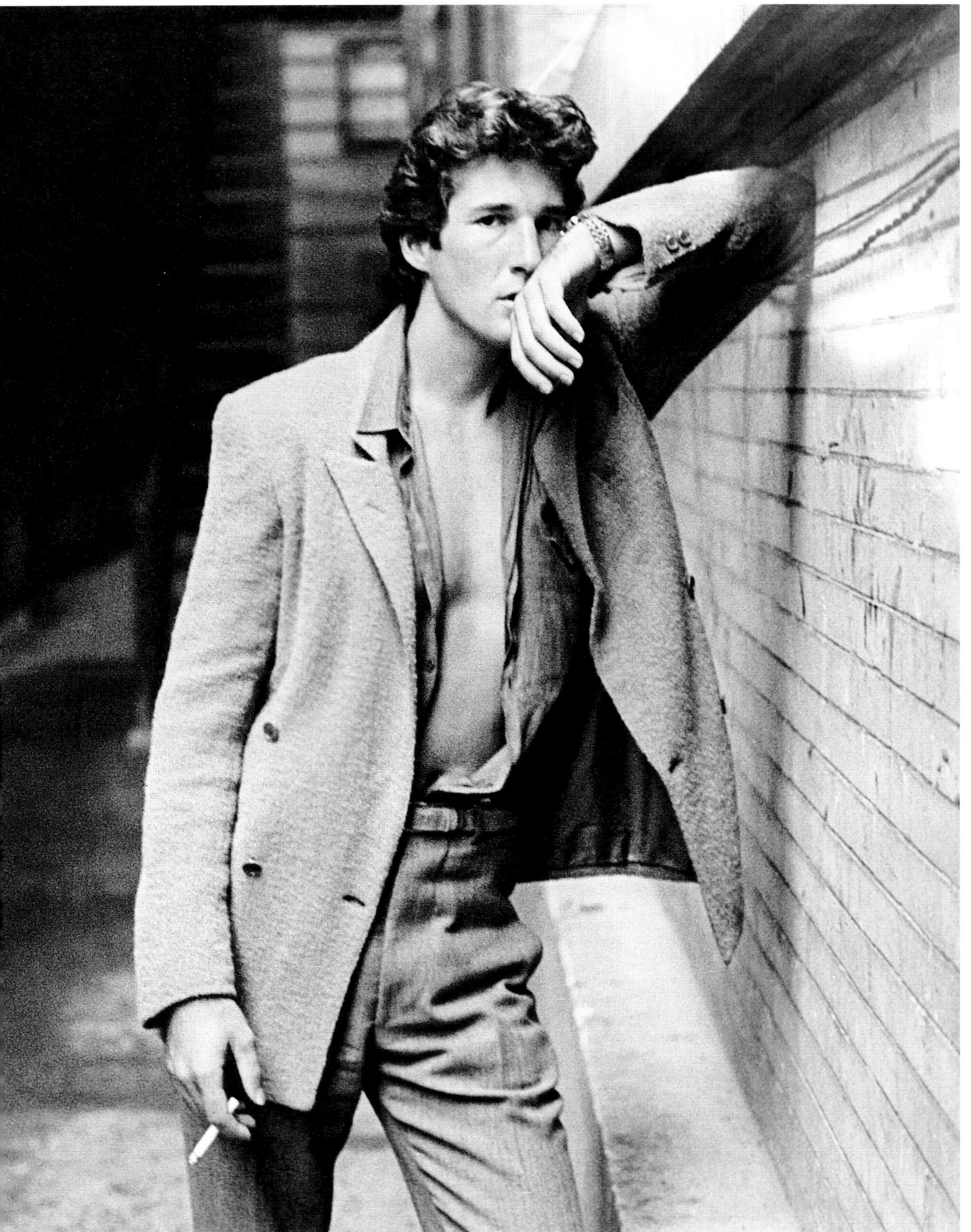

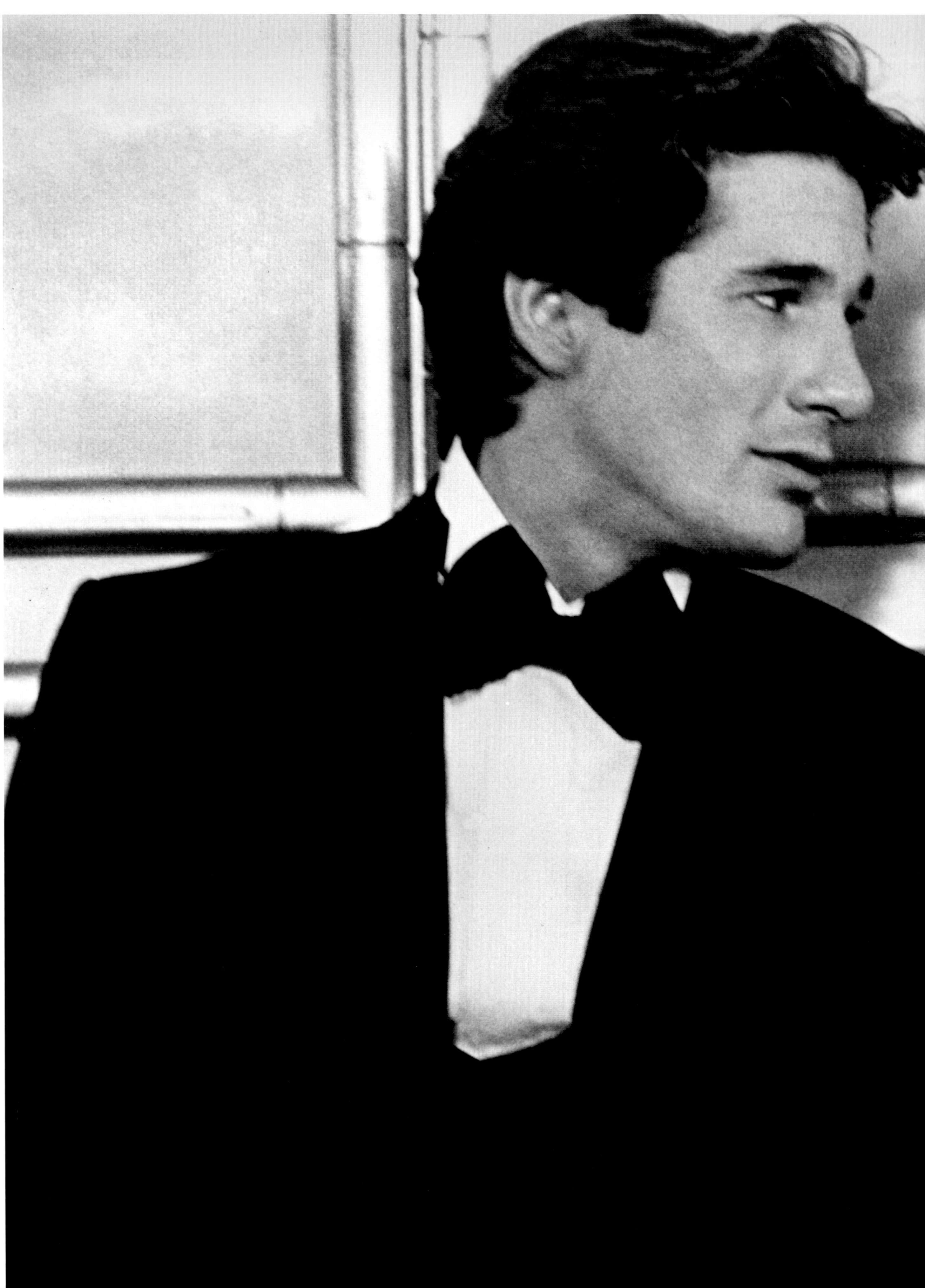

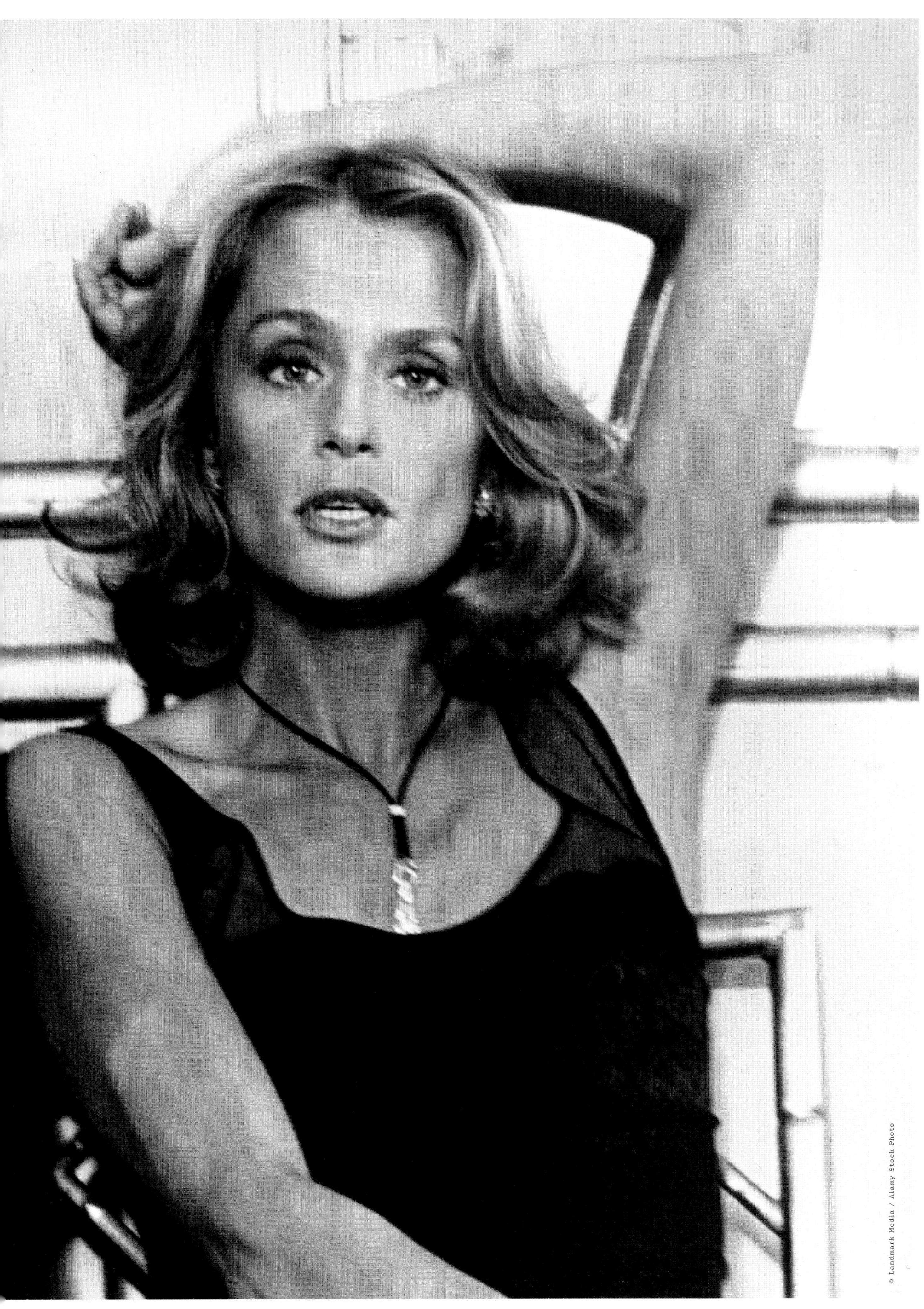

1.08

hard facts

EVERYTHING YOU SHOULD MORE OR LESS KNOW

WIKIPEDIA DEFINES "PERSONALITY" AS "ANY PERSON'S COLLECTION OF INTERRELATED BEHAVIORAL, COGNITIVE, AND EMOTIONAL PATTERNS THAT COMPRISE A PERSON'S UNIQUE ADJUSTMENT TO LIFE". PROOF THAT WE'RE ALL UNIQUE. STILL, SOME PEOPLE SIMPLY COME ACROSS AS HAVING MORE PERSONALITY THAN OTHERS. THERE'S NO EXACT FORMULA FOR THAT, OF COURSE. BUT HEY – WHY LET THAT STOP US?

(Self-Confidence + Authenticity) × (Empathy + Integrity) + Resilience − Fear of Mistakes =

(STRONG) PERSONALITY

THE KEY INGREDIENTS

☛ Self-confidence
Knowing who you are, what you're capable of – and what you can't do (yet).

☛ Authenticity
Being real and consistent – aligning your thoughts, feelings and actions. Authenticity can't be faked, which makes it all the more compelling.

☛ Empathy
People who can put themselves in others' shoes can lead, inspire – or simply connect.

☛ Integrity
A strong set of values that holds you up – especially when things get tough or unpopular opinions need voicing. Important in crisis situations.

☛ Resilience
The ability to handle setbacks without losing heart. Responding without drama (or only briefly) – giving you a chance to grow.

☛ Little fear of making mistakes
Strength doesn't mean aiming for perfection but owning your quirks and flaws – honestly and unapologetically.

BONUS TRAIT:

☛ A sense of purpose ☚
That thing we see in someone's eyes (or secretly envy): a sense of what gives their life meaning.

HOW COOL AM I?

The Coolness Test

It's official. After decades of being bullied and humiliated before finally landing an influential position in a leading research institution, a group of nerds set out to unravel the secret of what it takes to be cool. Their findings were validated using several select brands in order to define ten characteristics of brand coolness. We've translated these into personality traits and used them to develop ten questions that you can now answer in order to determine whether you're as cool as you think – or to find out just how cool you are.

Go on. What are you waiting for?

01 I'm special.

Untrue of me ① ② ③ ④ ⑤ Very true of me

02 I look good.

Untrue of me ① ② ③ ④ ⑤ Very true of me

03 I'm energetic and outgoing.

Untrue of me ① ② ③ ④ ⑤ Very true of me

04 I'm respected and have a good reputation.

Untrue of me ① ② ③ ④ ⑤ Very true of me

05 I'm rebellious, a nonconformist.

Untrue of me ① ② ③ ④ ⑤ Very true of me

06 I'm original. I do my own thing.

Untrue of me ① ② ③ ④ ⑤ Very true of me

07 I always say what's on my mind.

Untrue of me ① ② ③ ④ ⑤ Very true of me

08 I'm bored by the mainstream.*

Untrue of me ① ② ③ ④ ⑤ Very true of me

09 I'm iconic.

Untrue of me ① ② ③ ④ ⑤ Very true of me

10 I have fans, not followers.

Untrue of me ① ② ③ ④ ⑤ Very true of me

*Justin Bieber? Who's Justin Bieber?

Evaluation

100 points (mathematically impossible):
Still, or perhaps precisely because of this, you're the coolest! Congratulations! The only way to get 100 points is if you don't need a coolness test to prove you're cool.

40–50 points:
Pretty cool! But don't get too excited. Above all, don't tell anyone how you scored. Instead, read through our evaluation for 100 points above.

30–40 points:
Easy-going.

20–30 points:
Okay.

10–20 points:
Whew! You'd better take the test again.
Here's a little tip: cheat your way into being a little cooler. The way you see yourself doesn't necessarily have to match the way others see you.

0–10 points:
Too bad! But no worries: you've already taken the first step in the right direction.

TOTAL RECALL. OR: WHAT IS MEMORY?

Try to remember: not only does our ability to store memories slow down with age, our power of recollection also begins to fade. And worse: a lot of young people seem to have this problem as well.

Memory basically refers to nothing more than the ability of our nervous system to store information and retrieve it later. Depending on the period of time in which this content can be retrieved before it is forgotten, memory is divided into different categories:

Sensory memory is the first stage of our memory process and a sort of temporary buffer for sensory input. It holds a piece of information for a brief moment before it is further processed – or discarded.

Short-term memory, also known as working memory, forms the basis for conscious information processing. It stores a limited amount of information for immediate use.

Long-term memory is where information, experiences and skills are permanently stored. It enables us to access the past, recall knowledge and use skills that have been acquired over a longer period of time.

Declarative memory, a part of long-term memory, enables the conscious recall of facts, events and information. It includes semantic memory, which contains knowledge about the world

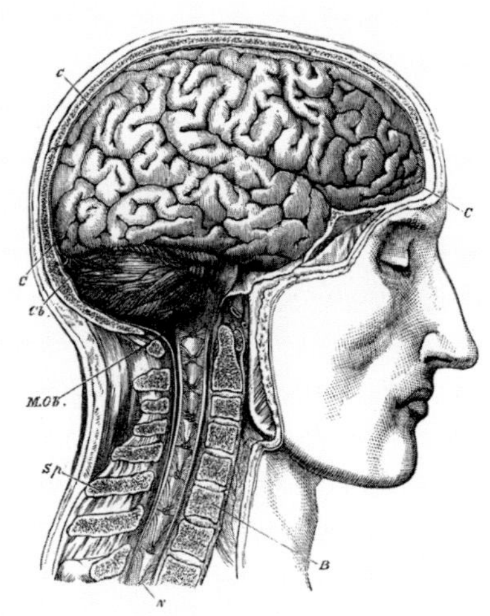

and general facts, as well as episodic memory, which stores personal experiences and events.

Procedural memory, also called behavioral memory, is another part of long-term memory. It allows skills, habits and motor sequences to be performed without conscious thought.

What is remembering?

Remembering refers to the ability of our long-term memory to consciously recall past content. The degree of retention in the brain increases with the importance of the information, the emotional significance and the association with other content. Remembering therefore involves consciously retrieving information from memory. Remembering, or recollection, also refers to the mental reliving of past experiences and events. A distinction is therefore made between the recollection of past events and the knowledge of those experiences.

What public pools and commercial television have in common

PUBLIC POOL

You rarely get in contact with water

The food is awful

You feel like you're constantly being watched

There's no end of body shaming

You hardly ever see any real celebrities

I'M A CELEBRITY...GET ME OUT OF HERE!

ON THE LAWN AT THE OUTDOOR POOL

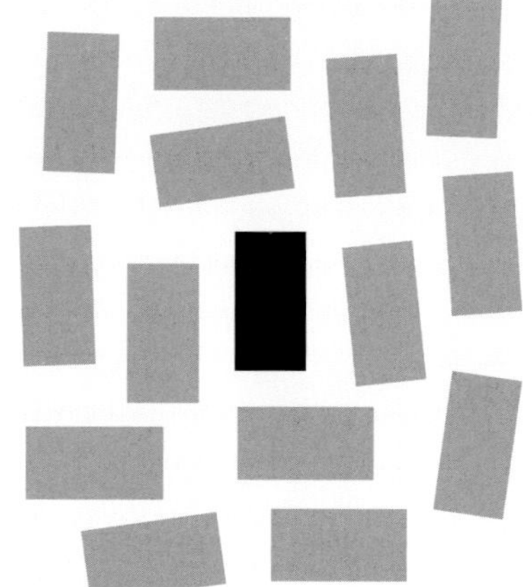

Towels with people lying in the sun

Towel that you're lying on

Towel that the soccer ball lands on

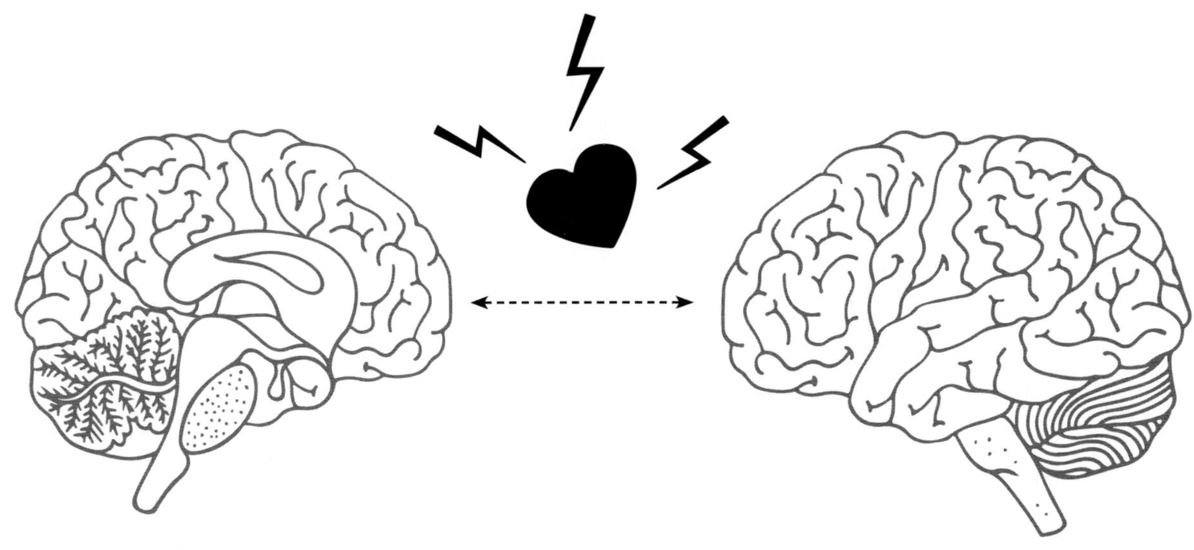

sapiosexuality

from Latin ***sapere***
("taste, know")
and ***sexus*** ("gender, sex")

A type of sexuality that involves attraction to a person's mind or intellect. The term therefore expresses a sexual preference for particularly intelligent people.

In other words, sapiosexuality equates smart with sexy. You could also call it the opposite of the popular misconception that smart people make poor lovers. In case you're now wondering whether women tend to be more sapiosexual than men, let's just say that there's evidence that semen quality increases with increasing IQ. At least according to the American evolutionary psychologist Geoffrey Miller, who has long studied the (sexual) advantages of the intellectually endowed. Some researchers even go so far as to say that the development of civilization was only possible because of the competition among men for women. We'll just leave it at that.

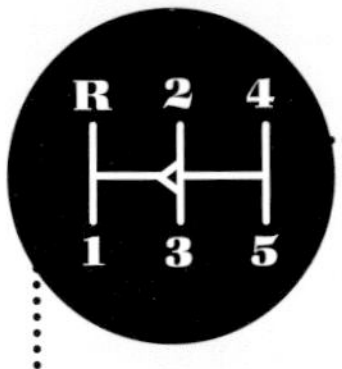

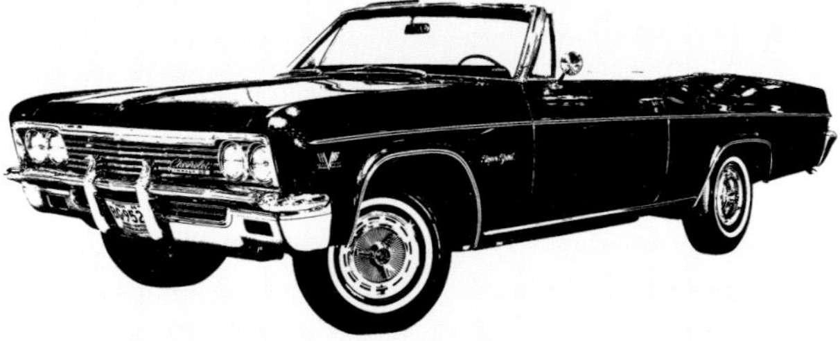

5 REASONS

WHY WE BURN MORE CALORIES DRIVING A STICK THAN AN AUTOMATIC:

Balancing the clutch on a hill
Starting uphill burns energy as we coordinate accelerator, clutch and brake pedal – a balancing act that challenges the body and, depending on the gradient, can even make you break a sweat.

Shifting gears
Shifting the gear lever engages the muscles in the arm like a light upper body workout – more so in the city than on the highway, of course.

Higher focus and concentration
Not only the physical exertion, but also the additional mental effort required to operate and coordinate the various pedals and gear stick results in a slight increase in calorie consumption.

Operating the clutch
Operating the clutch doesn't exactly match the exertion of a leg press at the gym, but the movements do come close to low-intensity fitness training.

Award-winning?
Yes, it depends on how you drive. You burn about 120 calories during a typical one-hour journey. A Grand Prix racer, on the other hand, will burn around 1,200 calories in the same amount of time.

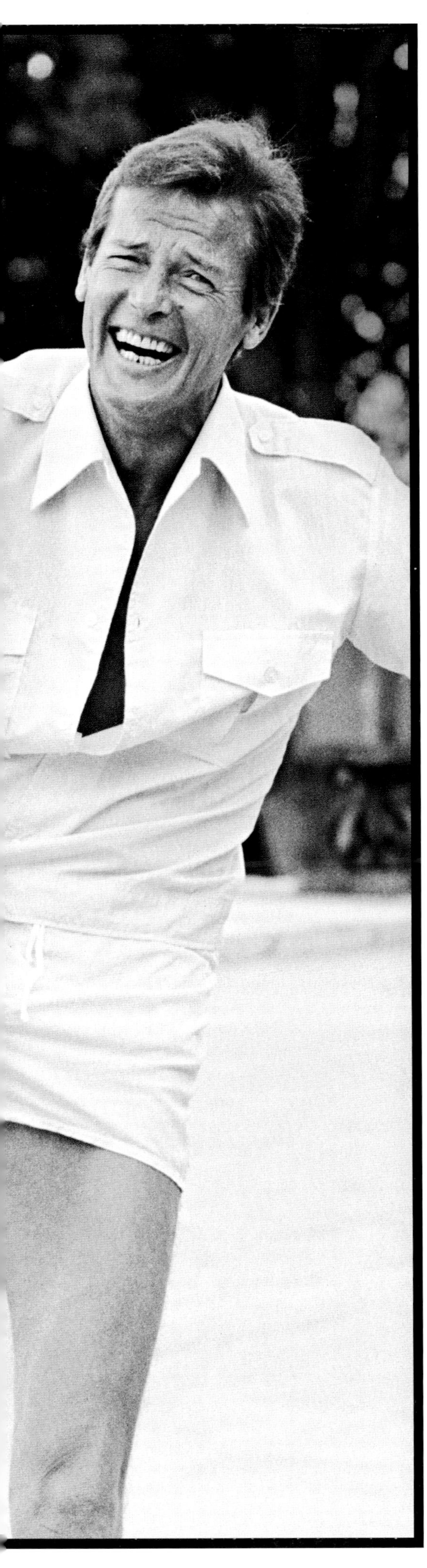

crack another egg on it 2

There was one thing Terry O'Neill could never understand: how fellow photographers would stop working once they thought they'd captured the shot. Because, as he put it, "Photography is all about shooting and capturing a moment spontaneously, not worrying about what picture you have already taken."

That must have been the case on this sunny day in the mid-1970s in Beverly Hills. Roger Moore, who was in the process of redefining the character of James Bond, did what you do when visiting the home of a mischievous fellow actor like Peter Sellers.

cool stuff 2.01

TEXT *Wiebke Brauer / Burkhard Maria Zimmermann*

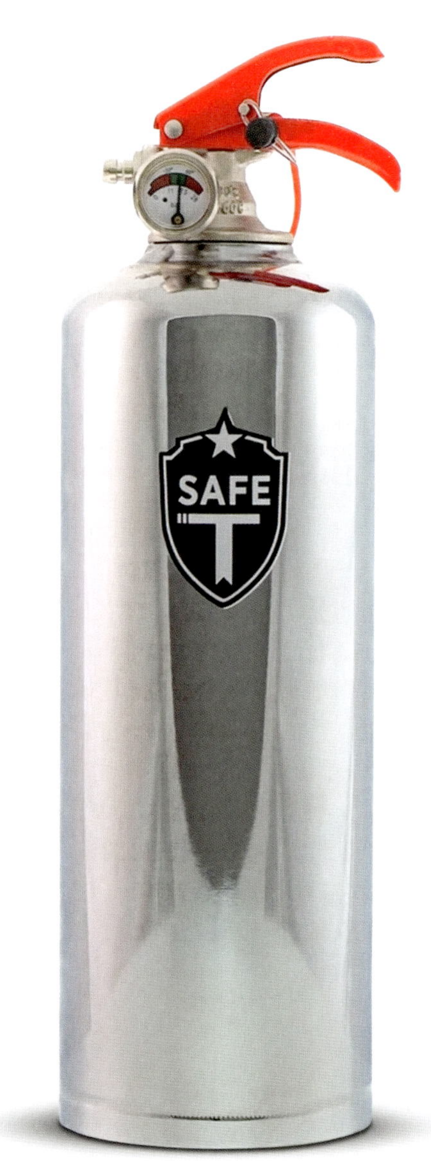

OPEN FIRE!

The bad news first: fire extinguishers in the European Union have to be red. Any deviation from this color would not be in compliance with European Standard EN3. The good news is that this regulation only applies to fire extinguishers in commercial buildings. So nothing stands in the way of a private purchase of this handmade and fully chrome-plated specimen.

→ safe-t.eu

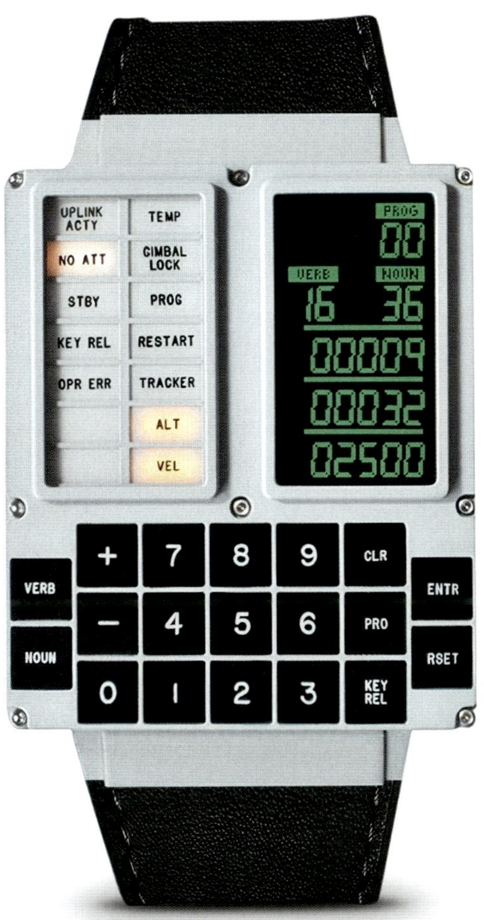

TAKE ME TO THE MOON

"This historic event perhaps taught us more about ourselves as human beings than about the moon itself," German newspaper *FAZ* once wrote, looking back at the moon landing of July 1969. And it clearly remains a source of fascination to this day. British start-up Apollo Instruments spent four years working on the DSKY Moonwatch, an exact replica of the Apollo Guidance Computer used on the Apollo missions. The watch features GPS navigation, an alarm, a stopwatch and a fully functional keyboard with the original, historical font.

→ apollo-instruments.com

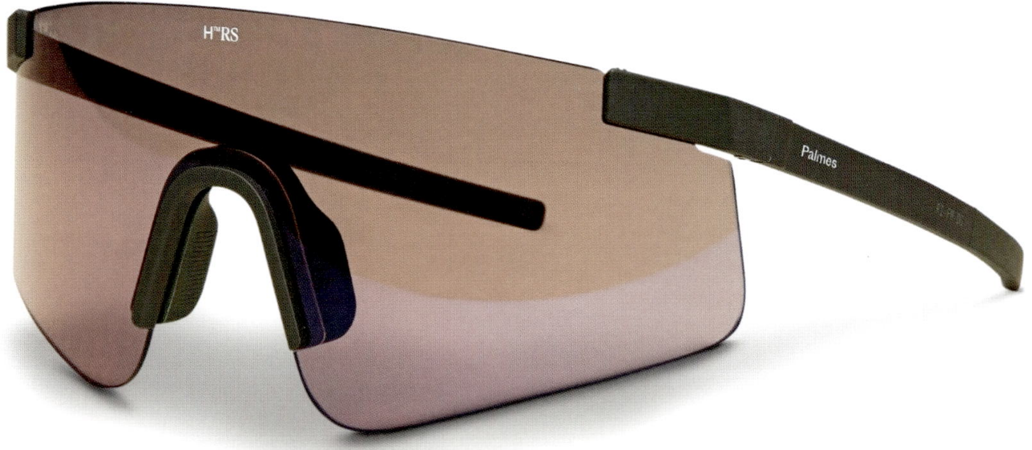

FAMILY RESEMBLANCE

Let's get this straight once and for all: *The Three Musketeers* and *The Count of Monte Cristo* were written by Alexandre Dumas père. His son, Alexandre Dumas fils, wrote *The Lady of the Camellias* – and the following sentence: "Life is enchanting; you just have to put on the right glasses to see it."

→ clothbase.com

APOTHEOSIS

The following quote is from Chilean writer Isabel Allende: “I carry around a little stool to stand on when people want a picture with their cellular phones.” With the vintage charm of the Cobardt bar stool, you’ll be sure to make a big impression.

→ fischers-lagerhaus.de

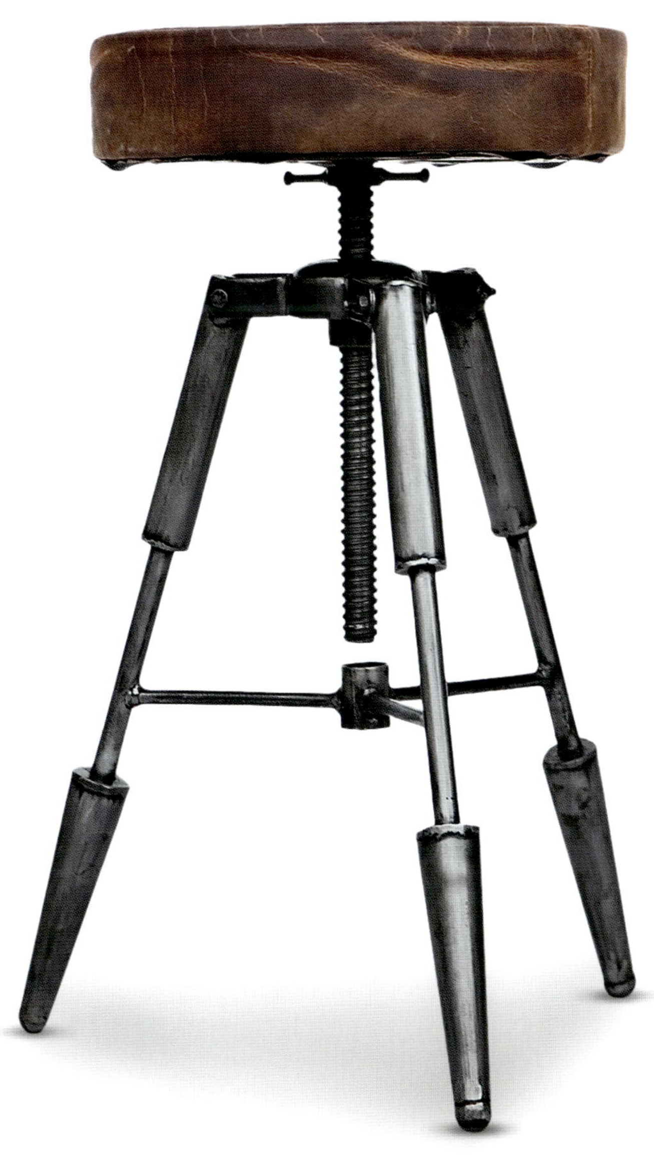

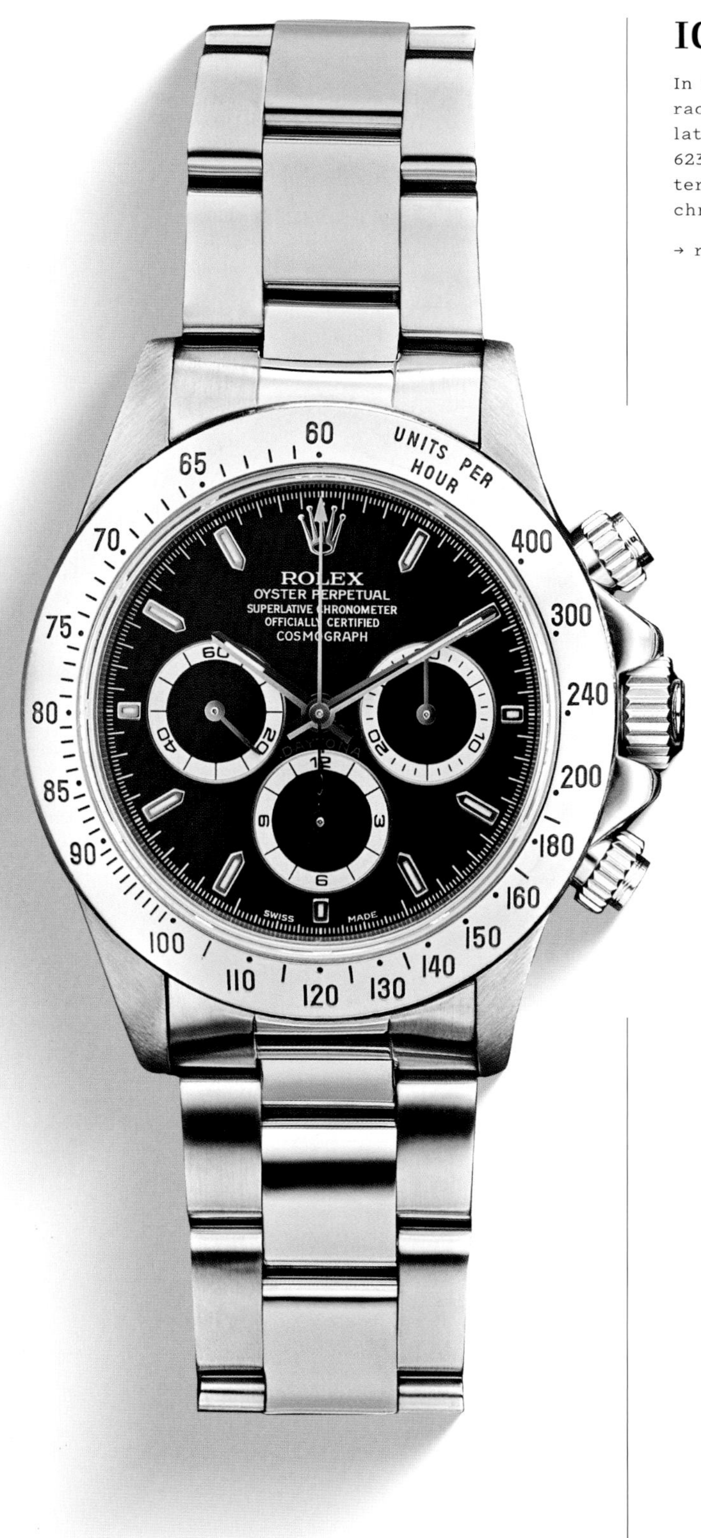

ICON OF COOL

In 1962 Rolex became the official timekeeper of the races at Daytona International Speedway. One year later, the company launched the Cosmograph Reference 6239 – soon nicknamed "Daytona". Incidentally, the term "Cosmograph" was coined exclusively for Rolex chronographs.

→ rolex.com

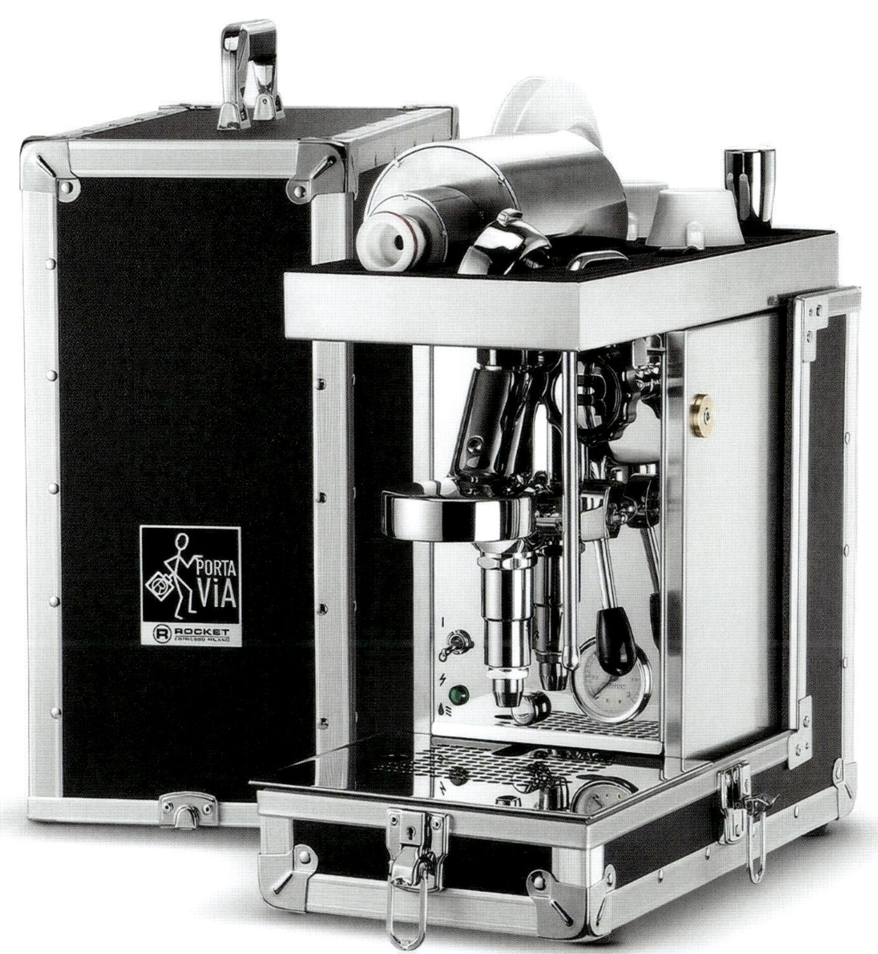

ROCKET SCIENCE

Coffee-to-go cups are a modern-day scourge, but it doesn't have to be that way. Italian manufacturer Rocket Espresso has long since come up with a solution: the Porta Via (literally: "take away"). This portable espresso machine comes with a milk frothing system and a robust case for transport. The only drawback might be that it weighs almost thirty kilos and needs electricity to work. But we're confident you'll come up with a solution.

→ rocket-espresso.com

WHAT PERFECTION SOUNDS LIKE

The 175 turntable from Burmester strives for nothing less than perfection. The platter features a brass core sandwiched in between two layers of aluminum to create optimum damping properties. The table is driven by four motors grouped around the sub-platter for absolutely quiet play. And the arm? Rests on a bearing of steel and ceramic and always delivers the needle so gently as if it were allowed to do it only this once and never again.

→ burmester.de

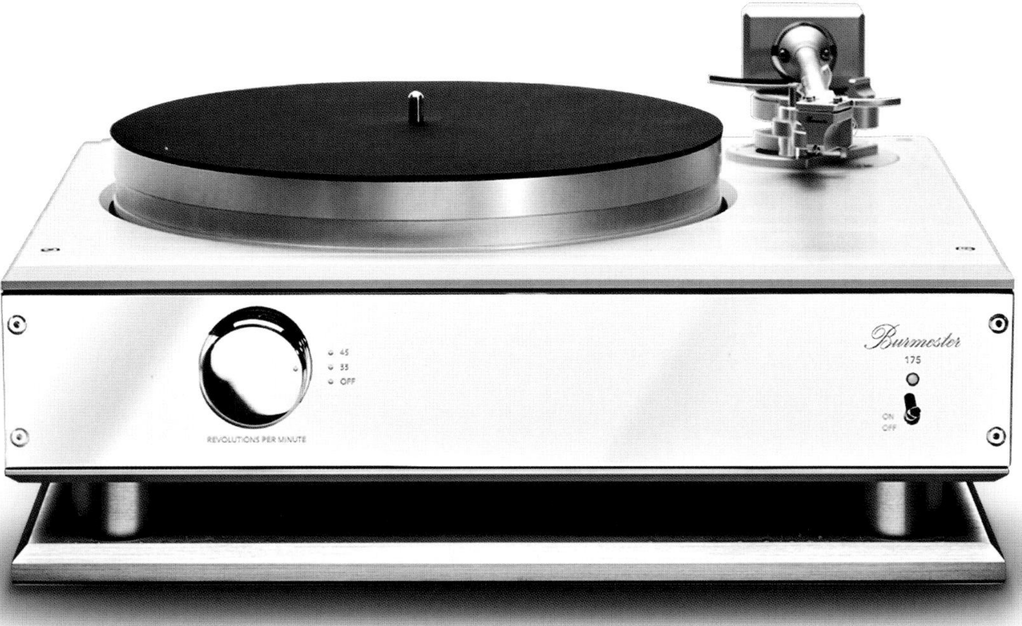

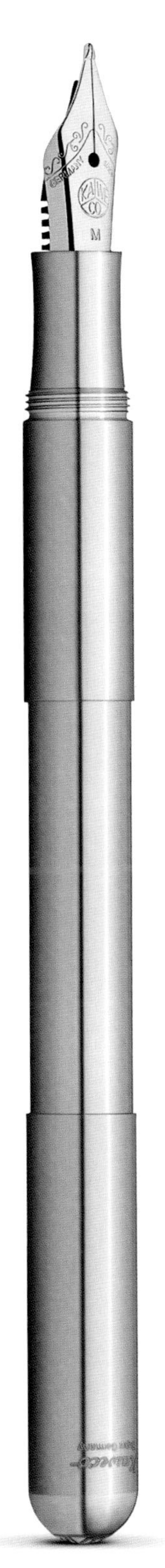

CLASSIFIED AD

"This is the cheaper, more practical version of a Mercedes. All I really need is this and a notepad. I could go for hours, days, weeks." That's how American playwright and screenwriter Jon Robin Baitz once described the Kaweco Sport in an interview with *The New York Times*. Sales of the fountain pen soared. The pen you see here is the Liliput – and as the name suggests, it is a particularly minimalist model.

→ kaweco-pen.com

measuring time 2.02

TEXT *Marko Knab*
PHOTOS *Richard Mille / DPPI*

1968 IS AN EVENTFUL YEAR, SHAKING UP NOT ONLY POLITICS AND SOCIETY BUT ALSO MOTORSPORTS. WINGS START APPEARING ON FORMULA 1 RACE CARS, AND TURBINE CARS ATTEMPT TO TAKE THE LEAD AT LE MANS. DPPI'S PHOTOGRAPHERS ARE ALWAYS ON SITE TO CAPTURE THE MOMENT. RECENTLY, THEIR ARCHIVE WAS OPENED TO THE PUBLIC.

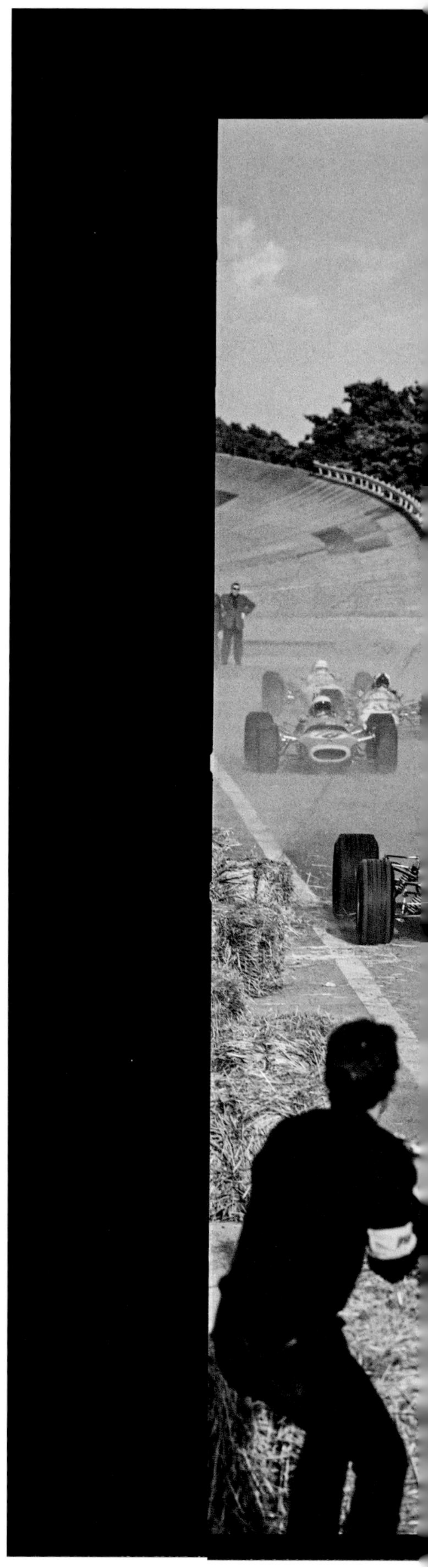

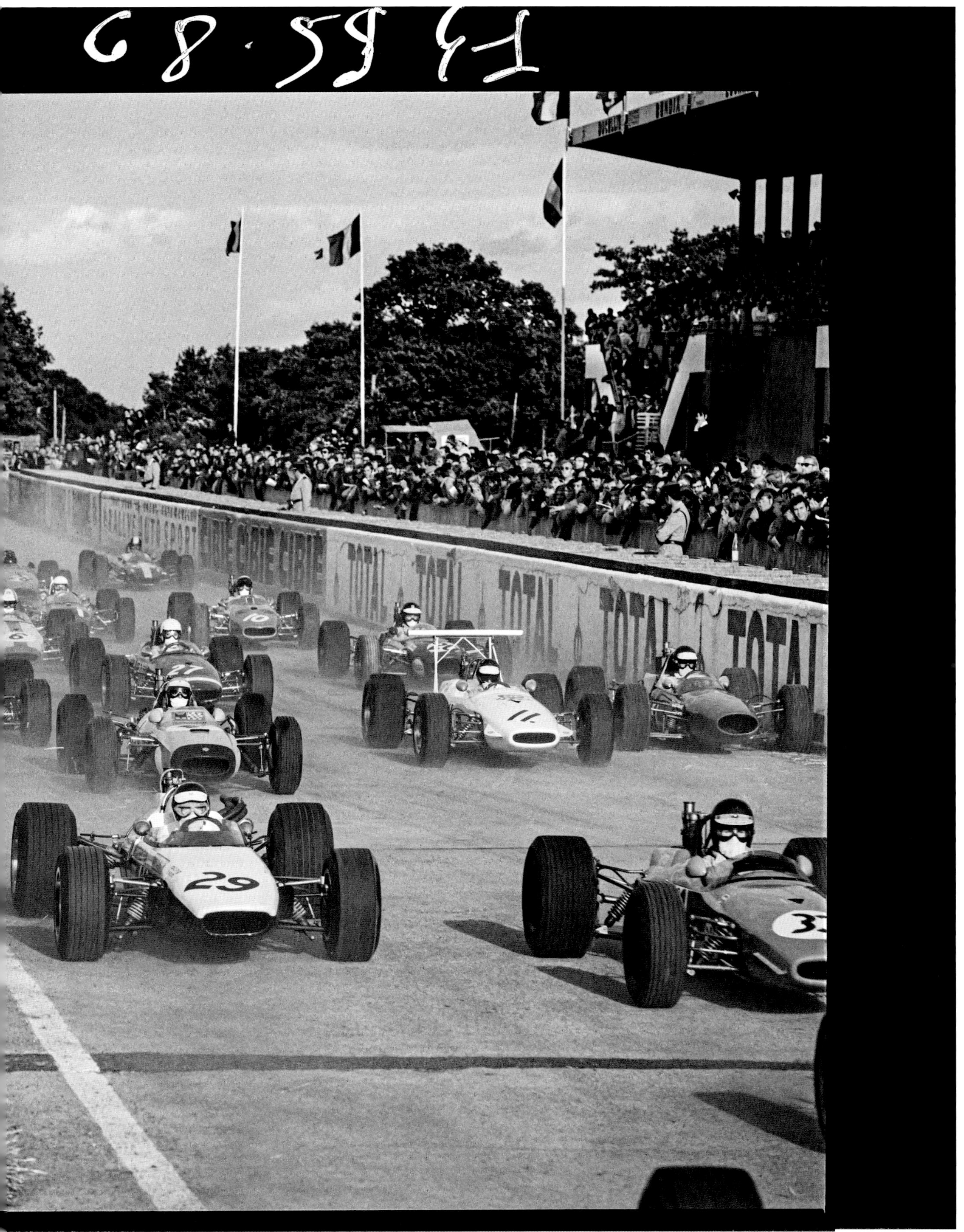
TOTAL
TOTAL
TOTAL
TOTAL
TOTAL

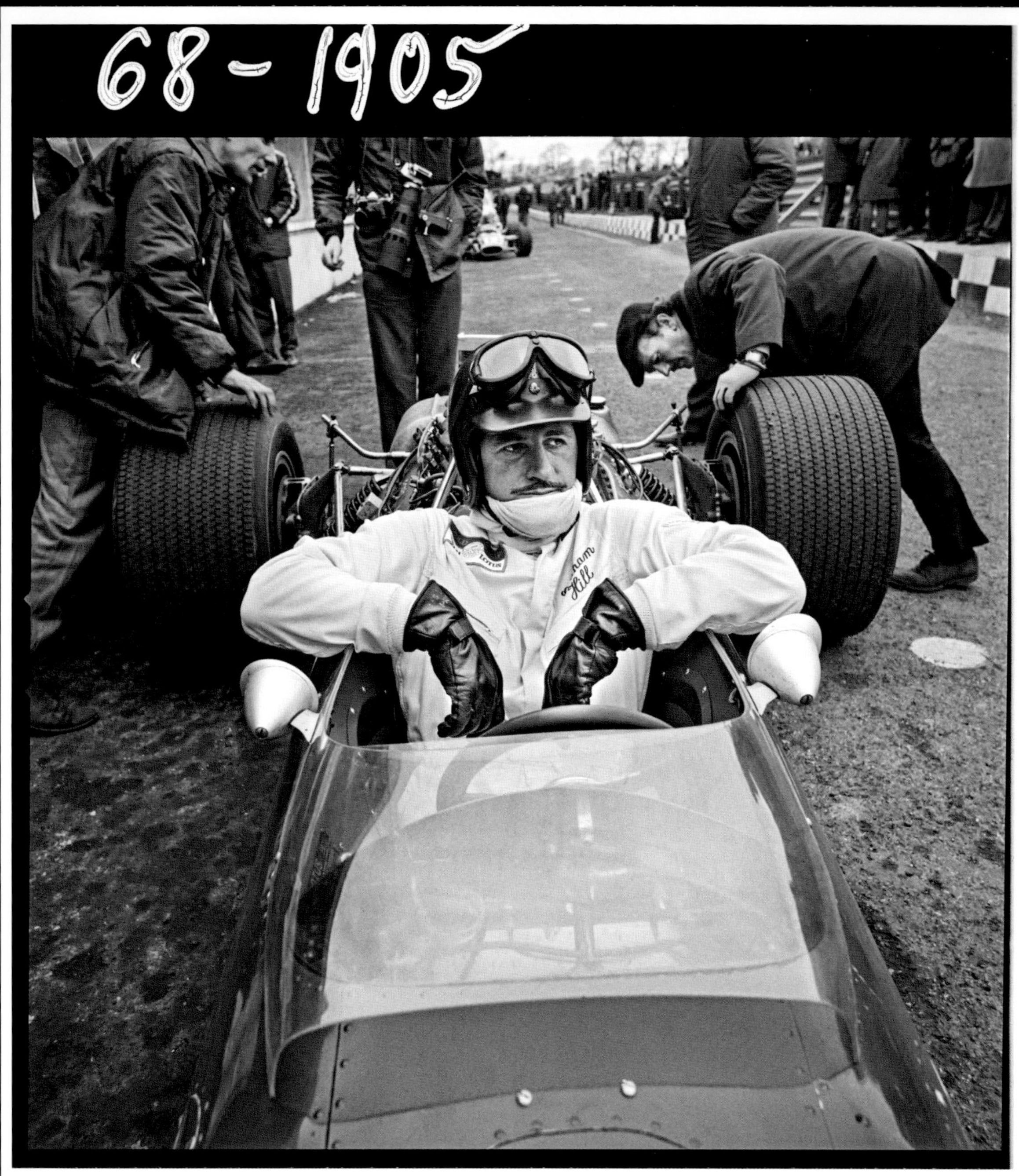

"I am an artist. The track is my canvas, and the car is my brush."

GRAHAM HILL

Graham Hill has to retire from the Race of Champions, which is not part of the World Championship, due to a drive shaft defect but still ends up F1 World Champion at the end of the year.

Season finale in Mexico in 1968. Jackie Stewart wins the World Championship a year later, with Jacky Ickx finishing second. Piers Courage ends up on rank eight. A year later, he will be killed in a fiery crash.

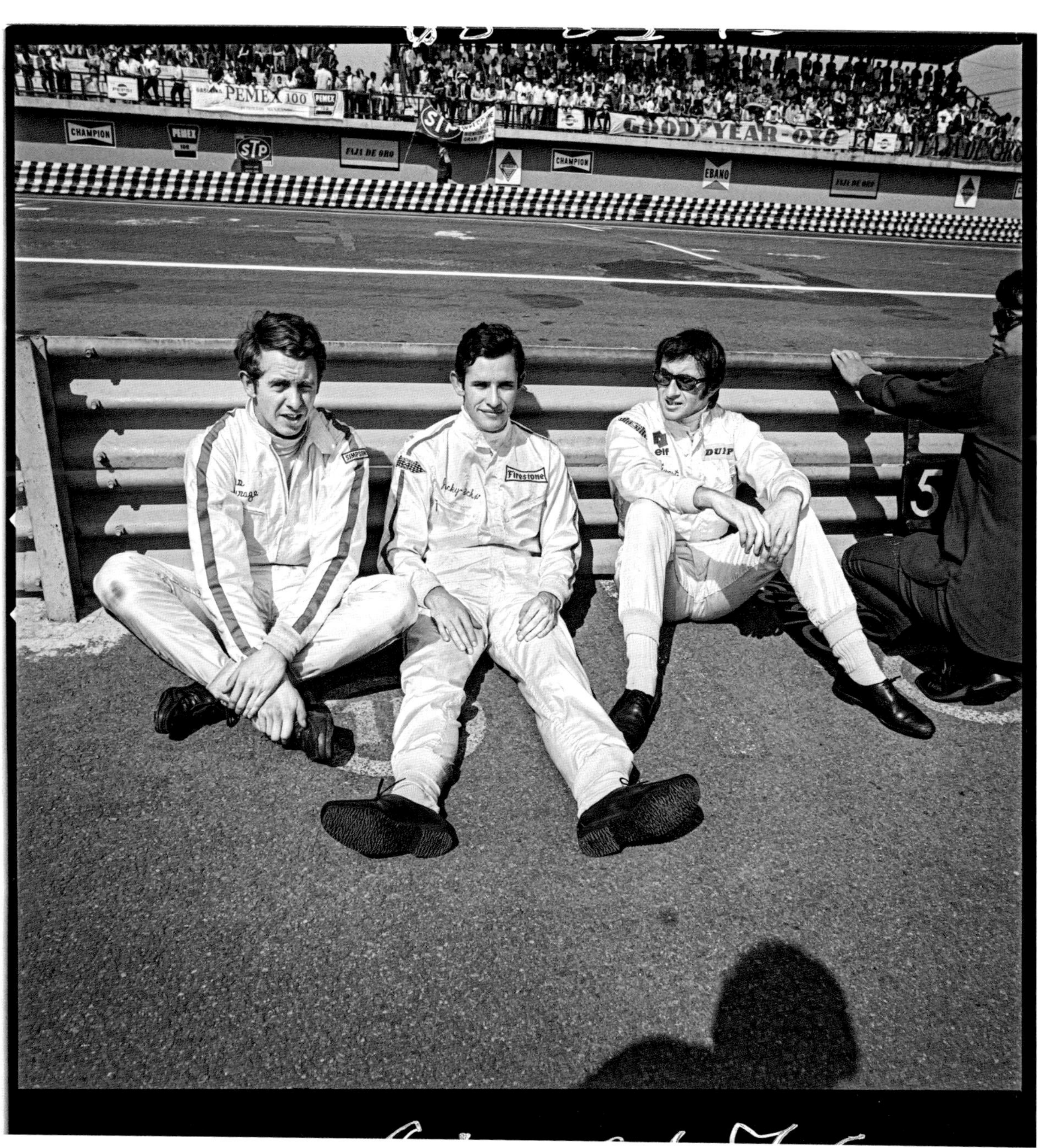

"In this sport luck and tragedy are only a few hundredths of seconds apart from each other."

JACKY ICKX

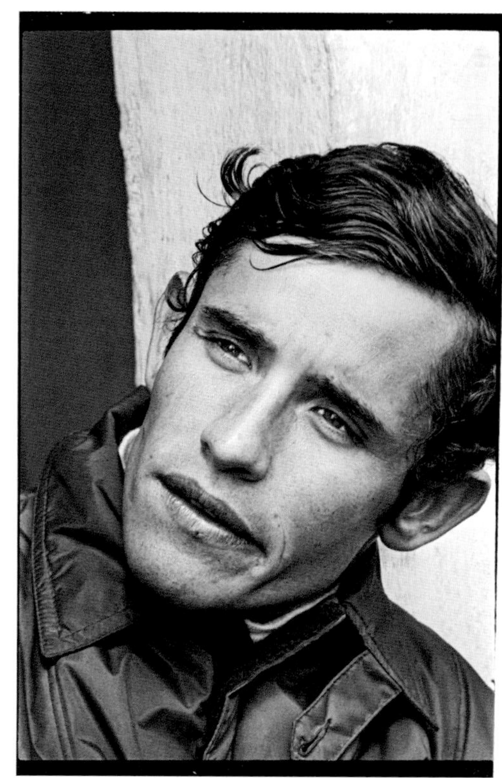

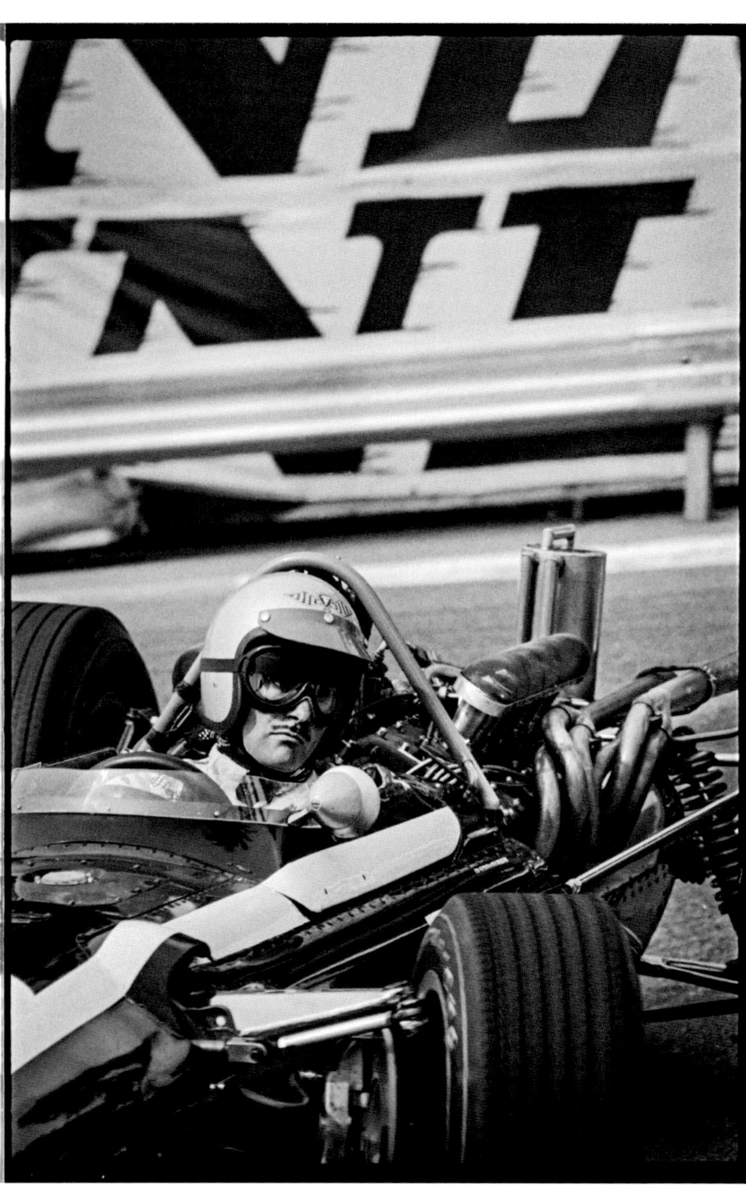

Left: In the 1968 Formula 1 season, Lucien Bianchi comes in third in Monaco, while Graham Hill wins for the fourth time.

Above: Jacky Ickx at the 1000-km race at the Nürburgring. In 1968 he finishes third together with Paul Hawkins in a Ford GT40.

Right: Dan Gurney has to drop out of the race due to a technical defect in the 1968 World Championship. A year earlier, on June 11, 1967, he spontaneously sprayed champagne on the spectators while celebrating his victory in the 24 Hours of Le Mans together with A. J. Foyt, inventing the ritual routinely performed on podiums today.

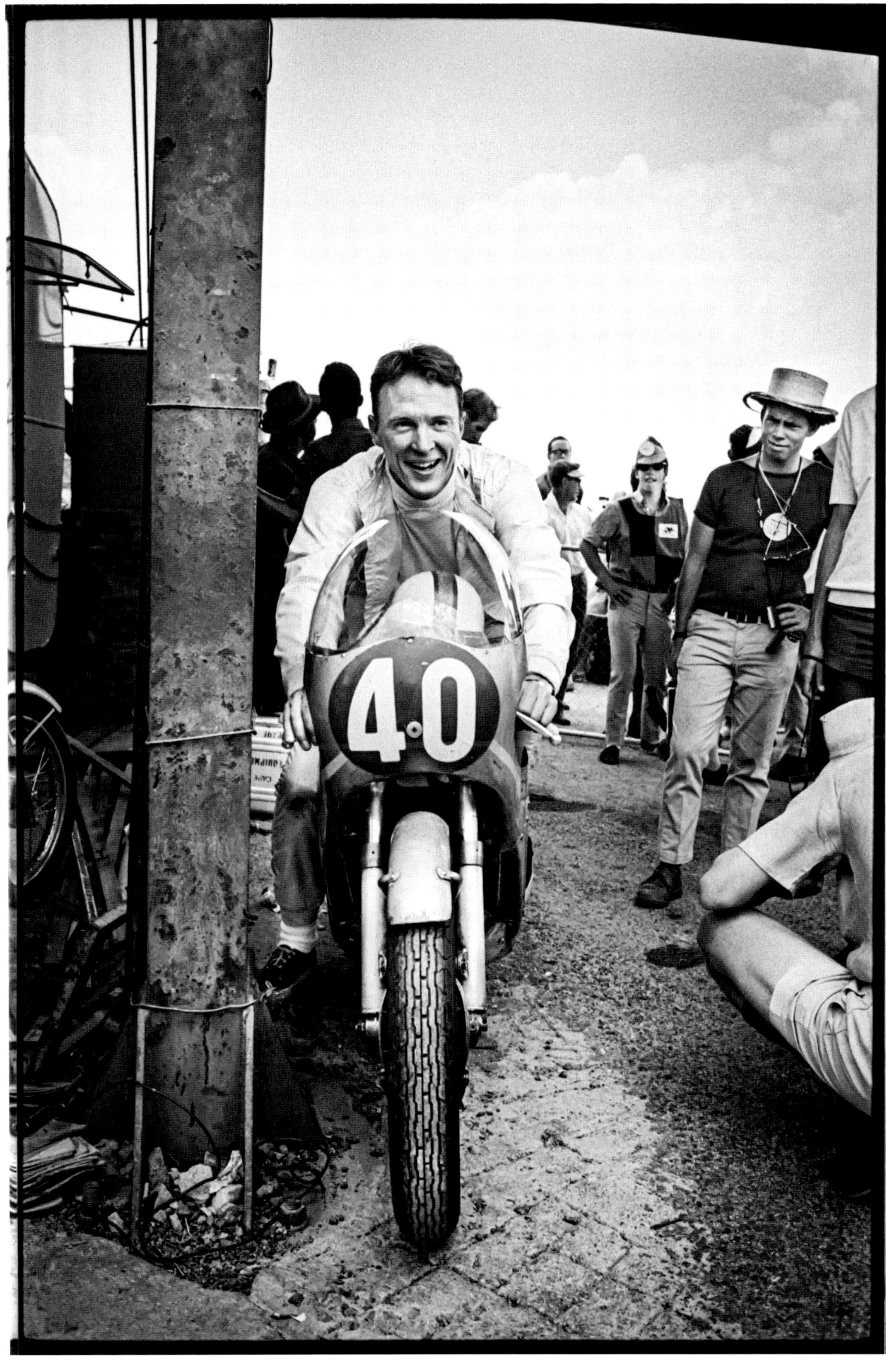
40

“If Jackie wants to say he knows Roman Polanski, Princess Grace and all those people, I couldn’t care less.”

DENNY HULME

Denny Hulme comes in second after Graham Hill at the Spanish Grand Prix. Hill had started sixth on the grid and worked his way to the top in an astonishing race.

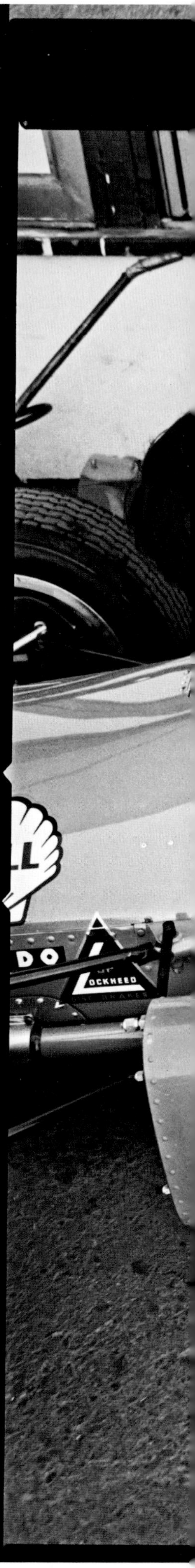

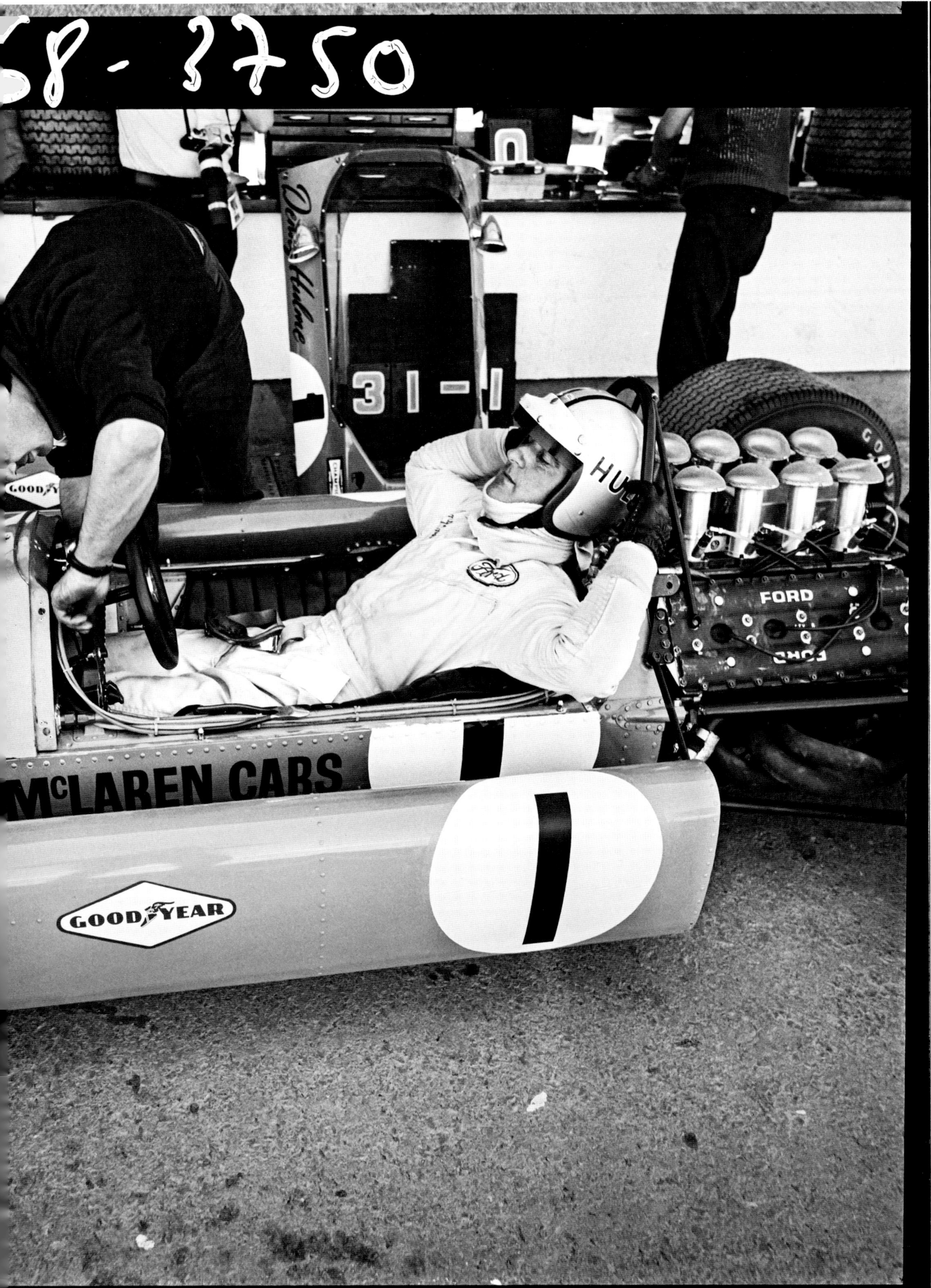

58- 3750
Denis Hulme
31-1
HULME
FORD
McLAREN CARS
1
GOODYEAR

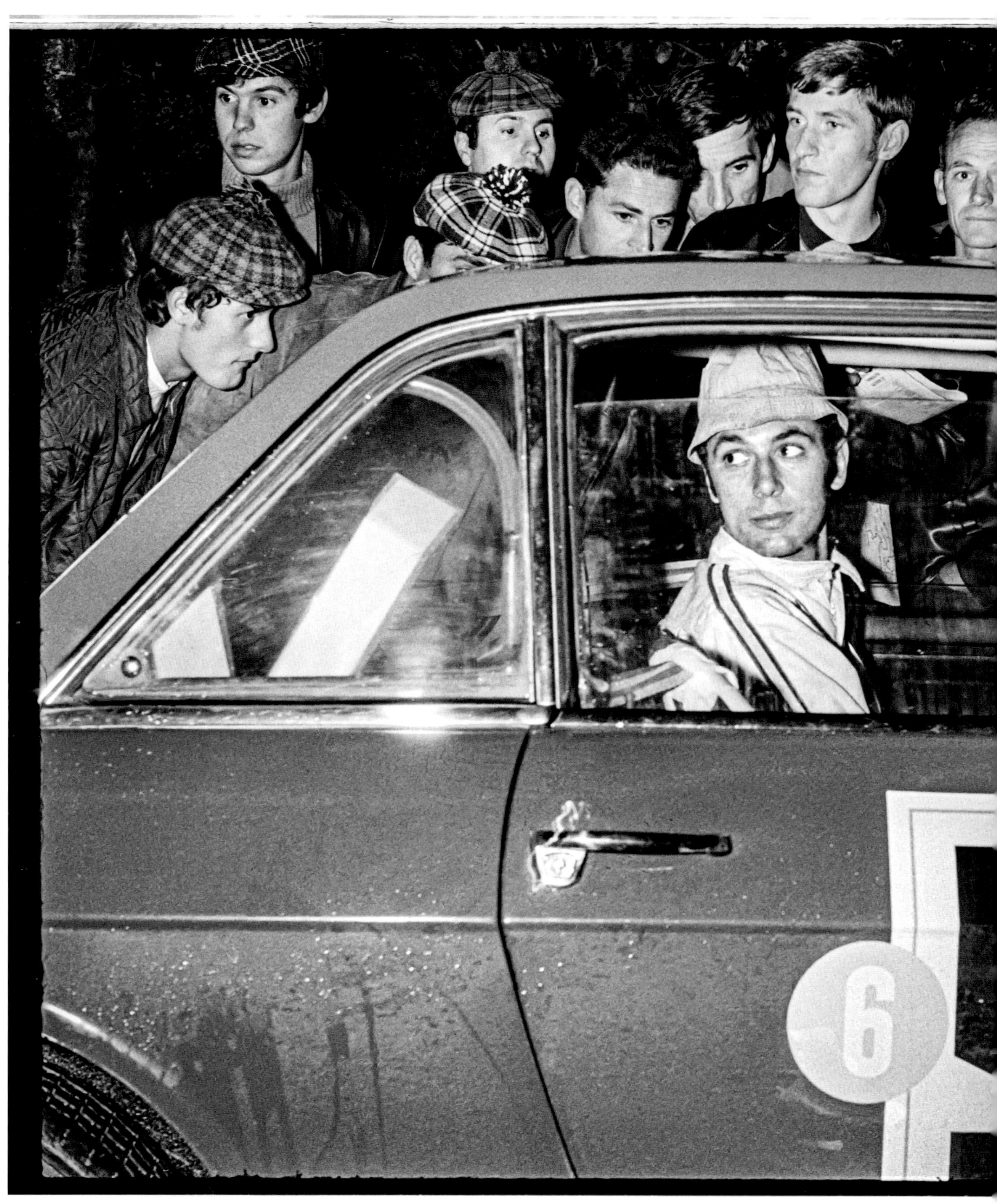

Sandro Munari's Lancia Fulvia HF 1.6 prototype suffers gearbox damage at the 1968 Tour de Corse. But the Italian driver later wins the European Rally Championship title in 1973 and the unofficial FIA Cup for Rally Drivers title in 1977. "Unofficial" because at the time only constructors were officially ranked.

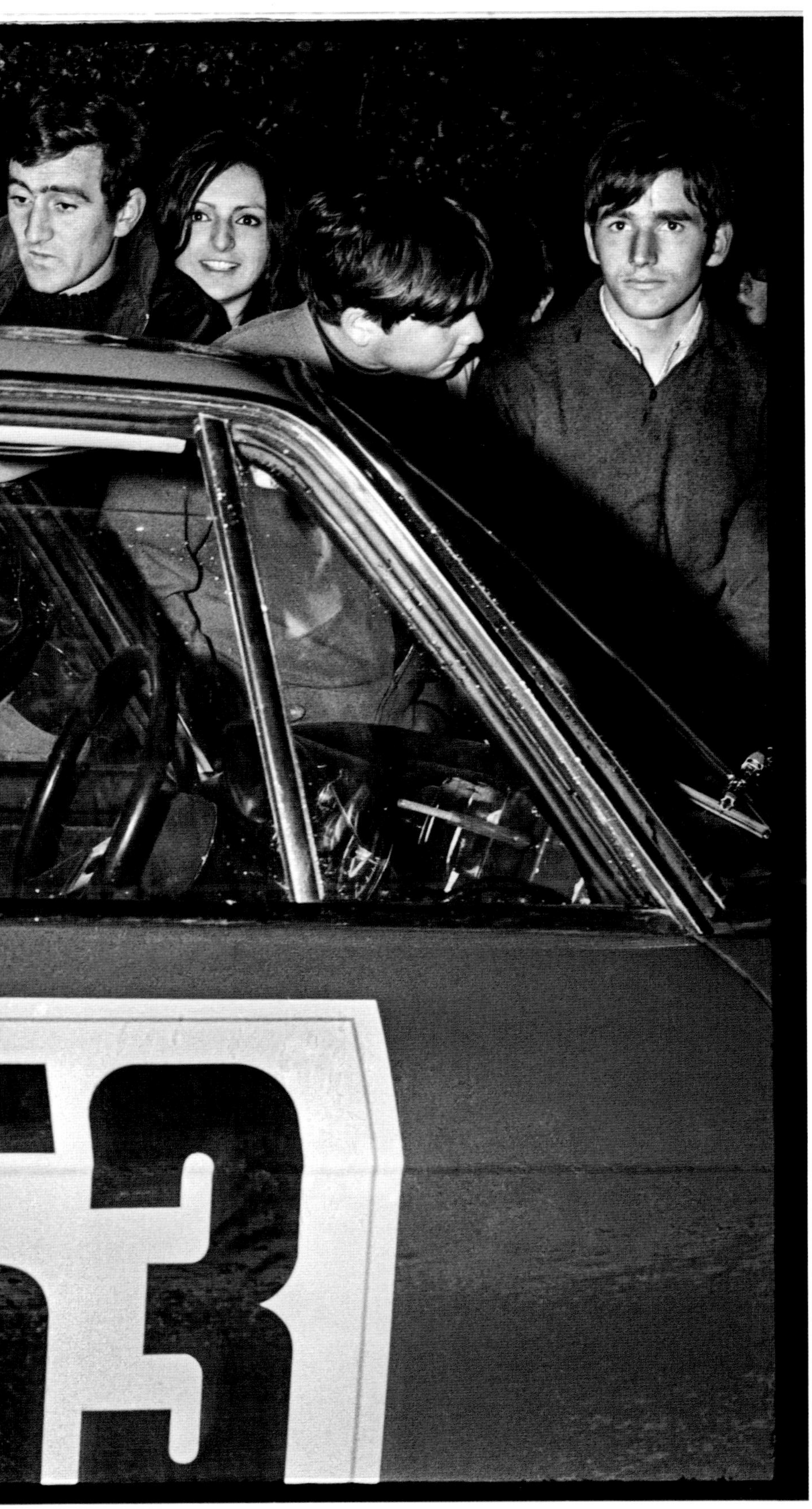

The photos in this story were taken from *Car Racing 1968*, the fourth volume in a series published by Cercle d'Art. The work was produced in collaboration with French photo agency DPPI and watch brand Richard Mille. The manufacturer of "racing machines for the wrist" is strongly rooted in motorsport due to the automotive passion of its eponymous founder. Richard Mille rewarded himself, as he says, with numerous sponsorships in various racing series and the establishment of an all-women's Le Mans team.

Manou Zurini: *Car Racing 1968*. Cercle d'Art. 240 pages. €95.00. Limited Edition: €250.00

"If Sandro Munari is driving one more time, I won't be."

WALTER RÖHRL

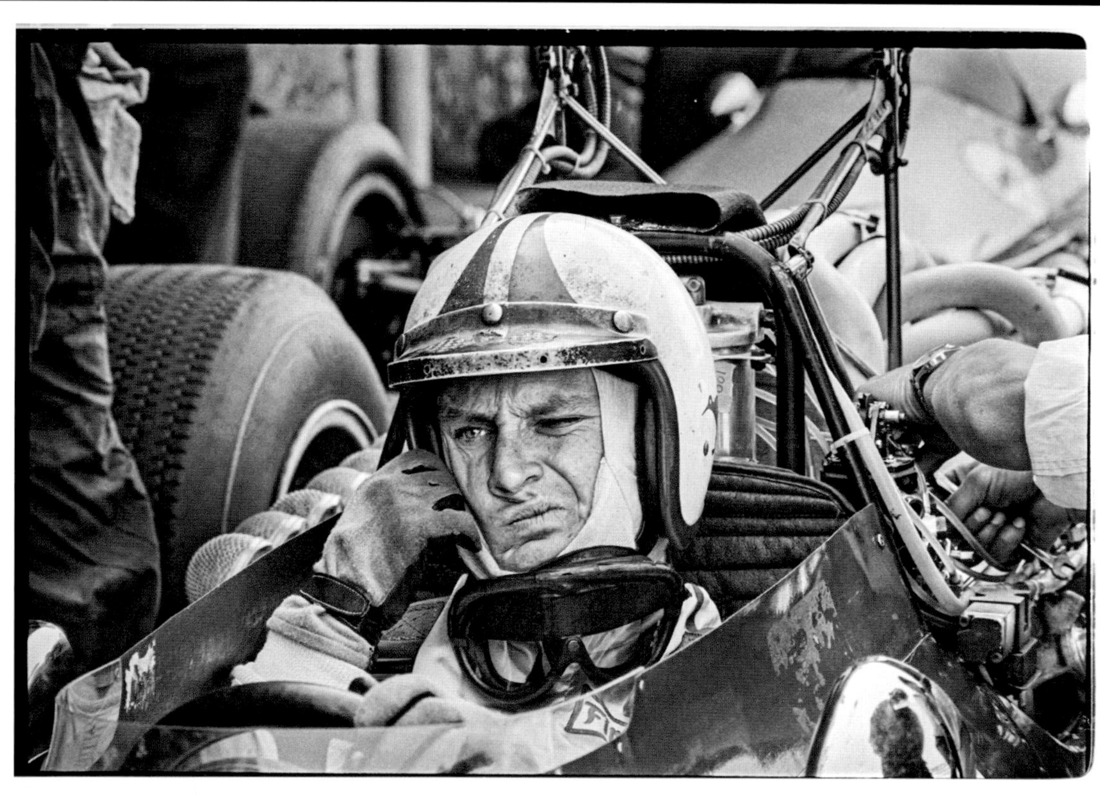

Above: Chris Amon and his Ferrari 312/68 have to retire in the season's last race in Mexico after 16 rounds.

Right: At the Formula 1 in Monaco, jerrycans sometimes end up being used as gambling tables and bolts and sockets as game pieces.

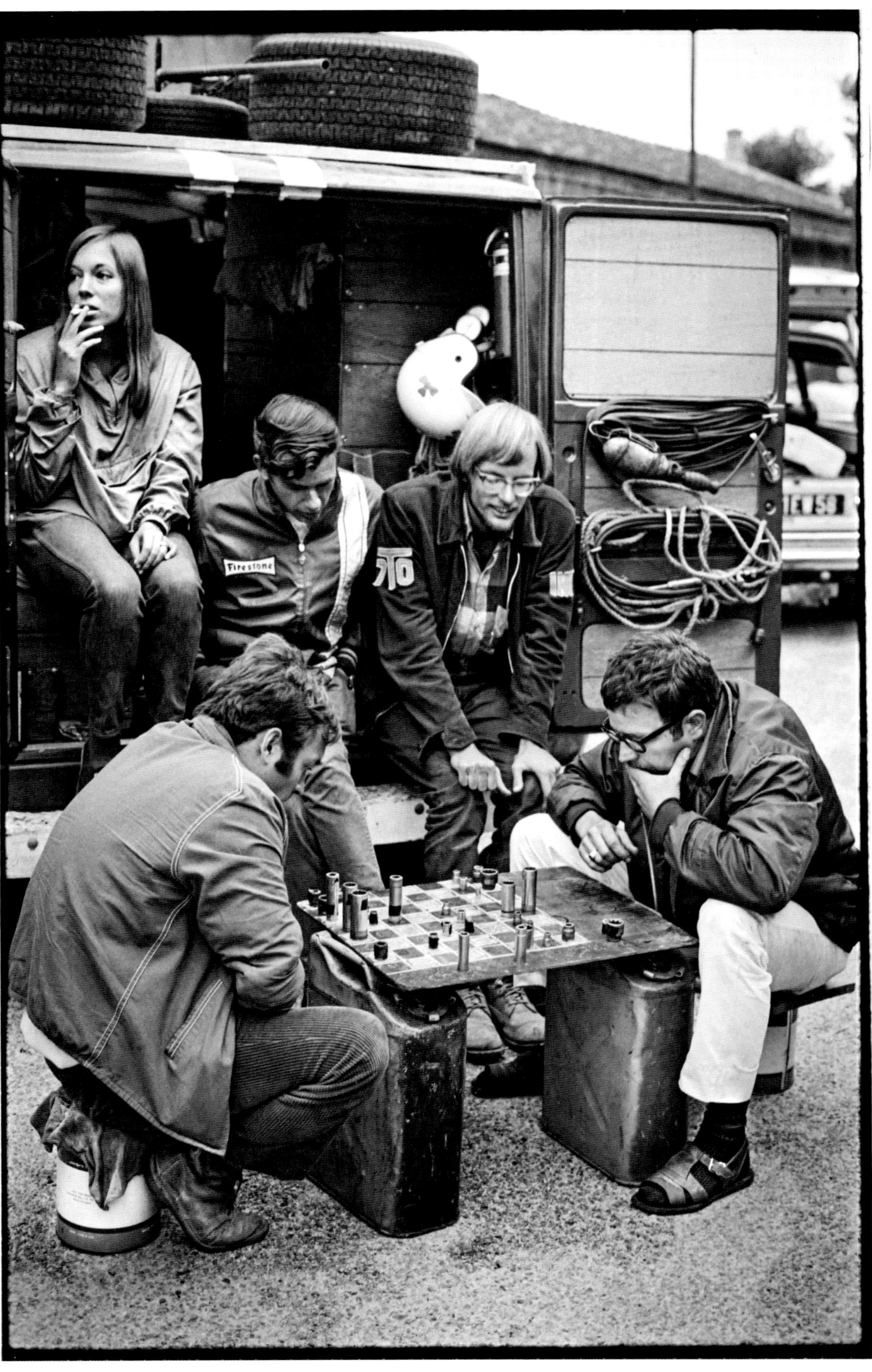
Firestone

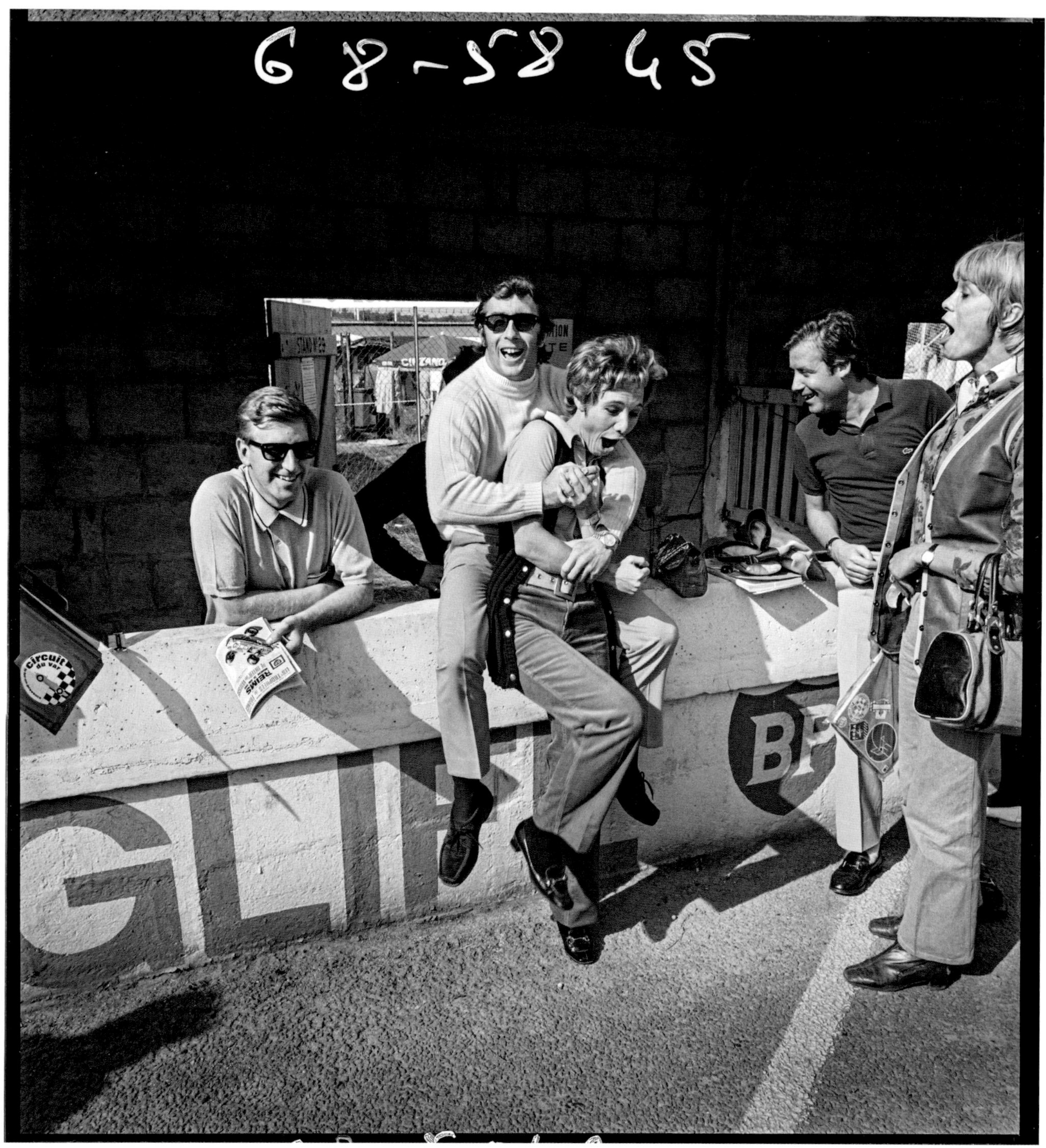

"The playboys weren't the great drivers, the ones who consistently won. At best, they were the number twos."

JACKIE STEWART

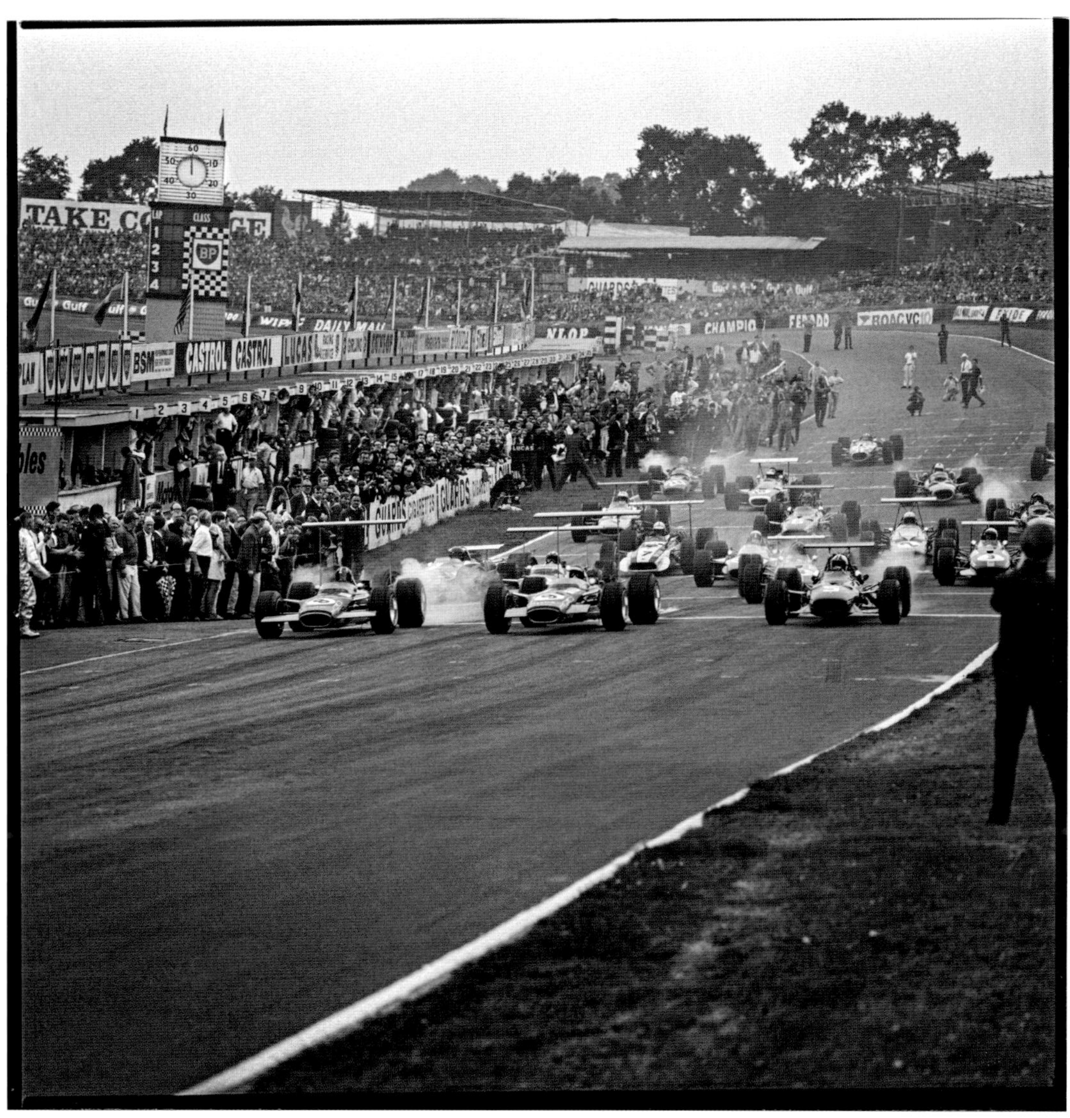

Left: Jackie Stewart with Matra timekeeper Michèle Dubosc at the Reims-Gueux Grand Prix, the French racing team's home turf.

Above: The Formula 1 in Brands Hatch in July of 1968. The evolution of the top level of motorsports is in full swing; the wings are a new addition. However, it's not the Team Lotus drivers Graham Hill and Jackie Oliver who take the win but privateer Jo Siffert.

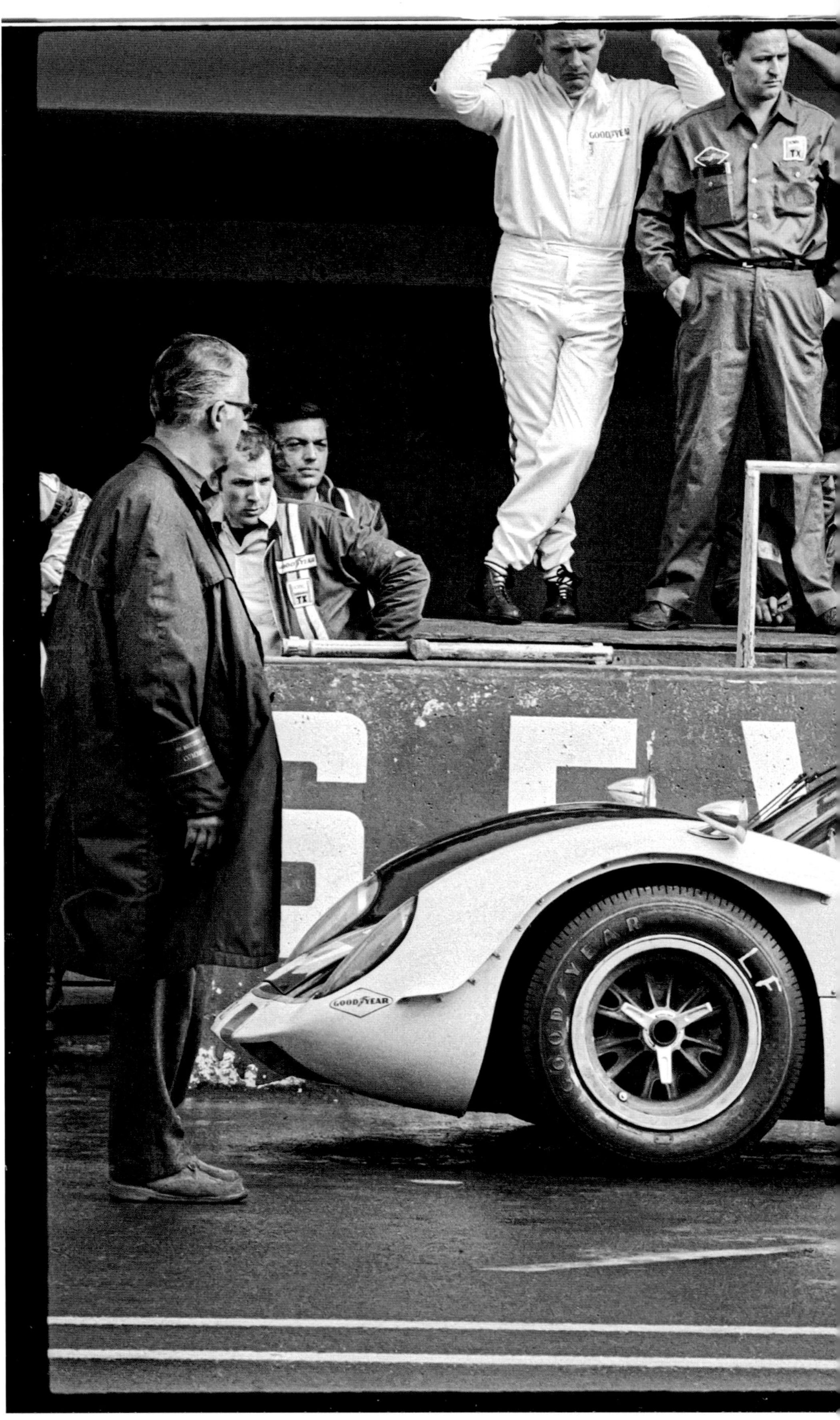

The Howmet TX equipped with a turbine powerplant is expected to trump combustion engines at Le Mans, but one of the two cars ends up being disqualified due to a lengthy repair and an insufficient distance, while the other car's driver crashes. Soon after, the program is discontinued.

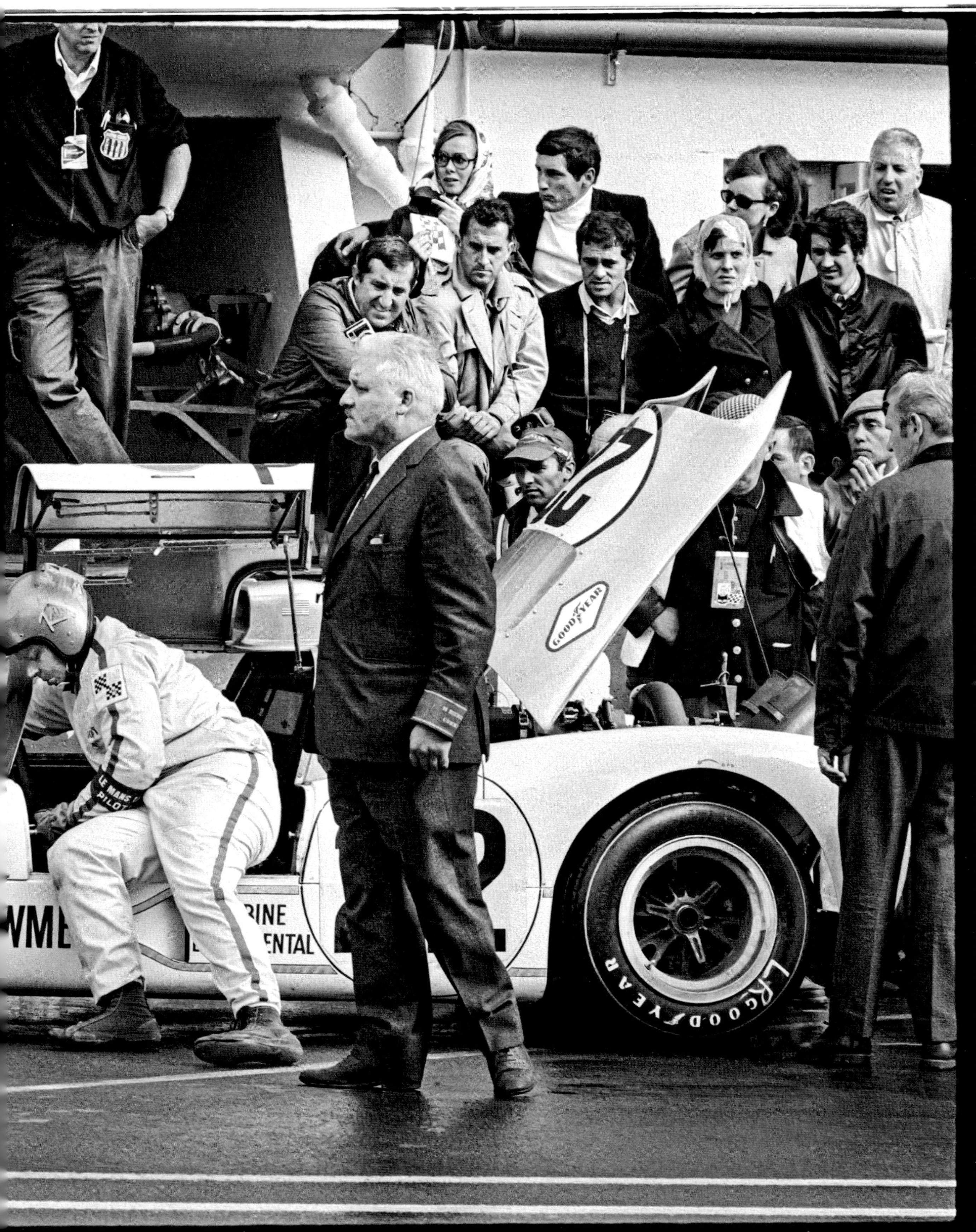
GOODYEAR
GOODYEAR

MICHEL BABIN HAS WORKED AT THE HÔTEL DU CAP-EDEN-ROC ON THE FRENCH RIVIERA FOR FIFTY YEARS. AND AS HEAD DOORMAN OF THE FAMOUS HOTEL, HE HAS WELCOMED ALL THE GREATS IN SHOW BUSINESS: ROGER MOORE, CHARLES BRONSON, MADONNA . . . JUST TO NAME A FEW.

BUT THE MOST BEAUTIFUL THING IS THAT WHEN HE'S ASKED ABOUT HIS ENCOUNTERS, HE ALSO HAS SOMETHING TO SAY – UP TO A CERTAIN POINT, OF COURSE.

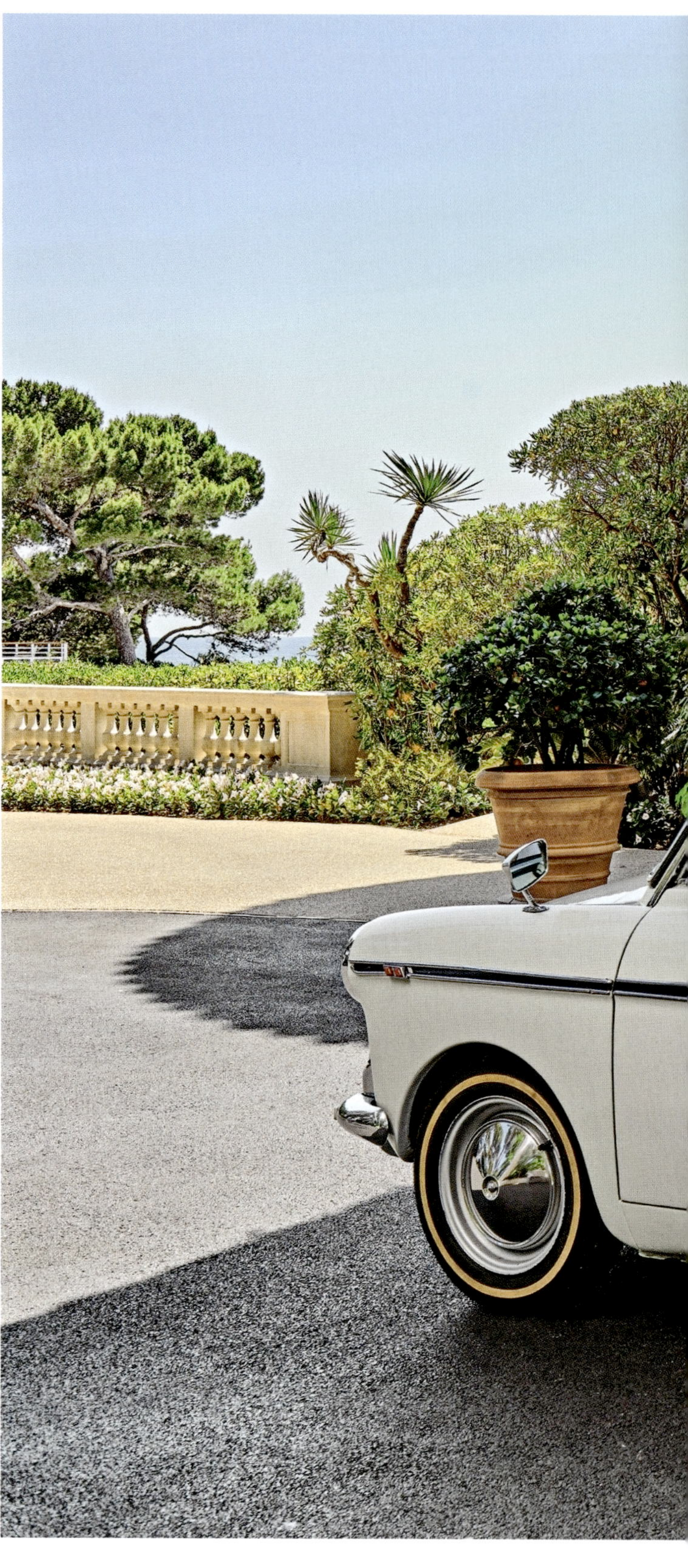

about egos

2.03

TEXT *Ulf Lippitz*
PHOTOS *Hôtel du Cap-Eden-Roc*

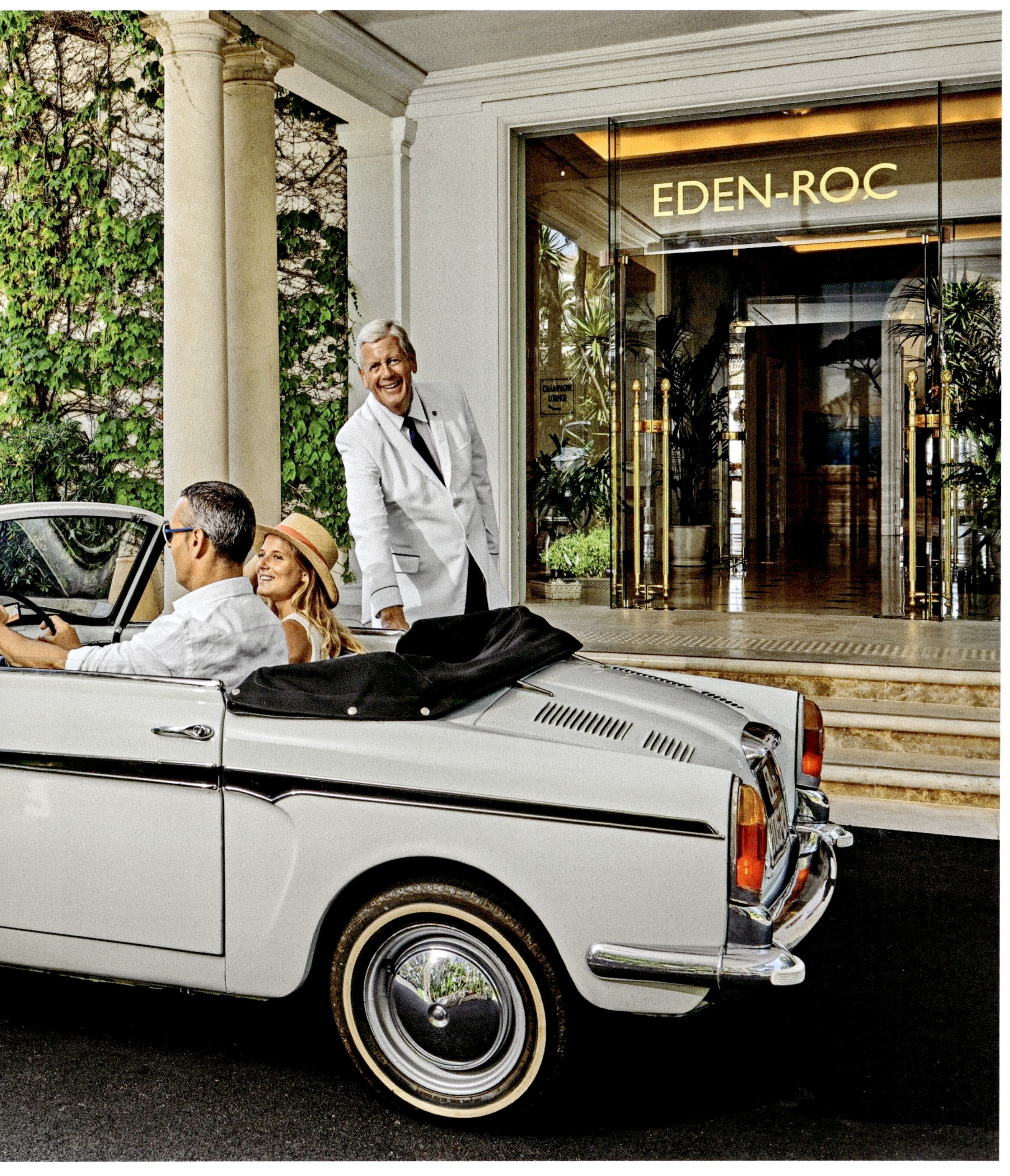
EDEN-ROC

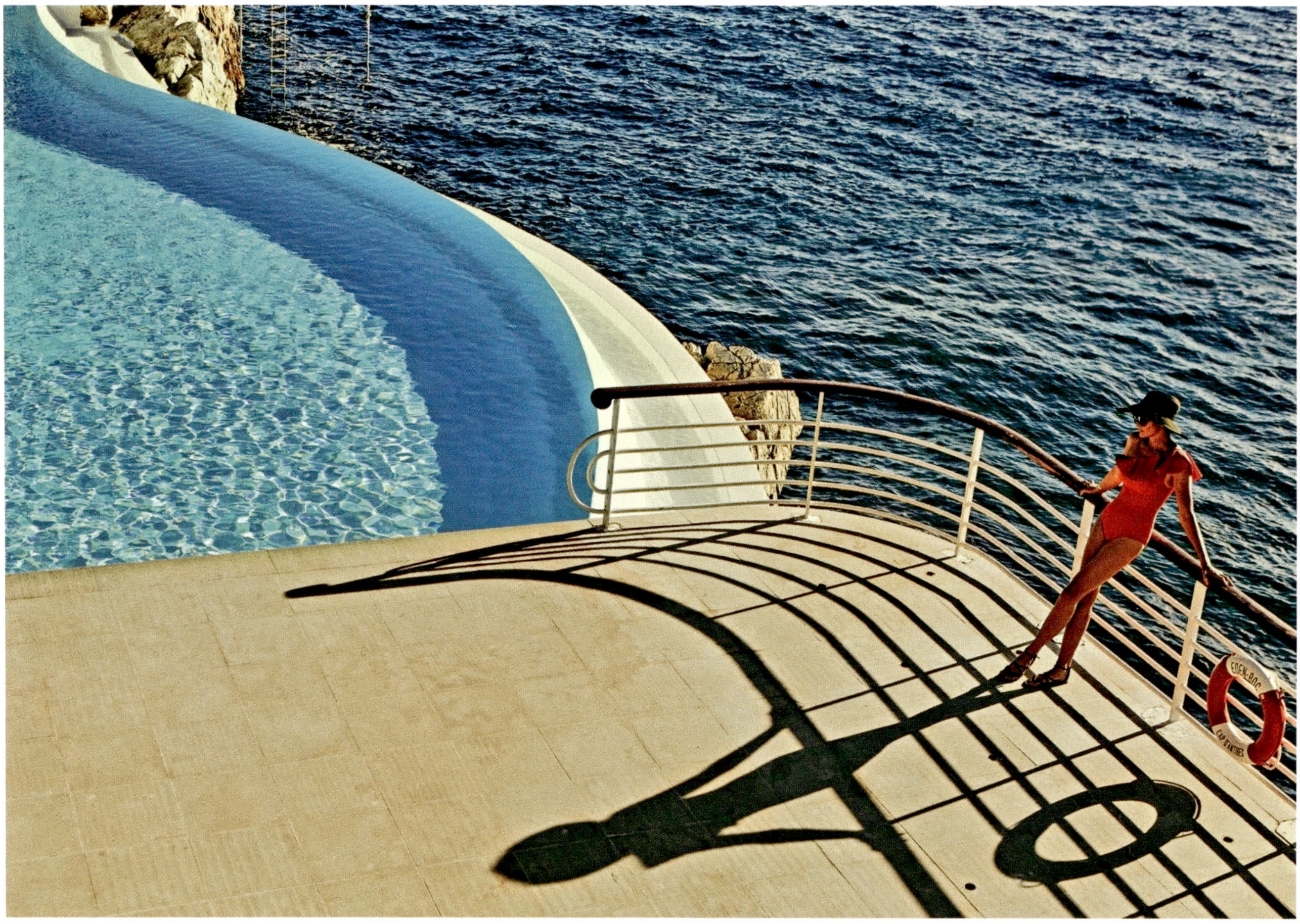

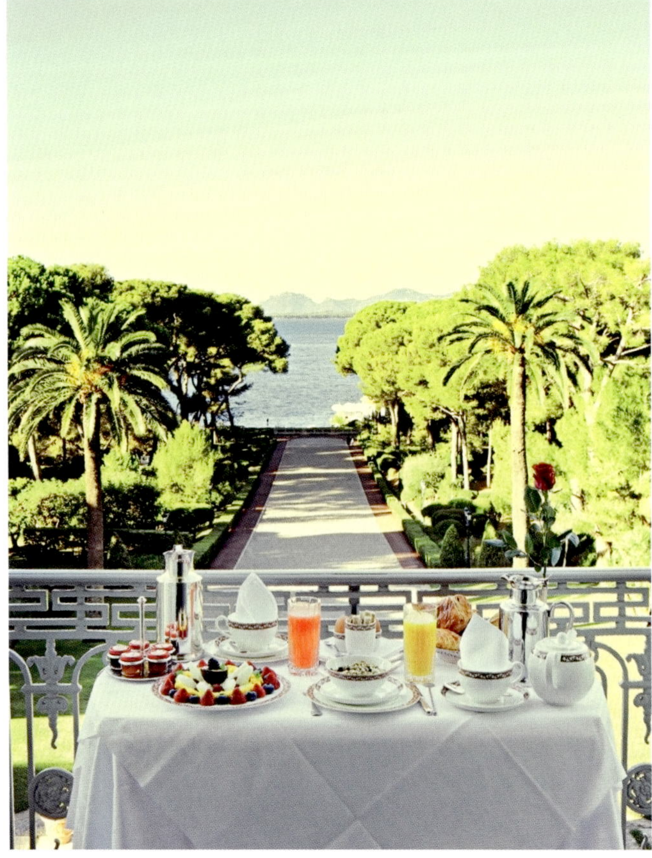

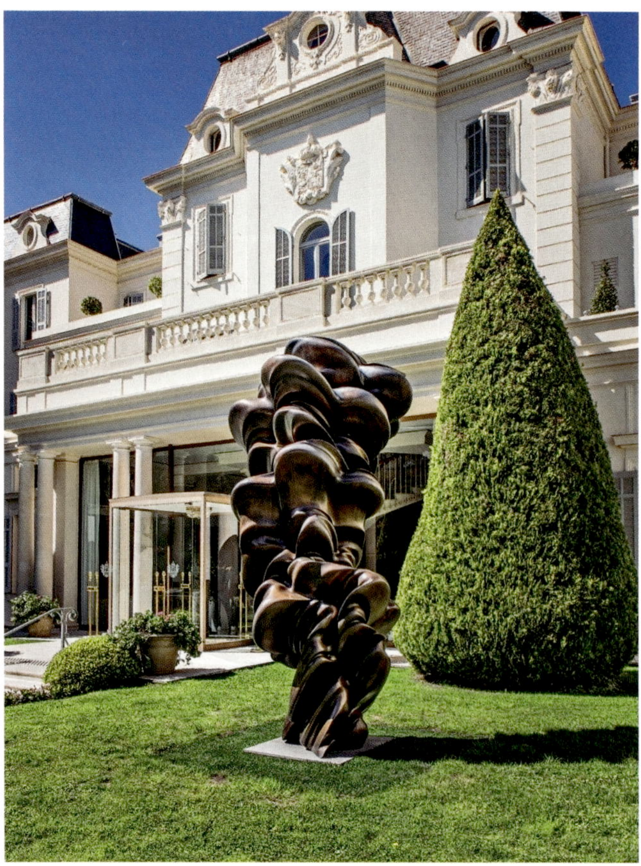

Should things ever get too indiscreet, Michel Babin smiles away any potential unease. *Have you ever been asked to score drugs for a guest? Has anyone ever tried to sneak their mistress into the hotel?* The seventy-two-year-old Frenchman then pretends that he simply didn't understand the question. Or looks at you with a disarming charm. That should come as no surprise. After all, the Hôtel du Cap-Eden-Roc is known for its illustrious guest list – but also for its strict rules. Photography is not allowed at the pool. Kate Moss was banned from the hotel because she shuffled through the lobby dressed only in a bikini. Until a few years ago, it was only possible to pay in cash, and there was no internet in the guest rooms either. The tall doorman just smiles: "The previous manager just wanted it that way." We spoke to Michel Babin about the art of forgetting, about good manners – and hoped for a couple of good stories along the way.

Monsieur Babin, with fifty years of service, you're the longest-serving employee at the Hôtel du Cap-Eden-Roc. Because of its discretion, the luxury hotel is especially popular with celebrities. How diplomatic do you have to be?
The first rule is not to interfere in the lives of the guests. In the evening, a man will arrive at the hotel with a pretty woman on his arm, and a day later he's sitting at the lunch table with his wife. As an employee, you say nothing, you keep your mouth shut. "Bonjour, madame." That's it.

Don't the wives ever ask questions?
That has happened. "Did you see my husband yesterday?" I simply respond, "I'm sorry, madame, but I do not recall."

"Madonna was a special person. She stayed at the hotel three times. But after that . . . pfff . . ."

"Charles Bronson – what a gentleman! He asked me if I would like to see the premiere of his film at the festival. Said he had two tickets for me."

So you lie.
No, I'm discreet. I play dumb.

Is that the core of your work as head doorman?
No, of course not. I'm the first person to greet the guests when they arrive, but the actual job is quite different: never forget the names, the titles or the stories that go along with a guest. The sequence is always the same. The first year it's, "Bonjour, monsieur." In the second year, the guests ask, "How are you?" And from the third: "Hi, Michel, nice to see you." The same families come on holiday every year.

About eighty percent of the guests are regulars . . .
. . . and the kids come back as adults. In the past, families still traveled with their own driver, maid and secretary. In some cases, if the family had booked for a month, an interior decorator visited the rooms beforehand and looked over the furnishings. Madame prefers the table here or the curtains in a different color? No problem at all. Nobody books for long stays like that anymore.

What do you do if you ever forget a name?
I go to the little niche where I sit. I keep a book there with all the names, so I look up who it could be and read the stories I've written down about them. In the worst case, I call the reception and ask who the guest is that's just walking

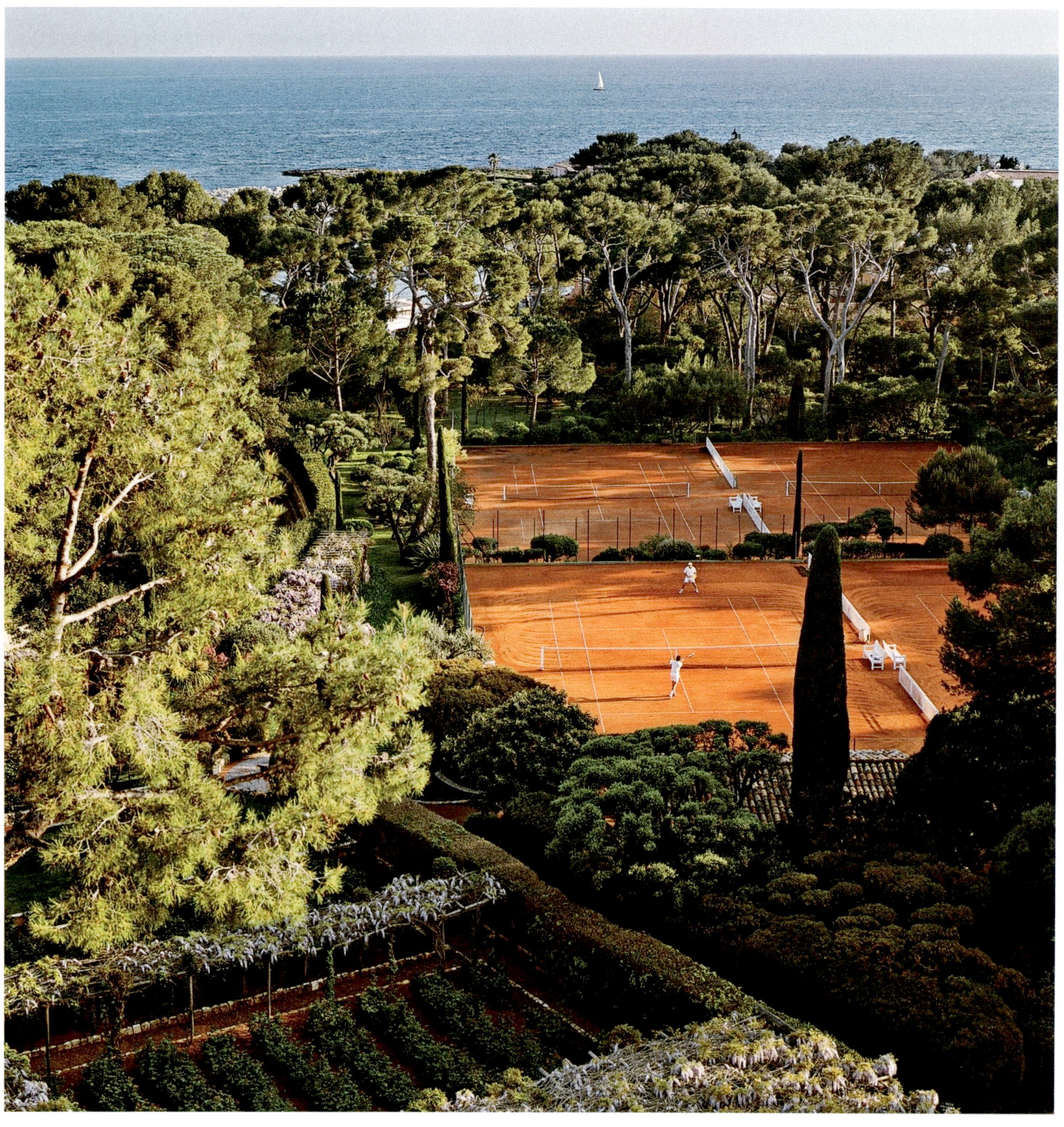

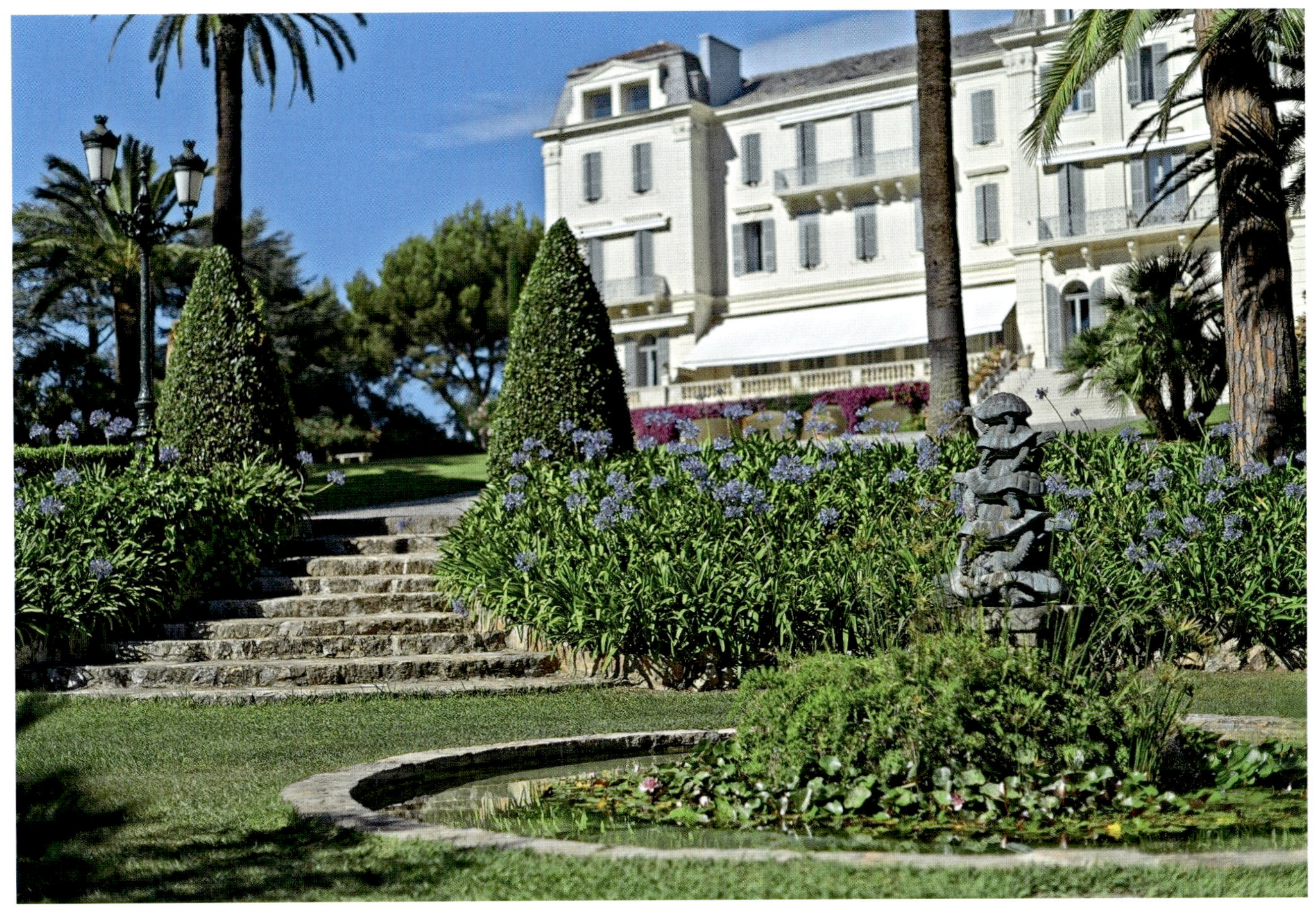

“Grateful for the sky, scenery and silence surrounding this blessed house.”

GUESTBOOK ENTRY BY STEFAN ZWEIG

down the gravel path to the beach wearing a Panama hat, and then I cordially greet the man: "How are you today, Mr. Smith?" The guest is surprised that after a year I've remembered his name. I just smile. "Of course, monsieur."

This refuge knows only one threat: the paparazzi.
When the Cannes Film Festival takes place every year in May, it's horrible. Dozens of photographers lurk around the hotel. We own a stretch of beach 300 meters to the yellow buoy, where the paparazzi are not allowed in with their boats. So they stand all around on the steep limestone cliffs and photograph everyone they catch sight of on the restaurant terrace. It was particularly awful when Madonna stayed here back in 1992. Not only did the paparazzi besiege us from the seaside, there were also hundreds of young girls camped out in front of the entrance at the park screaming, "Madonna, we love you!" day and night. We had to lock the gate.

Madonna hid in the back seat of the car. They threw a blanket over her and drove her out of the hotel.
I remember it well. *In Bed with Madonna* [*laughs*] . . . that's what *Truth or Dare* was called internationally.

"We make sure that guests walk through the lobby in proper attire – with shoes, not barefoot. Kate Moss didn't understand that."

Or more like: in the back seat with Madonna.
I must say, she was a special person. She stayed at the hotel three times. But after that . . . pfff . . .

That was quite the scornful pfff . . .
That lady had appalling manners. I can still see the little girl in front of me, a fan who had taken a picture of Madonna with her camera. Madonna immediately sicced her bodyguards on her. They took the camera from the girl and tore out the film. What a difference to Cary Grant.

The Hollywood star used to stay here in the seventies.
An elegant and polite man. He would always greet me with a warm "How are you, Michel?" Madonna didn't talk to the staff; we were nothing to her. When Cary Grant stayed with us, Grace Kelly popped over from Monaco to visit him. Two dogs on a leash, dressed in an elegant hat, a beautiful appearance. She had class. Or Charles Bronson. What a gentleman!

The actor became famous through films like Once Upon a Time in the West.
He asked me if I would like to see the premiere of his film at the festival. Said he had two tickets for me. All I had to do was get a bow tie and a dinner jacket and I was seated two rows behind the stars. The next day, he came to me to ask what I thought.

Naturally, you praised the film.
But of course. I'm not a film critic. I tell the guests what they want to hear. I keep my opinions to myself.

Not everyone was allowed to stay. Kate Moss was banned from the hotel for walking through the lobby wearing only a bikini. Would that still happen today?
We make sure that guests walk through the lobby in proper attire – with shoes, not barefoot. We are a luxury establishment, not a hostel. We don't want to frighten away our regulars. Kate Moss didn't understand that. She had to leave. Remember David Carradine?

The actor from Kill Bill. *He died in a hotel in Bangkok.*
He stayed with us once and organized a special Buddhist ceremony in his room. He lit loads of candles, and in the end the room was on fire. The manager threw him out.

"Johnny Weissmuller drank a bottle of whiskey per day, and then he would stand at the bar and imitate his famous Tarzan cry."

Twenty years ago, the hotel got a new manager who relaxed the dress code somewhat.
It used to be that you had to wear a tie to dinner. There was a special dress code for the evening. Gentlemen had to wear long trousers and a dinner jacket. One evening, an elderly lady called me to complain about a young American in the restaurant. "Michel, how can this happen? There's a man sitting at the table who is not wearing a jacket. And shoes without socks." Since then, we have kept spare jackets hanging in my office. Today, this rule no longer exists. When I ask young men to put on a dinner jacket, they give me a funny look and reply that such an impractical garment is too hot for them.

Is it true that Bruce Willis once booked a table for thirty people and then held a party with three hundred guests?
The hotel's former manager was seething. An unannounced party that went all night, not a drink left in the bar, the staff had to work until seven in the morning. Well, things like that happened thirty years ago during the film festival. That can't even happen anymore today. The bodyguards would stop you: "Where are you going?" "Who are you here with?" "What room are you staying in?" "I'm sorry, madame, I'm going to have to ask you to leave." The atmosphere has completely changed.

For a long time, you were also responsible for the guest parking area. What sorts of cars did you see drive up?
Bentleys, Ferraris, Rolls-Royces, Maseratis. Today, the guests fly to Nice and book a chauffeur or sometimes a small car.

It must have been awful when director Lars von Trier arrived at the hotel back in 2003 in a conventional camper van.
He announced it beforehand though. He said he couldn't travel by plane because he's afraid of flying. I parked the van in the employee car park. Sometimes he slept in it, though he still paid for the room. Roger Moore owned a villa near Antibes, but he came by every day to play tennis at our place. One day he drove up in his blue Rolls-Royce, got out and groaned: "Michel, don't tell anyone that 007 has back problems."

Besides the driving habits, something else has changed: the excess. In the past, people drank more than they do today.
Johnny Weissmuller used to come in and drink a bottle of whiskey per day, and then he would stand at the bar and imitate his famous Tarzan cry. Today, actors pay much more attention to their health, physique and what their doctor says. No heart problems! Nobody smokes like Bill Cosby anymore. He vacationed here with his children for a number of years. Every day he walked ten kilometers and rewarded himself afterward on the terrace with a big fat cigar.

MICHEL BABIN DE LIGNAC was born into a Breton noble family. When an acquaintance of his father's suggested he should go see the world, the young Babin began his career in the hotel business. He found work in Baden-Baden before coming to the Côte d'Azur in 1974. Sixty-seven years old today, Babin is the hotel's longest-serving employee, head doorman, valet – and go-to person for discretion.

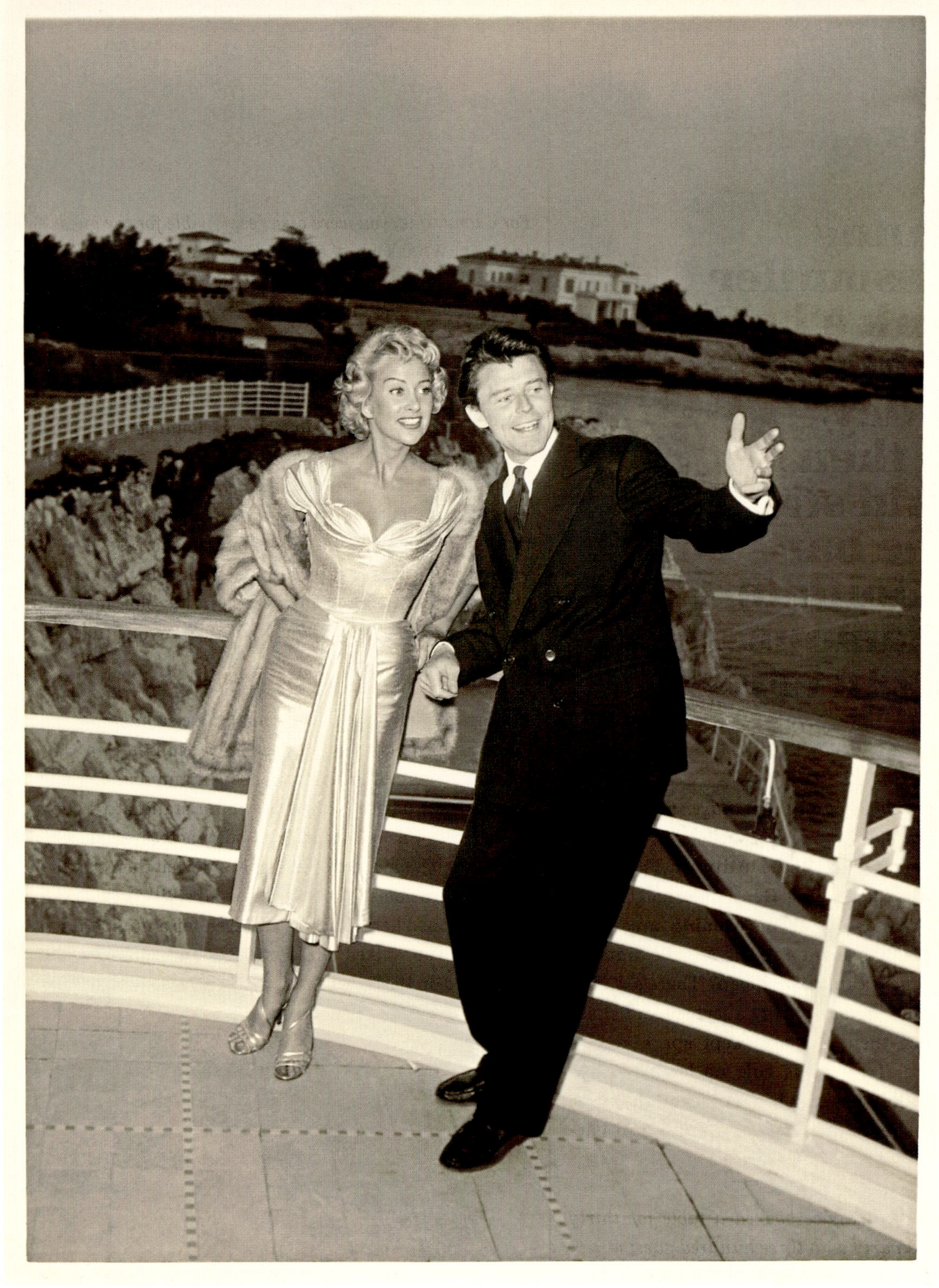

Actor Gérard Philipe was one of the biggest stars of the silver screen during the post-war period and a welcome guest at the hotel. (The woman at his side is not his wife, by the way.)

"On the pleasant shore of the French Riviera [. . .] stands a large, proud, rose-colored hotel. [. . .] Lately it has become a summer resort of notable and fashionable people."

F. SCOTT FITZGERALD IN HIS NOVEL *TENDER IS THE NIGHT* (1934)

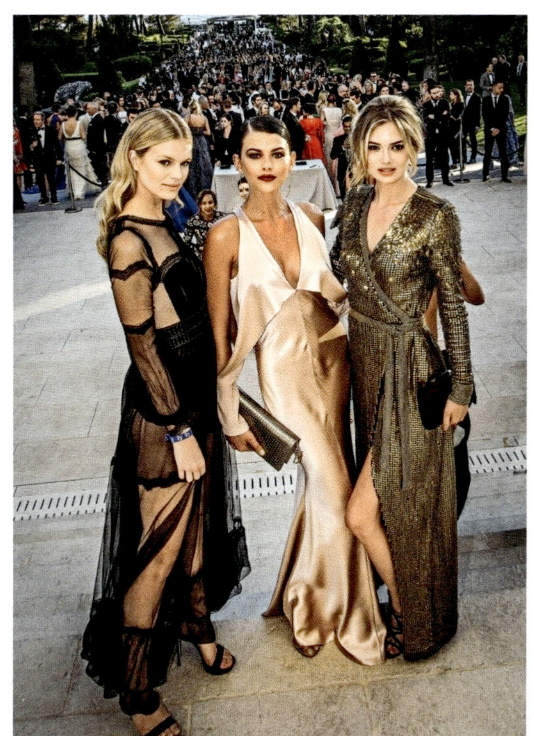

Right: The amfAR Gala at the Hôtel du Cap-Eden-Roc. Below: Marlene Dietrich, who allegedly began an affair here with Joe Kennedy, the father of JFK, despite having arrived with writer Erich Maria Remarque.

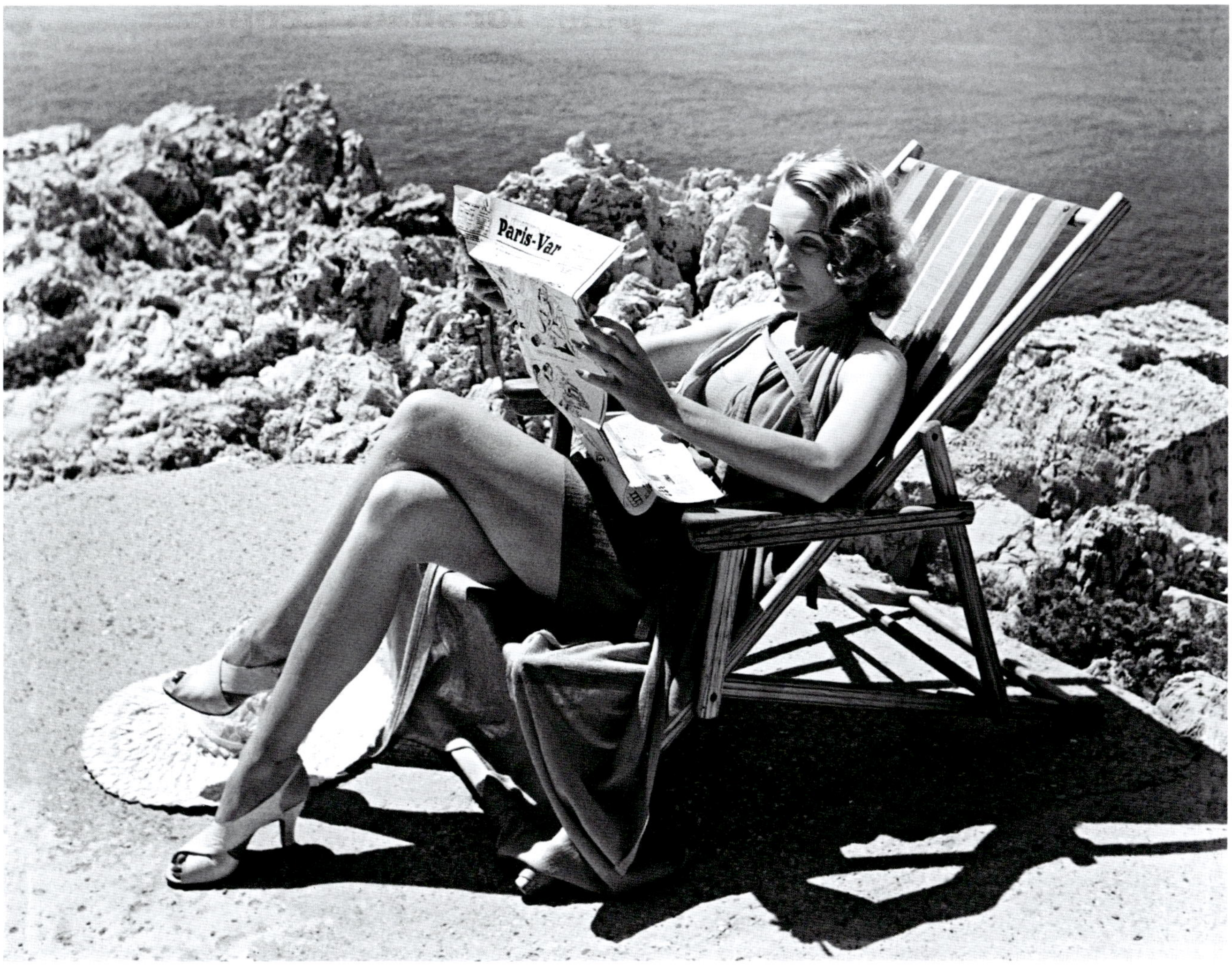

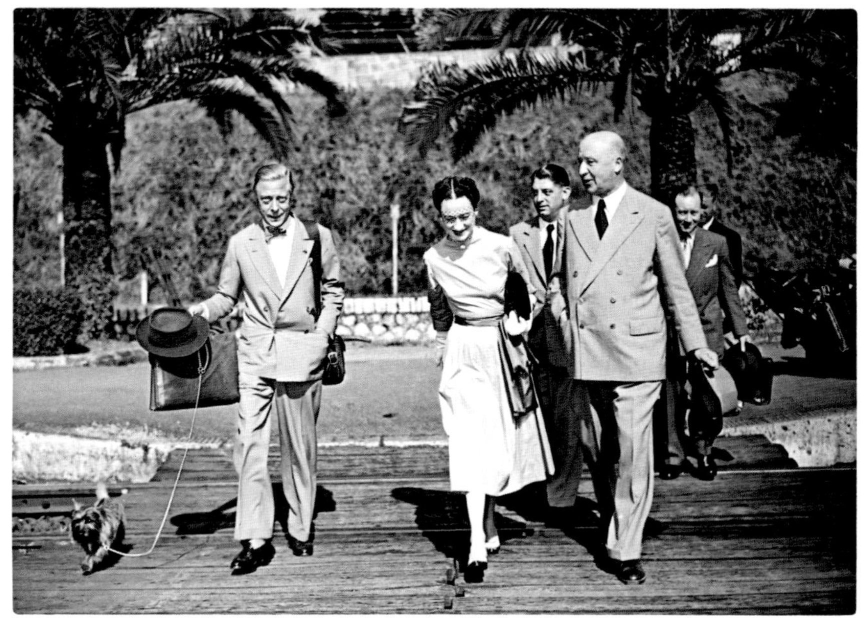

"The Riviera – a sunny place for shady people."

W. SOMERSET MAUGHAM

Above: For decades, "tout le monde" met at the Hôtel du Cap. The Duke and Duchess of Windsor honeymooned here in 1937.

Right: Europe's high nobility vacationed here during the Belle Époque, followed by the continent's super-rich and eventually by artists and celebrities from around the world. First port of call to enjoy outstanding cuisine, glittering balls and ostensibly relaxed mores: the Hôtel du Cap-Eden-Roc.

Opposite: French cinema actress Annabella (real name: Suzanne Georgette Charpentier), whose romance with Tyrone Power was widely reported by the tabloid press.

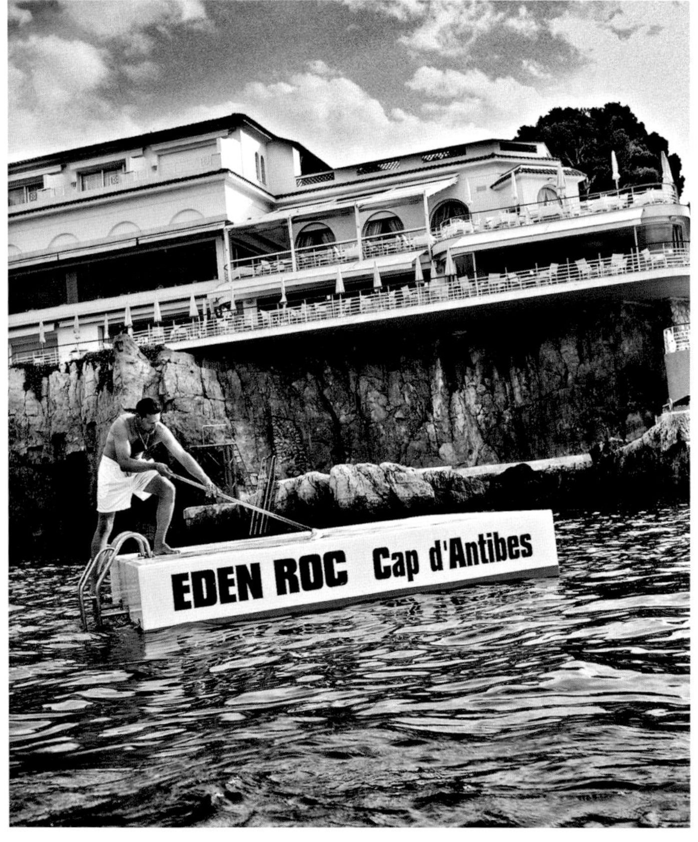

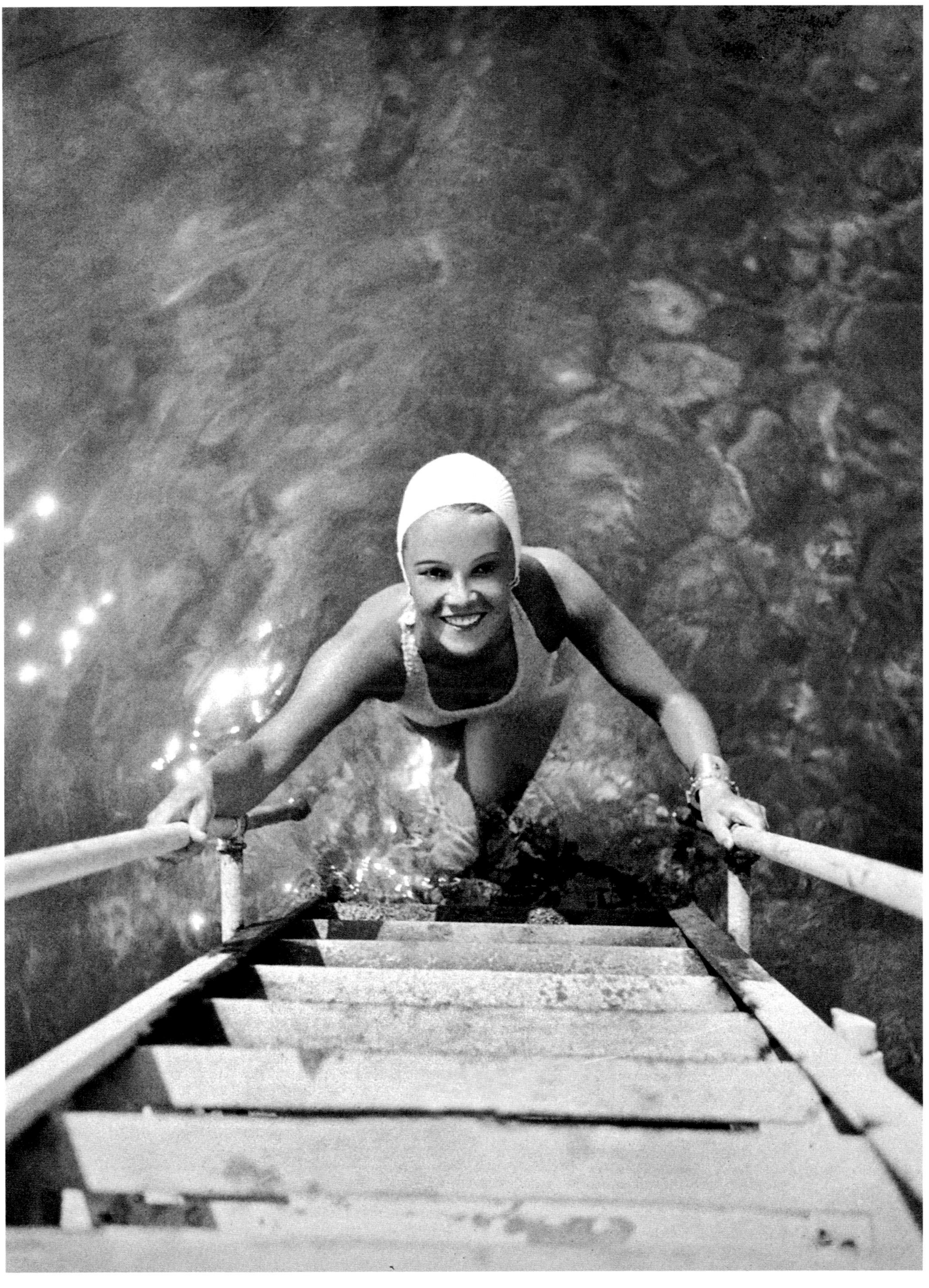

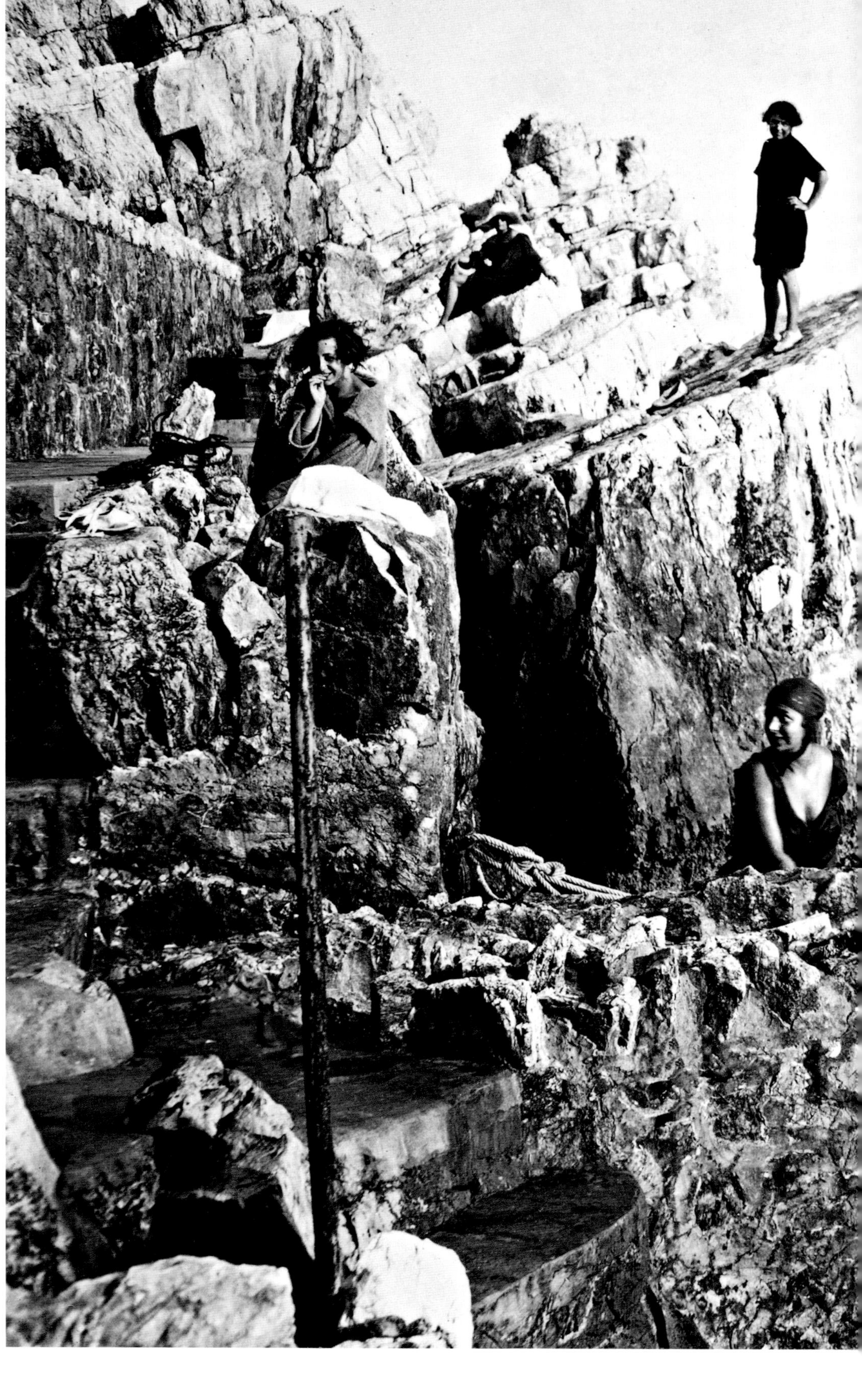

How it all began: Hippolyte de Villemessant, the founder of France's *Le Figaro* newspaper, wanted to turn his Villa Soleil into a "refuge for writers and artists". On February 28, 1870, the Grand Hôtel du Cap opened its doors. Seen here: Ernest Hemingway and screenwriter Anita Loos (*Gentlemen Prefer Blondes*).

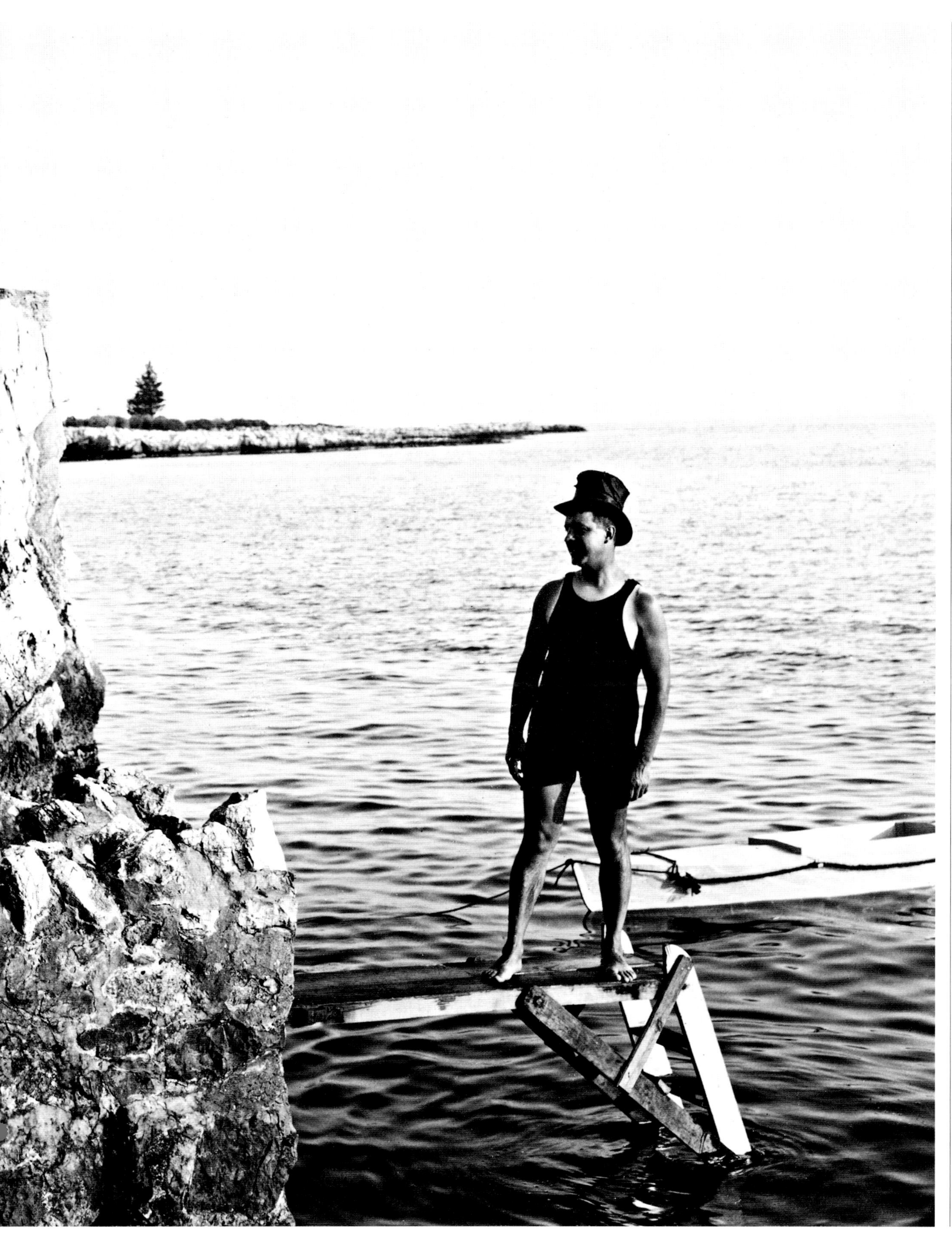

LUC DONCKERWOLKE IS CONSIDERED ONE OF THE MOST IMPORTANT AUTOMOTIVE DESIGNERS OF OUR TIME. AS CHIEF CREATIVE OFFICER, HE IS NOT ONLY RESPONSIBLE FOR THE DESIGN OF GENESIS VEHICLES, BUT ALSO FOR AN ENTIRE BRAND WORLD. BOTH ARE PROFOUNDLY INFLUENCED BY KOREAN CULTURE.

WHICH, IN TURN, IS ALL ABOUT BEING THERE FOR OTHERS.

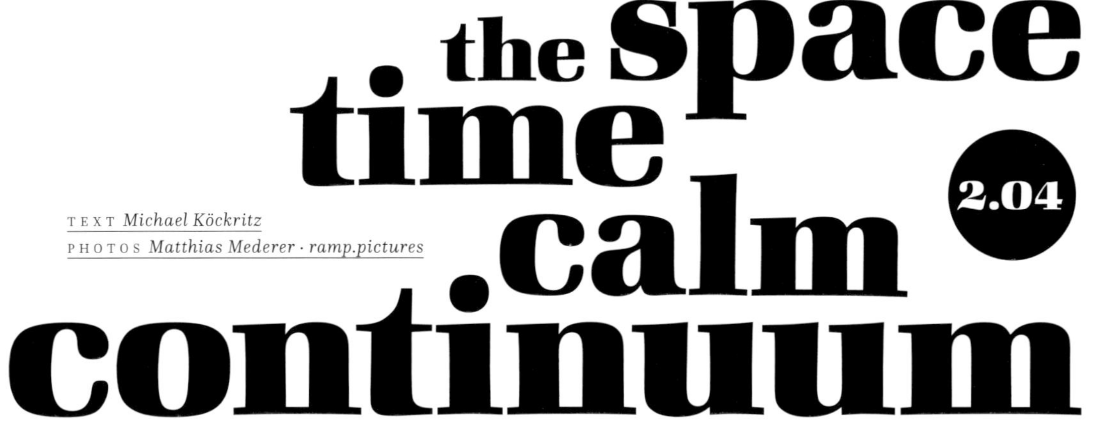

TEXT *Michael Köckritz*
PHOTOS *Matthias Mederer · ramp.pictures*

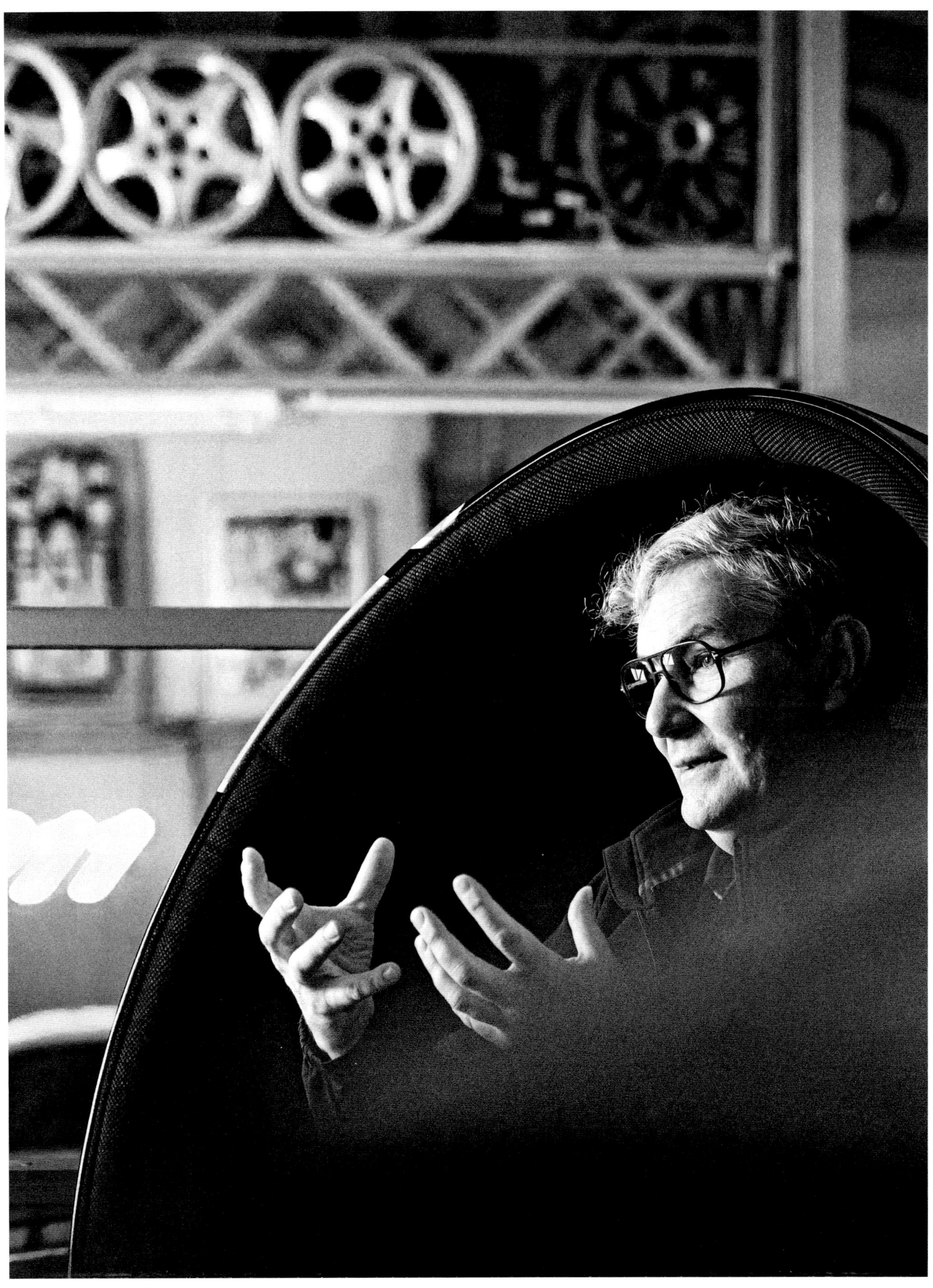

Mr. Donckerwolke, how important is automotive design in your life?
For me, it is a combination of my passion for cars and the gift of being able to draw, a way to illustrate things that didn't exist in my small world. I grew up in Africa and South America, where the roads were often in poor condition and you would see mainly Jeeps, Land Rovers and old pick-ups – but no Porsches, for example. So I started to draw them on paper. These drawings were my attempt at creating a world for myself, and that obsession continues to drive me to this day. Unfortunately, it doesn't always work.

Doesn't work? But here in your garage you've got six perfect Porsche 911s, from legendary classics to fairly modern models to highly sought-after collector's editions like a Speedster.
Well, yeah. But the problem is, you get used to things and then you want more. It's always like that.

Is this obsession with cars driven by their design or rather by the idea of the car as a symbol of freedom? Or is it a combination of both?
I think it's about my love for the product. Though I should elaborate on that a bit. Actually, I'm not all that interested in the finished car itself. For the most part, it's the process of designing and creating that I love. And I wouldn't confine that to only the design – that also applies to the product as a whole. Imagine taking a car apart and putting it back together again: I find every aspect of the car fascinating – the design, of course, but also the technology, the way a car functions mechanically. I love it when a product works. And that doesn't just apply to cars.

You work with nineteen design studios worldwide, a thousand people work for you. How do you manage all that? What do you see as your role here?
I see myself more as a kind of manager or coach, a trainer. I set the course and provide the motivation. I love working with such a big team because it gives me the opportunity to try out many different things. I'm very curious and want to see what happens when we try one thing or the other. And I always gamble on happy accidents.

Playful invention?
Exactly. Wherever you see bad design – and this is true not only in the automotive industry – it can be due to bad designers, but it can also be an indication of poor management. You need a form of management that places a high level of trust in the design department and gives them the freedom for inventive play. The awards I've won with my teams show that that's exactly what we have going for us. Yes, we have very good designers here, but we are also given the necessary freedom and trust. I have always worked a bit against the system. And here at Hyundai, I also understand my work in such a way that I manage my people as if it were my company, so I don't have the mindset of an employee. I've always done things that way. I didn't design the Lamborghini Murciélago for Lamborghini, I designed it for myself. [*laughs*] But I can only do that if I can identify with a product one hundred percent.

Though it is a bit unusual for a company like Hyundai to give you that kind of freedom, isn't it?
That's true. But I am also in a situation where I report directly to Chairman Chung Eui-sun. That means my boss is the owner himself. And he's a fantastic person whose main motivation is to make things that help people.

And what does that look like in practice?
Relatively unbureaucratic and probably somewhat unspectacular. Just one example: When I joined Kia in 2018, they weren't satisfied internally with the development of the Ioniq 6. I then secluded myself with three of the designers and we spent five weeks working intensely on this car. I kept sending our chairman some sketches and texted him play-by-play updates of our progress. And I always got immediate feedback. To put that into perspective, you have to understand that this guy runs a total of fifty-seven companies.

"I'm not all that interested in the finished car itself. For the most part, it's the process of designing and creating that I love."

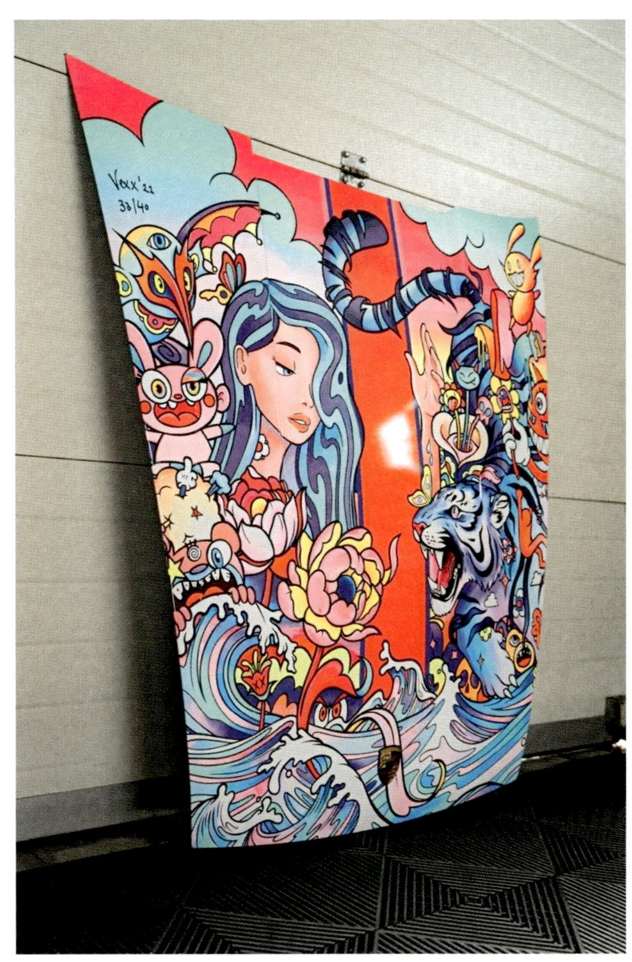

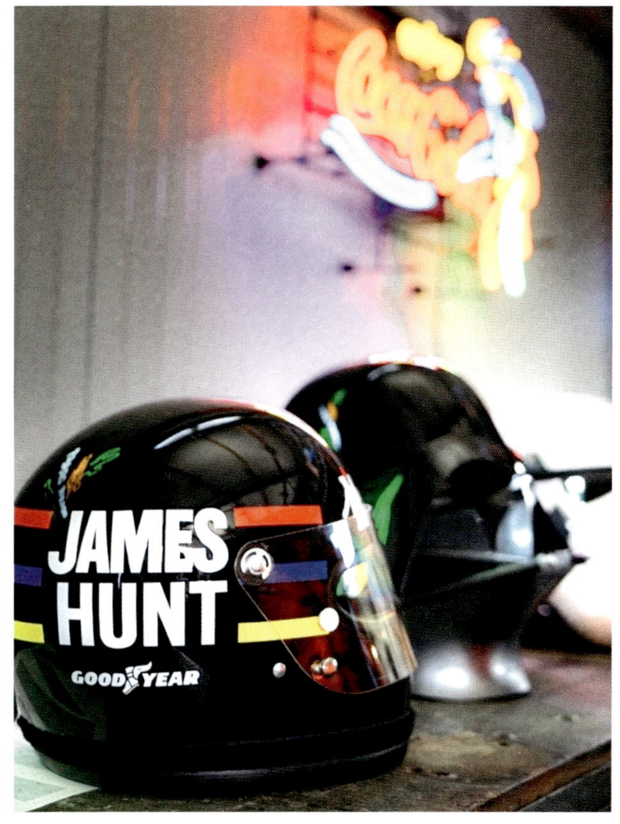
JAMES
HUNT
GOODYEAR

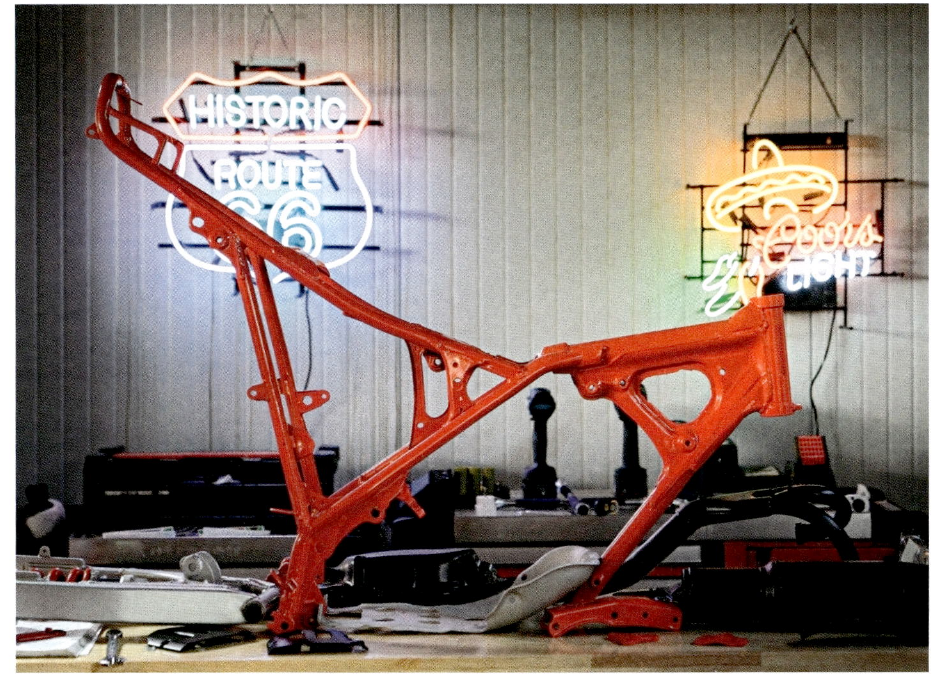
HISTORIC
ROUTE
66

The Ioniq 6's design does in fact polarize public opinion . . .

That's true. Actually, it all goes back to a suggestion from our chairman. He showed us a picture and said, "I could imagine it looking like this." That led to quite some heated debate internally. Several people said it wouldn't sell.

And what did the boss say to that?

"Have you talked to the customers from 2030? No? Then you should do that!"

That's pretty amazing.

He's always thinking ahead. And he believes in the design departments. When the iPhone came out, for example, he gave one to every designer. He wanted them to learn from and engage with the device in their daily lives in order to understand it. Because he was convinced that the iPhone was going to change the world.

So it's all about integrating the customer experience?

Something like that. For me, design has become so important in recent years primarily because it defines and delivers the user experience and because this user experience, with all its new digital possibilities, has become so much more complex. With electric cars, we are also seeing some new freedom in terms of previous technical specifications. An electric powertrain allows me to position the relevant components much more freely.

So a combination of functional quality and aesthetics. For a lot of people, this describes their understanding of luxury. What does luxury mean to you?

Quite simply and to the point: space, time and a sense of calm. No matter how fantastic your hotel room is, no matter how well you were taken care of on a flight or how expensive and exclusive your car is, if you don't have these three things, it's not luxury. So it's not only about material things. For me, luxury is something that I have to create myself because I'm responsible for making these three things happen. The greatest danger is being seduced by this and doing something just because you can. For me, the user experience and the formal implementation have to work together. They have to function together. Styling alone, just making something look good, isn't enough.

So it's about doing something for yourself?

Exactly. Of course, that isn't so easy when you live in a city with ten or twenty million other people. But here, too, I have to decide what's important to me. Let me give you another example: I had always dreamed of having HON Circle status at Lufthansa. Now I've been a member for the past seven years, enjoying all the first-class amenities, but I actually find the price to be too high. Because every time I get that new plastic card, all I can think is: "Oh dear, so much time wasted flying around all over the place instead of exploring the great outdoors or spending some quality time at home." I also don't like being constantly attended to by the flight attendants. I don't need that. It's these experiences from which I derive our understanding of luxury for Genesis.

Can you be more specific?

First of all, I'm reluctant to even use the word "luxury" when talking about Genesis. For me, Genesis is more about design, technology and hospitality. Why hospitality? Because I see this love of serving the guest as something deeply Korean, something I don't see in this form anywhere else. When it comes to hospitality, I haven't had a single negative experience in my seven years in Korea. Here in southern Germany, where I live, the Internet has been down for three weeks because a car crashed into some telecommunications box somewhere. When I called Deutsche Telekom, the first thing they did was to shift the responsibility back on me, telling me to buy a new router or get new cables. I had already done all that. But first I had to prove it. In Korea, that's one call: three hours later they're at my door and the matter is settled.

"I'm reluctant to use the word 'luxury' when talking about Genesis. For me, Genesis is more about design, technology and hospitality."

Sounds like confirmation of the cliché about Germany being a customer service wasteland.
But service is what it's all about! And that's why at Genesis the customer isn't simply called a customer, but a guest of honor, or *sonnim* in Korean. We do everything we can to bring that understanding to the road, which is why it might take a little longer. We don't have dealers. If you want to buy a Genesis, you call us or arrange a test drive online. The car is then dropped off at your place and picked up again later. It's the same with service and maintenance. You get a replacement car and don't have to worry about anything. For five years. As soon as you buy a car from us, you're our guest. That means everything is taken care of. For me, that's an enormously important topic that reflects exactly what I mean with luxury.

That's a clear explanation of your luxury understanding for the product. What about the brand?
Here we go several steps further. I'm actually an engineer and automotive designer, but the Genesis brand world also includes hotels and restaurants. We have the Genesis Lounge at the Shilla Hotel in Seoul, for example. Here, too, we implement our ideas in a consistent manner. When you make a reservation, you get a table in a room all to yourself. It's the best hotel in Korea. We have exactly the same concept at our Genesis House in Manhattan, which is considered the best Korean restaurant in the world. And I'm learning a lot in the process. The restaurant is always fully booked. When I asked for a report after six months on the job, I was surprised to read that we were far from breaking even every quarter. To my question as to how that could be, I was told, "You can't run a luxury restaurant, demand the highest standards of service, quality, staff and ingredients, and then aim for profit as your main goal."

How did you react to that?
I don't ask for any more reports! [*laughs*] But seriously, the standards for the food and the staff – not to mention the rent – are so high there's no way the model can turn a profit. I think that describes part of our understanding of luxury. If you really take the guest of honor philosophy seriously, you don't always have profitability as your first priority.

We go over to the cars. A Porsche 911 G in mint condition, a 993, a white 964 RS. Donckerwolke could tell a story about each one. But he also says, "Most of them aren't even registered anymore because I just don't have the time." He explains why each car is different, why some require more time and effort to be road-certified, and why that can't just be done by the inspection station around the corner. Donckerwolke collects almost exclusively Porsches. Besides the models here, he has two or three more stored away in another garage. If you ask him – keep in mind, this is the chief creative officer of Hyundai Motor's Genesis brand – where he got his enthusiasm for Porsche, he will tell you the following story:

When I was a teenager, I was in Senegal with my parents, and the Dakar 6 Hours race wasn't far away. So I went there and looked at all the cars. One of them was a 1974 Porsche 911 RSR, three-liter engine, which roared to life right in front of me. That experience, that feeling, has stayed with me ever since.

The spark that ignited your own enthusiasm, so to say.
Absolutely! And that enthusiasm remains alive and well. The sound of a 911 continues to have a profound effect on me. For my fourteenth birthday, I desperately wanted my parents to give me Paul Frère's book on the Porsche 911. It was in French. It became my bible. I knew it by heart.

By heart?
Word for word. Where we lived, as I said, there were no cars like that. Once a year my father had to go to Geneva for a debriefing at the UN. I stood all night at the window of the hotel and watched

"The standards for the food and the staff – not to mention the rent – are so high there's no way the model can turn a profit."

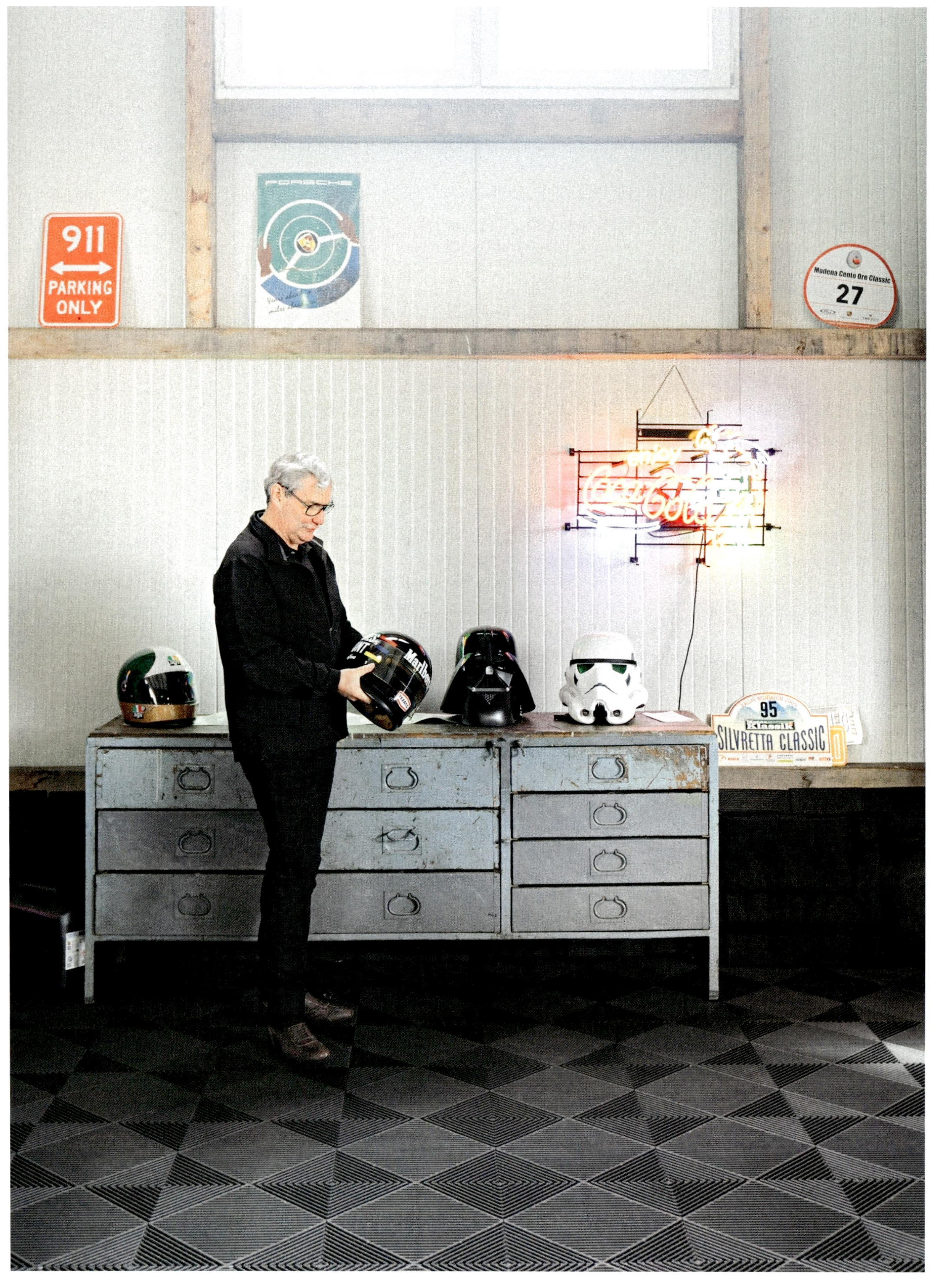
911
PARKING ONLY
PORSCHE
Modena Cento Ore Classic
27
95
Klassik
SILVRETTA CLASSIC

the cars drive by down on the street: Porsches, Ferraris, Lamborghinis, Maseratis. Then I started to draw the Porsche 911. It was a way for me to establish a relationship with this car. And that relationship turned into a long platonic love affair.

When did that love become more physical?
That took a while. I chose German as my second foreign language at school because I really wanted to work for Porsche. I then became an engineer and later a designer. To be honest, I was really a bit afraid of buying a 911. It was always my big dream and I was worried that reality wouldn't be able live up to the fantasy.

But your concern was unfounded?
Yes, and today it is more unfounded than ever. I'm not just talking about the 911 from an aesthetic point of view. I love things that work well. And that's also the reason why I have always owned significantly more Porsche 911s than cars from other brands. The 911 is unlike any other car.

You own both classics as well as newer models.
That's right. And I love them all. Each car has its own unique personality. And I like changing which one I drive because then I can feel how the chassis works differently, how the weight of the engine is different in each case and how that affects things.

Do you have a favorite?
Tough one. I love the 964, it still has those two cannon-like front fenders. It looks like Superman in flight. The 993 introduced a lot of changes: flatter in the front, much more complex in its shape. Because although the shape of a 911 seems simple, it's actually quite hard to sketch. I tried to model a 993 when I was still a teenager. That's when I first noticed it and was fascinated. It's nice when something seems very simple, but there's actually a lot of art behind it. It's like a very good dancer: you never see him sweat, but a lot of work takes place behind the scenes to make his moves look so effortless.

So the challenge is to get to the heart of the matter.
Exactly. And that's what the 911 delivers like no other car – across all generations! The 911 is designed by engineers for engineers. You like it – or you don't. It was always evolving, even when Porsche itself no longer really believed in it. That's one of the reasons why I think the Porsche 911 is the first global automobile. It's not the result of a survey of the individual markets to see what they wanted.

Do you have a favorite color?
There really isn't any color at Porsche that is as amazing as Oak Green. With Slate Gray following in a close second. I still don't own a car in either color. I like white a lot because it's from the world of racing, black because it's very elegant.

What is it about collecting that you find so fascinating?
I think it's the sheer pleasure. I always want more. Sometimes I think, "Okay, it's been a couple of years now, time to buy myself another Porsche." If it's a new car, I think to myself, I should go and buy another classic. And when I buy a classic, I think to myself, I should go and buy another new model.

LUC DONCKERWOLKE was born in Lima, Peru, in 1965 as the son of a Belgian diplomat. After studying in Brussels and at the ArtCenter College's former campus in Vevey, Switzerland, he began his career at Peugeot, moving on to Audi, Škoda and finally Lamborghini, where he first took on the position of chief designer, with responsibility for the design of the Lamborghini Murciélago and Gallardo, followed by positions at SEAT and Bentley. As chief creative officer of Hyundai Motor Group, he is in charge of the design language for Hyundai, Kia and Genesis and contributes creative input to corporate brands such as Boston Dynamics and the urban air mobility company Supernal.

"The 911 is designed by engineers for engineers. You like it – or you don't. It was always evolving, even when Porsche itself no longer really believed in it."

WE NEED TO START WORRYING ABOUT WHAT KIND OF A WORLD WE ARE GOING TO LEAVE FOR KEITH RICHARDS WHEN WE DIE.

Me as a teenager: "Don't tell me what to do!"
Me as an adult: "Can someone please tell me what to do? In detail and in chronological order?"

If you're not happy being single, try dating apps. You'll still be single, but you'll appreciate it a lot more.

I NEVER THOUGHT I WOULD GET UP AT 6 A.M. TO GO RUNNING.

I WAS RIGHT.

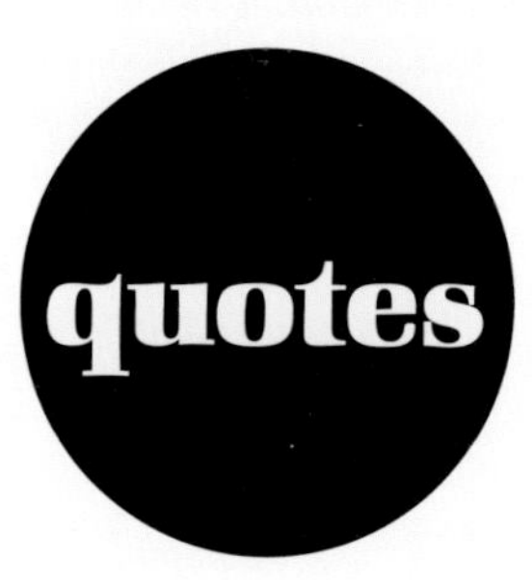

A GREAT BOSS IS THE KIND WHO SAYS: "DON'T WORRY ABOUT IT. WE CAN DO IT TOMORROW."

In ancient times cats were worshipped as gods; they have not forgotten this.

Before the internet, we thought the cause of stupidity was the lack of access to information. Well, apparently that wasn't it.

MINDS ARE LIKE PARACHUTES. THEY ONLY FUNCTION WHEN OPEN.

I cleaned out the candy drawer. Now I feel sick!

WHEN YOU'RE HAPPY, YOU ENJOY THE MUSIC. WHEN YOU'RE SAD, YOU UNDERSTAND THE LYRICS.

I DON'T KNOW HOW TO PLAY CHESS. BUT LIFE IS A CHESS GAME FOR ME.

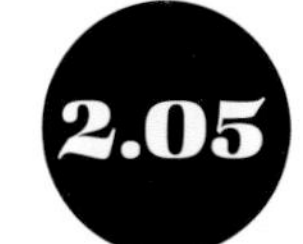

THIERRY GUETTA, BETTER KNOWN AS MR. BRAINWASH, FRENCH STREET ARTIST

DOING THE LAUNDRY: 40 MINUTES. DRYING: 60 MINUTES. FOLDING MY CLOTHES AND PUTTING THEM AWAY: 7-14 WORKING DAYS.

A boy helps an old nun to cross a busy road.

"Thank you so much, young man!" she says

"That's okay," he replies. "Any friend of Batman is a friend of mine."

Growing up is like getting a subscription to a service you didn't sign up for and can't cancel.

In my house, every Sunday everybody was cleaning. There was always music, and everybody was dancing, sometimes naked. Not hippie, but very free.

PENÉLOPE CRUZ

AN APPLE A DAY KEEPS ANYONE AWAY IF YOU THROW IT HARD ENOUGH.

Don't forget to drink water and get some sun. You're basically a houseplant with more complicated emotions.

I've decided to quit my job and travel until I run out of money.

I should be back by dinnertime.

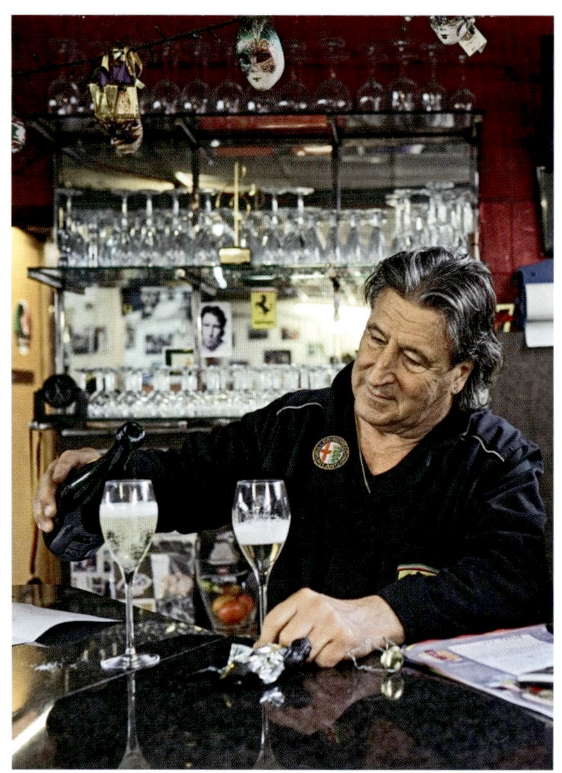

mr. ferrari 2.06

TEXT *Wiebke Brauer*
PHOTOS *Michael Nehrmann*

LUCIANO FAVARON HAS BEEN TINKERING WITH AND TUNING ITALIAN SUPERCARS IN HIS WORKSHOP IN NORTHERN HAMBURG SINCE THE 1980S. WHEN HE'S NOT BUSY MAKING MUSIC, THAT IS.

THE RED-LIGHT REGULARS AND SHOWBIZ STARS WHO USED TO FREQUENT THE AREA HAVE LONG SINCE DISAPPEARED. BUT A WHIFF OF THOSE FORMER GLORY DAYS STILL HANGS IN THE AIR.

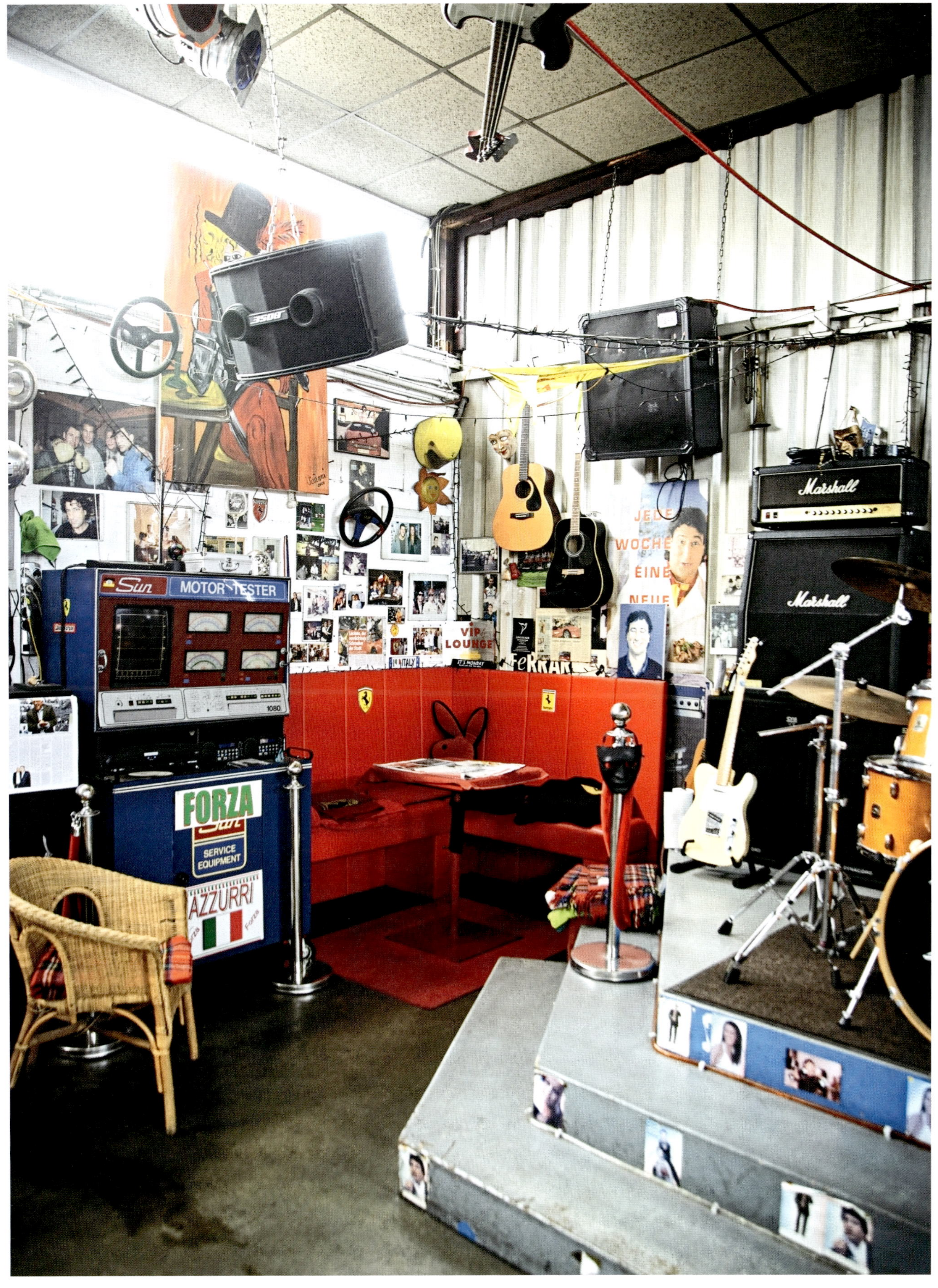
Sun MOTOR TESTER
FORZA
SERVICE EQUIPMENT
AZZURRI
VIP LOUNGE
FERRARI
JEDE WOCHE EINE NEUE
Marshall
Marshall

"You only live once, so you might as well make the best of it." Luciano Favaron beams like the rising sun over the Mediterranean as he says this. Then the Venice native opens the next bottle of Prosecco with a practiced hand. We're not on the Adriatic coast here, however, but in a backyard workshop in Hamburg, in an alley behind the rather unflattering Nedderfeld auto mile in the northern city district of Lokstedt. In the hall of a low-rise building stands a 1980 Ferrari 308 GTBi ("I bought it for DM 7,000 at the time."), next to it an Alfa Spider, in between an unadorned espresso machine on a small table, and opposite that a 1950 Fiat Topolino. Ferrari tools are neatly lined up on the walls, in the corner a drum kit sits enthroned on a small stage, guitars and Venetian masks hang from the ceiling, the fan heater roars, and Italo pop blares incessantly overhead. Photos cover every last bit of free space, among them F1 legends Michael Schumacher, Niki Lauda and Gerhard Berger, former soccer star Günter Netzer, legendary local pimp Handsome Klaus, German folk singer Heino and Italian actress Ornella Muti – just to name a few. Favaron also has several photos of television chef Steffen Henssler on his wall because he cooked with him on TV, and of comedian Alfons because his late-night show was recorded here. Everyone who is anyone has been to see Luciano, or "Luci", as people call him, especially local luminaries, show business greats, footballers and boxers. He's been working on Italian luxury cars here since the 1980s, though the occasional Rolls-Royce might find its way into his workshop as well. Favaron, who is seventy-four years old but looks more like he's in his late fifties, doesn't really need to work anymore. "But what would I do at home?" he asks, throwing his hands up in the air. "Have you eaten?" he then asks, before scurrying off to slice up some wild boar salami and parmesan.

Favaron was raised by his grandparents on a farm in rural Padua under extremely humble conditions. He learned the coachbuilding trade at Ferrari Mestre, near Venice, and dreamed of becoming a musician. "A man without dreams has missed out on life," says Favaron, adding that this also applies to women, of course. He may be old school, but he's not from yesterday. In any case, "visions", as he calls them, are important to him. In 1969 he grabbed his guitar and wanted to travel to London – but only made it as far as Hamburg Central Station. He still shudderingly remembers the stale smell of the cold deep-frying fat that wafted over the tracks back then. But he stayed. Not only because of the many bridges in Hamburg that reminded him of his home, but also because he fell in love. He is still married to Monika today, and photos of the two fill the workshop. A picture of their wedding can be found, of all places, on a pillar next to the lifting platform where quite a few items of female clothing are hanging about. Some are trimmed with delicate lace, others are covered with rivets and leather. How they ended up here is not immediately apparent, only that there were once many more of them and that a ride in Favaron's Ferrari had something to do with it. What Monika thinks of all this? "I was always faithful!" Luciano exclaims. For those innocently upturned eyes, he should get an award.

Everyone who is anyone has been to see Luciano, or "Luci", as people call him, especially local luminaries, show business greats, footballers and boxers.

Favaron's pronounced sense of showmanship led him to record albums with titles like *Pizza, Pasta e Amore* under the name Luciano Della Rosa and to go on tour with German musicians like Frank Zander and Bernd Clüver. When his music career slowed down, Favaron started working in a car repair shop where his brother Paolo, who had also come to Hamburg, was already employed. In the mid-eighties, the brothers set up their own business in the garage in Lokstedt. His success is due in part to the fact that Favaron was pretty much the only person in Hamburg who knew his way around Italian supercars. "They also call me Mr. Ferrari," says Favaron, raising his chin and tucking his hands into his smock. Not to mention that the gentlemen from the red-light district didn't necessarily have the patience to let the V12 of their Ferrari or Lamborghini warm up enough – and before you knew it, they were back in Favaron's shop. In the end, the entertainment industry's favorite Italian mechanic simply did an excellent job. To this day, he still has a penchant for meticulousness. Favaron: "First I polish the car, then I repair it." When no one is looking, he picks tiny bread crumbs off the red blanket on the small table in the corner.

"Luci is more German than the Germans," says Klaus Ottens, who dropped by for a drink that afternoon. "The Great White Shark", as he used to be called, played for FC St. Pauli from 1988 to 1993. At some point during this time, he also ended up at Luciano's, along with many other players from Hamburg's two soccer clubs. "Harry Bähre, who had the number 01 at HSV, was the only person who was ever allowed to smoke in here," recalls Ottens, before launching into the next story from the old days.

It's not always a happy story, with plotlines including players who couldn't cope when their time in the limelight was over, or the tragedy of "Handsome Klaus" from the Reeperbahn, who stopped by even after he had to sell his Countach, his Mercedes convertible and his Silver Shadow, who washed his own espresso cups and said, "Luci, you have it so nice here." Favaron is still irritated at how everyone who had turned their backs on Klaus Barkowsky when he ran out of money showed up at his funeral. "Criminals, every last one of them!" he says. Asked about the fact that Barkowsky and his ilk weren't exactly law-abiding citizens themselves, Favaron takes it all in his stride: "I'm a criminal too!" he exclaims, grinning from ear to ear.

"I was always faithful!" Luciano exclaims. For those innocently upturned eyes, he should get an award.

How you interpret this remark is up to you. That's what's so special about this place: there are always more truths here than guests. Favaron takes care not only of valuable (and meanwhile no longer so expensive) vehicles but also speaks to the Germans' eternal love for all things Italian – and for a bygone era. The golden eighties, when money was no object, sports cars were still racy, and the world seemed a more simple place. Though maybe it still is – at least here, at this workshop. "My nonno always said, 'When you're happy, the whole world is happy,'" says Favaron, before he raises his glass with the words, "Viva la vita!"

Favaron takes care not only of valuable vehicles but also speaks to the Germans' eternal love for all things Italian – and for a bygone era.

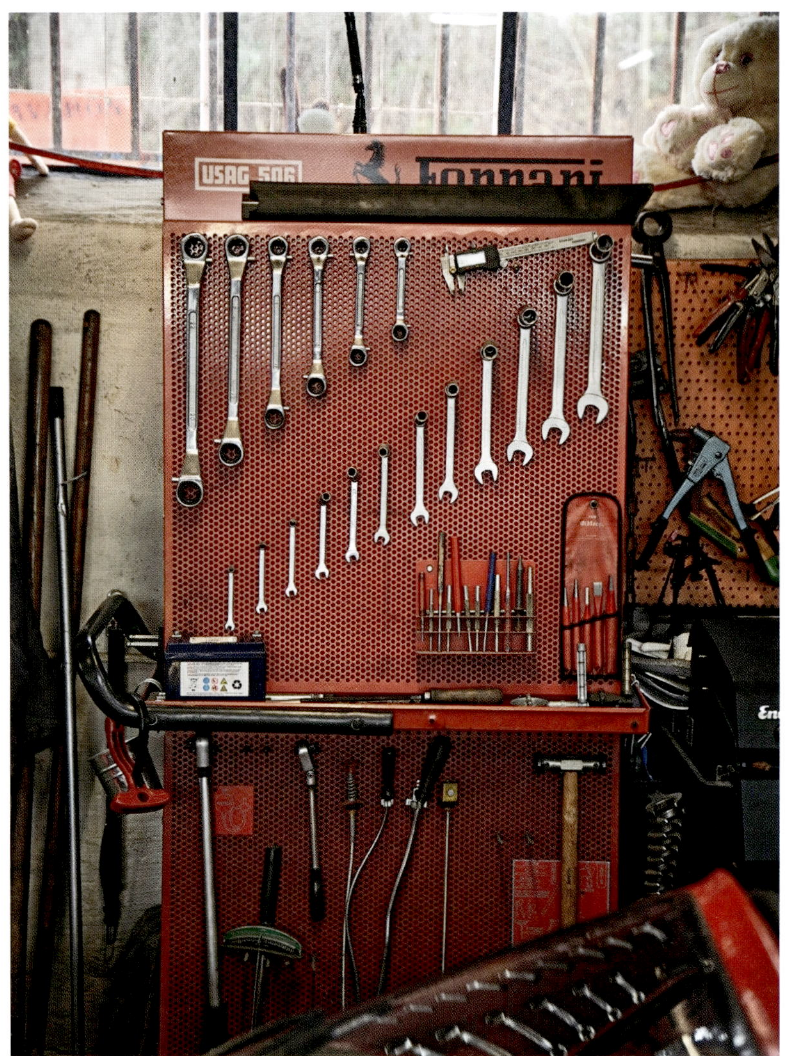

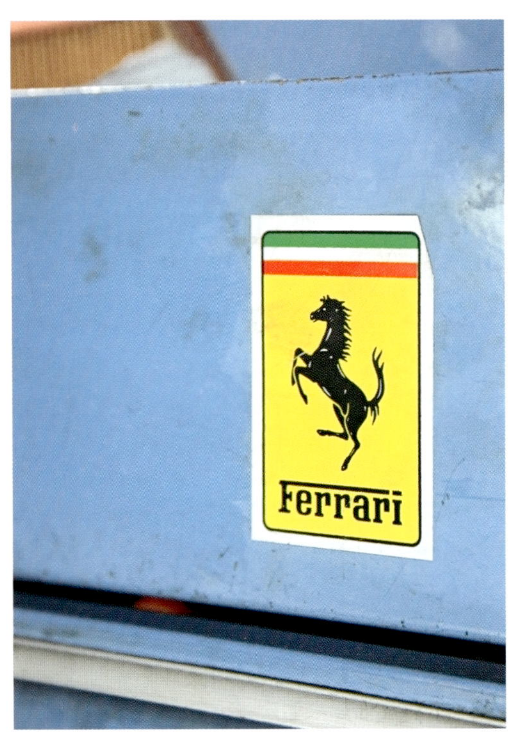

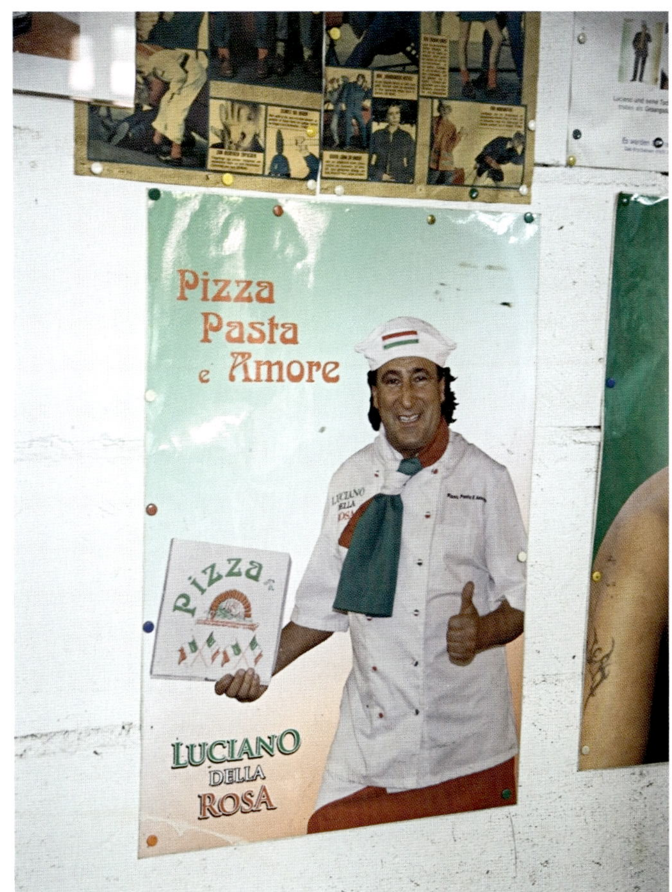

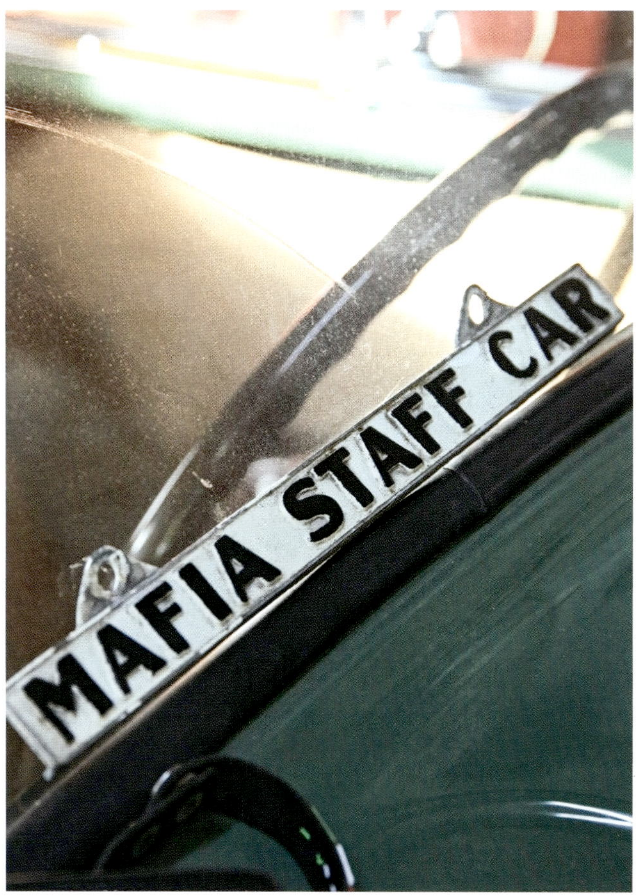

Under the name Luciano Della Rosa, he recorded albums with titles like *Pizza, Pasta e Amore* and went on tour with German musicians like Frank Zander and Bernd Clüver.

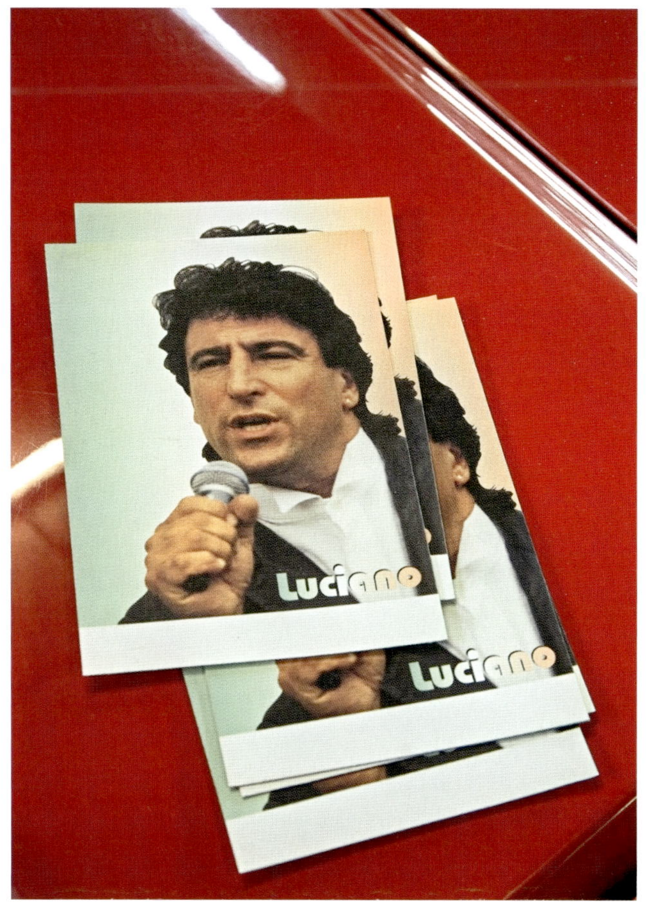

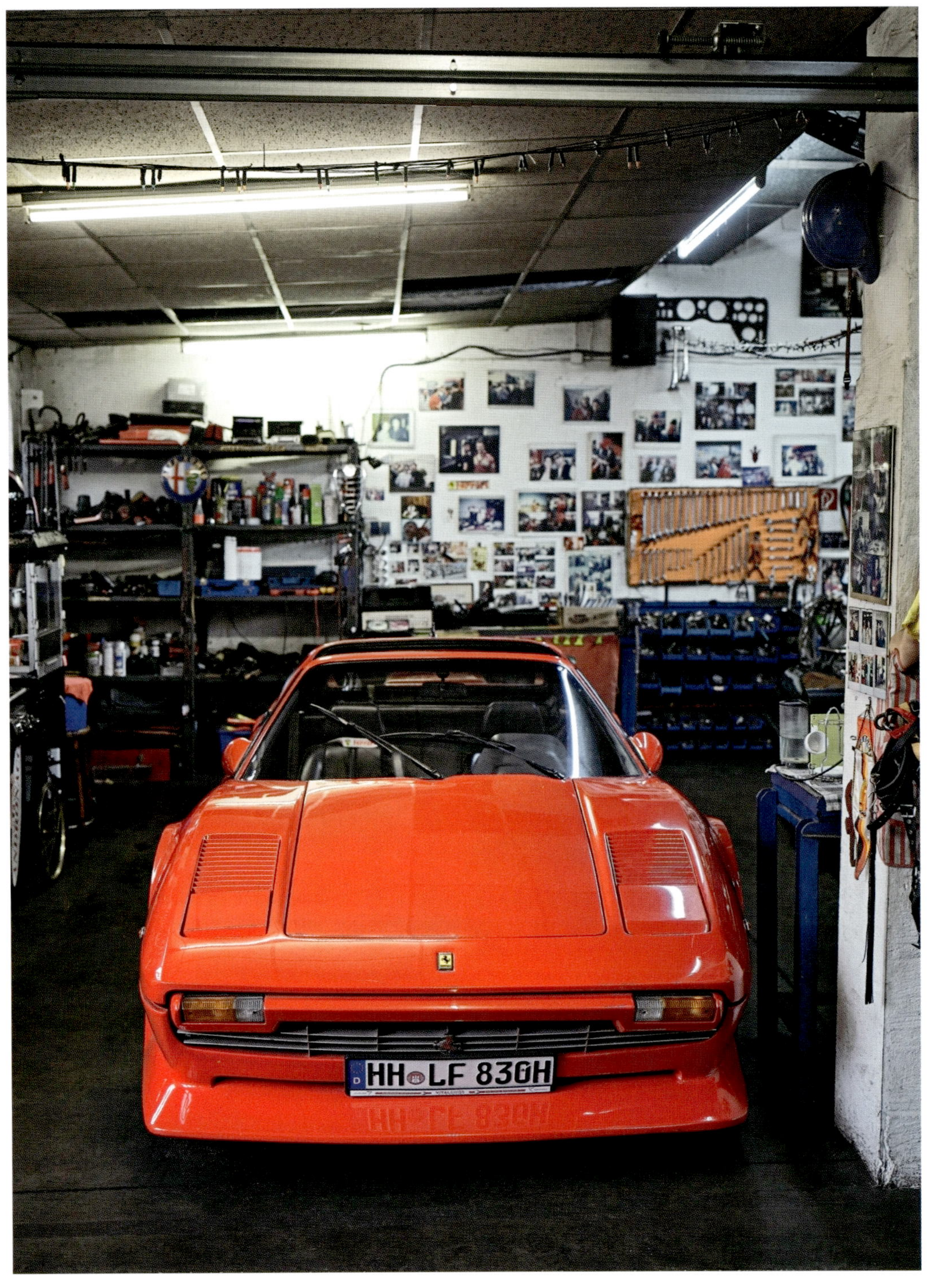
HH LF 830H

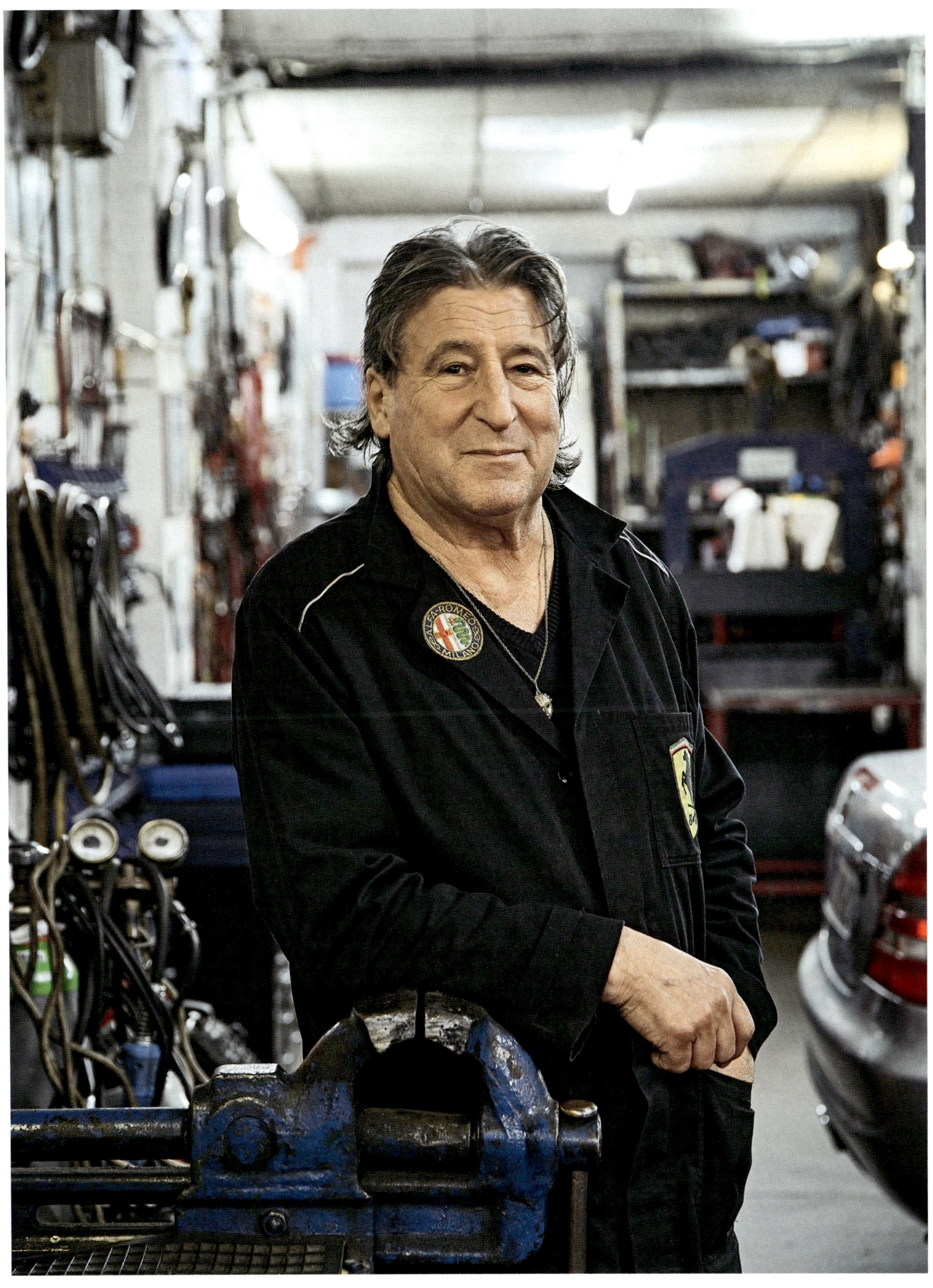
ALFA-ROMEO
MILANO

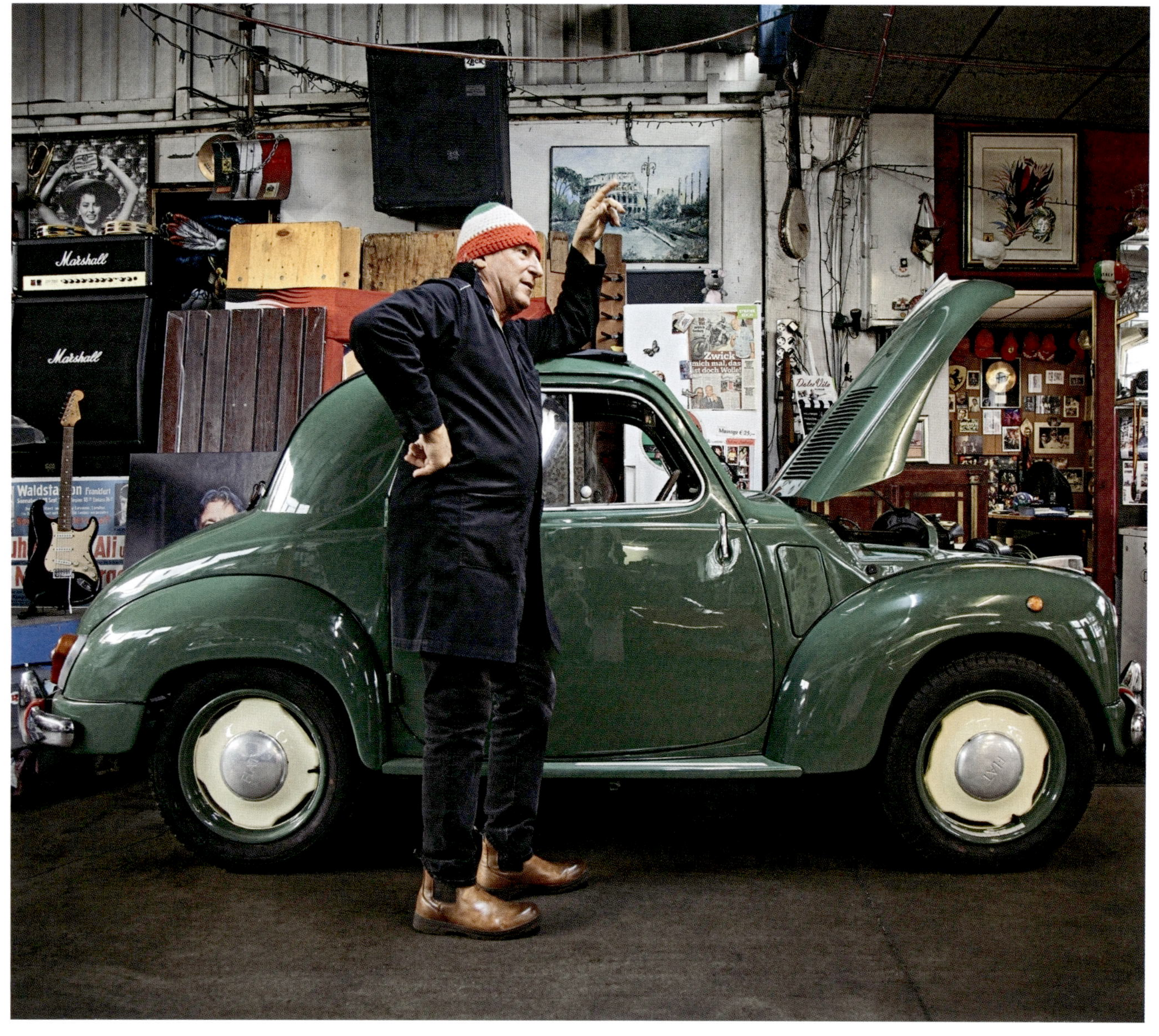

Favaron was raised by his grandparents on a farm in rural Padua under extremely humble conditions. His first job was at Ferrari Mestre.

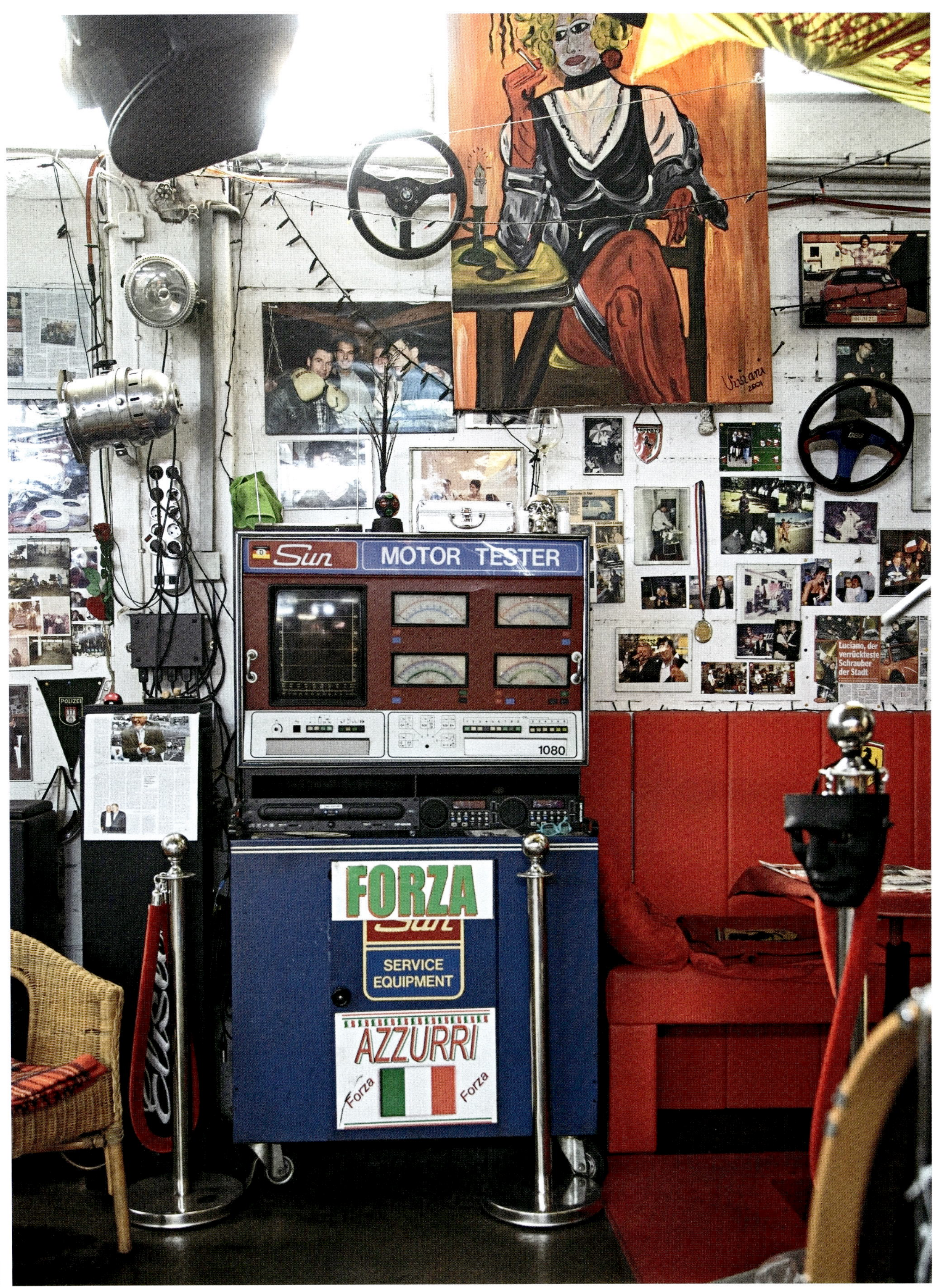
Sun
MOTOR TESTER
1080
FORZA
SERVICE
EQUIPMENT
AZZURRI
Forza
Forza
POLIZEI
Luciano, der verrückteste Schrauber der Stadt

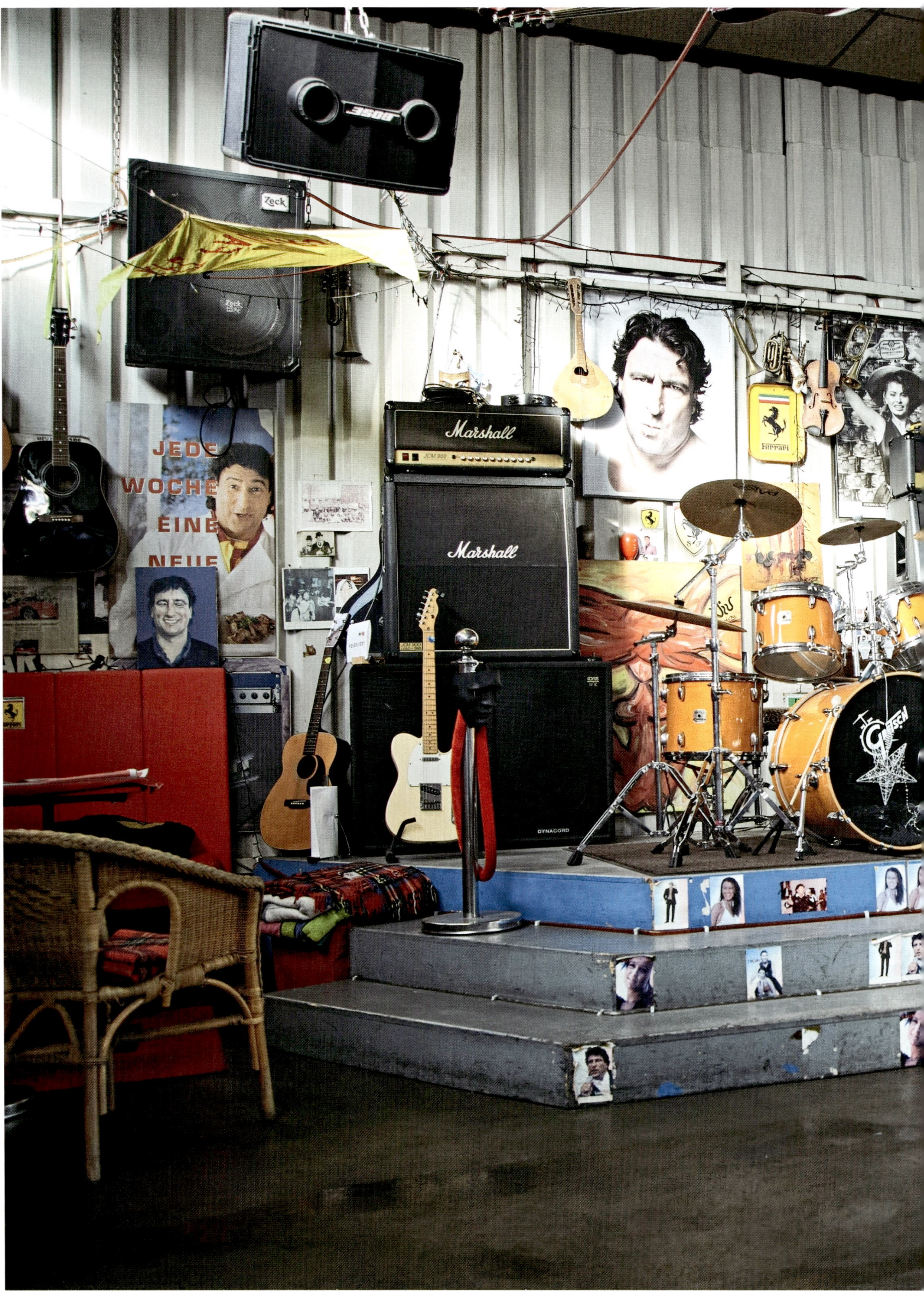
Zeck
JEDE
WOCHE
EINE
Marshall
JCM 900
Marshall
Ferrari
DYNACORD

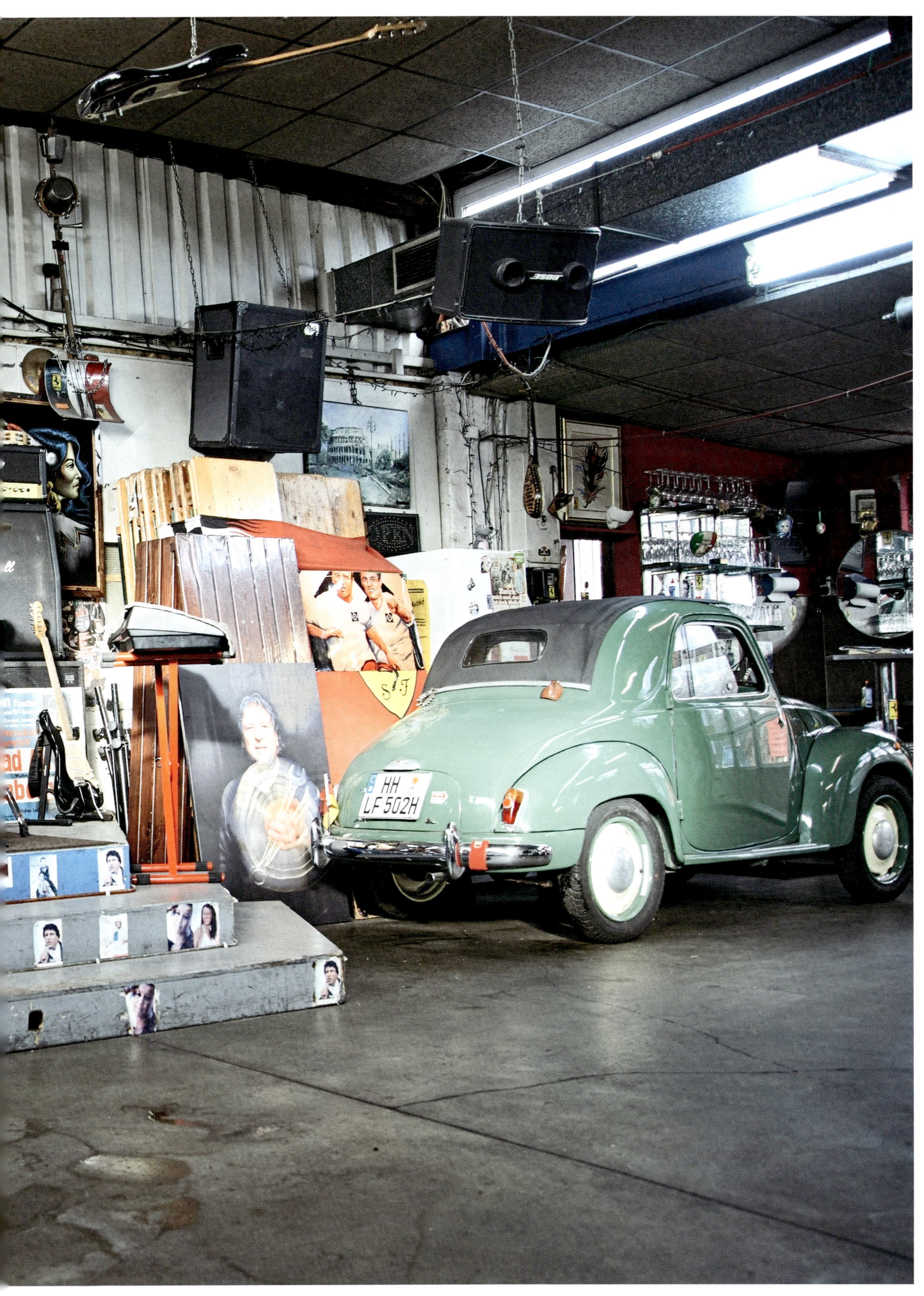
HH
LF 502H

2.07

hard facts

EVERYTHING YOU SHOULD MORE OR LESS KNOW

JOMO*

*** Joy of Missing Out**

part of speech: **noun**

pronunciation: **[joh-moh]**

Not so long ago, we learned that FOMO stands for "fear of missing out" – the feeling of apprehension that you are missing out on some (subjectively) important information, event or experience. The symptoms: constantly checking your emails or looking for status updates and messages on Instagram, Facebook or X (formerly Twitter). (According to unconfirmed reports, men suffer from FOMO more often than women; in either case, however, this fear is driven by our compulsive need to be part of the in-group.) The acronym JOMO, on the other hand, describes the opposite phenomenon: taking pleasure in digital detox. You can either force yourself to have a timeout by going someplace without network coverage, for example, or you could just voluntarily drop out every now and then. Smartphones today offer various options for reducing your screen time, although this feels more like being reprimanded than like a joyous experience. A more effective approach is to simply abandon the idea that life would be better or that you will be smarter or more popular if you are constantly doing something new. So just switch off – and enjoy life as it is!

se • ren • di • pi • ty

noun: the occurrence and development of events by chance in a happy or beneficial way

Viagra, penicillin, the Post-it Note – all these inventions are the result of happy accidents, also known as serendipity. These accidents can even be categorized. In 2018 Ohid Yaqub of the University of Sussex studied the mechanisms of serendipity and published a paper listing four basic types:

Yaqub calls the first type **Walpolian serendipity**, the discovery of things which the discoverers weren't searching for. In 1943, for example, a study of the victims of a mustard gas explosion led to the development of chemotherapy. The second type is **Mertonian serendipity**, where the discovery may lead to the solution of a given problem via an unexpected route. This is what happened to Charles Goodyear, who had spent many years unsuccessfully searching for a way to make rubber thermostable when a rubber-sulfur mixture accidentally splashed onto a hot stove. The third type is **Bushian serendipity**, in which the discovery leads to a solution that hadn't been sought because the research was untargeted, or it was not research at all. The example given here is the discovery of the anesthetic properties of laughing gas. The fourth type, called **Stephanian serendipity**, refers to untargeted research that leads to an unsought-for solution to an unsought-for problem that arises later. The most famous example here is the invention of safety glass when in 1903 the chemist Edouard Benedictus accidentally dropped a flask that did not shatter because of the collodion film inside.

> **"Life is like a box of chocolates. You never know what you're gonna get."**
>
> FORREST GUMP

Hey Google, what's wrong with me?

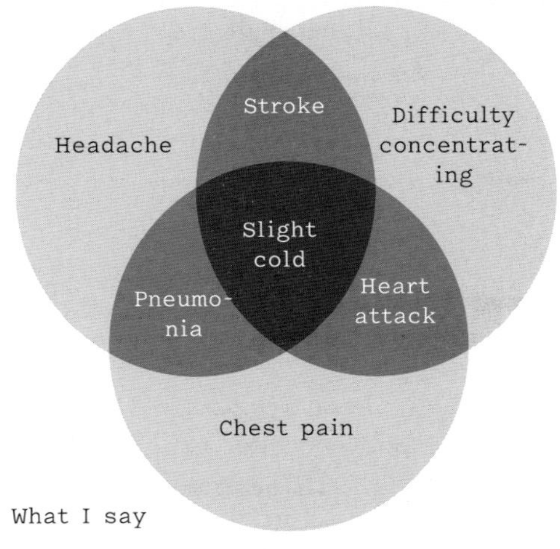

What Germans do when the person they're talking to doesn't understand German:

Switch to English

Try using hand gestures

Speak more loudly!!!!

THERE AND BACK AGAIN

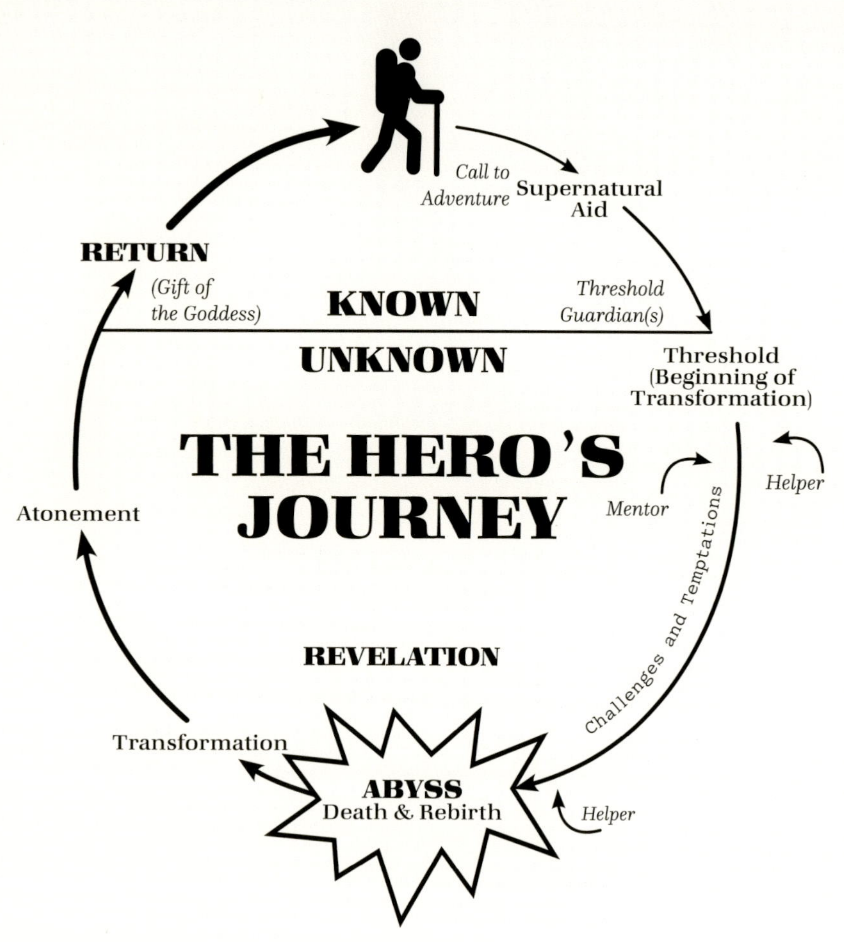

Not pictured: the fire-breathing dragon, the great white shark or the alien, not to mention the cat that needs to be rescued as well. Also unforgettable: Darth Vader or the Ford Falcon XB GT coupe. Joseph Campbell's ideas influenced filmmaker George Lucas in the development of his *Star Wars* saga and director George Miller in the design of his protagonist Mad Max in the movie of the same name.

So there you are, sitting comfortably in front of your cave smoking your pipe, when a wizard comes along talking of adventure. The next day, you've got twelve dwarves sitting in your den, and before you know it, you're on a hero's journey, find a ring that makes you invisible, and in the end, the dragon dies. If this sounds vaguely familiar, it's the abridged plot of *The Hobbit, or There and Back Again* by J. R. R. Tolkien. Which, by the way, is a very classic hero's journey with typical situations and characters. A "monomyth" is what James Joyce called this story template. According to the model proposed by American mythologist Joseph Campbell, the journey always begins with the call to adventure, followed by refusal, challenges and temptations, and, if all goes well, the return from the quest. In the end, you're sitting back home again, feeling out of place. Because nothing is the same anymore.

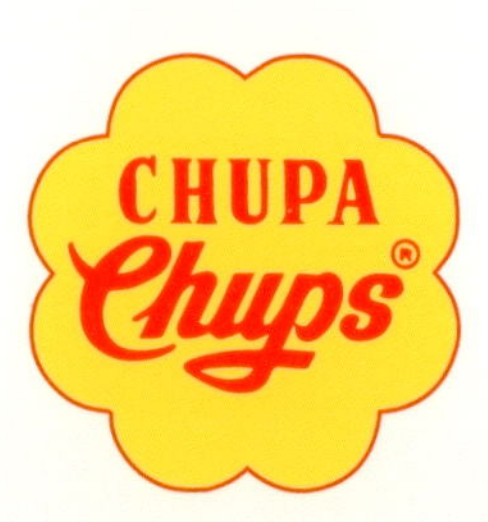

Revealed: Famous Lollipop Logo a Dalí Doodle!

We all know Chupa Chups, the Spanish lollipop brand founded by Enric Bernat in 1958. Bernat, a friend of Salvador Dalí, in 1969 persuaded the surrealist artist to design the logo for him. Dalí scribbled a daisy on a napkin – and the logo, which has remained nearly unchanged to this day, was born.

THE QUEEN'S PROFIT

Just like chess, the business world is all about strategic planning, calculating risks and anticipating your opponent's moves. Seems only logical, then, to pick up some business tips from chess professionals.

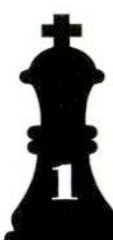

1 THE ART OF LOSING WITH DIGNITY

Learn to embrace failure as an opportunity. Grandmasters of chess know that defeat is an essential part of the game. They analyze their losses with relentless objectivity and look for patterns of error and missed opportunities. This way of thinking differs significantly from that of businesses, which prefer to stigmatize failure instead of celebrating mistakes. The result: they become blind to necessary changes.

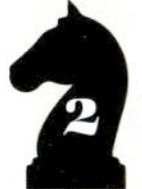

2 FOCUS

In chess, several variations have to be considered at the same time. That will only succeed if the player manages to stay focused even under stress. In everyday working life, our effectiveness is often hindered by the constant flood of decisions that have to be made and by our culture of multitasking. When our brain tries to complete several complex tasks at once, its performance drops considerably. Chess teaches us the need for disciplined concentration – and how to say no to unnecessary distractions.

3 RECOGNIZE PATTERNS

Chess professionals have the uncanny ability to immediately recognize recurring patterns on the board. Studies show that experienced players not only see the individual pieces, but also entire constellations that are of strategic importance. This gift can also be transferred to the business world. Entrepreneurs who can quickly identify patterns in market trends, customer behavior or internal workflows save valuable time, enabling them to take a proactive approach instead of merely reacting to events as they happen.

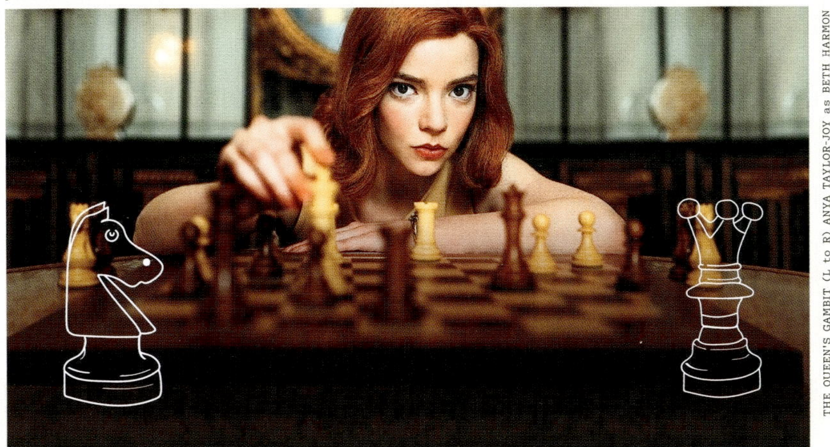

THE QUEEN'S GAMBIT (L to R) ANYA TAYLOR-JOY as BETH HARMON
Cr. COURTESY OF NETFLIX © 2020

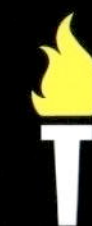

OLYMPIC TRIVIA

WINNER OF THE DAY

The longest Olympic match in history lasted for more than eleven hours. It was the 1912 wrestling semifinal between Martin Klein (Russia) and Alfred Asikainen (Finland). Klein won, but he was unable to wrestle for the gold the next day because he was too exhausted from the bout.

FLYING FISTS

Boxing legend Muhammad Ali was certainly not afraid of his opponents, but he was afraid of flying. That's why, before the 1960 Olympic Games, he initially insisted on traveling to Rome by boat and train. In the end, he did take a plane, though he also bought a parachute beforehand that he wore on his back for the entire flight.

ROLL IN THE HAY

In case things got physical between the athletes during the 2004 games in Paris, the organizers made 300,000 condoms available for free at the Olympic Village – to prevent any unforeseen consequences nine months later. There was also an athletes' bar, though only non-alcoholic drinks were served.

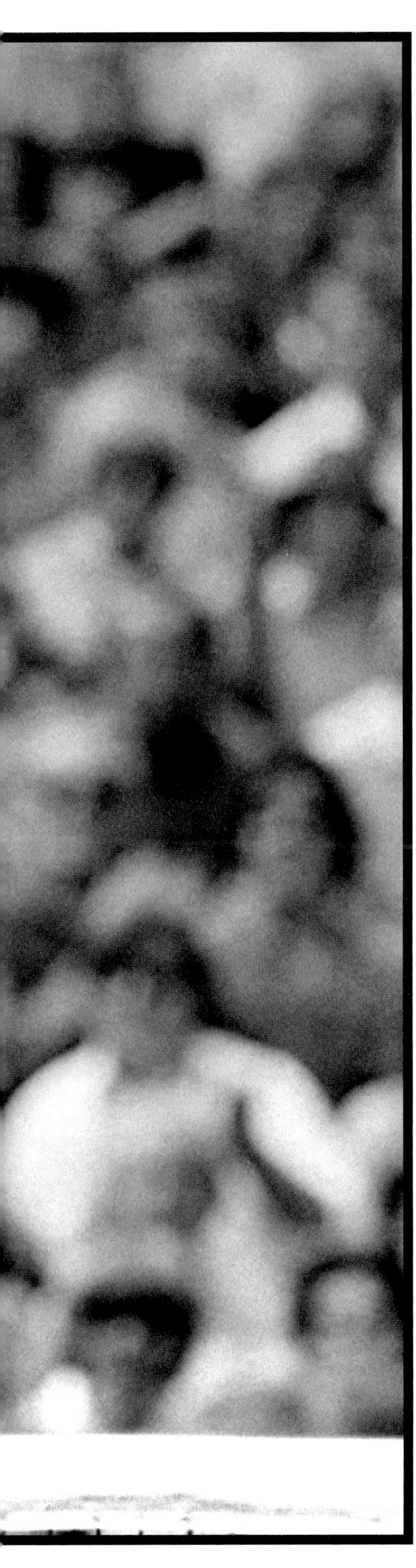

the cool elegance of freedom 3

When Björn Borg swept past Peter McNamara in straight sets in the quarterfinals of the 95th Wimbledon Championships in 1981, he was already a legend. He had won Wimbledon five times in a row and brought a new kind of cool to tennis: long hair, headband, two-handed backhand – but above all, it was his calm presence on court that sparked a wave of "Borgmania" which pulled the sport out of its formerly elitist corner. And then? "The Ice Man" lost to John McEnroe in the final. In 1982 he played just one more tournament before announcing his retirement one year later.

The fact that he was just twenty-six at the time? Only made him more of a legend.

cool stuff

3.01

TEXT *Wiebke Brauer / Bernd Haase / Martin Trockner*

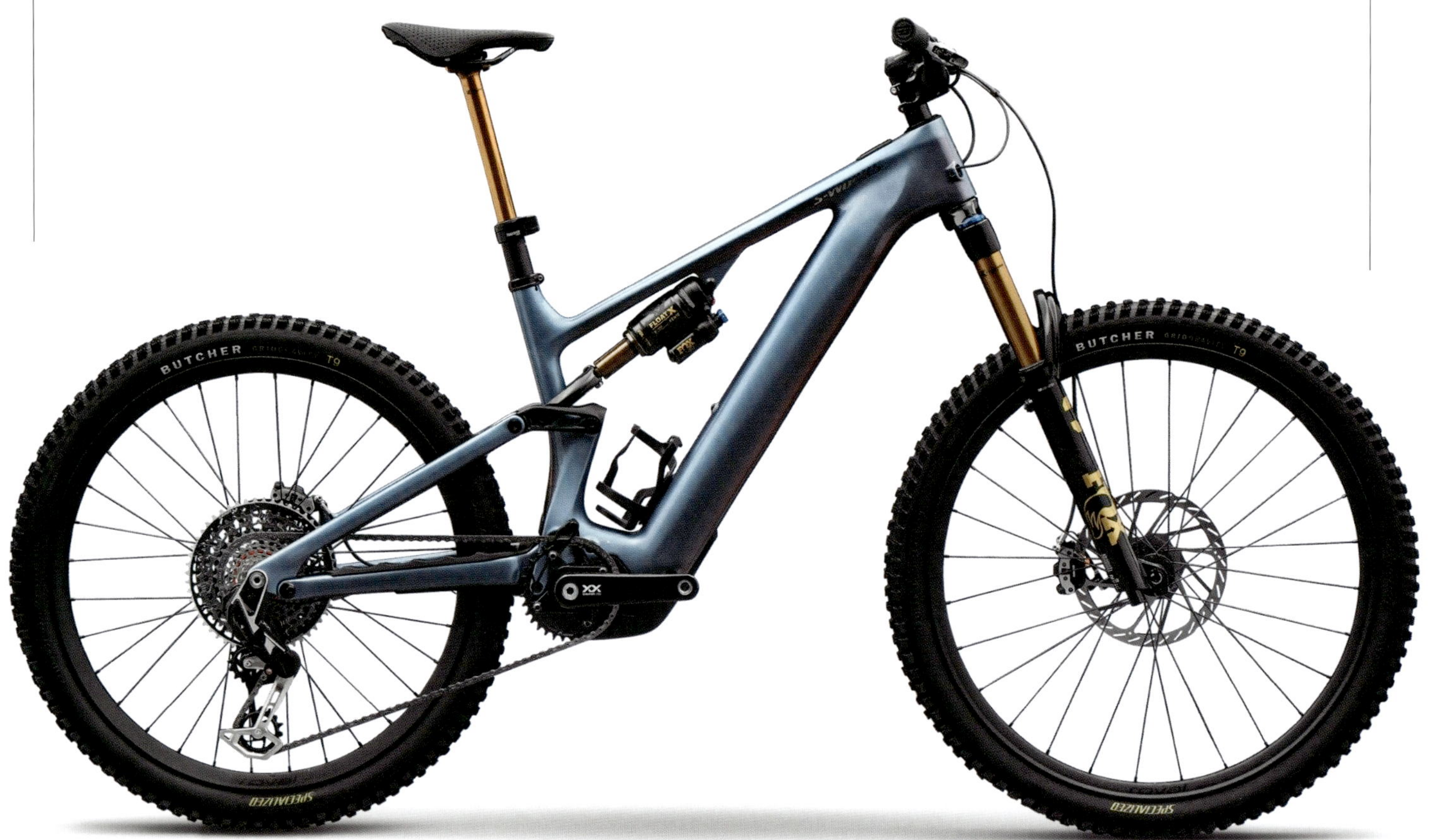

WINNING FORMULA

The S-Works Turbo Levo 4 was just crowned *E-Mountain-bike* magazine's Best eMTB of 2025. Specialized describes its winner as so innovative, it practically turns you into a cycling cyborg – which, naturally, you'll want to test for yourself.

→ specialized.com

KEEP YOUR HEAD

"Sometimes you want to do everything right in life, and then a truck driver from Heilbronn fails to see you in time." From: *Möchte die Witwe angesprochen werden, platziert sie auf dem Grab die Gießkanne mit dem Ausguss nach vorne* [When the Widow Wants Someone to Talk to Her, She Puts the Watering Can on the Grave with the Spout Facing Forward] by Saša Stanišić. Hmm, okay. What you see here is the Paul Smith + Kask "Motion Blur" Wasabi Cycling Helmet.

→ paulsmith.com

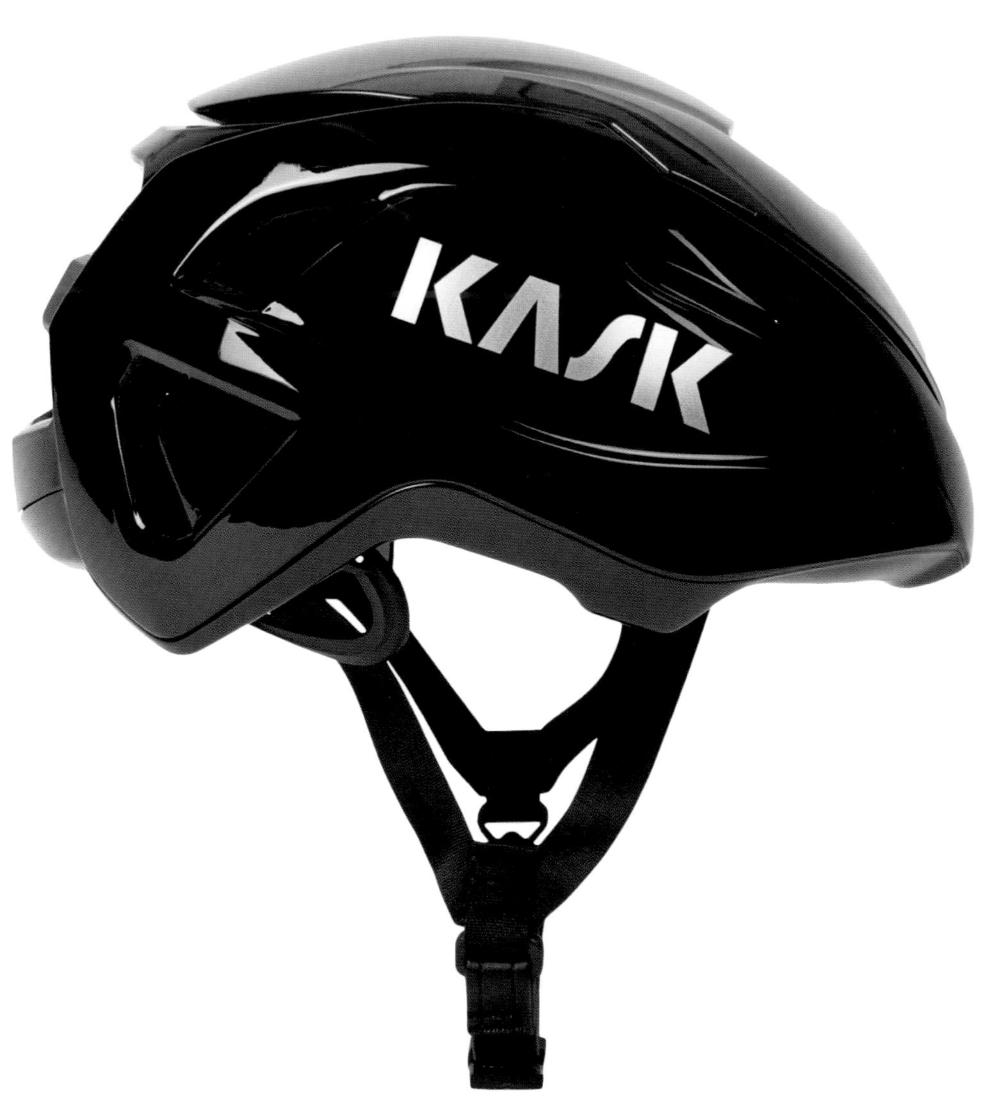

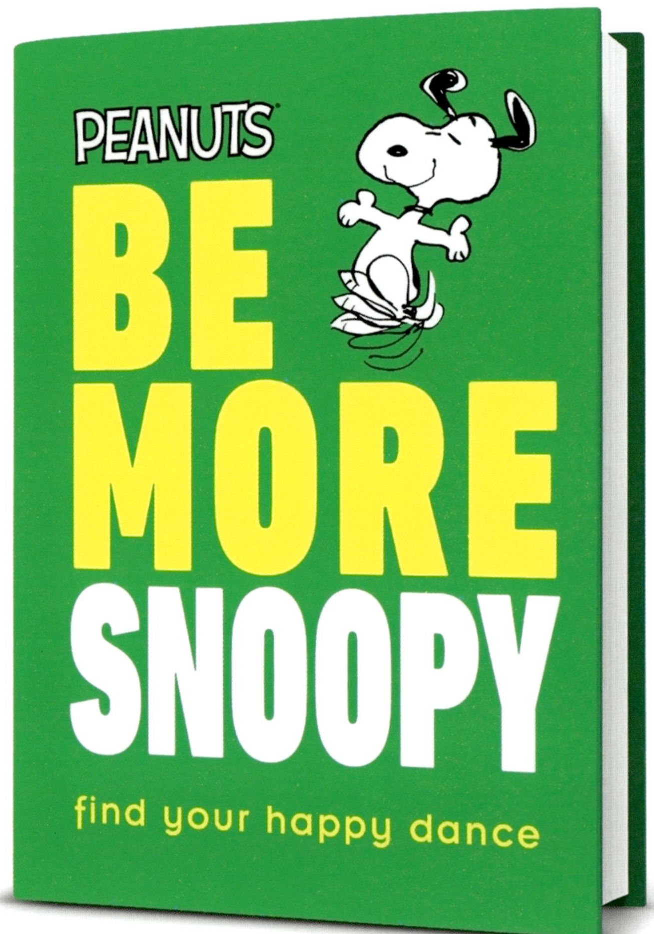

IT'S A DOG'S LIFE

The book *Be More Snoopy* features original comic strip artwork by Charles M. Schulz accompanied by comments from writer and publisher Nat Gertler on why sometimes we should learn to be more like the world's most famous beagle.

→ dorlingkindersley.de

STILL ROLLING STRONG

Because it needs to be said: skateboards count as sustainable mobility too. Which makes it all the more fitting that, more than four decades after its first inception, the legendary skateboard brand Banzai was revived in 2020 - along with its classic 1970s boards. Made from anodized aluminum, they come as an Artist Edition in five colors, complete with art print and delivered in a collector's box.

→ banzaiskate.com

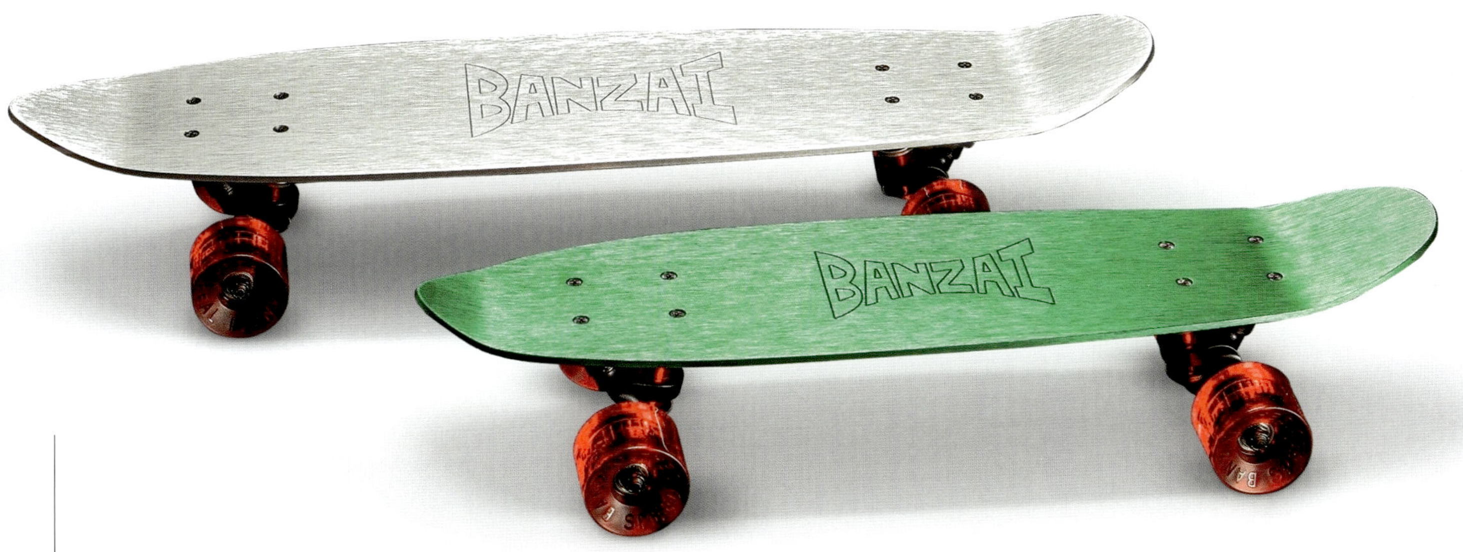

HIP TO BE SQUARE

No, Mel Gibson is not trying to monetize memorabilia from his *Mad Max* films. The T-005 Cross is the wonderful pioneering work of Thrive Motorcycles, a custom shop based in Jakarta, Indonesia. The rough-edged one-off is based on a 2008 Yamaha Scorpio 225 and has wowed at several exhibitions since its completion in 2015.

→ thrivemotorcycle.com

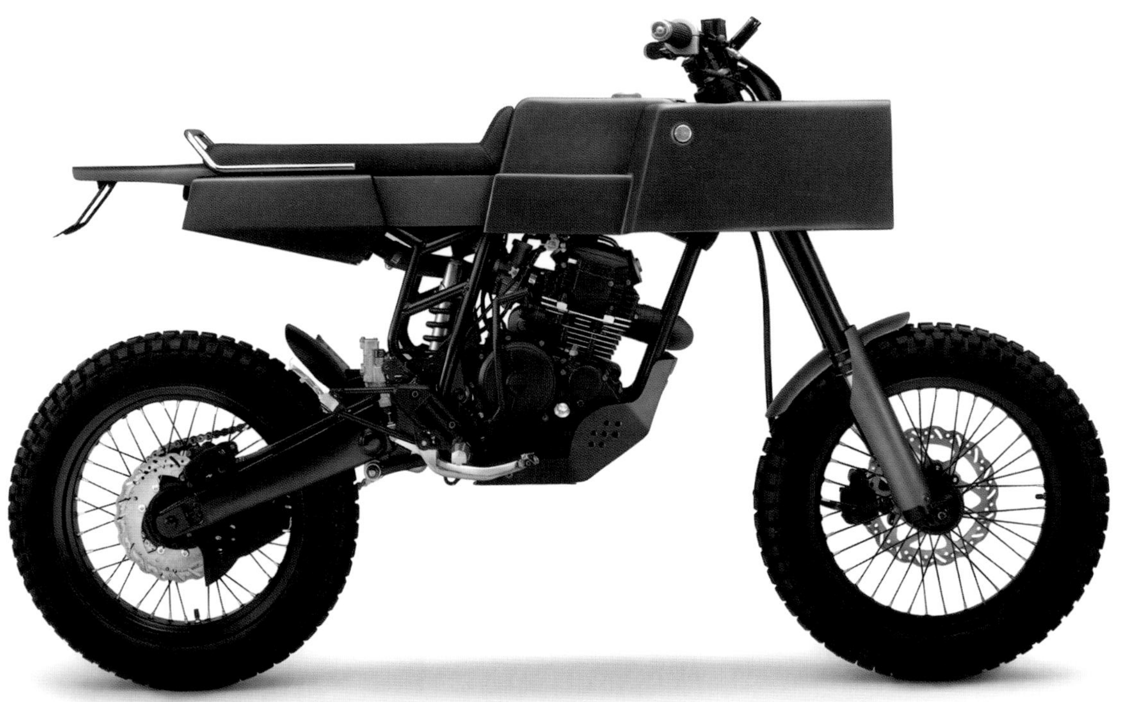

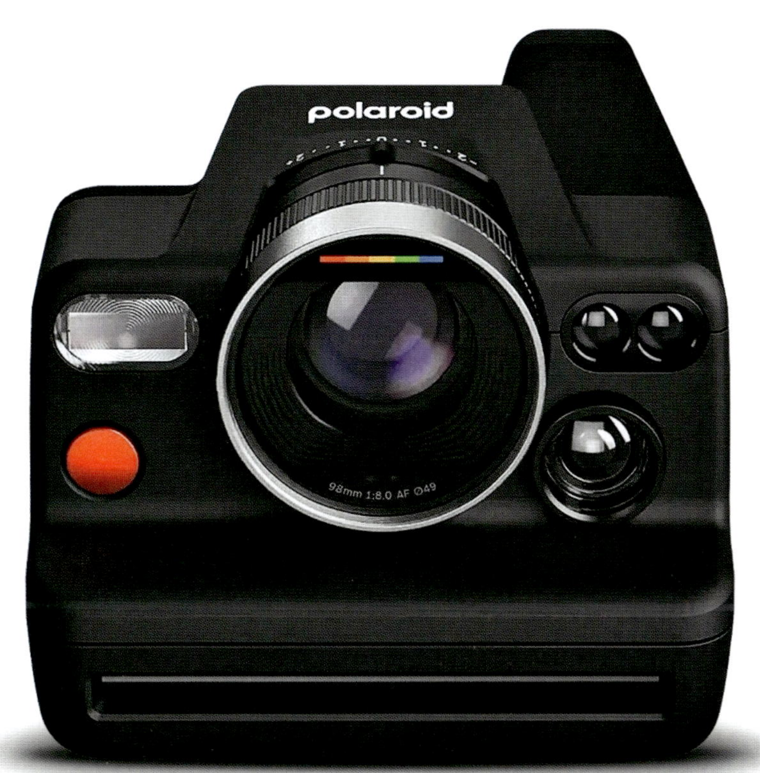

PICTURE IMPERFECT

"Life isn't perfect. So why should art be?" A fair question from photographic artist Max Siedentopf, who grabbed the top-of-the-range Polaroid I-2 and set out to explore Berlin's more ordinary corners in search of the extraordinary. The result? A bold collaboration between the photographer and the camera maker – and a campaign confident enough to call itself *The Imperfectionists*. What more do you need to know about the adventure of photography?

→ polaroid.com

THE ART OF THE DUNK

In 2023 Leo van Gemmern decided to found his own company, Comrade Berlin, because he couldn't find a unique basketball that wasn't just suited for playing but would also look good as decoration in his flat. He still works at his regular job by day, but at night he is busy designing balls and building his brand.

→ comrade-berlin.com

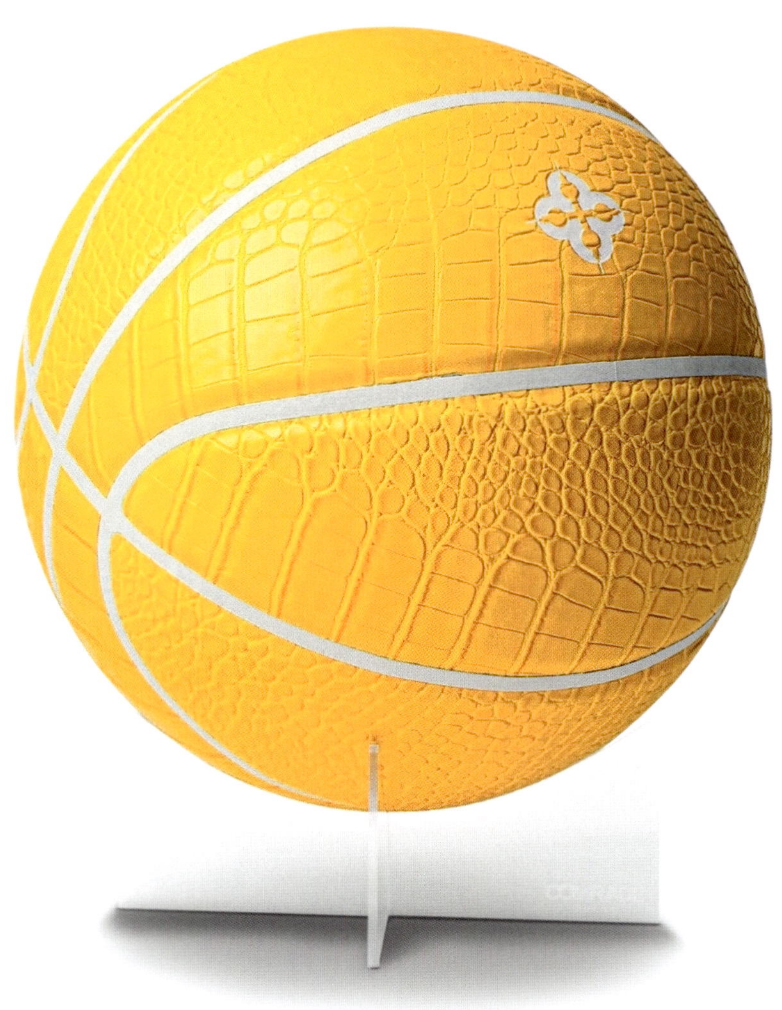

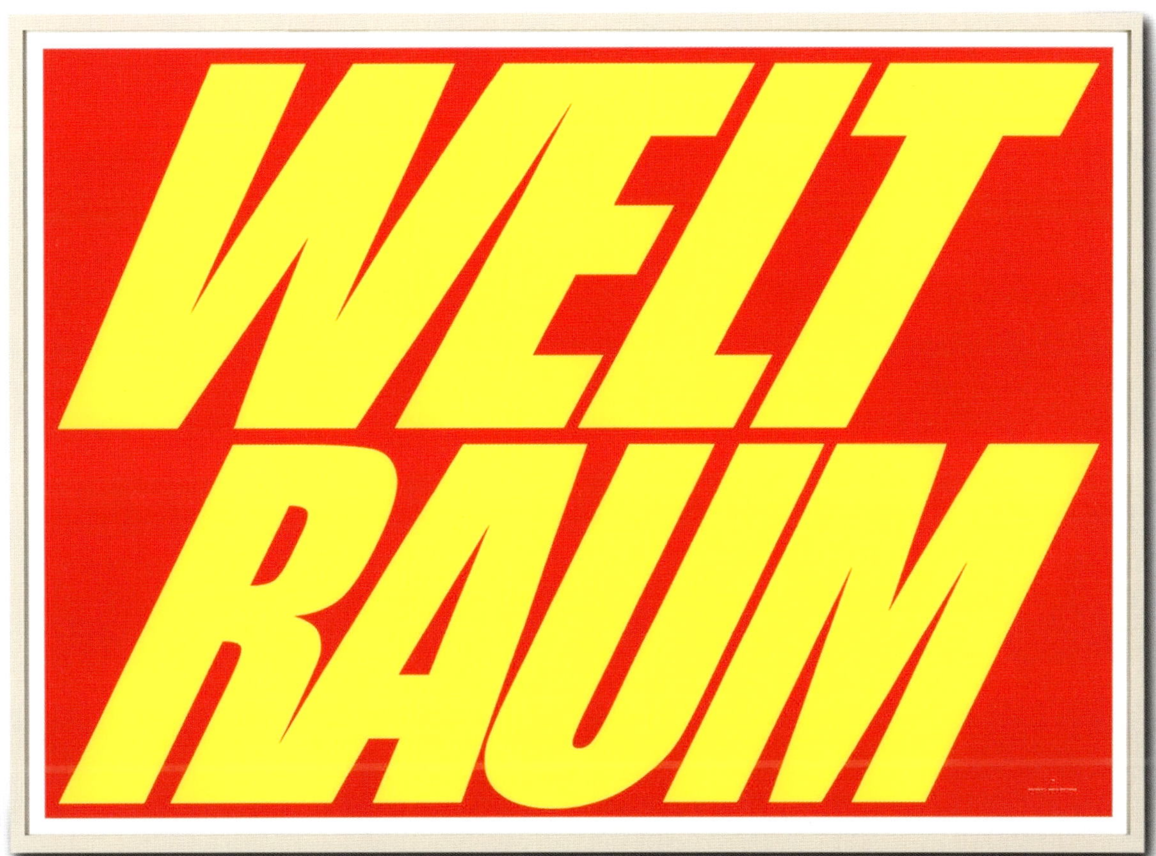

COLOR SPACE

"'Yellow,' he thought and stomped off back to his bedroom to get dressed. Passing the bathroom he stopped to drink a large glass of water, and another. He began to suspect that he was hung over." From Chapter 1 of Douglas Adams's *The Hitchhiker's Guide to the Galaxy*. Obviously. A fitting companion: the limited-edition screen print *Weltraum I* [Space I] by Martin Grothmaak.

→ united-landscapes.com

thirteen shades of black

3.02

YOHJI YAMAMOTO, BORN IN 1943, HAS BEEN CALLED THE "GODFATHER OF AVANT-GARDE FASHION" FOR HIS RADICAL DESIGNS, ALWAYS IN HIS FAVORITE NON-COLOR: BLACK.

WHAT ISN'T IMMEDIATELY APPARENT IS THAT WOMEN HAVE ALWAYS PLAYED AN IMPORTANT ROLE IN THE DESIGNER'S WORK. ESPECIALLY HIS MOTHER.

TEXT *Wiebke Brauer*
PHOTOS *Getty Images*

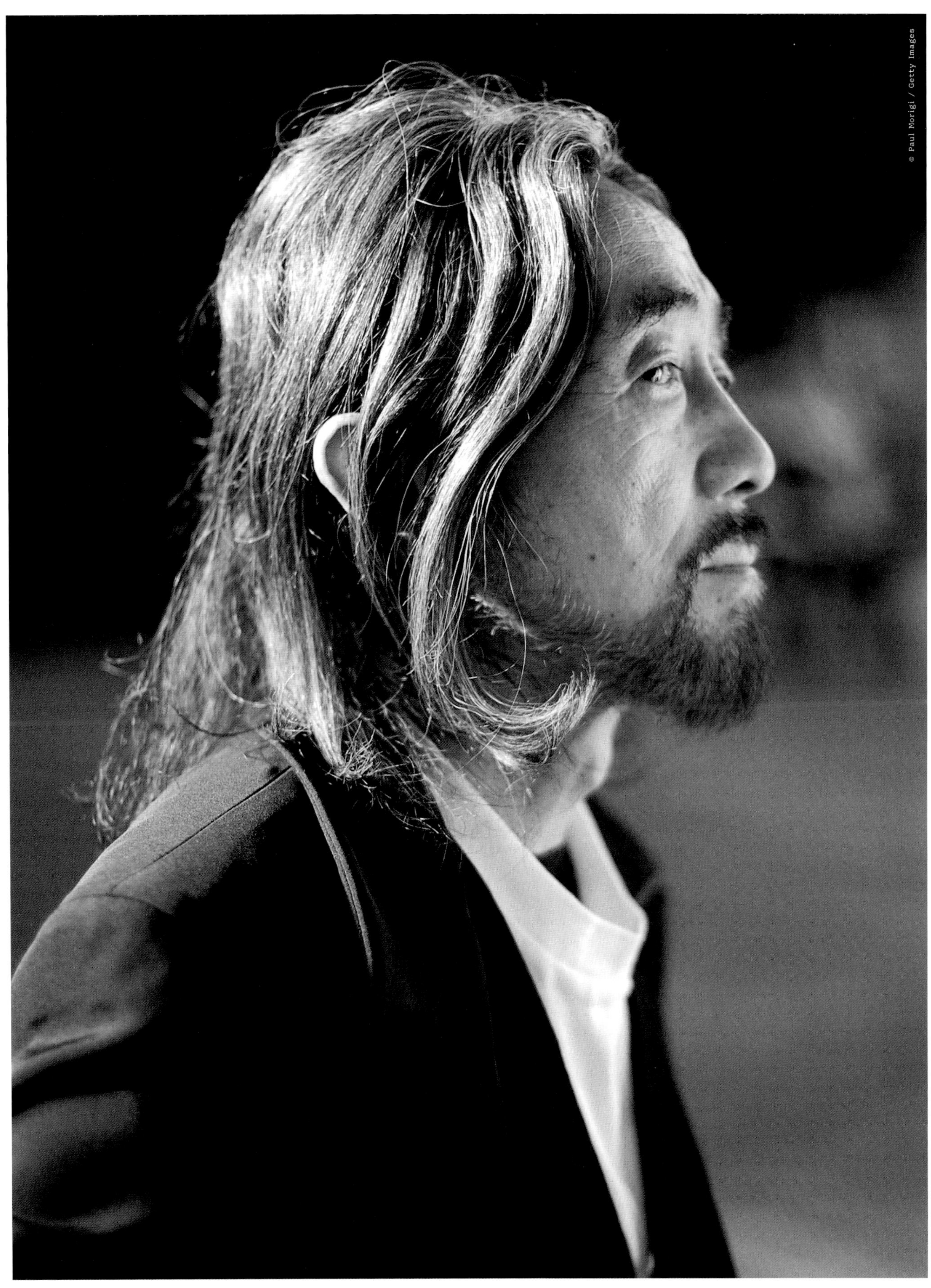

If you want to tell a story about Yohji Yamamoto, you have to start with his mother. This may seem surprising at first, especially since the fashion designer's creations have nothing warm, soft or comforting about them. Rather, his creations convey a sense of darkness, an amorphousness, perhaps even something disturbing, but in any case a remoteness from the body, due to the wide cuts, unhemmed edges and often asymmetrical silhouettes. If you want to understand why he once said, "Everything I know, I owe to her," and to what extent Fumi Yamamoto continues to influence her son today, you have to take a closer look at their respective life stories.

Yamamoto has a radically different idea of sensuality – abstract, but always intelligent.

Yohji Yamamoto was born on October 3, 1943, in Yokohama. His father died in a prisoner of war camp when Yohji was just two years old. Like many other war widows in Japan, his mother opened a dressmaking shop, located in Tokyo's red-light district. Day and night, she would sit at the clattering sewing machine, determined that her child would have a better life. She wanted her only son to study law – a classic. And he obeyed – for a while. In 1962 he enrolled at Keio University in Tokyo to study law, initially with the goal of becoming a prosecutor. After graduating, however, Yamamoto boarded the Trans-Siberian Railway instead of looking for a job. "I didn't want to become a businessman," he told the *Süddeutsche Zeitung* in 2016, "I wanted to drift, travel around." Upon his return, he asked his mother if he could help out in the shop.

One can only imagine her shock. It took two weeks before his mother gave him permission to work with her – and only on one condition: he should learn the art of pattern cutting so the seamstresses in her employ wouldn't make fun of him. In 1966 he enrolled at the Bunka Fashion College in Tokyo, where his mother had also studied. Yamamoto graduated at the top of his class. It is also worth mentioning that among the nine hundred graduates, there were only two men. The clientele of his mother's shop was also almost exclusively female. Some came to have dresses made to please their paying husbands, others were mistresses, barmaids or prostitutes. Yamamoto took measurements, drew sketches and sewed by hand. Most of the time, the customers wanted revealing, figure-hugging clothing that would please their men, which didn't appeal much to Yamamoto. He was surrounded by hard-working women in a patriarchal society. That left its mark. Also important is the fact that Fumi Yamamoto had decided not to remarry. And she dressed only in black, which is not necessarily a color of mourning in Japan, but in any case has a masculine connotation. After all, the samurai usually wore black.

Yamamoto's fashions suggest that he wanted to protect women, to give them a sort of armor or uniform. He also had a radically different idea of sensuality. It was – and still is today – abstract and at first glance not organic, but always intelligent. One thing that his fashion certainly is not is simple. As he told the *Süddeutsche Zeitung*: "People who want to wear my clothes have to change their lives." What he meant by that is: if you wear Yamamoto, you make a decision. His designs are not accommodating; they are different, they require you to reorganize your entire wardrobe, perhaps even change your way of thinking, because by wearing his fashions you set yourself apart from others and move through the world in a different way. Just how unconventionally he thinks as a designer was evident as early as 1983: "I always wonder who decided that there should be a difference in the clothes of men and women," Yamamoto told *The New York Times*. "Perhaps men have decided this."

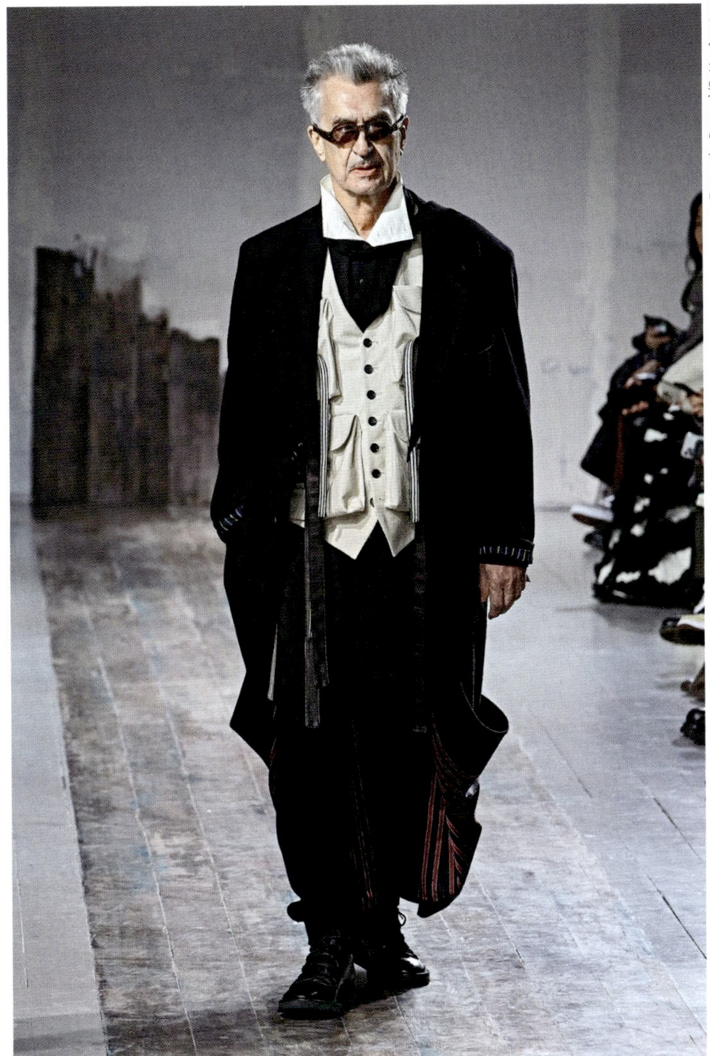

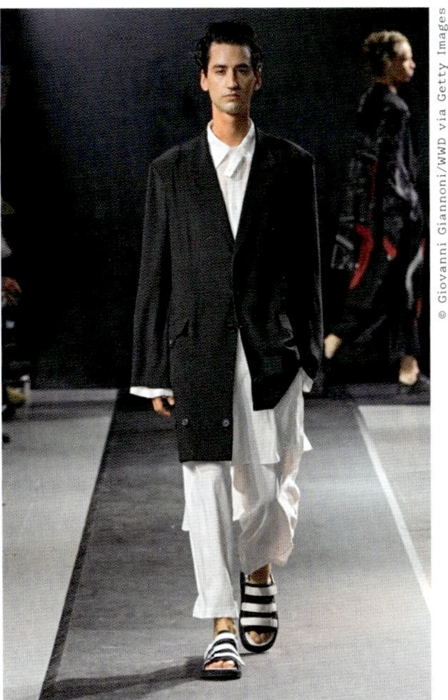

Yohji Yamamoto and Wim Wenders (left) have been friends for years. In 1989 the German director made a documentary film about the Japanese designer called *Notebook on Cities and Clothes*. At the Paris prêt-à-porter show in January 2024, the then seventy-nine-year-old even walked the catwalk for Yamamoto, and he wore the same look again at the Oscar ceremony. Speaking of his friend in German newspaper *Die Zeit*, Wenders said: “He really is like the older brother I never had. We realized how much we have in common, he from post-war Japan and I from post-war Germany.”

In 1972, at the age of twenty-nine, he founded his prêt-à-porter line for women. Its name: Y’s. Five years later, he successfully presented his collection in Tokyo, and in 1981 for the first time in Paris. From that moment on, Yohji Yamamoto’s designs changed the history of fashion. He was called “fashion’s poet of black”. Countless exhibitions, biographies and films have paid tribute to him. But it was a long road getting there.

Yohji Yamamoto was not the only Japanese designer in Paris in 1981. Kenzō Takada had arrived in the fashion capital of the world nearly ten years earlier. And joining Yamamoto were Rei Kawakubo [founder of Comme des Garçons and a long-time partner of Yamamoto] and Issey Miyake. For the first collections by Yamamoto and Kawakubo, the models were dressed in tatters, and no rouge was allowed. Kawakubo’s catwalk show was titled “Destroy”. The critics were shocked, the French créateurs de mode knocked out of their complacency. Just to recap: this was the time when Thierry Mugler was dressing his models more revealingly than ever and Gianni Versace was favoring flowing, transparent fabrics.

The Japanese designers took the traditional clothing of their homeland as their starting point – like the kimono, with its geometric panels of fabric that tend to shroud the body somewhat ungracefully rather than clinging to it. Combined with impressions of post-war Japan, the dropping of the atomic bombs, and the country’s lost past, this perhaps inevitably resulted in a new beginning

"I always wonder who decided that there should be a difference in the clothes of men and women."

Yohji Yamamoto

based on deconstruction. In an interview with the German weekly newspaper *Die Zeit*, Yamamoto said: "Some people called what Rei Kawakubo and I did a revolution. Our designs polarized, especially because of their sometimes morbid look. We even tore up some of our garments. Suddenly everyone was talking about 'Hiroshima chic'. Without meaning to, we had started a trend."

But trends were precisely what Yamamoto was not interested in. "Fashion has no time. I do," he once told Swiss daily *Neue Zürcher Zeitung*. He always found the image of the fashion creator to be tiresome, even incomprehensible. Instead, he dressed exclusively in black, always wearing a felt hat and smoking a cigarette, with his hair down to his shoulders. Another thing you should know about Yamamoto: he's a black belt karate master and president of the World Karate Federation. "For my total life, I am comfortable being in black, not in the light," he says in Theo Stanley's 2011 biographical film *Yohji Yamamoto: This Is My Dream*. Of course, not all black is the same. His first creations included thirteen different shades of black, and the definition of black that he gave Suzy Menkes twenty-five years ago in the *International Herald Tribune* is almost famous: "Black is modest and arrogant at the same time. Black is lazy and easy – but mysterious. It means that many things fit together, but it takes on different aspects in many fabrics. You need black to have a silhouette. Black can swallow light, or make things look sharp. But above all black says this: 'I don't bother you – don't bother me.'"

Black may say many things, but what is truly astonishing is the long period of time during which the designer reinvented himself over and over again, constantly presenting new collections or entering into new collaborations. The most famous and longest-lasting of these is the one with Adidas, which has endured since 2002. Speaking with *GQ*, Yamamoto once explained the reason for the partnership quite succinctly with the words: "I felt I wanted to make sneakers." It's as simple as that.

For the first collections by Yamamoto, the models were dressed in tatters. The critics were shocked.

Yohji Yamamoto is the last of his kind as a designer: Issey Miyake died in August 2022, Kenzō Takada two years earlier. At a lecture at the Oxford Union Society in 2018, he said that no other fashion designer was his equal, though he did admit that he admired Alexander McQueen. Despite his age, retiring is not an option. He will continue until he dies with scissors in his hand. "Real fashion is disappearing," he told *GQ*. "But as long as I'm alive, I will stop it."

Getting back to Yamamoto's mother, who died three years ago at the age of 106 – he once commented on the subject in the *Süddeutsche Zeitung* as follows: "My mother happened to be a seamstress. And I just wanted to help out in the shop. But actually, that's what I still want to do today."

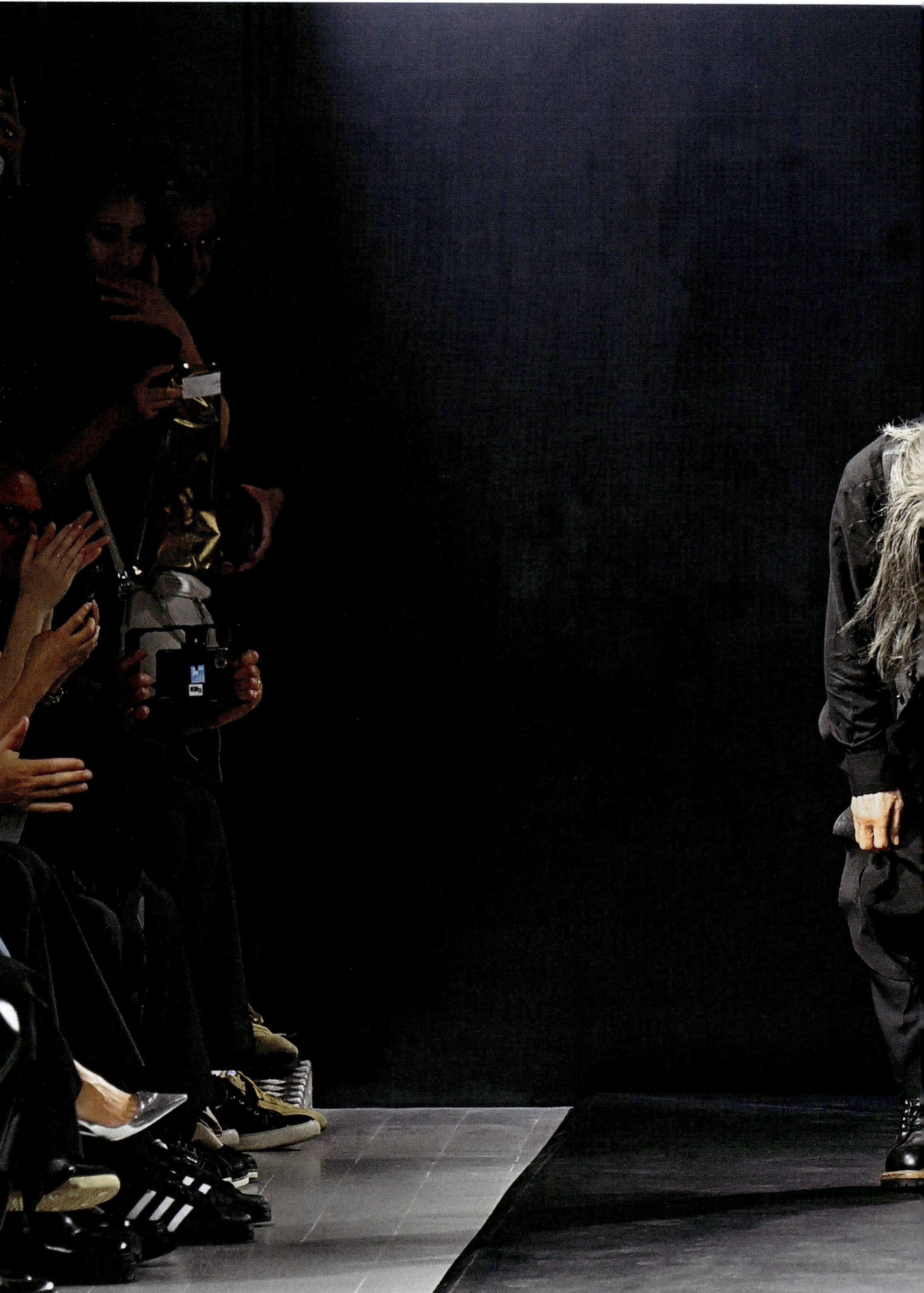

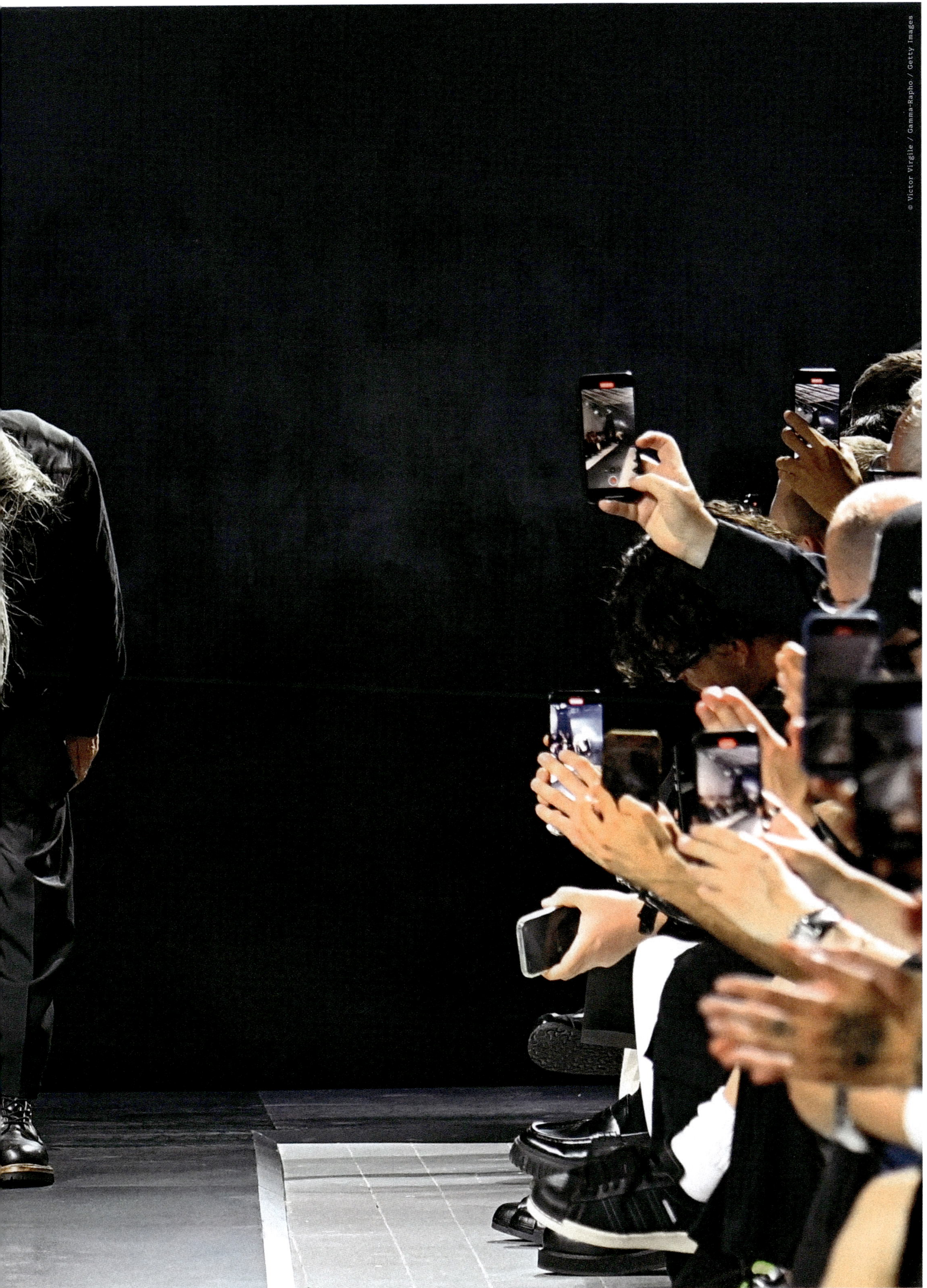

I should just do nothing, but what?

3.03

TEXT *Philipp Tingler*
ILLUSTRATIONS *Gregory Gilbert-Lodge*

SUNDAYS CAN GO EITHER WAY. WHEN THEY'RE GOOD, THERE'S A SENSE OF PURPOSE AND JOY EVEN WHEN YOU DON'T PURSUE ANY REAL GOAL. THAT'S THE MAGIC OF ATELIC ACTIVITIES. THOSE ARE THE SUNDAYS OF DOING. SOMEWHERE BETWEEN RAWDOGGING AND THE PROGRESS OF CIVILIZATION.

So I'm at my dentist's, looking out at Lake Zurich, and the hygienist says everything's perfect. The only thing that might be better would be to use a fluoride gel on Sundays. And I ask, "Why Sundays?"

And she replies: "Oh, that's right. For you, every day is Sunday."

THE UNEASE OF REST

I really hope not. That every day is Sunday, I mean. Because I'm *a priori* not a big fan of Sundays. Here I agree with Karl Lagerfeld, who once said: "Every day is and is not a holiday for me." Sunday is a day of rest. At least in Central Europe it is. Though rest has a double-edged quality to it. The abyss of idle time. And, in the words of the French Enlightenment philosopher Blaise Pascal, you may come to see your own isolation, insignificance, dependent nature and powerlessness. We are thrown into a world that doesn't care about us. Suddenly, the chasm opens up wide. On any Sunday.

We may live in a twenty-four-hour society, but for us, Sunday is still different. Sunday has a special feel to it, it is one of those days with a specific mood, like Monday, Friday and Saturday. Only the middle of the week is neutral. On Sundays, the mood is one of elation and freedom,

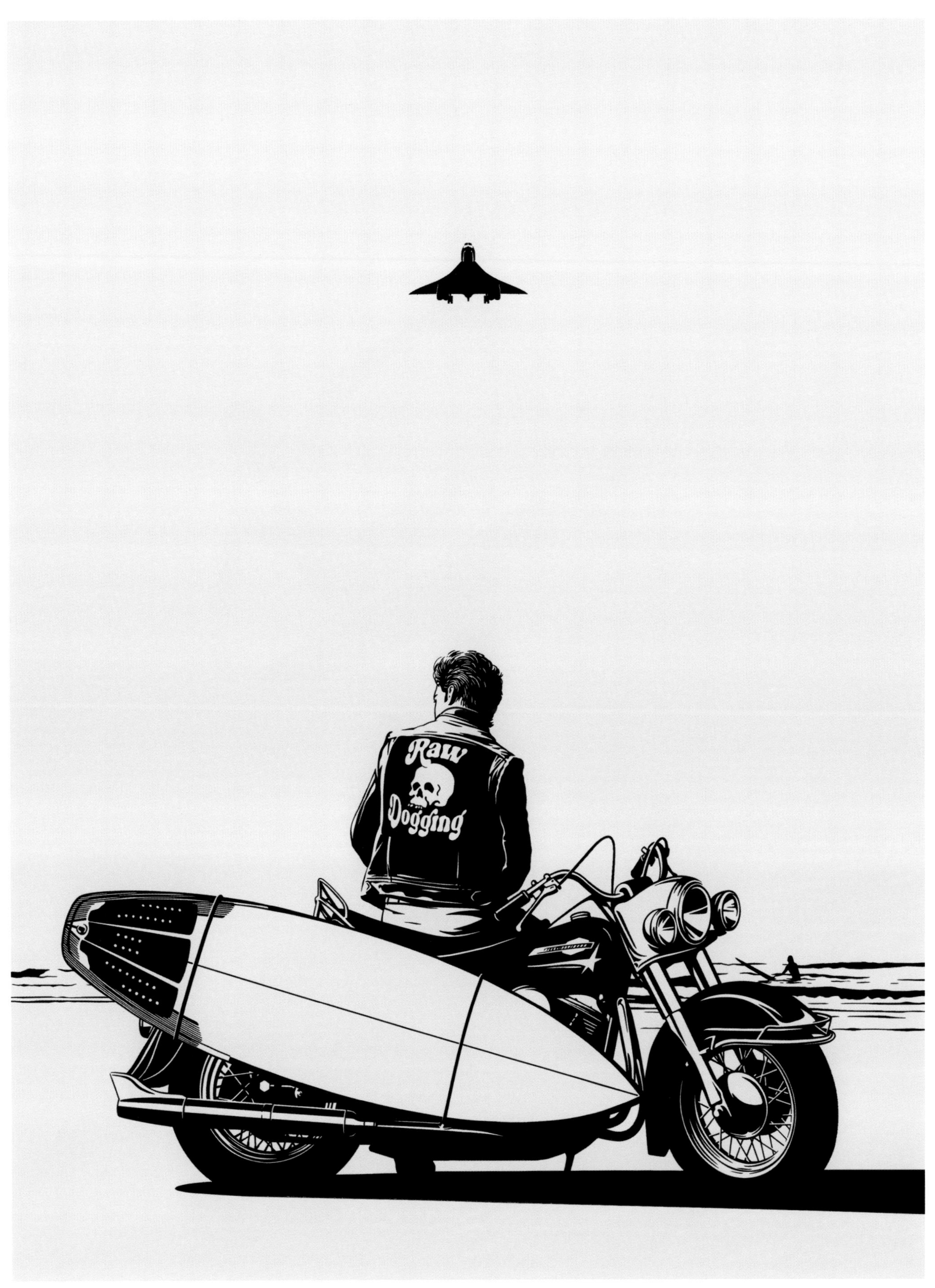
Raw
Dogging

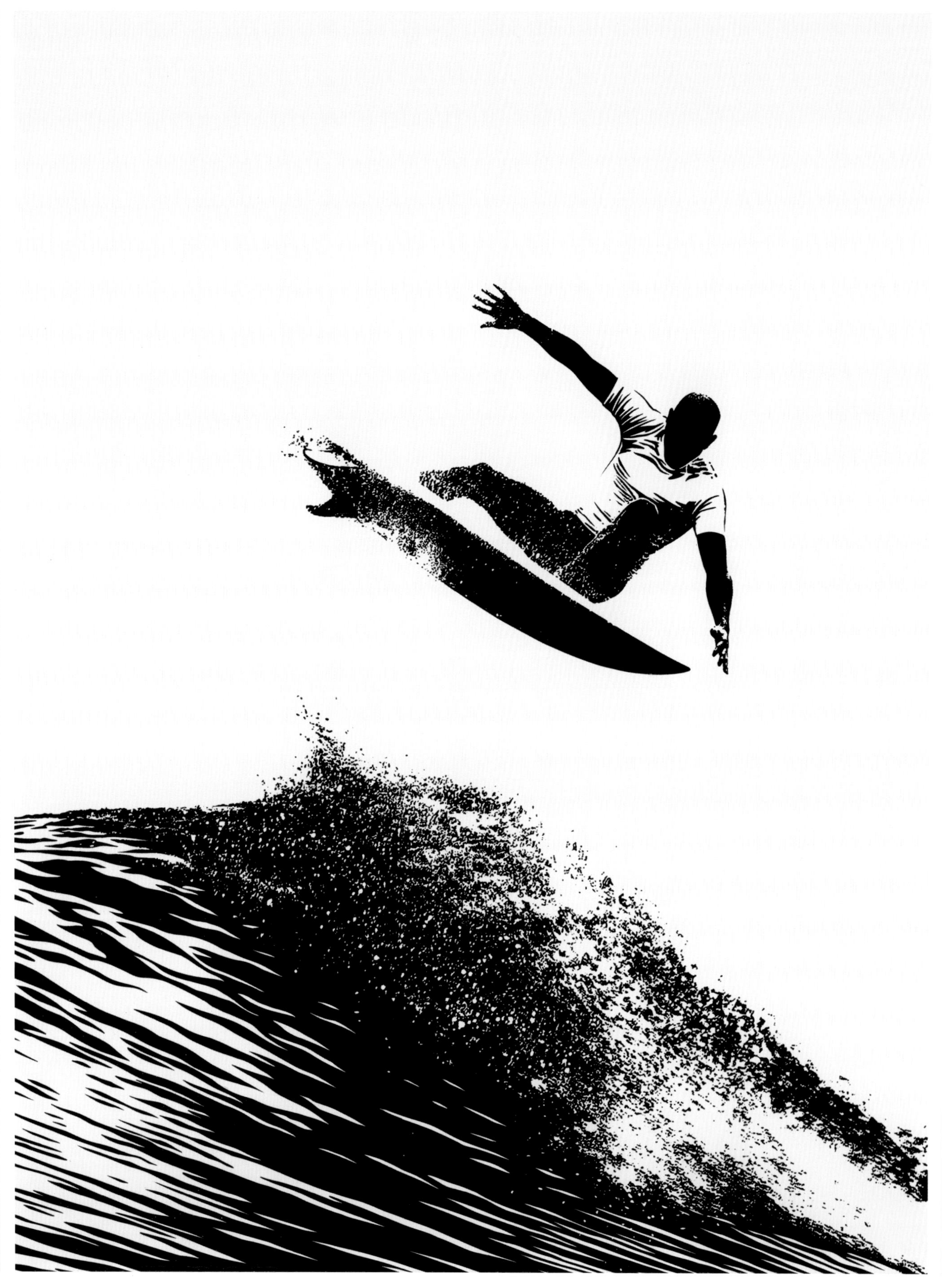

but possibly also of melancholy or even despondency. This is not least due to the fact that Sunday marks an end, especially Sunday evening. That's when the *Sunday scaries* or the *Sunday night jitters* set in. That sense of unease about the end of the week and the weekend, the transition to the everyday routine, if you have one. But even if you don't have an everyday routine, the coming week is finite.

We also live in a society fixated on mindfulness, where we are constantly urged to reflect on and observe ourselves. The problem is that reflection and self-observation aren't always so easy to bear. Sundays tend to offer fewer distractions than other days, which may make us more aware of our own problems, insecurities and existential doubts. This potential for unease is the source of a certain ambivalence about slowing down, cocooning, hygge and all those other idealized Sunday comforts that hipsters rave about when they have themselves photographed for dating sites in front of their flatpack shelves and LED rope lights. Because in the end, no amount of rope lights can save us from confronting the darkness of mortality.

IS HAVING NO GOALS THE ANSWER?

But the melancholy of Sunday also has a poetic dimension, precisely because it reminds us of our own mortality and the deeper meaning of life. Approached with awareness, this wistfulness can become a source of inspiration and reflection. Mindful of the contemporary debate surrounding the undervaluation of atelic activities, i.e. activities that are not directly goal-oriented (such as surfing, walking or philosophizing), we could reflect on the fact that these kinds of activities or processes, which have no culmination or particular end, are meaningful. And that they can potentially be continued indefinitely. Sundays, with their prescribed period of rest, seem to be a magical external framework for the rediscovery and re-evaluation of such activities, for a "refusal to obey Western demands for an active life", as Thomas Mann wrote in *The Magic Mountain*. The atelic opens up a completely different form of existence for precisely that individual of whom the sociologist Alain Ehrenberg stated a few years ago in his famous book *The Weariness of the Self* that late modern society categorically demands personal initiative.

I'm *a priori* not a big fan of Sundays. Here I agree with Karl Lagerfeld, who once said: "Every day is and is not a holiday for me."

Atelic does not mean *rawdogging*. The latter term, originally with purely sexual connotations, has had a remarkable career since 2022 and, according to *The New York Times*, can now be used to describe "almost any activity accomplished without the assistance of a buffer". Probably the best-known example last year was rawdogging long-haul flights. On social media, people gave testimonials of how they flew from London to Sydney and deliberately avoided any form of entertainment, apart from staring at the in-flight map. But you can also practice rawdogging when cooking, for example, by not using a recipe, or when you're sick by refusing medication, or when you go to a concert by staying sober. And so on. It's mainly a question of declaring your intent, and that is readily done. After all, we live in the age of declarations.

A NEW KIND OF ATTENTION

Rawdogging is more or less intelligent. Usually less. But staring straight ahead for eleven hours with a flat, nervous hyperattention at the screen position of a virtual airplane isn't atelic. One indication of an atelic activity

Atelic does not mean _rawdogging_. The latter term, originally with purely sexual connotations, has had a remarkable career since 2022.

is that it is done for its own sake and contains a certain fulfillment in itself. In a society that is often strongly fixated on productivity and on achieving certain goals, atelic activities promote a form of being that is separate from performance or success. Atelic activities can encourage creative thinking and fresh associations, offering opportunities for a new kind of attention. One that is deep and profound. The philosopher Byung-Chul Han, who in his book *The Burnout Society* notes a change in the nature of attention due to general the acceleration of contemporary life, writes: "We owe the cultural achievements of humanity – which include philosophy – to deep, contemplative attention." That's what Sundays are for, isn't it? Incidentally, Friedrich Nietzsche knew this already, as he stated in *Human, All Too Human*: "From lack of rest, our civilization is ending in a new barbarism. Never have the active, which is to say the restless, people been prized more. Therefore, one of the necessary correctives that must be applied to the character of humanity is a massive strengthening of the contemplative element."

The contemplative element. That is what Sundays are all about. If you see Sundays that way. And if you criticize the loss of contemplation, the absolutization of the *vita activa*, as partly responsible for the exaggerated nature of the late-modern active society, then you should also not overlook the fact that the boundaries are fluid. What I mean to say is that in many fascinating activities, their atelic parts cannot be clearly distinguished from the telic, i.e. result-oriented, parts. For example, when writing a book. Or this essay. So what about surfing or riding a motorcycle? These activities are perhaps not goal-oriented, but they do have a result. Needing or requiring a goal can also act as a constraint, even for the progress of civilization, which is why I recommend watching the legendary BBC series *Civilisation*. As its creator, the British art historian Kenneth Clark, recognized more than half a century ago: "It may be difficult to define civilization, but it isn't so difficult to recognize barbarism." There's also a less dramatic way of putting it: the essence of inspiration is that it happens spontaneously, often just when things are particularly hectic. Or during your dental hygiene appointment.

The contemplative element. That is what Sundays are all about. If you see Sundays that way.

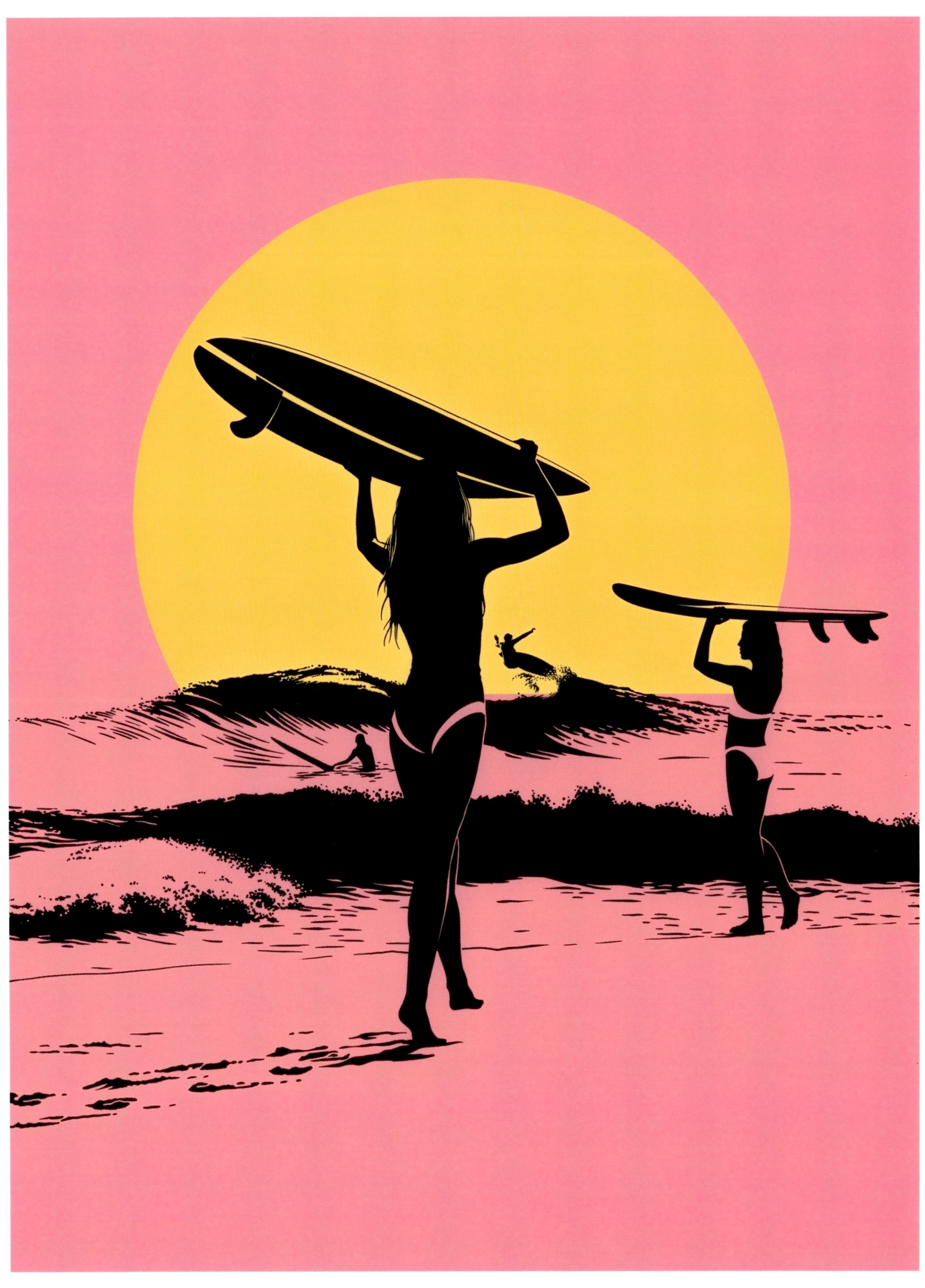

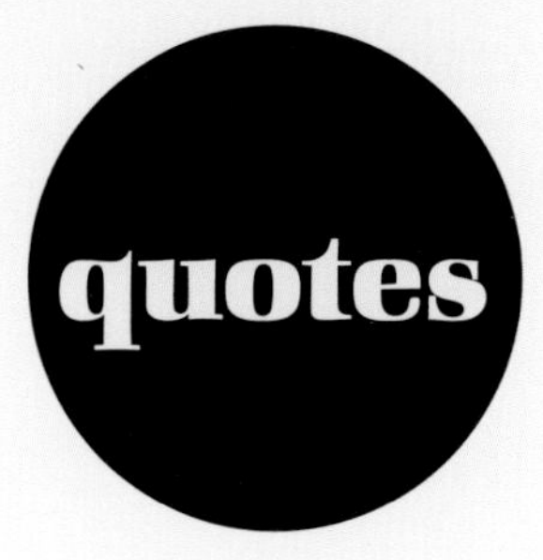

IF YOU WANT YOUR CHILDREN TO BE INTELLIGENT, READ THEM FAIRY TALES. IF YOU WANT THEM TO BE MORE INTELLIGENT, READ THEM MORE FAIRY TALES.

I have never tried that before, so I think I should definitely be able to do that.

PIPPI LONGSTOCKING

I LIKE PEOPLE WITH WHOM I DON'T HAVE TO WATCH WHAT I SAY.

I TRIED BEING REASONABLE. I DIDN'T LIKE IT.

If you get on the treadmill one minute before midnight and get off at one minute past, then you've exercised for two days in a row.

I CAN'T DO THE SPLITS, BUT THEN AGAIN I'VE NEVER BEEN IN A SITUATION WHERE I'VE THOUGHT, "THE ONLY THING THAT CAN HELP NOW IS THE SPLITS!"

WE HAVE A SAYING: IF A PROBLEM CAN BE SOLVED, THERE IS NO USE WORRYING ABOUT IT. IF IT CAN'T BE SOLVED, WORRYING WILL DO NO GOOD.

"Carpe diem" means "seize the day". You should do that too and turn off the TV.

PETER LUSTIG

When she texts you saying, "We need to talk," answer with, "I agree, and the sooner the better!" That way at least both of you are nervous. For more relationship advice follow me on Tinder.

It is through wonder that men now begin and first began to philosophize.

ARISTOTLE

I HAVE NOT FAILED. I'VE JUST FOUND TEN THOUSAND WAYS THAT WON'T WORK.

THOMAS EDISON

I ain't tryna say nothin', but in 132 years the USS Enterprise is takin' off, and all we've managed to invent so far is Uhura's Bluetooth headset.

Why do things that only happen to stupid people keep happening to me?

HOMER SIMPSON

MUCH TO LEARN, YOU STILL HAVE.

YODA

NOTHING IN LIFE IS TO BE FEARED, IT IS ONLY TO BE UNDERSTOOD.

MARIE CURIE

STRESS IS A FORM OF SELF-ABSORBED HYSTERIA THAT ONLY LEADS TO YOU LOSING CONTROL. THE IMPORTANT THING IS TO NOT TAKE THE WORLD AND YOURSELF TOO SERIOUSLY.

ATTRIBUTED TO KARL LAGERFELD

OF ALL THINGS, I LIKED BOOKS BEST.

NIKOLA TESLA

Philosophy is like being in a dark room looking for a black cat that isn't there. Theology is like being in a dark room looking for a black cat that isn't there and shouting, "I found it!"

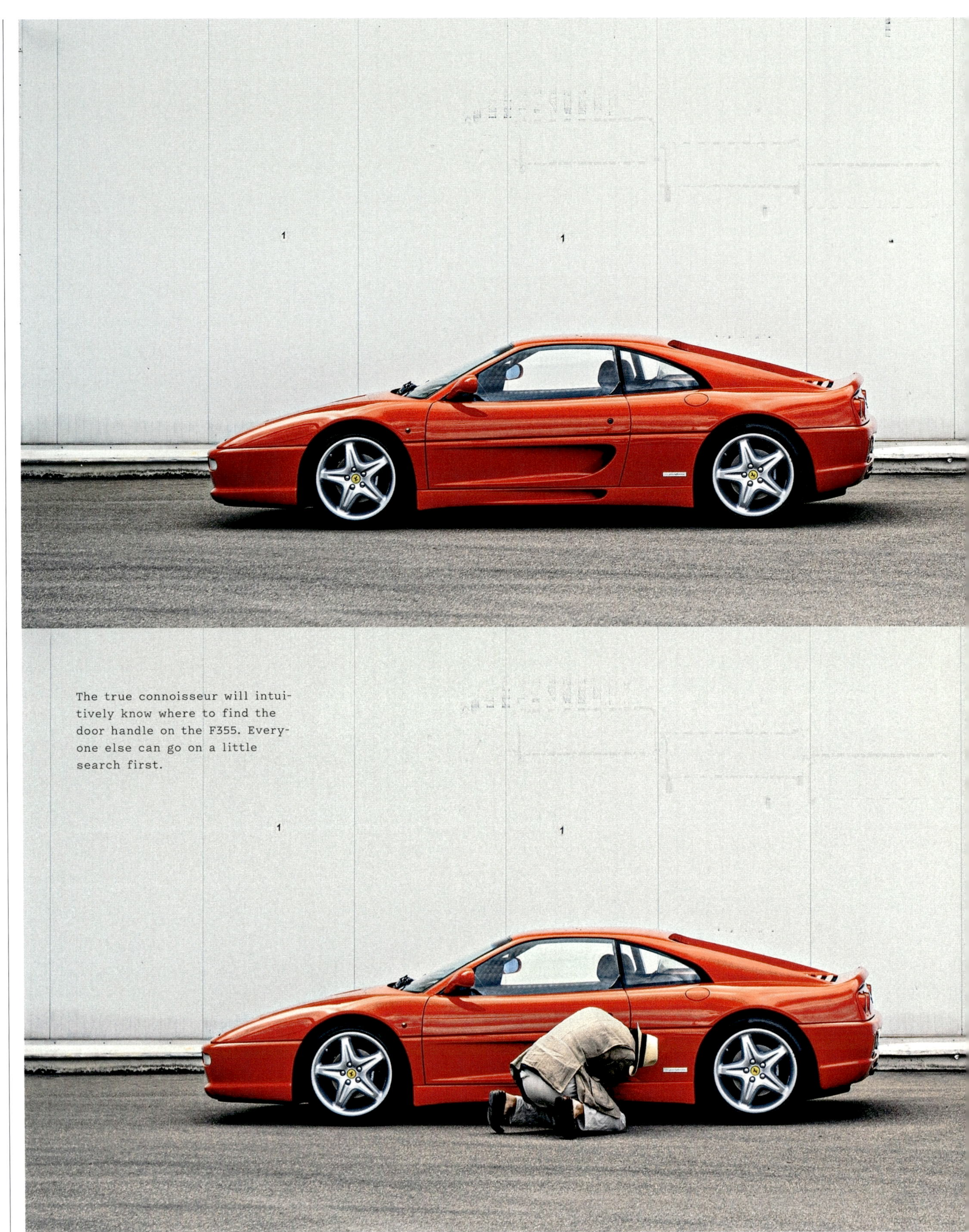

The true connoisseur will intuitively know where to find the door handle on the F355. Everyone else can go on a little search first.

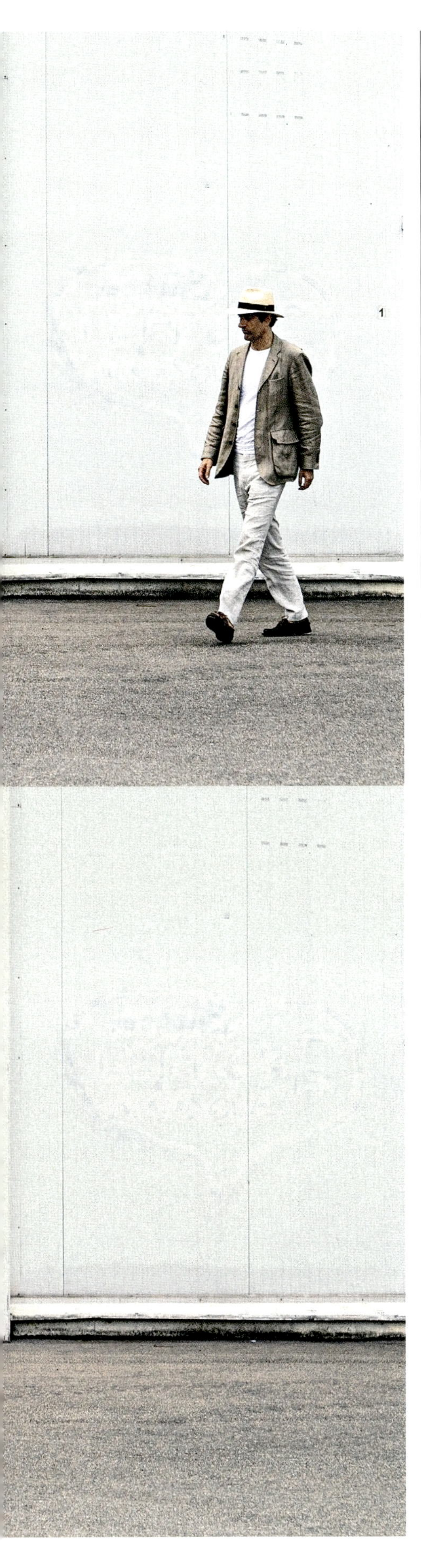

a ferrari like a ferrari

3.05

TEXT *Kurt Molzer*
PHOTOS *Matthias Mederer · ramp.pictures*

THE F355 – THE BEST V8 FERRARI EVER BUILT – ROLLED OUT OF MARANELLO IN 1994.

IT STILL LEAVES US SPEECHLESS.

It has to have been one of the most shameful moments in the life of Luca Cordero di Montezemolo. The year was 1989. A red traffic light in Italy. Luca, a handsome man who always looked spruce and smartly dressed, is at the wheel of a yellow Ferrari 348 with Testarossa-style gills. Next to him is some kind of Abarth-tuned Fiat. First row on the starting grid, if you like. The aristocratic "Nobile dei Marchesi di Montezemolo" (the most noble Marquess of Montezemolo) usually doesn't engage in duels of speed within city limits, preferring to leave that up to the rabble. But this time his right foot is itching and twitching (he's only human after all), and he wants to teach the plebe a lesson. He's got the Ferrari in first gear and is ready to go. But when the light turns green, the unspeakable happens: the Fiat makes the Ferrari eat dust! South of the Brenner Pass, this is called blasphemy. If the Inquisition had still existed, the guy in the Fiat would have been burned at the stake.

For Montezemolo, the world was turned on its head. As if sheep were suddenly eating wolves. He may even have thought to himself that the two letters "MO" on his license plate didn't stand for Modena, but for Moscow. Monte, as he was known, then manager of the organizing committee for the World Cup in Italy, was made chairman of Ferrari two years later. He asked his old friend Niki Lauda to test the 348 (Montezemolo had been Ferrari's racing director and won the Formula 1 championship with Lauda in 1975 and 1977). The Austrian driver did him this favor, returning the car with the comment: "Makes funny noises and drives jerkily." In other words: a clunker.

Largely inspired by Lauda's remarks, Montezemolo would later get a bit carried away, saying that the 348 was the worst Ferrari ever built. That makes me want to spontaneously say two things and pose an interesting question. Comment number one: You don't want to have been the engineer in charge, do you? Comment number two: My deepest sympathy to anyone who bought one of those jalopies. And last but not least: Did Ferrari offer to pay the therapy sessions for those poor bastards who saved half a lifetime or more to buy themselves a 348?

They had a lot to make up for in Maranello. You can bet that those heads that didn't roll were on fire from morning to night. I can just see Montezemolo, that mercurial bundle of energy, drumming everyone together, the man for the engine, the man for the gearbox, the man for the chassis and so on – all of them men, nothing has changed since then, just try a little harder, ladies, it can't be that difficult to design a decent supercar engine in the twenty-first century – and how, gesticulating wildly, he impresses upon them that the successor to the bumbling 348 must make amends with the disappointed Ferraristi

On the outside, overwhelmingly alluring. On the inside, innovative down to the last bolt.

and show the world that Via Abetone Inferiore No. 4 is still the first place to go for the ultimate sports car. Or did they really want to become the laughing stock for their dearest enemies in Zuffenhausen?

It helped. Ferrari brilliantly turned the rudder around. What came onto the market in the spring of 1994 under the designation F355 was nothing short of a masterpiece. A Ferrari like a Ferrari. On the outside, overwhelmingly alluring. On the inside, innovative down to the last bolt. Gazing at the newborn at the Geneva Motor Show, you could see the features of the iconic 308 and 288 GTO shimmering through, like when happy parents discover certain physiognomic features of a particularly attractive grandmother in the face of their infant. It was curvier and more seductive than its predecessor and once again had the four characteristic rear lights, so you knew with one hundred percent certainty who had thundered past you at 295 km/h, even at night. To summarize the design: Pininfarina made a backwards somersault towards classic elegance that deserves top marks.

As far as the mechanical aspects were concerned, this Ferrari showed the competition how a technology transfer from F1 can be exploited to the maximum. Its kinetic energy was stimulated by a 3.5-liter naturally aspirated V8 with titanium connecting rods, a flat crankshaft and lightweight forged alloy pistons. The biggest advantage, however, were the five valves per cylinder, which were proudly immortalized in the model designation: 355 = 3.5 liters, 5 valves. That made for a total of 375 hp. The last hand-built Ferrari (mass production began with the successor 360) generated more horsepower per liter than the V12 in the McLaren F1! The fighting weight was also right: at 1,350 kilograms, it was two Great Danes lighter than the 348 (1,440 kilos). Price tag: about $120,000.

Three years after its launch, the Italians felt they had to give their superstar the proverbial icing on the cake. As an option to the beguilingly beautiful six-speed manual gearbox, it was the first road car to be available with the semi-automatic gearbox that was originally used in F1. They could have saved themselves the trouble. The shift paddles may have looked futuristic, but the gear changes were rustic and took too long. A production-ready car this was not. In city traffic, the Ferrari jolted from one intersection to the next like an old Butterfield Overland Mail stagecoach on its way from El Paso to Tucson. You don't want to know what Lauda would have thought of that.

It was by no means a foregone conclusion that I would be allowed to drive this ravishing Ferrari on the occasion of its thirtieth birthday. When the F355 first saw the light of day, I was in the middle of my *Sturm und Drang* period – which meant that my various speeding violations had finally landed me in traffic school and that I had to submit to my first traffic psychology examination. (The whole ordeal would repeat itself just a few years later.) The psychologist, who was wearing a brightly colored short-sleeved shirt and had hair like Guildo Horn (use Google if you must), said I was in real danger of being banned from driving for life. Given my record, any judge could easily rule in favor of permanently revoking my license once the maximum suspension period had expired. I started to feel queasy. I slowly began sliding off of the couch and seriously contemplated suicide. "Relax," Guildo Horn said as he hurriedly handed me a glass of water, "you're with me for now. And I'm not working against you, I'm working with you." I was incredibly lucky to have Guildo Horn as my psychologist, and after paying a shockingly high fine, I got my driver's license back a few months later. The psychologist had written an extremely sympathetic letter oozing with (invented) admissions of remorse on my part.

The last hand-built Ferrari generated more horsepower per liter than the V12 in the McLaren F1.

My inner voice is telling me that I should be taking this opportunity here to publicly thank this man, who has since retired and who I now count among my friends. My inner voice is female, dark and smoky timbre, probably puffs filterless Gitanes, and I think she wears shoes with high heels. I always do everything she asks of me, I've been in bondage to her since puberty. Here goes: Dear Guildo (I've only ever called him that, his real name doesn't really matter anyway), old chap, if you're reading this, you'll be pleased, and I know you are, because you're totally into *ramp*, even though you keep saying the price is the ultimate in gall, but it's not your fault, because you're descended from stingy East Westphalian philistines, so I'll ask you anyway: please keep quiet, you've been getting a free copy for years (I spoke to Köckritz about the price and that it came from you, by the way, but Michael just shrugged his shoulders indifferently, he doesn't give a damn), please don't bother me with it anymore, but I actually wanted to thank you: Guildo, I know I'm deeply in your debt, without you I would probably have lost my license for good and would long ago have ended up in the gutter, with intermittent stays in the drunk tank, without you I wouldn't have been able to drive the F355 on its anniversary and tip my Panama hat to it with all due devotion, believe me, I'm realizing this very clearly right now, I'm going into myself and am lost in thought like Petrarch on his descent from Mont Ventoux. Hugs, your only Kurt.

The red car with the black interior that became mine for the twenty-four hours left the factory in 1997 with the full name of F355 Gran Turismo Berlinetta. A small aside here: "Why do you always say that Berlin is nicer when you're on the phone these days? Nicer than what?" my current significant other, who has become a little hard of hearing from too much acid techno, asked me recently. (I should clarify that the German for "nice" is "nett".) "I'm not saying *Berlin is netter,* you deaf little nut, I'm saying *Berlinetta.*" In the distant past, I really wanted an Opel Manta CC Berlinetta, and I made many long-distance calls across the old Federal Republic of Germany to try to get one: "Hello, I'm calling about the Manta Berlinetta you've advertised. Is it still available?" – "Nope, already sold." I was always at least one phone call too late and was never able to claim the most exclusive of all Mantas as my own.

As soon as I took a look at the circular instruments, I knew what I had signed up for: rev counter up to 10,000 rpm (red zone at 8,500).

The F355 was also available as a Targa and a Spider. But the Targa was the no-fish-and-no-meat version for all people who don't really know what they want. And the Spider was, for example, designed for the wannabe show-offs on Munich's Maximilianstraße or the stars and starlets rolling along Hollywood Boulevard. The true sports driver opted for the closed version, because he didn't want any blackbirds shitting on his skull during a neat four-wheel drift.

As soon as I got in and took a look at the circular instruments, I knew what I had signed up for: rev counter up to 10,000 rpm (red zone at 8,500). I could already hear the trumpets of Jericho in my head. I set out to adjust the steering wheel for ergonomic perfection. By today's standards, it is tilted a little too far forward. My search for a lever was unsuccessful, however. In retrospect, I would have been interested to know whether other car brands – let's say something halfway sensible like Porsche, BMW, Mercedes or Audi – also offered only such stubbornly set-in-their-ways steering wheels thirty years ago. My immense laziness did not allow me to research this question.

But let's let the steering wheel be a steering wheel and turn our attention to the truly surprising spaciousness of the cockpit. Surprising, because you don't get into this Ferrari, you squeeze into it like the Viet Cong into the tunnels of Cu Chi. You feel cramped and closed in when you crouch down into the car like a worm through the open door, but once inside there is so much space that even a driver with a hat on has enough clearance at the top. That's a good thing, because why should hats-on drivers like me be denied the orgiastic pleasure of driving a Ferrari? We hat drivers have rights just like everyone else, though we are much maligned. The general populace, in all its wickedness, doesn't mean us well. Just because the occasional hatted person behind the wheel is so slow they end up leading a

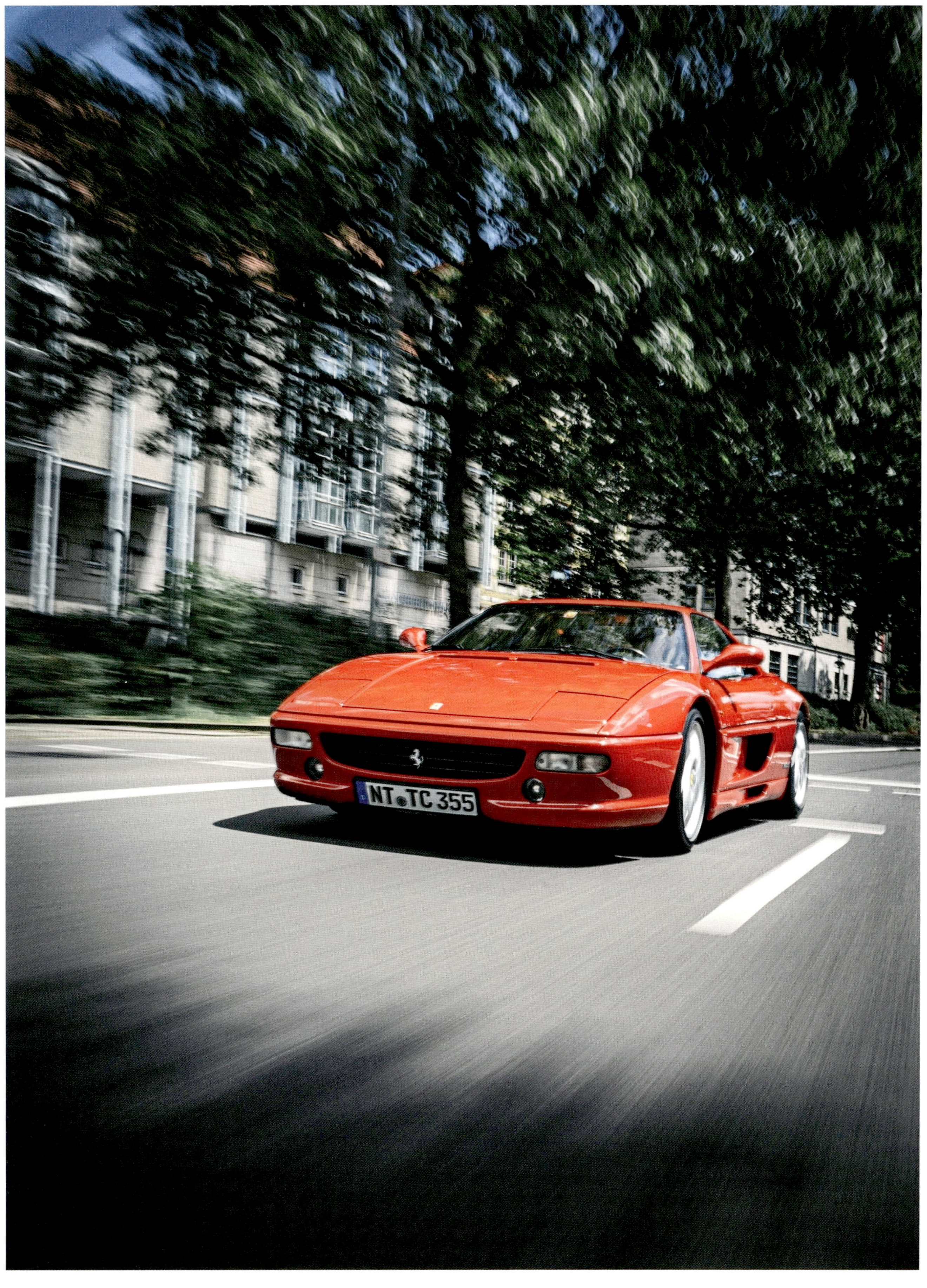
NT TC 355

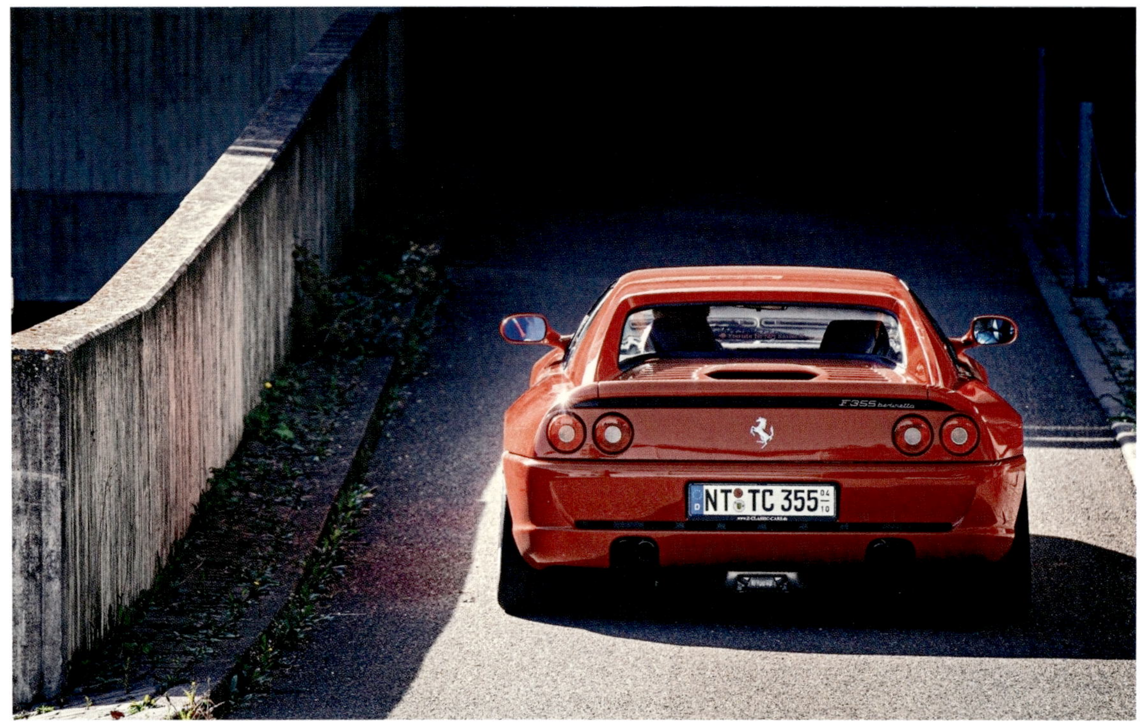
NT TC 355

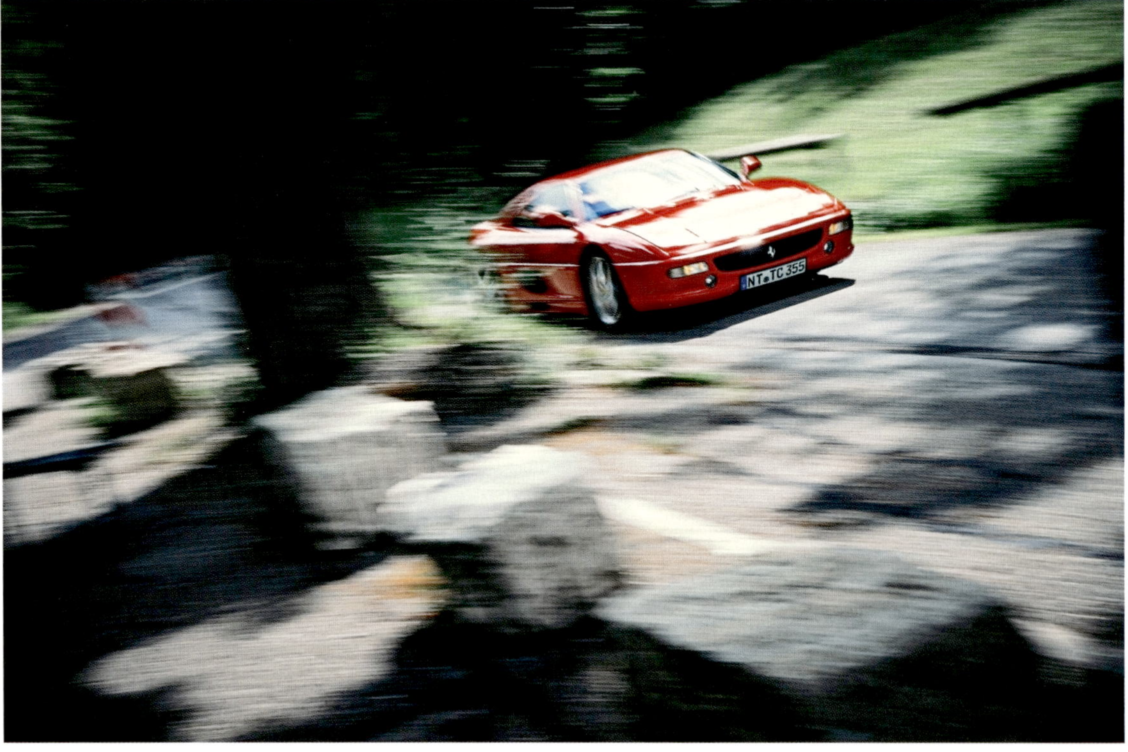
NT TC 355

line of frustrated drivers along the highway waiting for a chance to pass you don't have to say that it's always that way.

I fastened my seatbelt and turned the ignition key. The F355 doesn't roar like its ancestor, the 458 Italia. It hums unobtrusively after starting up. You could even call it unspectacular. But it could also be interpreted as a message. This Ferrari – or rather: this engine – tells you from the outset that it is not a servile American V8 that climbs to the highest mountains of torque merely by stroking it. Forget it. It doesn't do the work, you do. It's southern European, after all. If you want to properly feel its power – the message continues – you need to rev it up until your hair bleeds, which means that you only have your left hand to steer, because your right hand is constantly glued to the stick to make sure you're always in the right gear. Your feet won't be allowed a break either, the left hand clutches firmly on the wheel, the right hand is in a constant up and down between full speed ahead and reduced speed, you're heel is nimbly on the brakes in the double-clutch position (exception granted for left-foot brake maneuvers). It's not going to be a Sunday in the park.

Understood. Best to get everything right right from the start. I revved it up to 6,000 at idle. A brilliant squeal. Cast off. One leap forward and from zero to a hundred in four-point-seven. Unless you've just stepped out of the abnormal power rocket that is the Rimac Nevera (zero to 100 km/h in 1.9 seconds), that still seems pretty fast today. Thirty years before, it must have felt unworldly. I stayed in attack mode and did as described in the previous paragraph, always keeping one eye on the rev counter, because nothing happens below 4,000. A warning light flashed in the back of my head: caution, mid-engine rear-wheel drive, no ESP! The mid-mounted engine is undoubtedly the last word in wisdom for a sports car. Placing the heavy components (engine, transmission) as close to the center of the vehicle as possible results in an agility and light-footedness that cannot be achieved in any other way. Because everything is concentrated so close to the pivot point, however, the car suddenly goes into an uncontrollable spin. The limit comes unannounced. Suddenly, it's just there. But you're not.

I revved it up to 6,000 at idle. A brilliant squeal. Cast off. One leap forward and from zero to a hundred in four-point-seven.

Two years before, I had driven the McLaren 750S at Estoril. In a fit of megalomania, I activated the variable drift control with the most extreme angle. What had to happen happened: at the exit of a left-hand bend, I was half a second too early on the gas. Spurred on by its primal instinct, the beast suddenly swerved wildly to the right. It was only thanks to the ESP being switched on that I was able to prevent the car from taking off. How would the Ferrari behave? I don't know. At the crucial moments, I lifted my foot off the gas every time. But not out of cowardice – out of common sense. This F355 hadn't seen a single scratch in twenty-seven years of existence. I had no intention of changing that. As we all know, the devil never sleeps. At worst, I would have had to stand in front of the owner and say: "You can have your Ferrari back, it's stuck to a tree ten kilometers from here. Actually, it's not stuck to the tree, it's more wrapped around it. I mean: was wrapped around it, because when the fire department tried to remove it from the tree, it broke in half. I'm so sorry. Can I buy you a small beer in return?"

The F355 felt neutral right up to that line where things could (perhaps) have become dicey. It let itself be pitched around the corners with almost Lotus-like agility. Abrupt load changes were welcome. In other words, in a quick succession of bends it remained true to its line, meaning that it didn't sway in such a way that you would have lacked the momentum for the next bend. The brakes instilled me with confidence right from the first negative acceleration maneuver (I like the word because of its rarity, it occasionally flies at me like a white raven, in the future I want to use it more often). The pressure point on the pedal is not too hard and not too soft, it is perfectly at the golden mean. The Ferrari also behaved very well in a straight line, with no nervous to and fro on the front axle at high speeds or similar antics. The steering is more sensitive than the ABS, where you can feel that this is a car from the nineties.

In short, I felt very comfortable in and grew fond of this Ferrari in no time at all. I stopped keeping it constantly on the move. Wouldn't that have degraded it to a mere barrel organ? No. We glided leisurely through the countryside in unison and marveled at each other, the F355 and I, and I can assure you, friends, I could tell by the looks on their faces that a driver with a hat like that in a Ferrari completely confuses people, it throws those nitwits out of their clichéd thought patterns, almost squares the circle. Hey, if the hat fits . . .

This story began with Luca Cordero di Montezemolo. It should also end with him. As the F355 was the first road-going model built under his aegis, I often had to think of him while driving this car – and of this story from twenty years ago. It shows what a fun guy this successful man and workaholic could be (and still is): I had traveled to Milan to interview Diego Della Valle, CEO of luxury fashion manufacturer Tod's, at his company headquarters. His secretary greeted me at the reception and escorted me into the conference room. Signor Della Valle was on an urgent phone call, I was told, and it would take a few more minutes. Five minutes later, the door opened. But it wasn't Diego Della Valle who entered the room, but one of his best friends: Luca Cordero di Montezemolo. Hey, would you look at that, I thought. He shook my hand and introduced himself. Not as Luca Cordero di Montezemolo, but as Michael Schumacher: "Michael Schumacher," he said, pronouncing the name the English way, "nice to meet you." (Montezemolo and Schumacher were about to win their fourth F1 title in a row.)

I went along with the joke: "This is such an honor, such a pleasure to meet you." Montezemolo, as Michael Schumacher, told me that Diego Della Valle was still on the phone. Could he keep me company in the meantime? Supposedly a certain Luca Cordero di Montezemolo was also in the house, had I ever heard of him? No, I said, who would that be? Not important, he replied. It went on like that for ten minutes. Among other things, I asked "Schumacher" how he rated his own driving skills. Answer: "I'm the best, all the others are just nosepickers." Then came Diego Della Valle. "Michael Schumacher" said: "Ah, there's that Montezemolo." It was just wonderful, and if I had been driving the birthday car at the time, I would have said to the Nobile dei Marchesi: "Michael, I love the F355!"

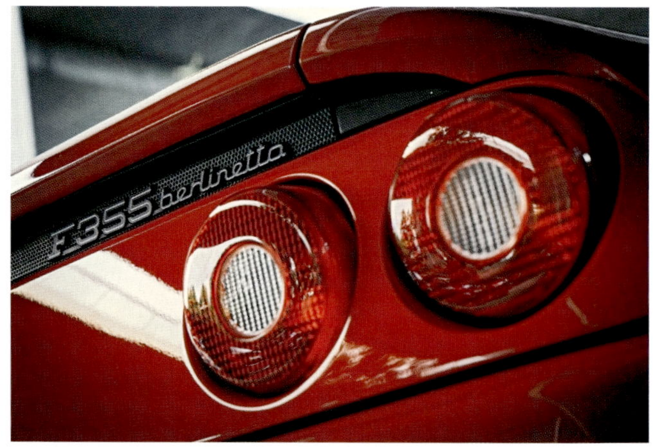

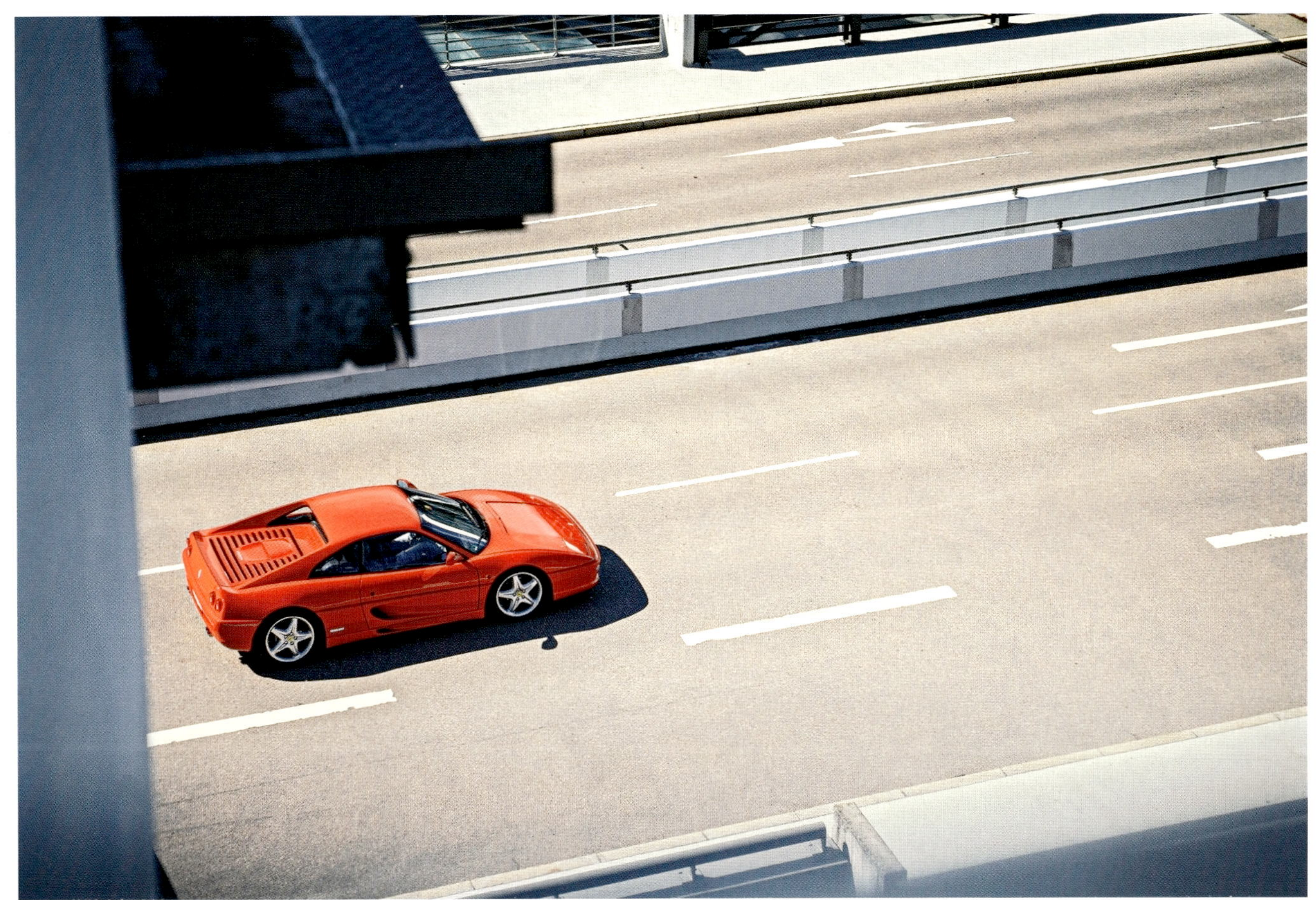

A warning light flashed in the back of my head: caution, mid-engine rear-wheel drive, no ESP! The limit comes unannounced. Suddenly, it's just there. But you're not.

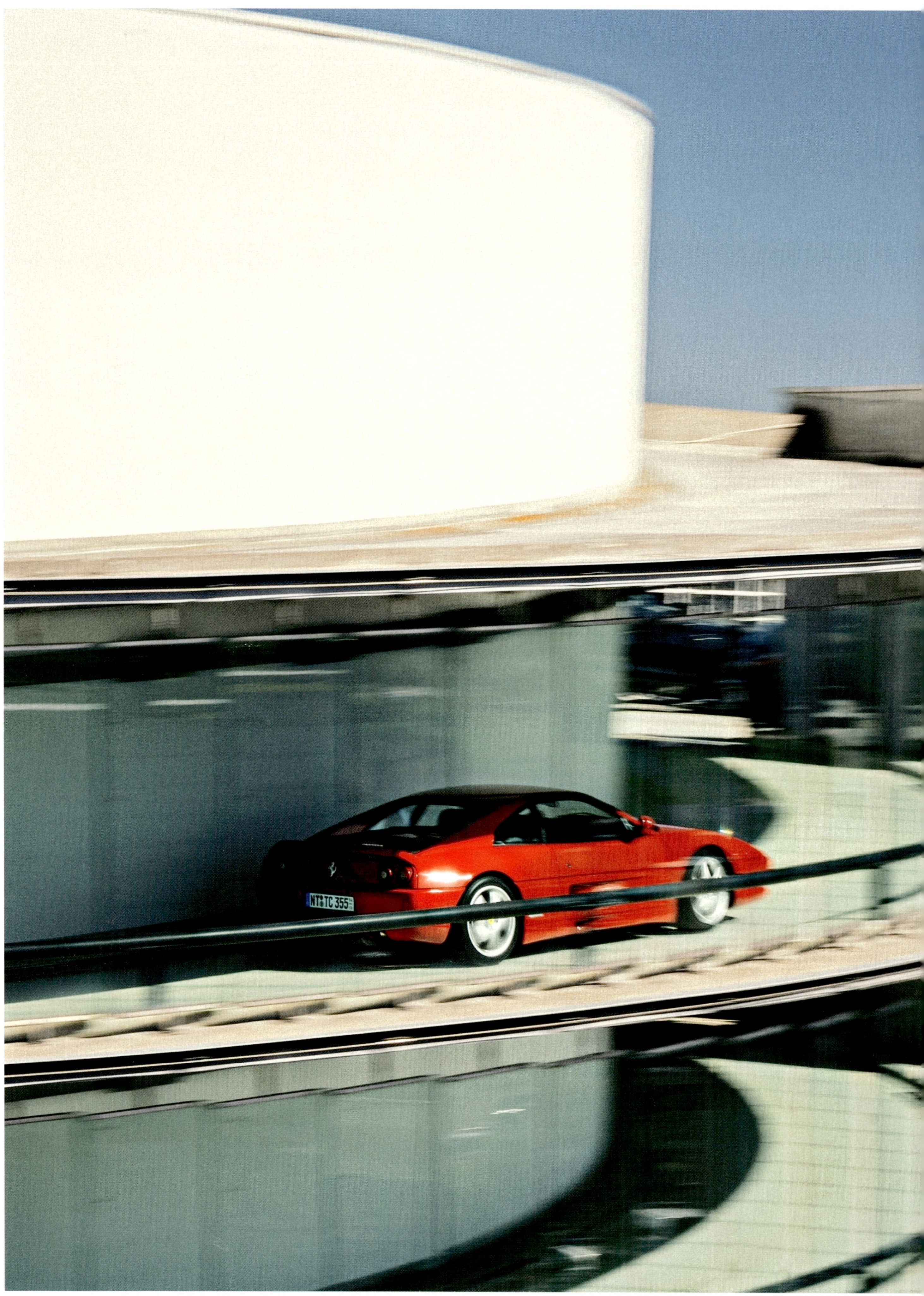
NT TC 355

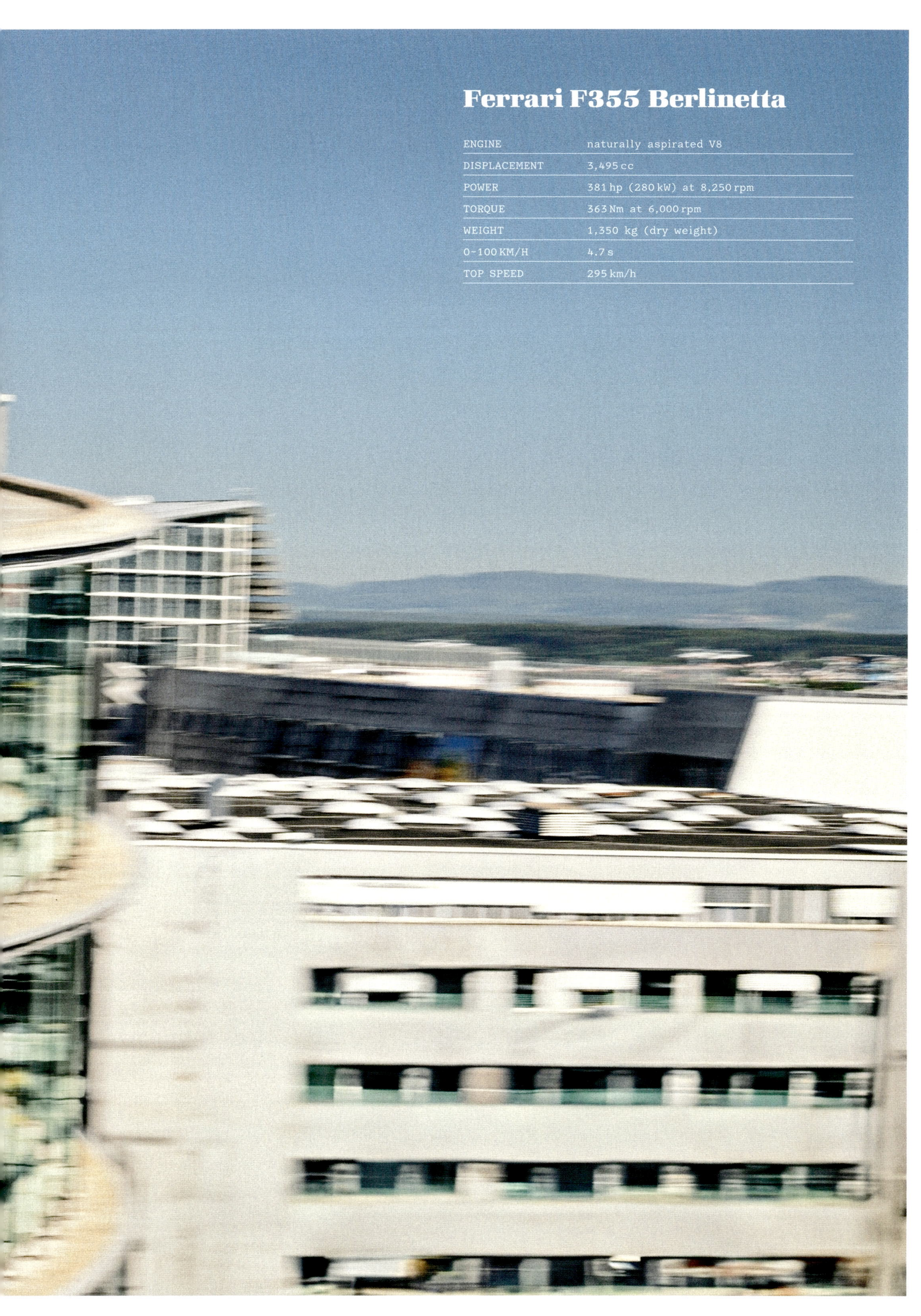

Ferrari F355 Berlinetta

ENGINE	naturally aspirated V8
DISPLACEMENT	3,495 cc
POWER	381 hp (280 kW) at 8,250 rpm
TORQUE	363 Nm at 6,000 rpm
WEIGHT	1,350 kg (dry weight)
0-100 KM/H	4.7 s
TOP SPEED	295 km/h

IT PAYS TO BE OPEN TO THE SPECIAL THINGS AND MOMENTS IN LIFE, YOU DON'T NEED TO CONSTANTLY CHASE AFTER THE LATEST FADS TO STAY ON THE LEADING EDGE.

THE SAME CAN BE SAID FOR THE WORLD OF SUPER SPORTS CARS.

NEED PROOF? WE RECOMMEND A PORSCHE 911 TURBO S AND A LAMBORGHINI GALLARDO LP 560-4.

3.06 stay cool

TEXT *David Staretz*
PHOTOS *Matthias Mederer · ramp.pictures*

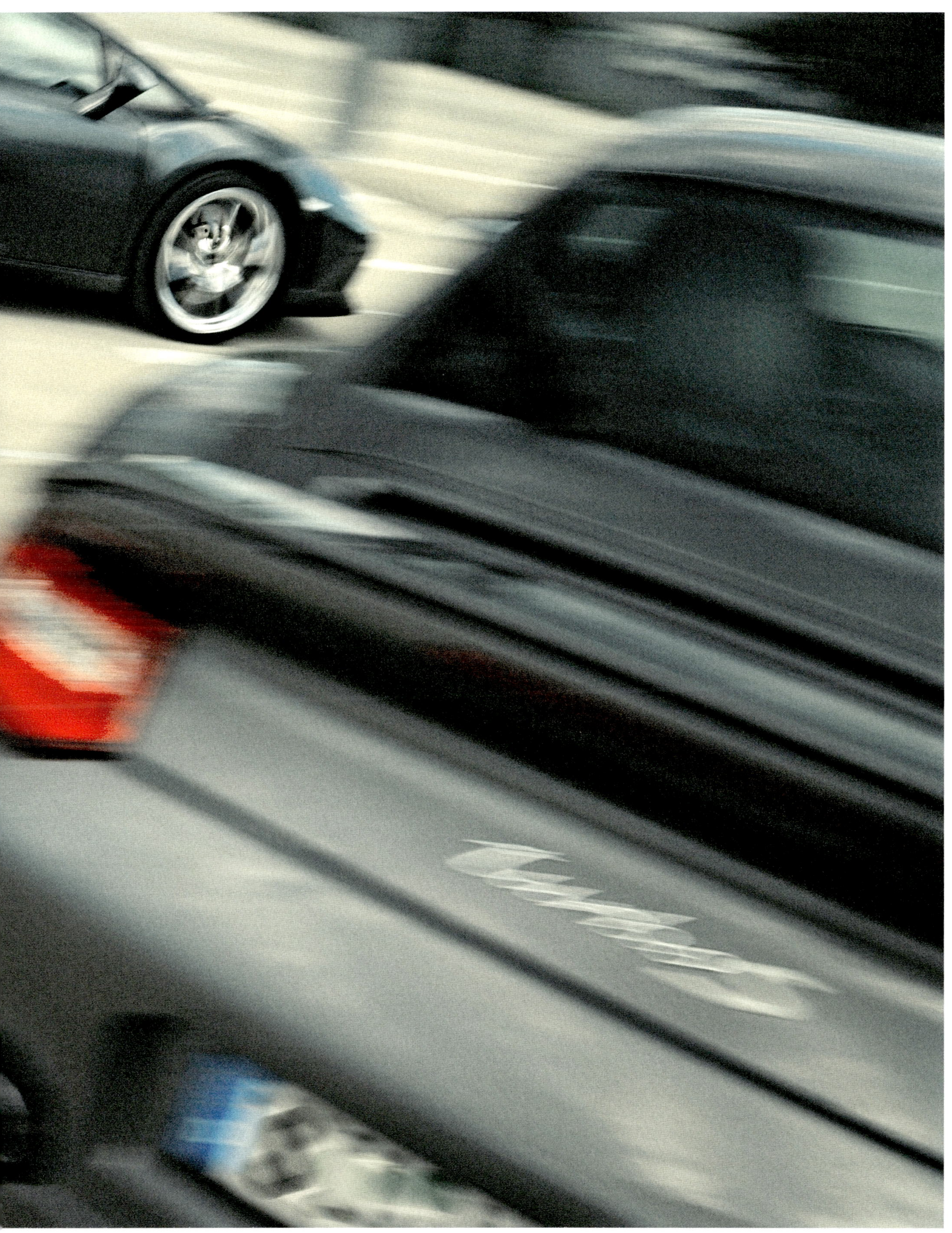

"Stay cool" is more than just an empty slogan. It expresses a way of life, reminding us not only to be cool, but also to stay that way. Like these two cars.

Porsche 911 Turbo S (997.2)

ENGINE	twin-turbocharged flat-six boxer
DISPLACEMENT	3,800 cc
POWER	530 hp (390 kW) at 6,250-6,750 rpm
TORQUE	700 Nm at 2,100-4,250 rpm
WEIGHT	1,660 kg
0-100 KM/H	3.3 s
TOP SPEED	315 km/h

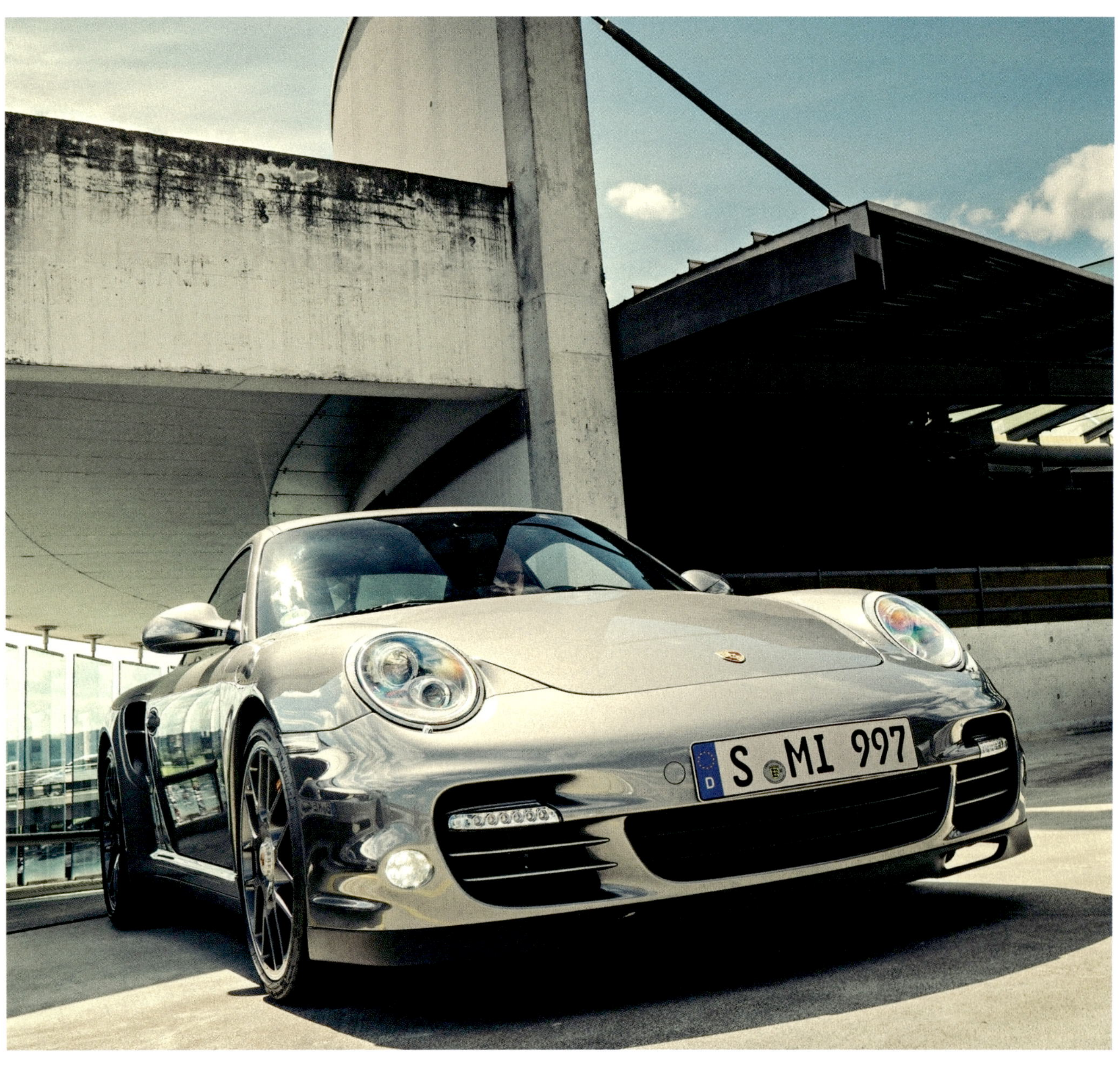

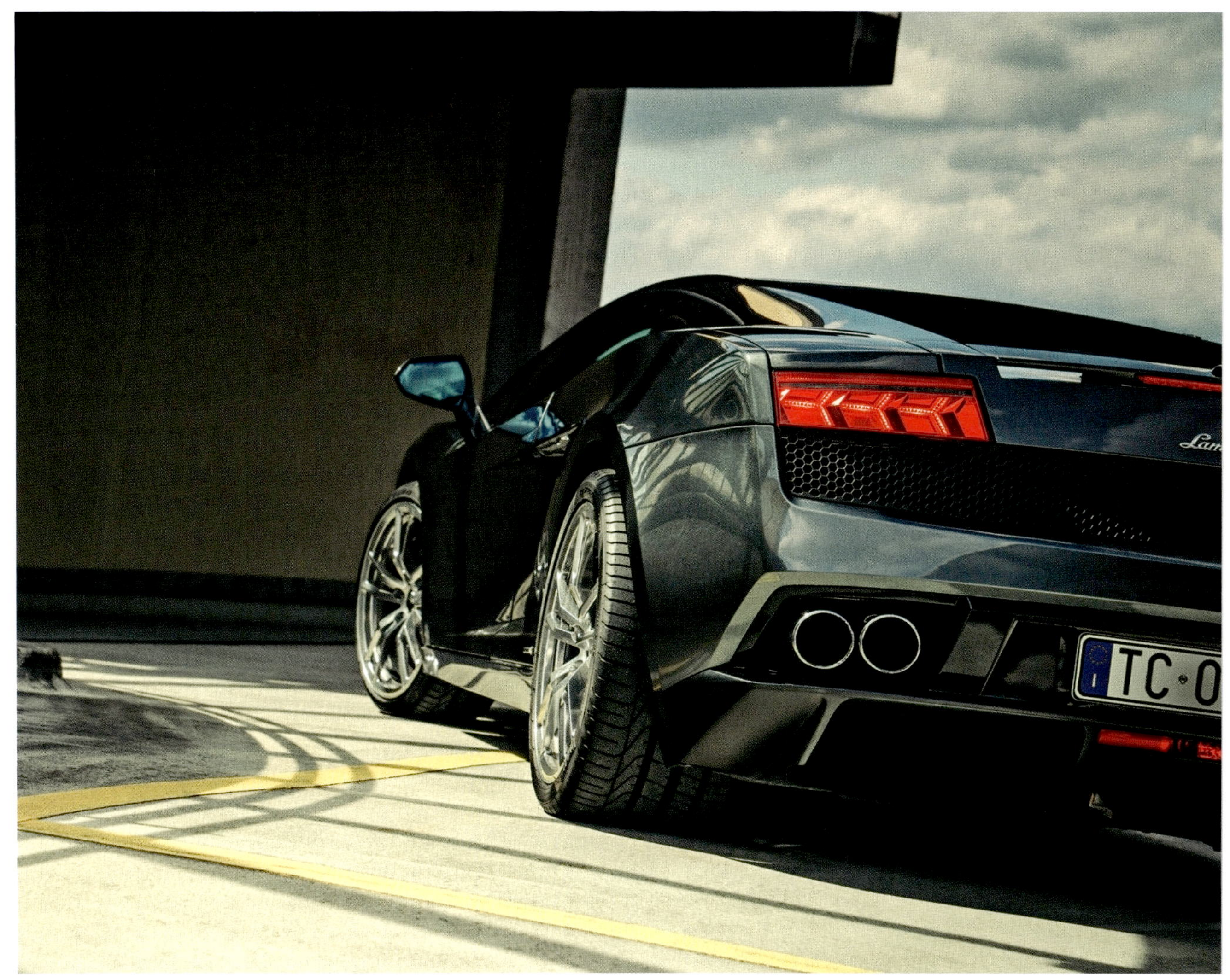

Two cars that seem so effortless in their appeal, their ingenuity, their radical nature and their talent for timeless perfection.

Lamborghini Gallardo LP 560-4

ENGINE	naturally aspirated V10
DISPLACEMENT	5,204 cc
POWER	560 hp (412 kW) at 8,000 rpm
TORQUE	540 Nm at 6,500 rpm
WEIGHT	1,500 kg
0-100 KM/H	3.7 s
TOP SPEED	325 km/h

We've made it, we have nothing left to prove to anyone, only to ourselves. This philosophy can be attributed to and experienced in an astonishingly congruent manner in two super sports cars. Rarely have two cars been so closely aligned with the theme of "cool stuff" as these two.

And speaking of cool: the saying "stay cool" is more than just an empty slogan. It expresses a way of life, reminding us not only to be cool, but also to stay that way. Like these two cars, which seem so effortless in their appeal, their ingenuity, their radical nature and their talent for timeless perfection.

2010 was obviously a good year, perhaps it even held that moment we are all looking for, the moment in which time stands still. We're constantly searching for moments of happiness, inventing fashions in order to chase after them posthaste, but the impression is mounting that it may be worth turning back a few chapters. Steve Jobs presented the first iPad. Sebastian Vettel became the youngest Formula 1 world champion to date. And the Siberian iris was flower of the year in Germany. Still with us? We don't want to overdo it either.

The Porsche 911 Turbo and the Lamborghini Gallardo are reliable benchmarks for technical and conceptual endurance; they stand for an avant-garde class of practical supercar that has proven itself over the vector of time, something that perhaps wasn't even listed in the product specifications. Because you can always rely on their essential consistency, the constant evolution of their technology. It's a fine line, both for experts and connoisseurs: driving a well-aged car with all of its primal power and beauty without having to join a vintage club or take part in Sunday drives over the Stelvio Pass.

What is really fascinating about these two cars in the fifteenth year of their existence is the seriousness with which they commit to their vision and the focus with which they still confront the poetic questions of high-speed driving today. These two driving machines are accessible for effortless straightforward lifestyles because they themselves still belong to the no-fuss generation: get in, fasten your seatbelt and drive off with a casual glance in the rear-view mirror – the equivalent of a motorcyclist who slowly and theatrically lifts his booted left leg from the asphalt as he accelerates rapidly down the road.

In this Turbo and Gallardo, there's no one constantly trying to take the wheel from you, there are no grandpa apps that are constantly pushing your coffee cup more snugly into its holder, any electronics that are on offer are there for a reason, have been thoroughly tested, and are helpful in the best sense of the word. Which means we can get down to business on the performance side of things; the Gallardo's 560 hp have not been relegated to retirement. An alert mind, vigilant reactions and real skills are required to drive it – or to handle the acceleration of the 911 Turbo with its challenging and explosive character. One thing reinforces the other here, because the car needs you as much as you depend on the car. This Gallardo and this Turbo, completely different in their concept, are so similar when it comes to the sheer power, the hard braking, the tight steering, the taut seating position, everything as matter of fact as you would expect from a super sports car – and yet without causing you any fatigue or exhaustion, always full of response and information, from the front axle, from the rear slip, from the depths of the all-wheel gearing, bursting from the dynamically mounted furnace, the fervent machine, frenetic in its revs, milling and howling in the extremes. Wicked, yes, but – the years are our witnesses – still reliable after all this time.

Before we get completely carried away in our euphoric enthusiasm, let's take a small break with the most important specs to catch our breath:

Porsche 911 Turbo S (997.2): meteor grey metallic, natural leather interior in cocoa brown

Lamborghini Gallardo LP 560-4: also

2010 was a good year. Sebastian Vettel became the youngest Formula 1 world champion to date. And the Siberian iris was flower of the year in Germany. Still with us? We don't want to overdo it either.

grey metallic, black Alcantara interior

Both sports cars impress the observer as timelessly modern driving machines with the ultimate in connoisseur quality; owners of one or the other are guaranteed to be an established sports car enthusiast, while the choice of color reflects their stylistic restraint. A profound appreciation for aesthetics and design is obvious. They are character actors of a fading era, a time when you still had something real in your hands in the sense of direct access to the machine, to the road, to life, before the generation of digital natives took over. These automobiles are no referential marketing tools with a driving experience button but exist in and of themselves, just like animals – or children.

At this point, we would like to shout a word onto the stage: *sprezzatura*. This is the Italian term for effortless grace and casual elegance. Germans aren't very good at it, of course, but we don't want to get into that here, we just want to mention it as an essential character trait. Though if you think about it carefully, the Gallardo actually benefits from the best of both worlds, as it contains a lot of components from the VW Group, developed in advance and in parallel. In particular, it shares more than a few parts with the Audi R8.

As an evolution of the old-school Porsche, the 997.2 is fundamentally rooted in a strong tradition, a classic rear-wheel car for the daily drive, an icon, a consistent and logical continuation of the technical and model developments. In this respect, the sixth 911 generation continues to embody the incredible evolution of the classic rear-engine sports car concept, the image burned into our retinas from childhood. But, hello, we're talking about 530 hp in the Turbo S version, dynamic engine mounts, brake-based torque vectoring and the ultra-quick seven-speed PDK for top acceleration values.

And, yes, Porsche is the braking world champion, especially when, as in this model variant, the carbon-ceramic option is fitted behind the center-lock rims. Center-lock rims! The highest distinction of racing-orientated track suitability.

But it is precisely in this discipline that the Gallardo holds a subjective trump card. And that has to do with the seating position. The driver directly faces the road, without any distractions, in a line of sight that is not even clouded by self-perception, as the front end ducks out of the way. Porsche, as a classic example of fine driving, attaches great importance to the guiding edge in the form of the right-side headlight dome. The classic vertical dashboard also causes a certain amount of visual inhibition, whereas in the Gallardo the visual flow pulls your sight forward with the momentum of a river's rapids. Still, the Lamborghini always lets you feel as if you could stop at any time should a cornering situation become too dicey.

To fully exploit the potential of the Turbo S, press the Sport Plus button. Then the PDK relinquishes all composure, shifts late and hard, skips up to gear level seven, and the variable turbo blades ensure optimum throughput. The suspension is in merciless mode and has a banging hardness. Now you really appreciate and feel the Porsche's bolt-tight workmanship.

On the other hand, the Gallardo brings an element of the exotic to our daily lives, characterized by its stringent design, with which Luc Donckerwolke created a modern classic right from the start.

Unfortunately, we have abandoned and given up so much from this era. New cars today are constantly pestering us with their electronic interventions, interfering in our driving maneuvers, which we protest in the strongest possible terms, because ultimately we still want to bear full responsibility, and full freedom of choice is only logical. The Lamborghini Gallardo and the Porsche Turbo are an exciting and intense reminder of those times.

And of the fact that you really only stay cool by living free.

What is really fascinating about these two cars is the seriousness with which they still confront the poetic questions of high-speed driving today.

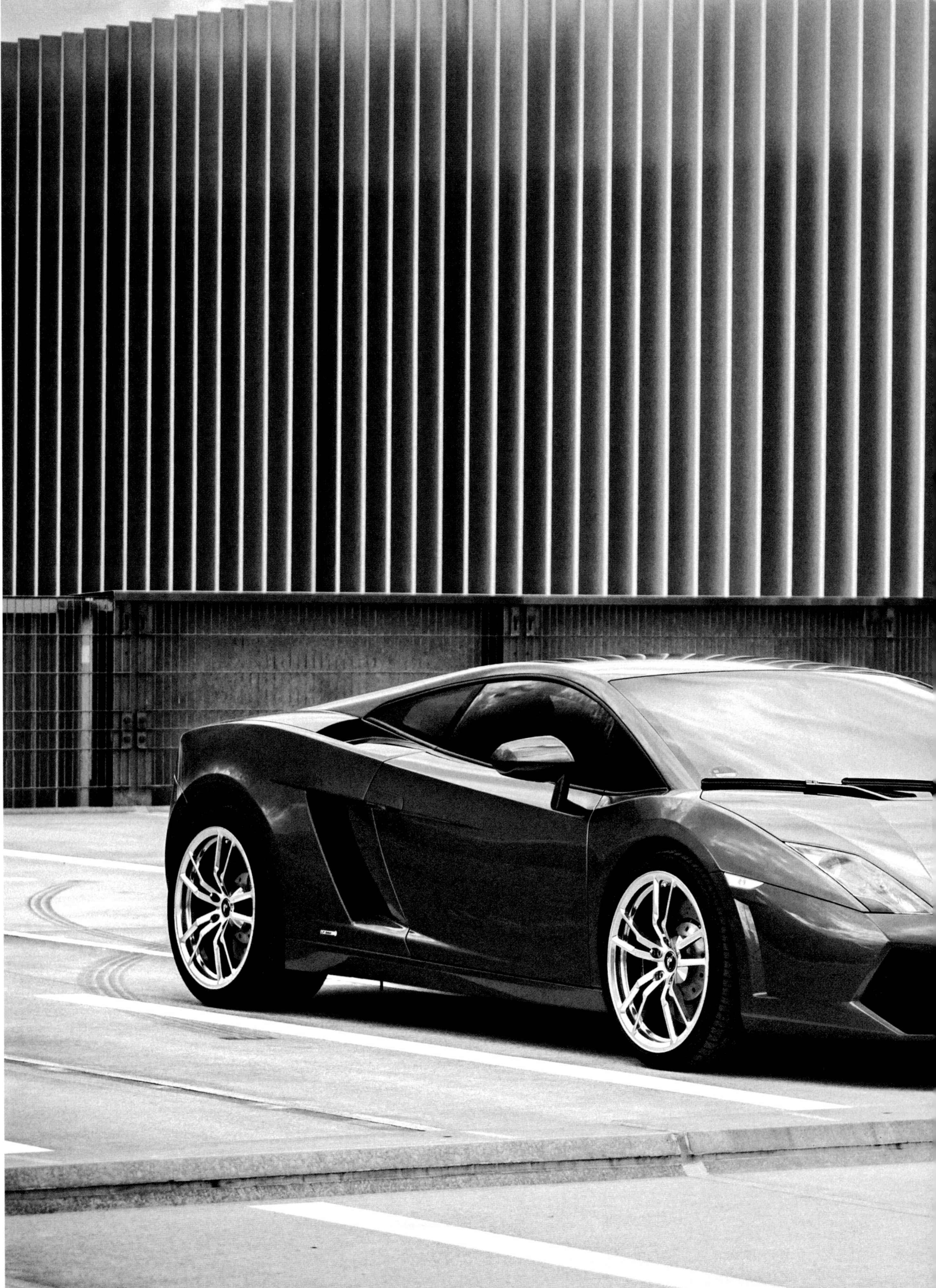

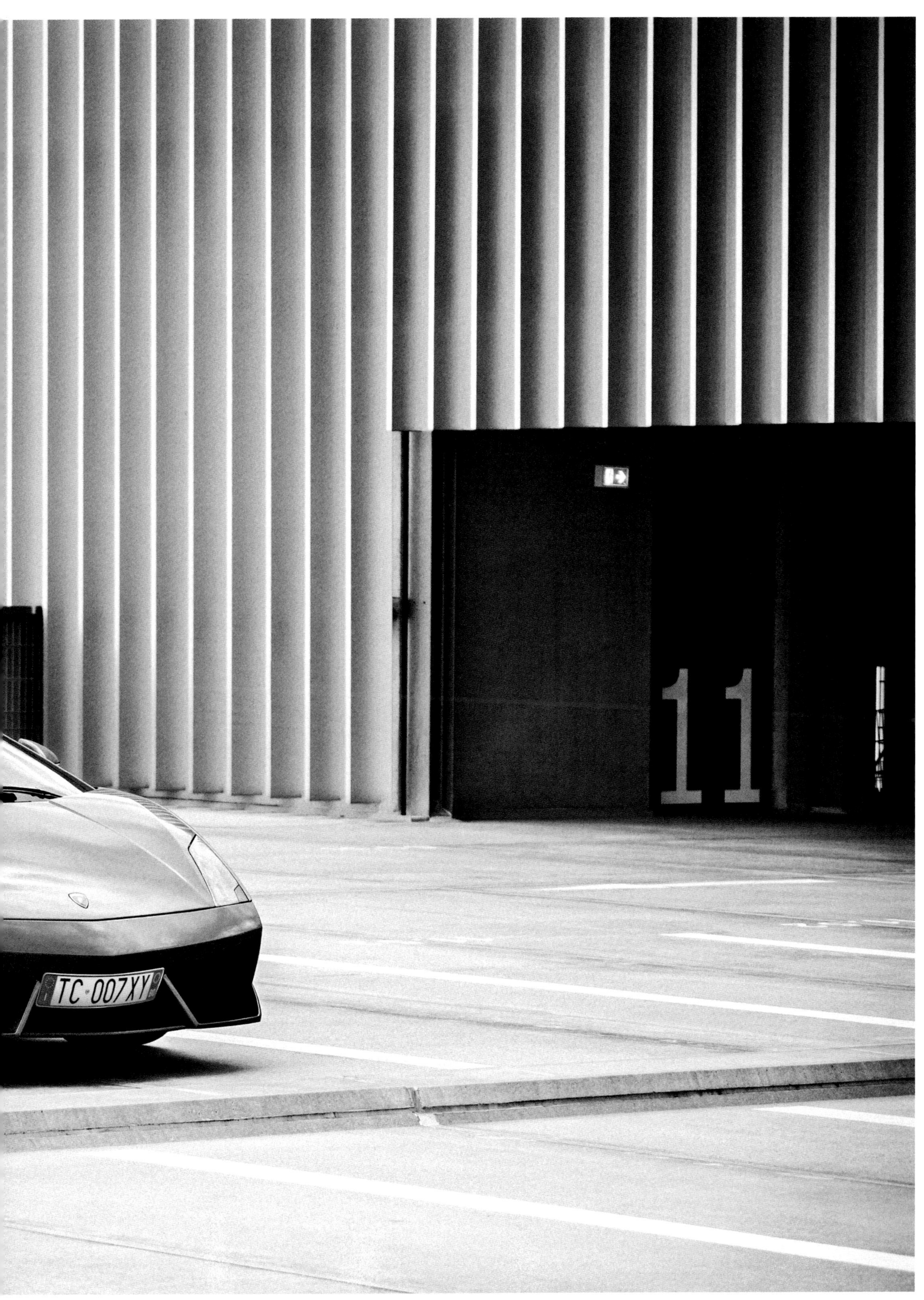
11
TC 007XY

3.07

hard facts

EVERYTHING YOU SHOULD MORE OR LESS KNOW

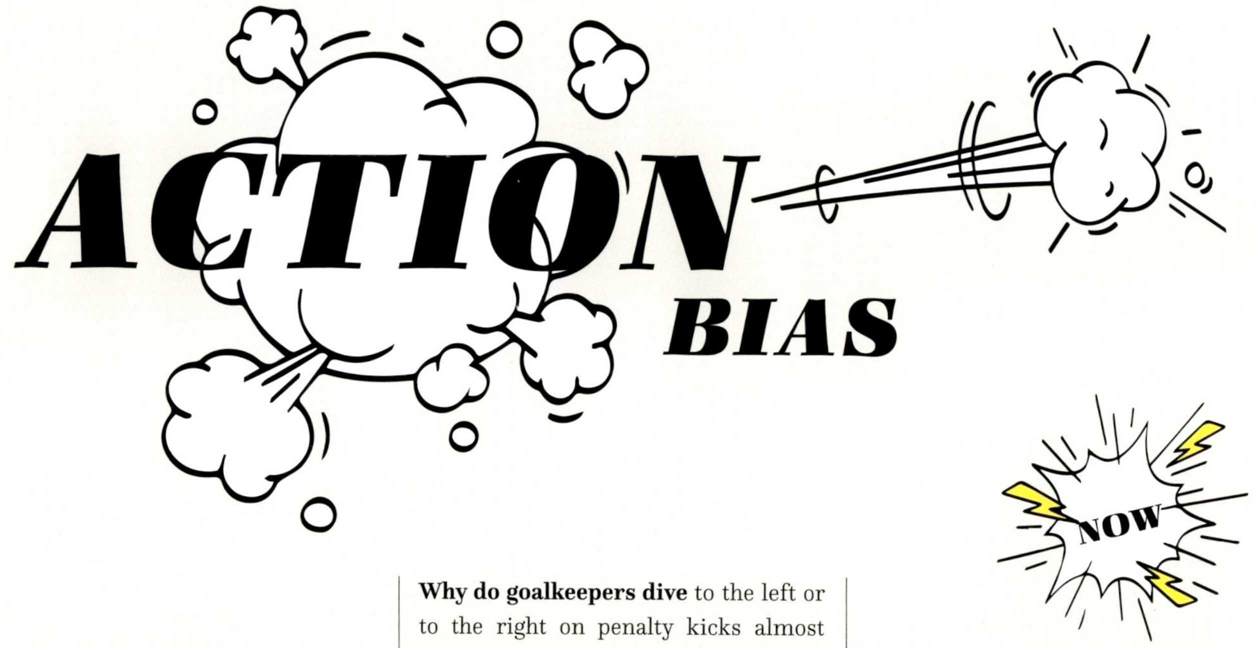

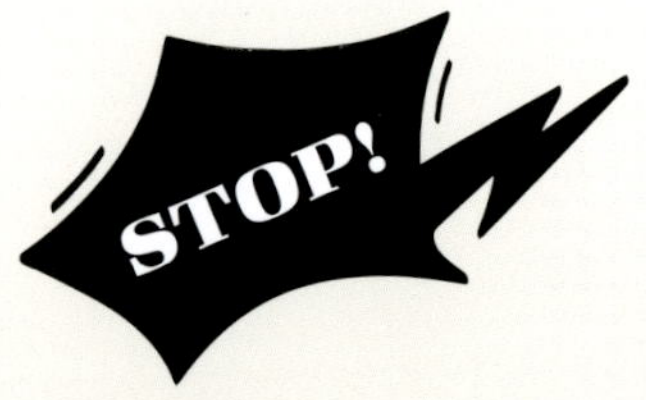

Why do goalkeepers dive to the left or to the right on penalty kicks almost every time, even though the chance of stopping the ball is statistically greatest if they simply stand still? The answer: **action bias**, the urge to do something even when doing nothing would be the better alternative. The underlying cause is an error in our thinking called a cognitive bias – our brain's attempt to simplify the complex world around us. In evolutionary terms, it may have made sense to act quickly in order to survive. Today, however, this primal instinct often leads to hasty decisions. Panic selling, for example. Action bias fuels us with energy, but in the end the question remains: Do we have the courage to do the right thing – even if it means doing nothing?

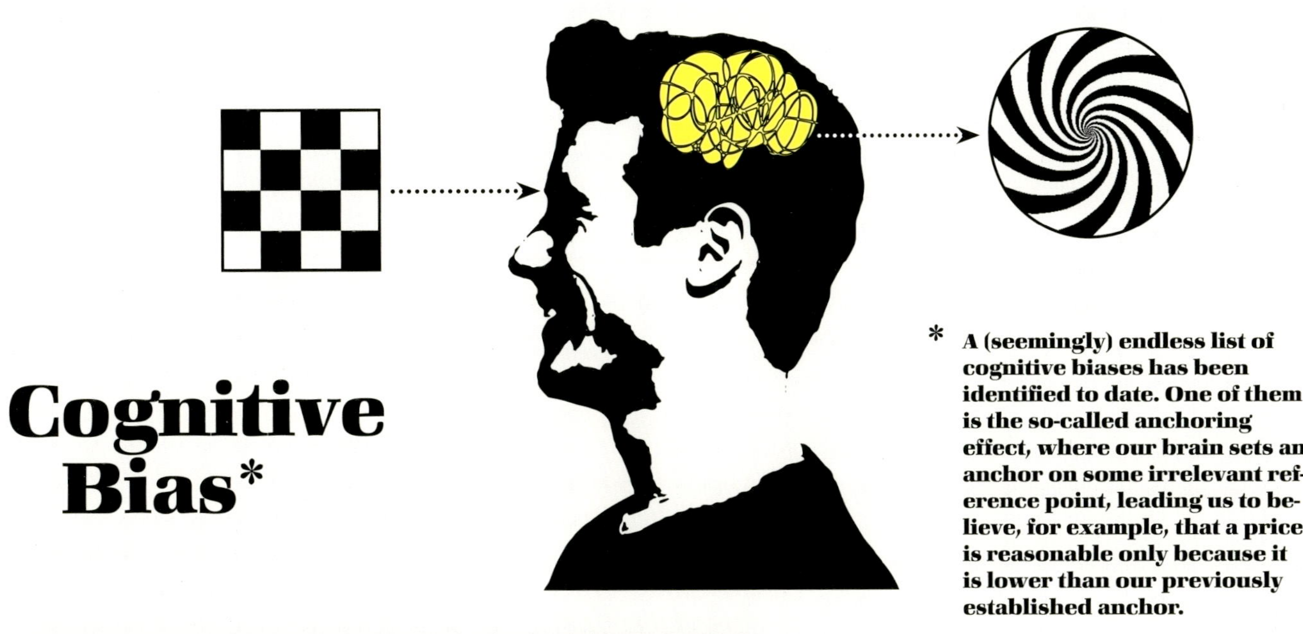

Cognitive Bias*

* A (seemingly) endless list of cognitive biases has been identified to date. One of them is the so-called anchoring effect, where our brain sets an anchor on some irrelevant reference point, leading us to believe, for example, that a price is reasonable only because it is lower than our previously established anchor.

A cognitive bias involves a systematic error in our thinking and observation, a pattern of deviation from norm or rationality in judgment. The term has its origins in cognitive psychology, the subdiscipline of psychology that studies mental processes. First introduced in the 1950s, the concept of cognitive biases became known to a wider audience with Daniel Kahneman's 2011 book *Thinking, Fast and Slow*.

One reason for our faulty observations, memories, thoughts and judgments is that our brain is constantly trying to find simple answers to complex problems. That may sound like a good strategy, but it has one small downside. This (over-)simplification of the world unknowingly leads us to make an ever larger number of irrational and even harmful decisions.

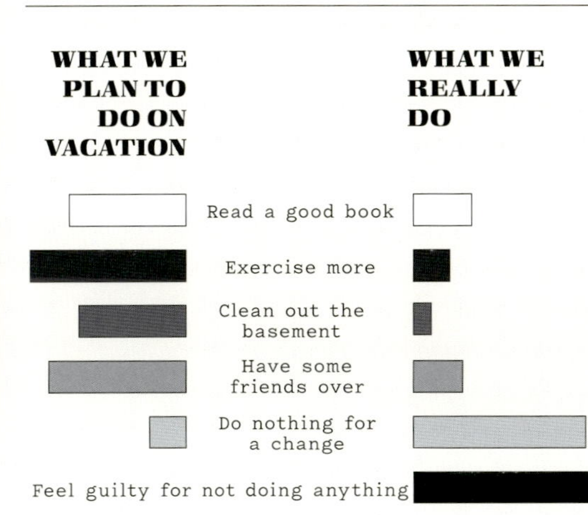

No such thing as the perfect pie chart? Think again!

Sky

Sunny side of pyramid

Shadow side of pyramid

> ***"Hectic action masks mental distraction."***
>
> Eugen Bleuler, Swiss psychiatrist

Don't Tolerate the Intolerant

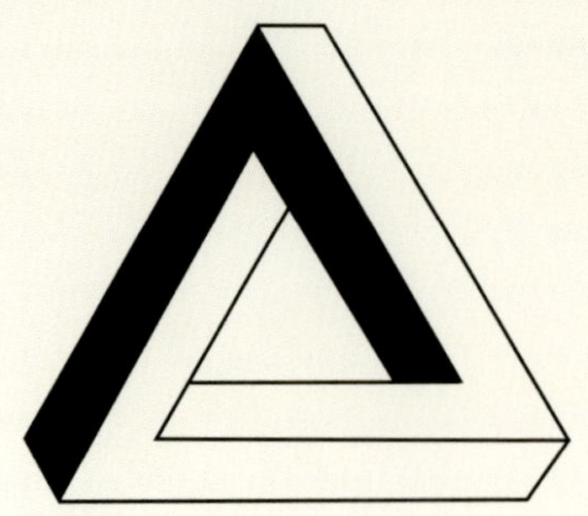

There are two things you should know about the following excerpt from Karl Popper's *The Open Society and Its Enemies*. First, it is considered one of the most important works of political philosophy in the twentieth century. Second, the Austrian-British philosopher made the decision to write the book following Austria's annexation by Nazi Germany in 1938.

The paradox of tolerance: unlimited tolerance must lead to the disappearance of tolerance. If we extend unlimited tolerance even to those who are intolerant, if we are not prepared to defend a tolerant society against the onslaught of the intolerant, then the tolerant will be destroyed, and tolerance with them.

In this formulation, I do not imply, for instance, that we should always suppress the utterance of intolerant philosophies; as long as we can counter them by rational argument and keep them in check by public opinion, suppression would certainly be unwise. But we should claim the right to suppress them if necessary even by force; for it may easily turn out that they are not prepared to meet us on the level of rational argument, but begin by denouncing all argument; they may forbid their followers to listen to rational argument, because it is deceptive, and teach them to answer arguments by the use of their fists or pistols.

We should therefore claim, in the name of tolerance, the right not to tolerate the intolerant. We should claim that any movement preaching intolerance places itself outside the law, and we should consider incitement to intolerance and persecution as criminal, in the same way as we should consider incitement to murder, or to kidnapping, or to the revival of the slave trade, as criminal.

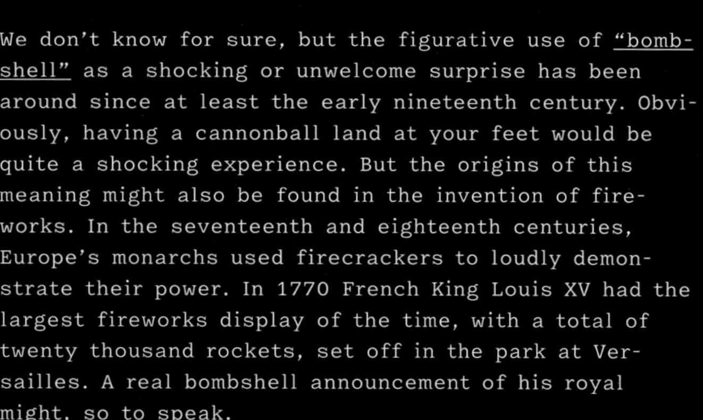

BOMB-SHELL

We don't know for sure, but the figurative use of "bombshell" as a shocking or unwelcome surprise has been around since at least the early nineteenth century. Obviously, having a cannonball land at your feet would be quite a shocking experience. But the origins of this meaning might also be found in the invention of fireworks. In the seventeenth and eighteenth centuries, Europe's monarchs used firecrackers to loudly demonstrate their power. In 1770 French King Louis XV had the largest fireworks display of the time, with a total of twenty thousand rockets, set off in the park at Versailles. A real bombshell announcement of his royal might, so to speak.

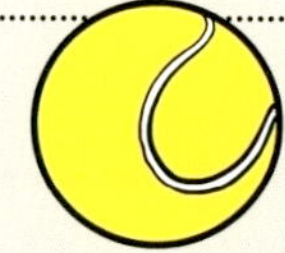

YELLOW INSTEAD OF WHITE

Tennis balls were originally either black or white. So why are they yellow today and what does Sir David Attenborough have to do with it? One of Attenborough's early positions at the BBC was as controller overseeing the switch to color television. The first color broadcast of Wimbledon took place in 1967, but it was almost impossible to see the white balls on the TV screen. Attenborough made his case for a fluorescent color. The International Tennis Federation (ITF) then conducted extensive research and introduced yellow balls into the rules of the sport in 1972.

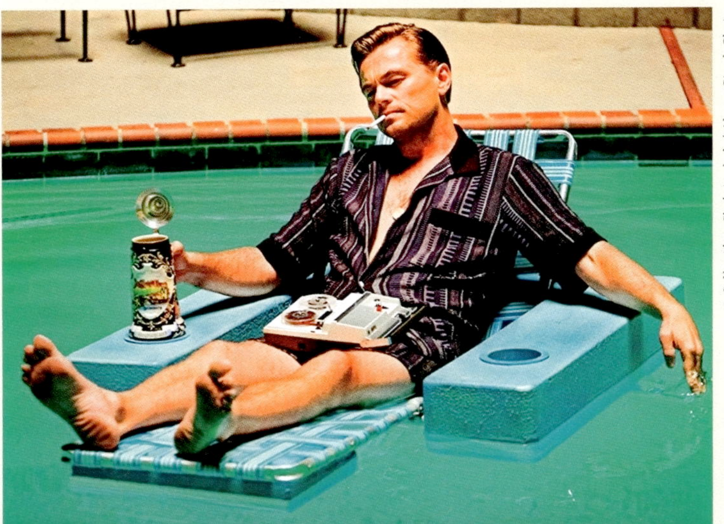

© Collection Christophel / Alamy Stock Photo

POOL ETIQUETTE

TIP 1 *Just for the record, jumping into the pool without taking a shower first contaminates the water up to sixty times more with sweat, residual make-up and dirt than swimmers who shower off beforehand.*

TIP 2 *A public pool is a great place to meet people. But you should still keep a respectful distance to others. Remember Covid? Stretch out your arms. The other person should be two arms' lengths away.*

TIP 3 *Are you an athletic god who needs to show off their frisbee skills at the poolside? Please don't. To avoid collateral damage with the other bathers, go play on the grass. Preferably the lawn without beach towels on it.*

TIP 4 *Where worlds collide: semi-professional athletes on a training plan, recreational swimmers, and chatterboxes bobbing in the water doing the breaststroke. Suggestion: keep the designated lanes clear for swimmers and go to the snack stand if you want to socialize.*

TIP 5 *Want to do a fast crawl? Assess the situation first: Are there different lanes for different speeds? Are the others circle swimming or splitting the lane? Then you can find the right lane for you and be happy that everything is going so smoothly.*

TIP 6 *We're at a public pool and not in a commercial for Caribbean rum. So please put something on before going to the restaurant. Nobody wants to sit on a chair that is still sopping wet from your bathing shorts.*

TIP 7 *Only flying is more fun. If you feel compelled to do a cannonball, please check in advance whether there are people sunbathing nearby. Not everyone will be excited by the prospect of an unsolicited shower. Same thing when diving off the ten-meter board.*

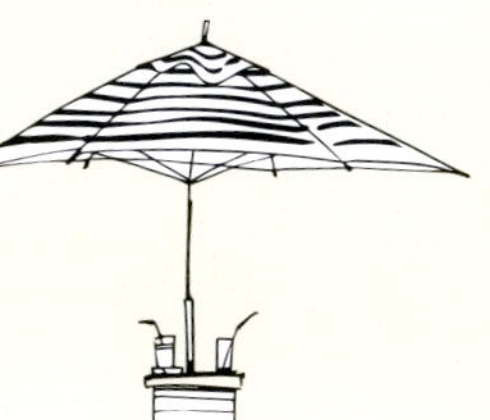

COOL IT DOWN

These foods can help to lower your body temperature

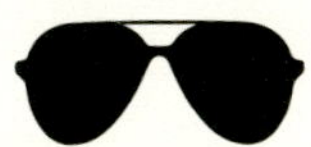

A WARM DRINK ON A HOT DAY

The clicking of ice cubes in a glass sure is a lovely sound. But a cold drink is not recommended on a really hot day. The body then produces additional heat to try to compensate for the temperature difference. Lukewarm tea is the better way to go. Peppermint is an especially good choice.

*

EAT YOUR VEGGIES

Traditional Chinese medicine recommends asparagus, cucumbers, tomatoes, carrots, celery, spinach, eggplant, radishes . . . and tofu. Because tofu is made from soybeans. And soybeans, after all, are a vegetable.

*

"I CARRIED A WATERMELON"

Don't let the *Dirty Dancing* quote confuse you, we just want to advertise the best fruit for battling the heat. According to TCM, it's a watermelon. Cherries, peaches and Mirabelle plums are not recommended.

*

HOT IN HERE

Spicy food can help to regulate your body temperature. If you don't tolerate chilies, ginger or cayenne pepper, you can always try basil, thyme, rosemary or parsley.

*

THE GRILL STAYS OFF

Steamed and raw foods cool more than fried or grilled. Heavy food with lots of fat also heats you up.

*

SOUR, SOUR, SOUR

Acidified dairy products such as yoghurt, cultured buttermilk or kefir will kill the inner heat. So now you know why they're so fond of lassis in India.

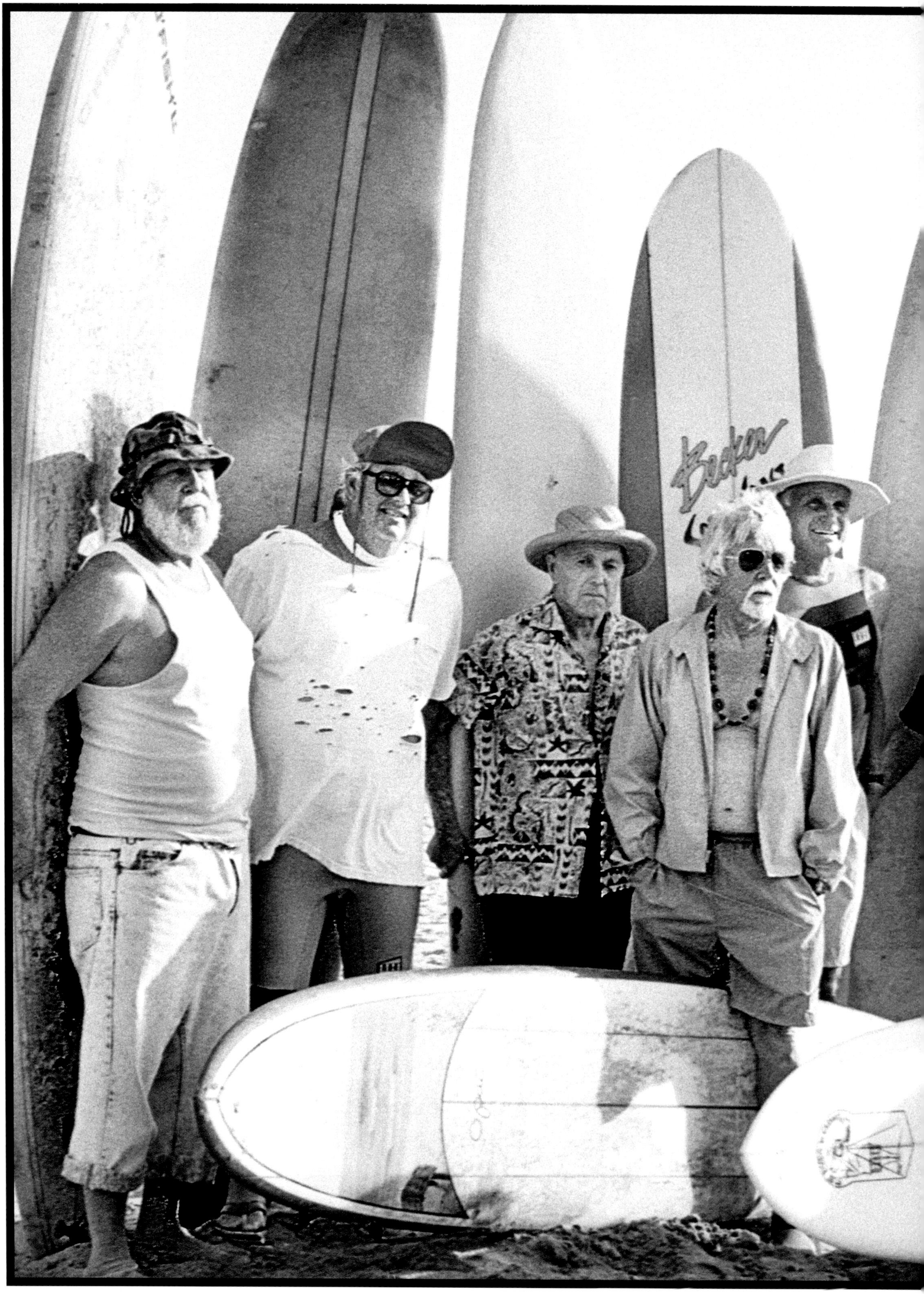
Becker

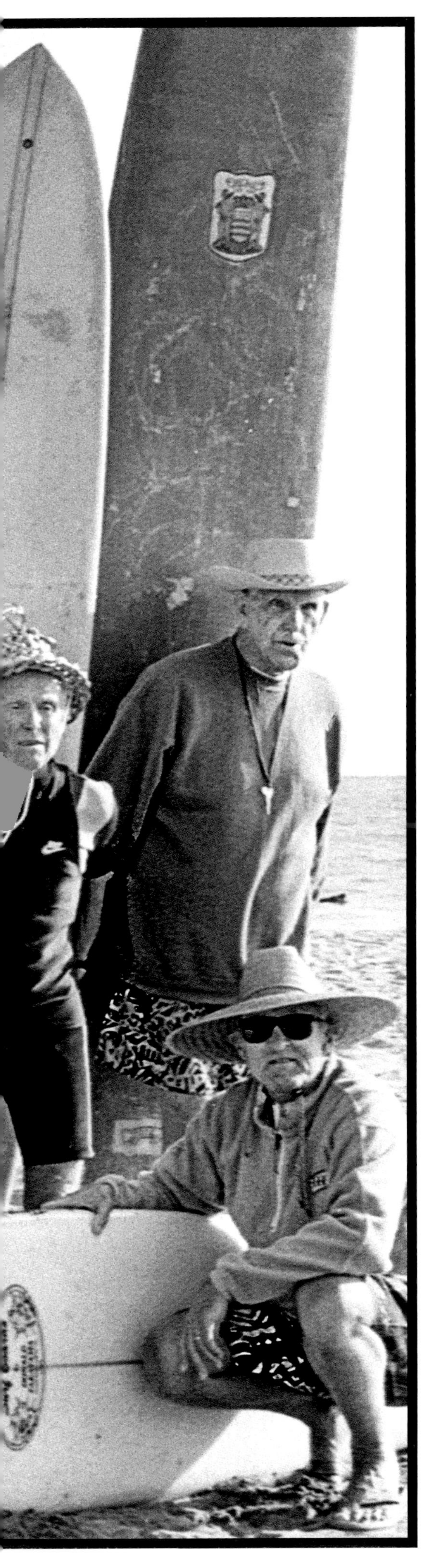

play it as it was

4

"Surfing, alone among sports, generates laughter at its very suggestion, and this is because it turns not a skill into an art, but an inexplicable and useless urge into a vital way of life." Says Matt Warshaw. As a former pro surfer and current executive director of the *Encyclopedia of Surfing*, his words carry some weight – especially when you look at this 1990 photo from an ad shoot in San Onofre State Beach in California. It shows a group of older guys with their boards who, thanks to their chosen way of life, had earned a certain reputation in surfing circles – even beyond the West Coast.

And from what we hear, they had the skills to back it up – effortlessly.

cool stuff 4.01

TEXT *Wiebke Brauer*

BOING BOOM TSCHAK

The products from Swedish consumer electronics company Teenage Engineering all have one thing in common: you want them even if you don't need them – and you definitely want to listen to Kraftwerk while you caress the surface of the sleek devices. Which certainly is true for this OP-XY performance sequencer, sampler and synthesizer.

→ teenage.engineering

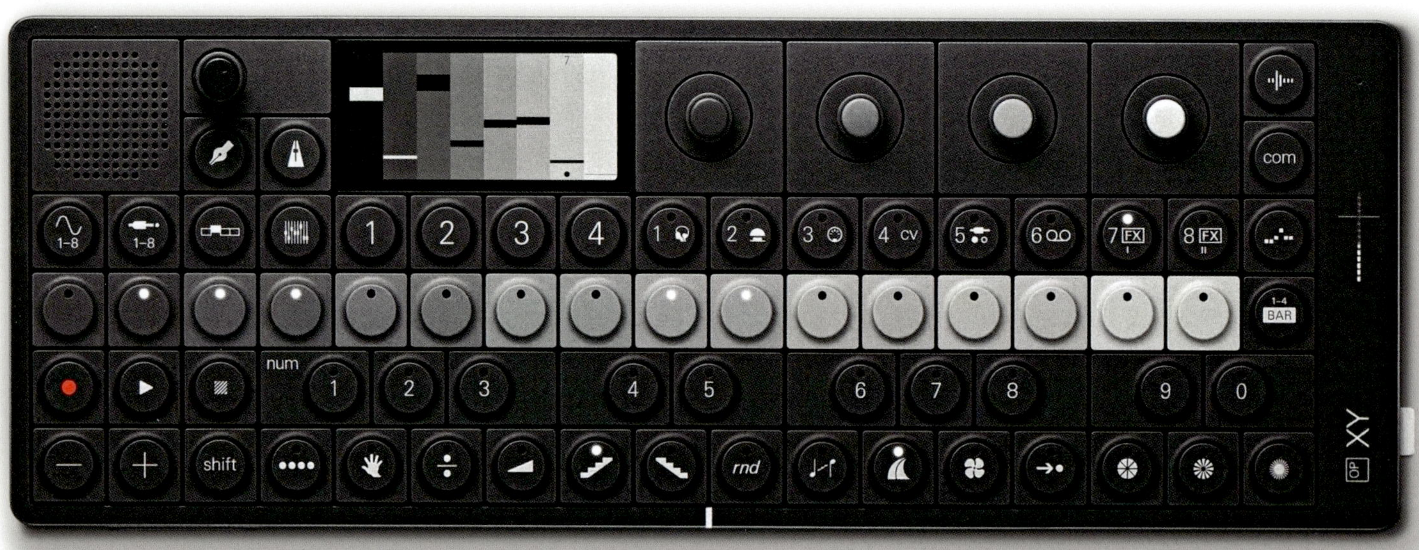

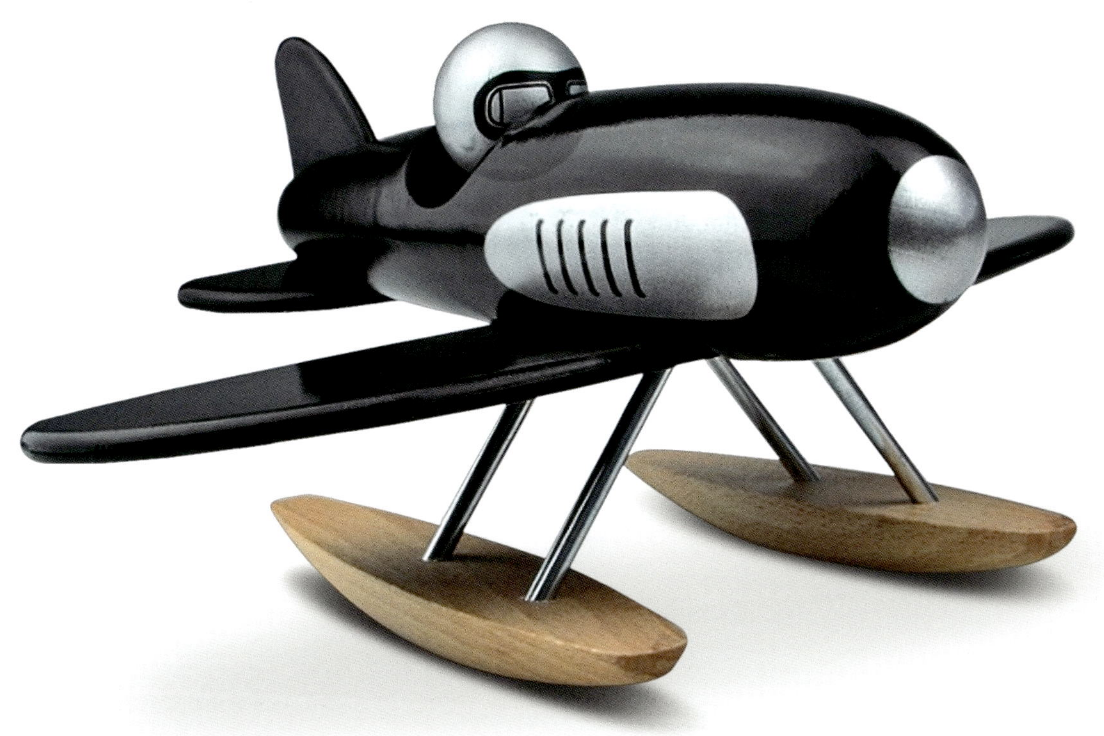

WINGS OF DESIRE

Business magnate and aviation pioneer Howard Hughes once dreamed of building giant seaplanes for use during World War II. But by the time his H-4 Hercules, commonly known as the *Spruce Goose*, was completed, the war was already over. Still, with a wingspan of 97.5 meters, it held a record for seventy-two years. This toy plane from Vilac may not quite match that - but at 26 centimeters, it's doing its best.

→ playoffside.com

AN EVEN SPREAD

The perfect distance for spraying on perfume? Between 20 and 30 centimeters. The result is a fragrant mist that settles evenly over your skin. Something to think about the next time you apply Armani Code Eau de Toilette.

→ armanibeauty.com

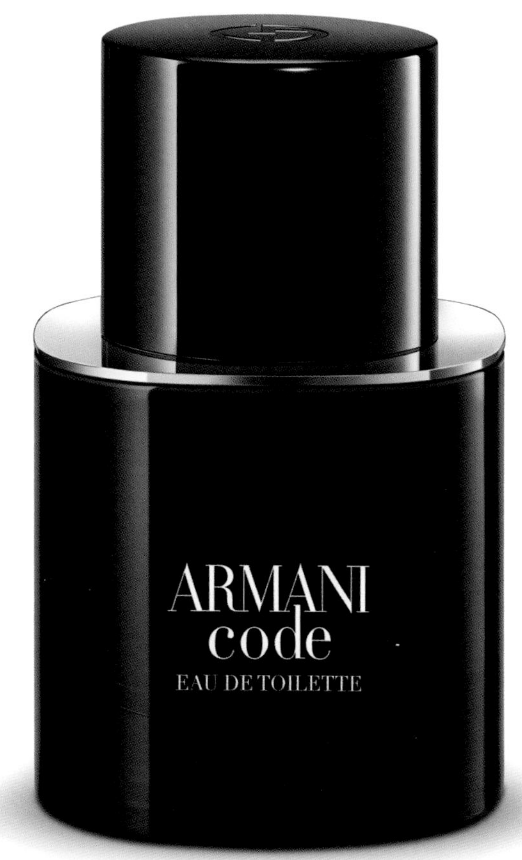

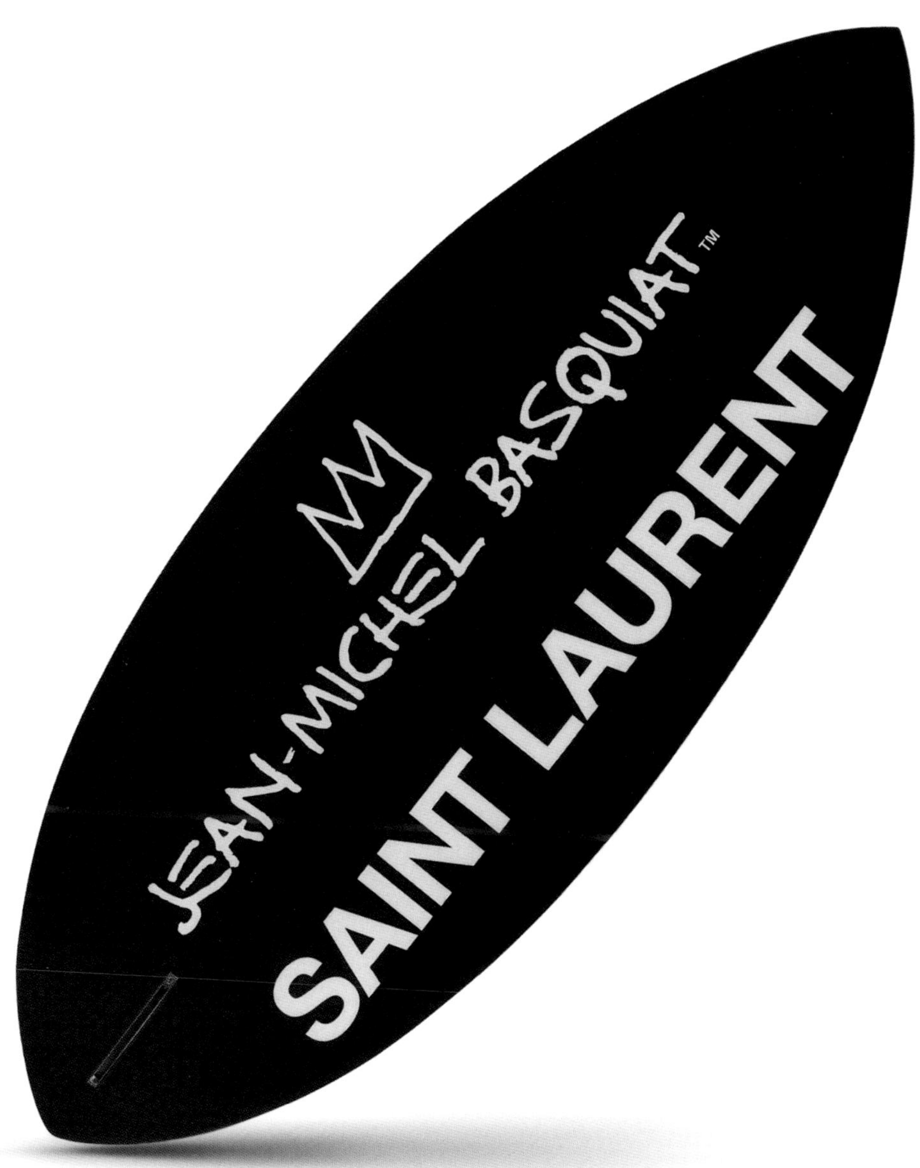

AQUAPLANING

The Stribeck curve shows how friction in a hydrodynamic contact varies with viscosity, speed and load. Three so-called lubrication regimes can be identified, the third being hydrodynamic lubrication – which influences fluid friction and is of interest to skimboarders. Admittedly, none of that has anything to do with Jean-Michel Basquiat. Except that the American artist's signature looks fantastic on the underside of this 2021 board from Saint Laurent.

→ ysl.com

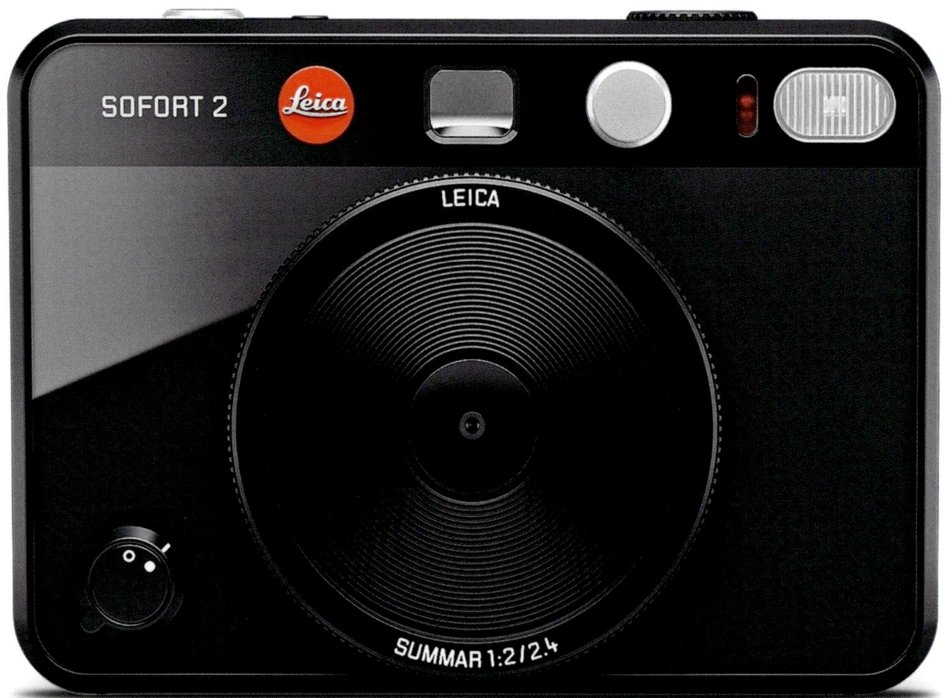

INSTANT SOUP

"There's only one rule in photography - never develop color film in chicken noodle soup." This quote is attributed to Canadian photographer Freeman Patterson. If you're tempted to try it anyway, don't worry: the Leica Sofort 2 instant camera prints the photos with no soup needed.

→ leica-camera.com

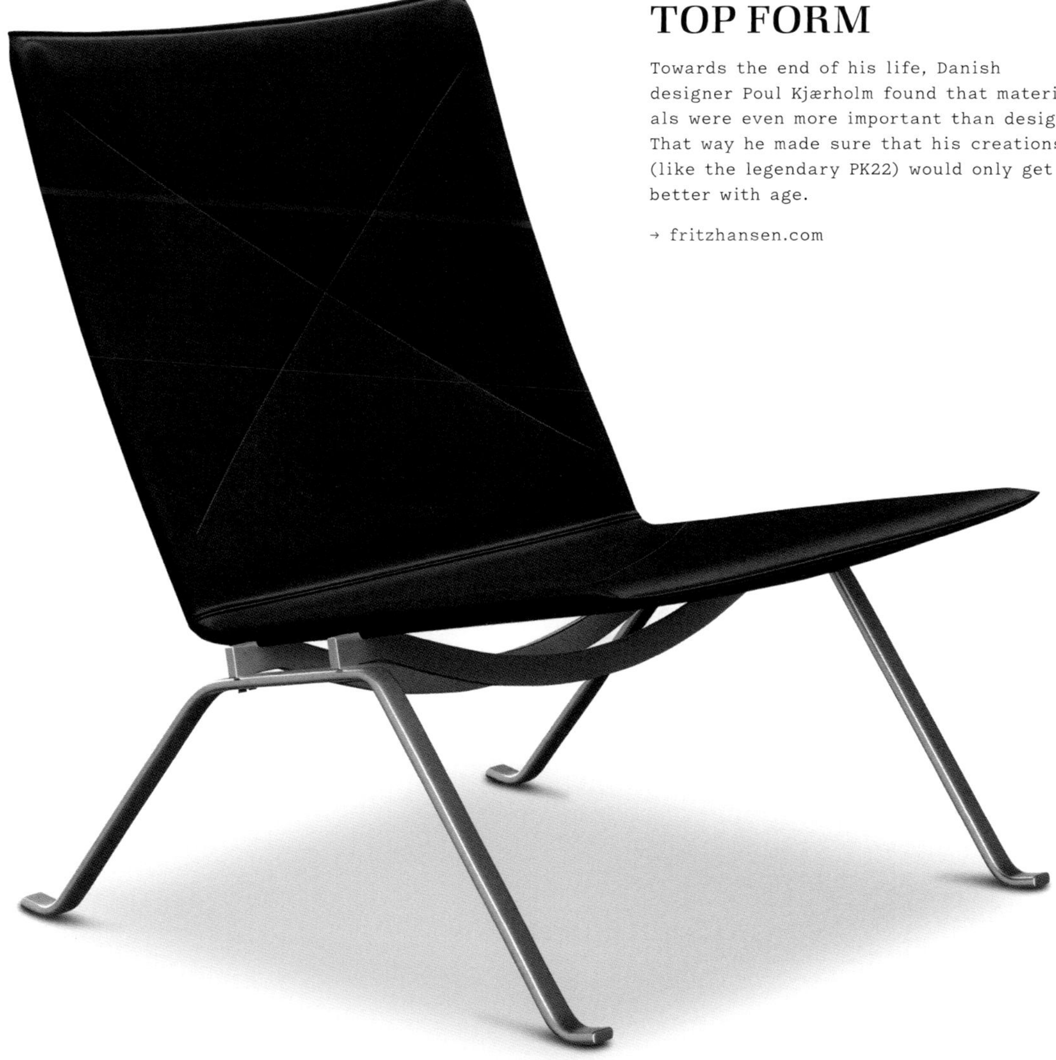

TOP FORM

Towards the end of his life, Danish designer Poul Kjærholm found that materials were even more important than design. That way he made sure that his creations (like the legendary PK22) would only get better with age.

→ fritzhansen.com

CREDIT WHERE CREDIT IS DUE

In his 1888 utopian science-fiction novel *Looking Backward*, Edward Bellamy was the first to come up with the idea of a credit card. Okay, and what does that have to do with this multi tool in the shape of a Land Rover Defender? Well, it's the size of a credit card.

→ parts.jaguarlandroverclassic.com

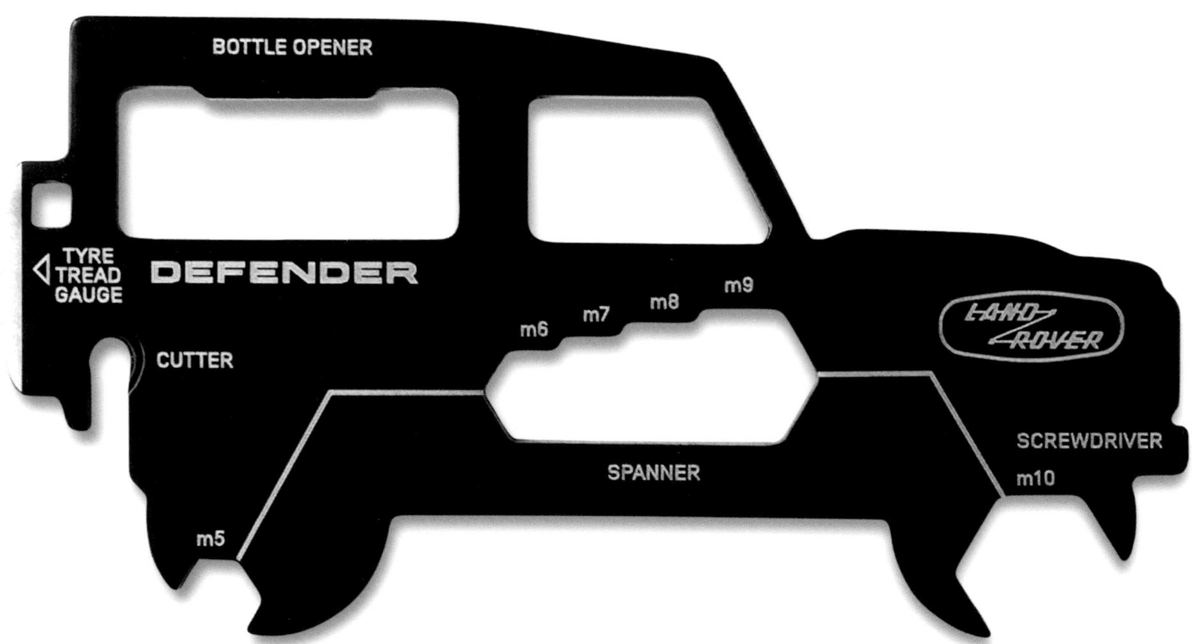

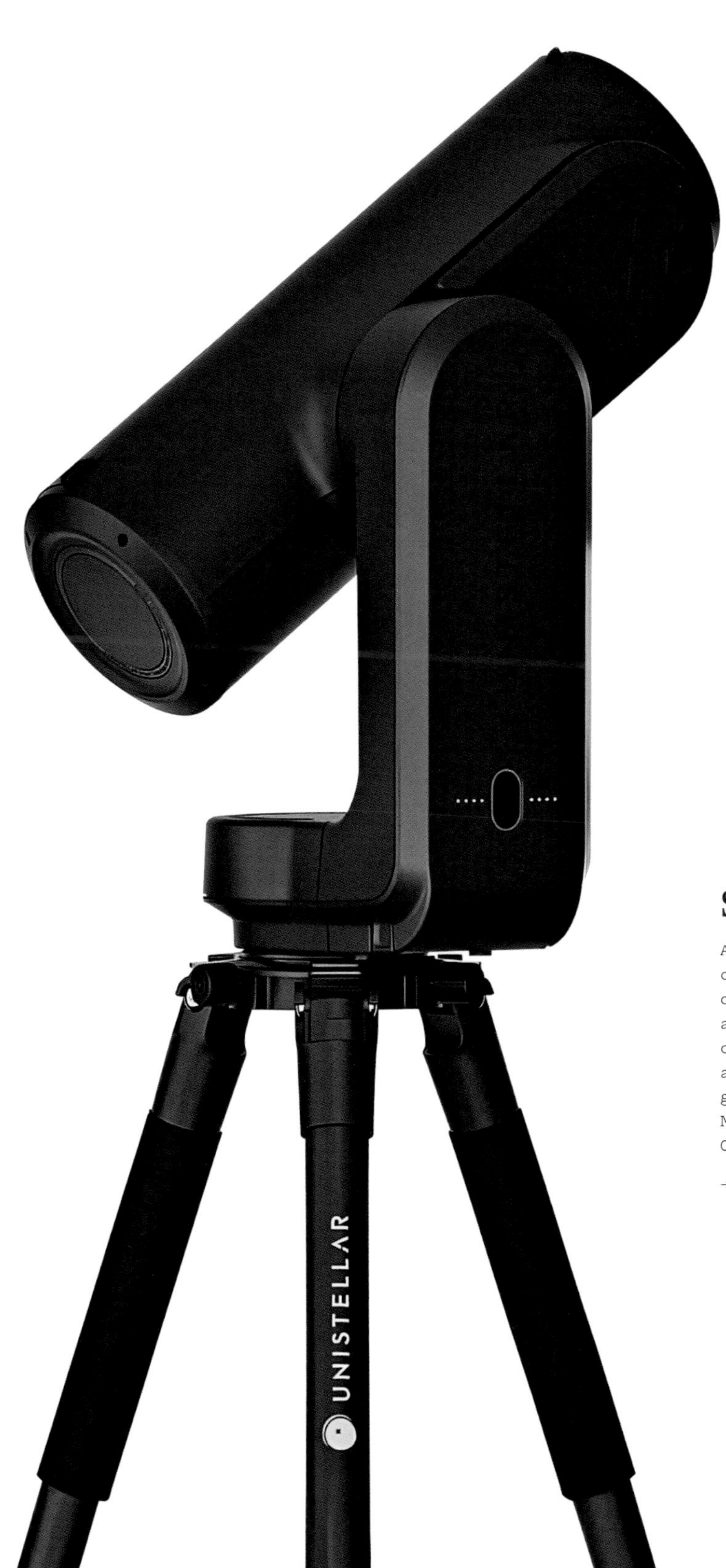

STARSTRUCK

According to a more or less recent survey conducted by the dating app Tinder, almost one in three users between the ages of 18 and 24 believes that astrology has a significant influence on their love life. The study also revealed that Virgos, Gemini and Libra get the most matches. Well, what can you say? Maybe just this: What you see here is the Odyssey portable telescope.

→ unistellar.com

quality time

TEXT *Michael Köckritz*

4.02

WE ARE LIVING IN A WORLD THAT IS RAPIDLY ACCELERATING INTO THE FUTURE, BECOMING MORE DYNAMIC AND COMPLEX THAN EVER BEFORE. EVERYTHING IS CHANGING, GETTING FASTER.

AND US, RIGHT IN THE MIDDLE OF IT.

An increasing number of things is happening in an increasingly short amount of time. The accelerations of our knowledge and communication society serve as a guiding principle here, always tempting with new options that fill our lives even more, even as an endless onslaught of new needs demand our attention and energy. The result of this modern pace of life is that time is always in short supply. We are constantly running out of time.

It's important to note that our lives are shaped by the way we deal with time. If we were to live our lives in sync with our biorhythm, a day would have more than just twenty-four hours – it would have twenty-five. And that twenty-fifth hour would be pure luxury – as time itself is increasingly experienced as a luxury good these days.

Time, according to sociologist and time researcher Karlheinz Geißler, is for humans what water is for fish. We swim in time without thinking about what it is that we are actually moving through. But as humans – and this is the big difference between us and fish – we have the ability to contemplate the element through which we move. And the truth is: people don't have time – we are time. So saving time actually means saving your own life.

The more we experience, the longer a period of time appears when looking back. When we have exciting experiences, time seems to fly by.

But what is time? "When it comes to time, scientists quickly reach the end of their abilities," says Geißler. "They don't even know what time really is." But this not-knowing, he goes on to say, does not stop the various disciplines from defining time according to their respective needs. For physicists, time is a fundamental variable, while social scientists regard it as a way of bringing order to the impermanent. For economists, the matter is quite simple; they cite Benjamin Franklin: "Time is money." Philosophers see this question as related to the nature of time – and offer some very divergent answers. To ask, "What is time?" is, according to Wittgenstein, not even a meaningful question. Kant, on the other hand, does provide an answer in his transcendental philosophy: he sees time as a pure form of intuition. "Time is a necessary representation, lying at the foundation of all our intuitions. [...] Time is therefore given a priori. In it alone is all reality of phenomena possible."

Albert Einstein also had his answer: "Time is what you measure with a clock." What may at first seem like a rather flippant response is in truth an expression of his years of grappling with the principles of space and time. This pragmatic approach was in fact key to developing the theory of relativity, which introduced a radical rethinking of what space and time actually are. By simply looking at the clock, it became possible to ignore all subjective elements so that only the measurable counts.

"Time is life, because I can only experience myself in time," said the psychologist and biologist Marc Wittmann. Together with colleagues, he succeeded in identifying the insular lobe – a specific area of the cerebral cortex – as the primary centre for body awareness. It's here that all the sensory input received at any given moment – feelings of cold, thirst, even emotions – merge with our awareness of time to create a sense of self. In other words, the way we perceive ourselves and the way we experience time are inextricably linked – the sensations originating in our own bodies set our biological clock.

As human beings, we have two ways of experiencing time: there's the experience of the moment, and then there's the retrospective recall. We vividly remember the many "first times" in our lives: our first kiss, our first party, our first car.

The more we experience, the longer a period of time appears when looking back. When we have exciting experiences, time seems to fly by. To "extend" our lives, therefore, all we have to do is break through the routines and give new experiences a chance.

But first we need to know how people spend their time and what sorts of things are important to them. Studies have shown that we have five modes of time that fundamentally define how we go through the day.

"Quality time" refers to the time we take for ourselves, for family and friends and for our hobbies. During "productive time", we work. "Necessity time" is devoted to the obligations of our lives. And when we finally get to put the daily grind behind us, that's when we experience "down time". Finally, "transition time" refers to those times when we shift from one time mode to the next.

Ideally, we move with style and ease through all the exciting moments that time has to offer. Inspiration and experience, combined with time for ourselves, self-awareness and self-fulfillment. Then a world of personal discovery opens up, a space where we can encounter ourselves.

A glance at the right watch can certainly help to reinforce that feeling.

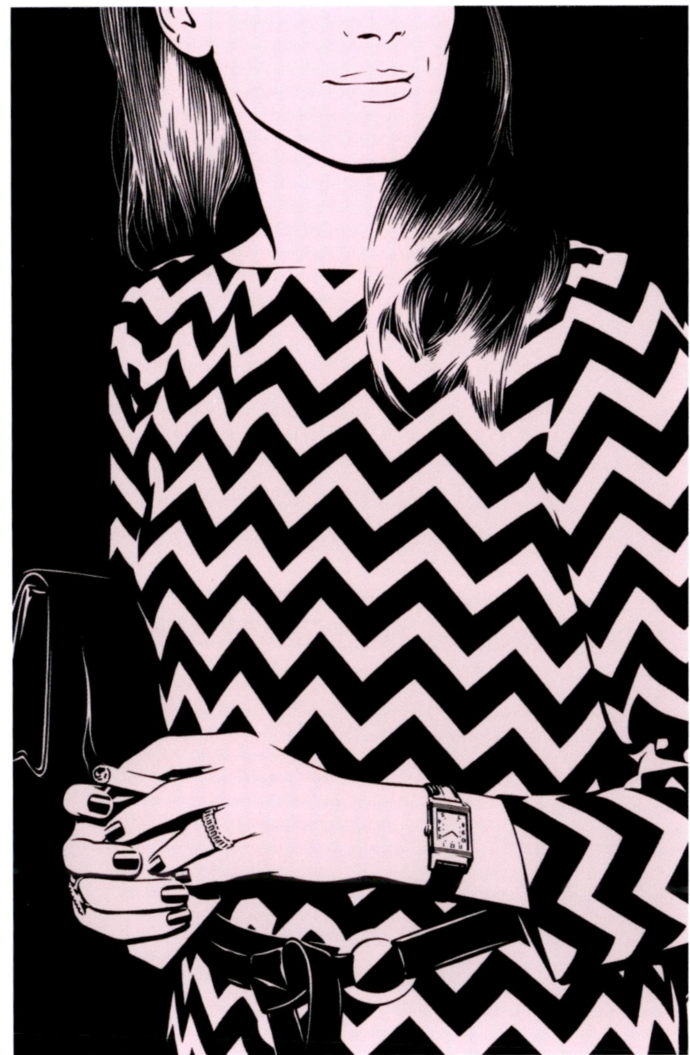

The result of our modern pace of life is that time is always in short supply. We are constantly running out of time.

play time

4.03

TEXT *Wiebke Brauer*
PHOTOS *Steffen Jahn*

WHEN WE WERE KIDS, WE WOULD SIT DOWN WITH OUR TOY CARS ALL AFTERNOON AND FORGET THE TIME. WHICH IS UNLIKELY TO HAPPEN WITH THESE WATCHES – THOUGH IT IS NO LESS ENJOYABLE.

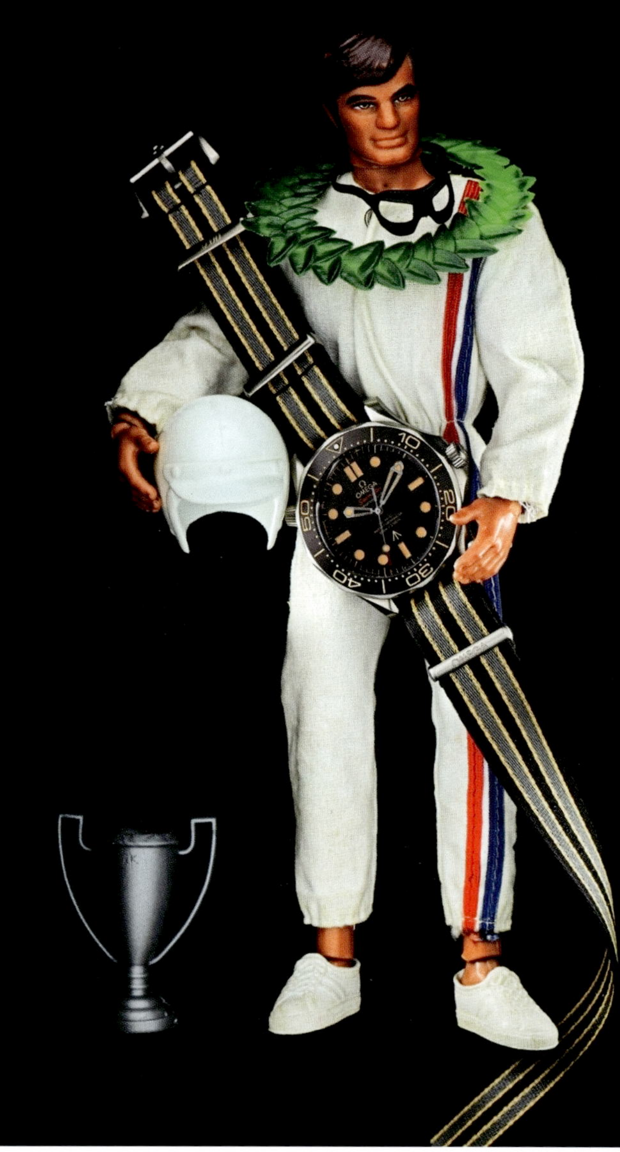

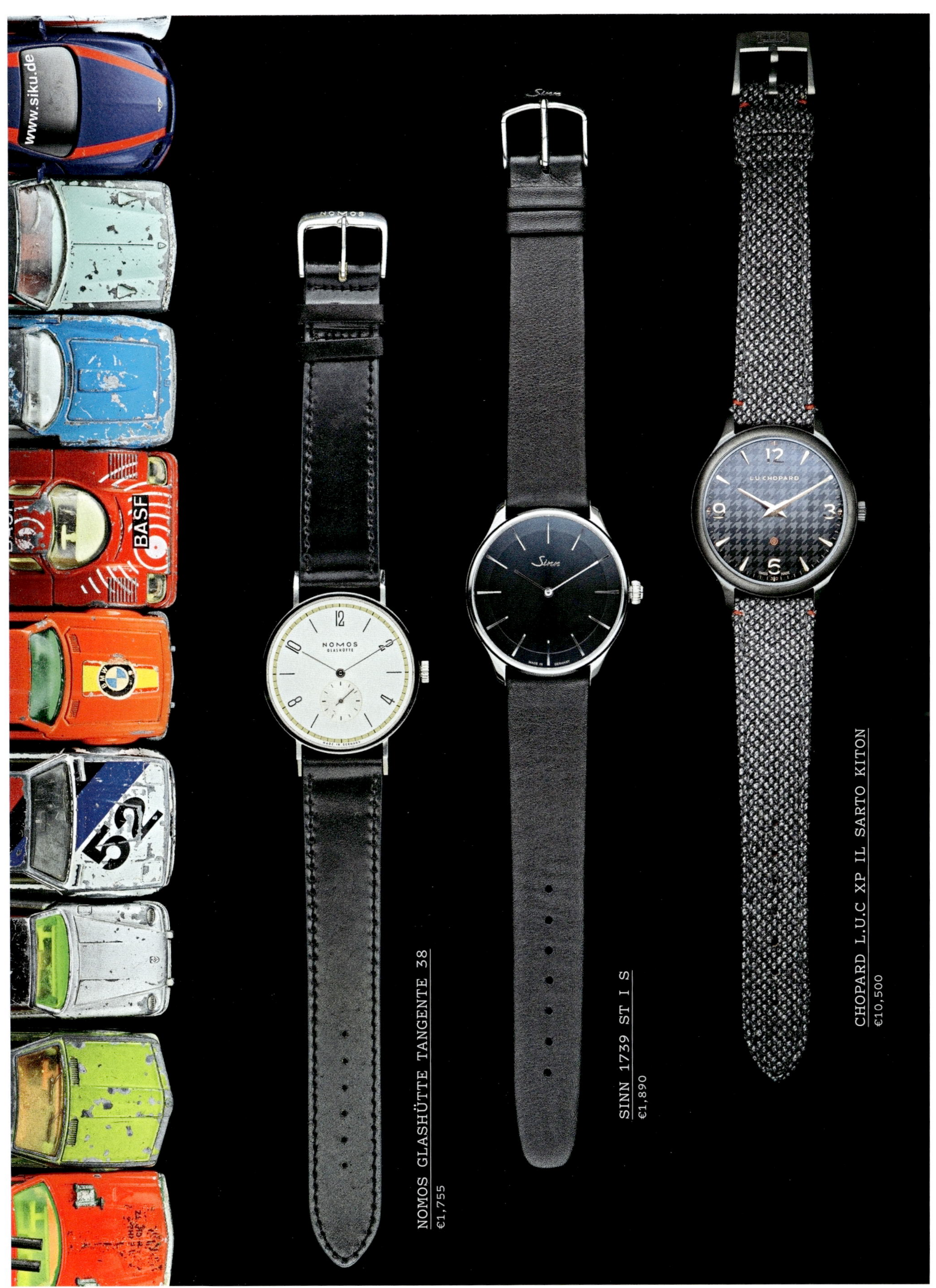

NOMOS GLASHÜTTE TANGENTE 38
€1,755

SINN 1739 ST I S
€1,890

CHOPARD L.U.C XP IL SARTO KITON
€10,500

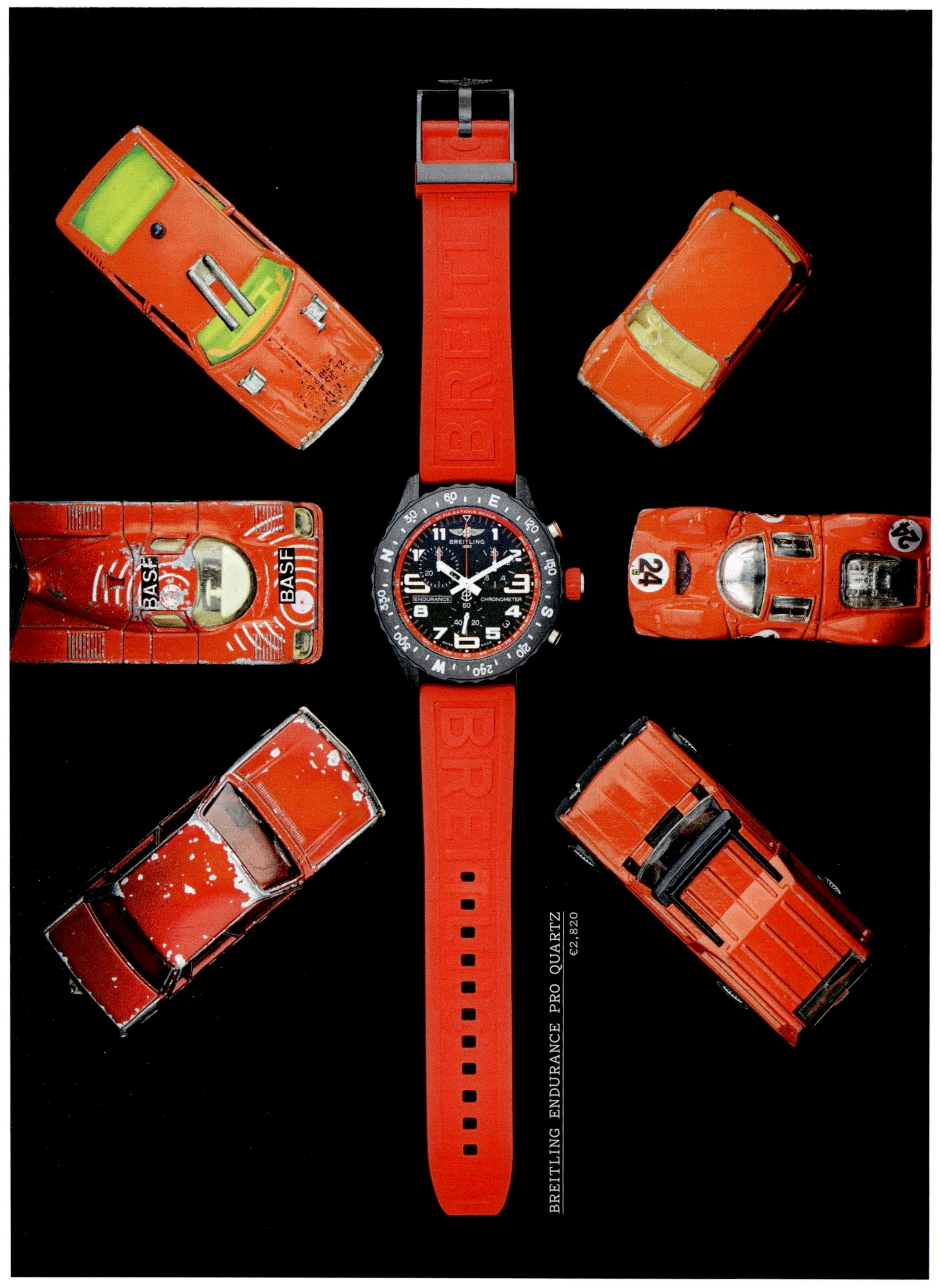

BREITLING ENDURANCE PRO QUARTZ
€2,820

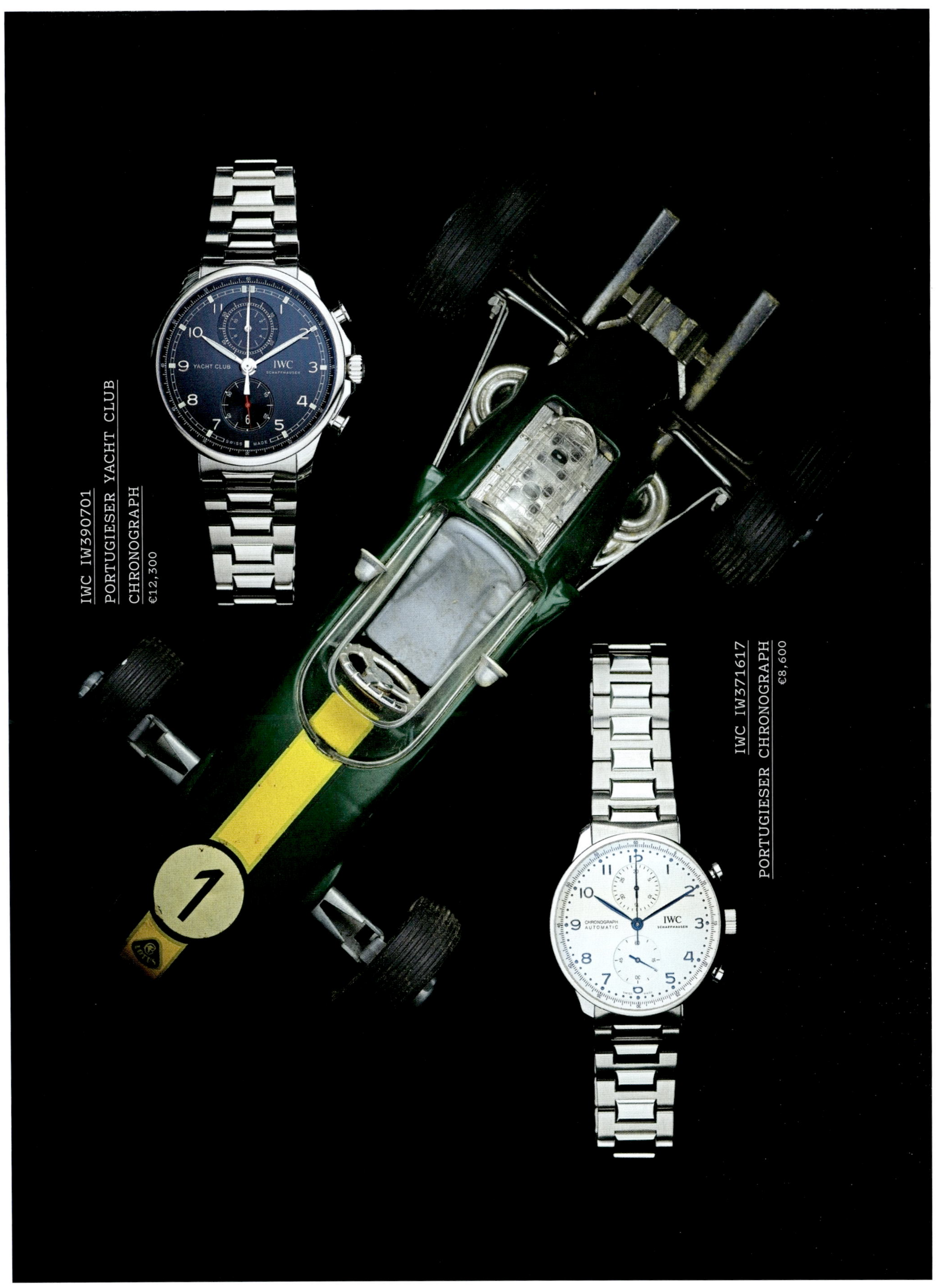

IWC IW390701
PORTUGIESER YACHT CLUB
CHRONOGRAPH
€12,300

IWC IW371617
PORTUGIESER CHRONOGRAPH
€8,600

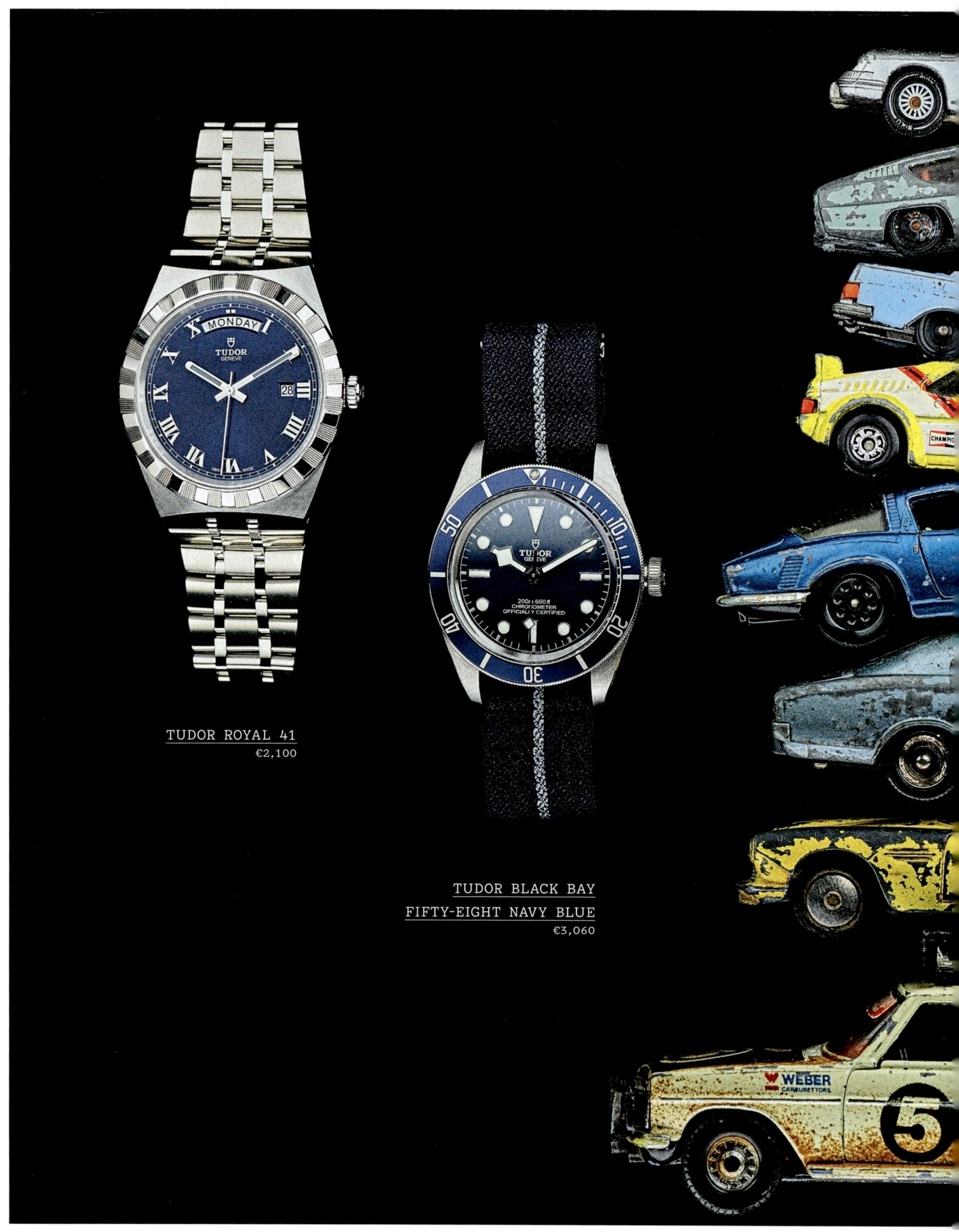

TUDOR ROYAL 41
€2,100

TUDOR BLACK BAY
FIFTY-EIGHT NAVY BLUE
€3,060

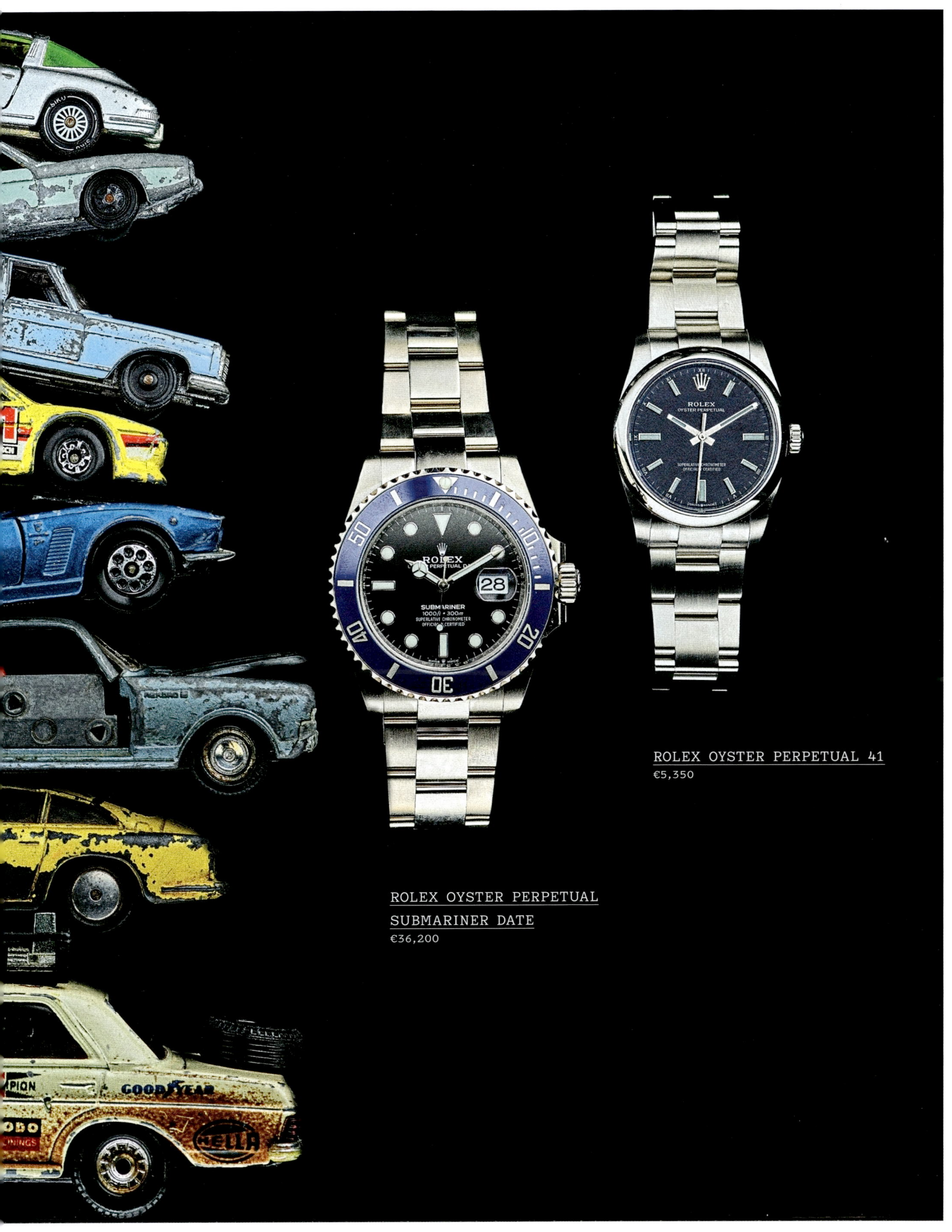

ROLEX OYSTER PERPETUAL 41
€5,350

ROLEX OYSTER PERPETUAL
SUBMARINER DATE
€36,200

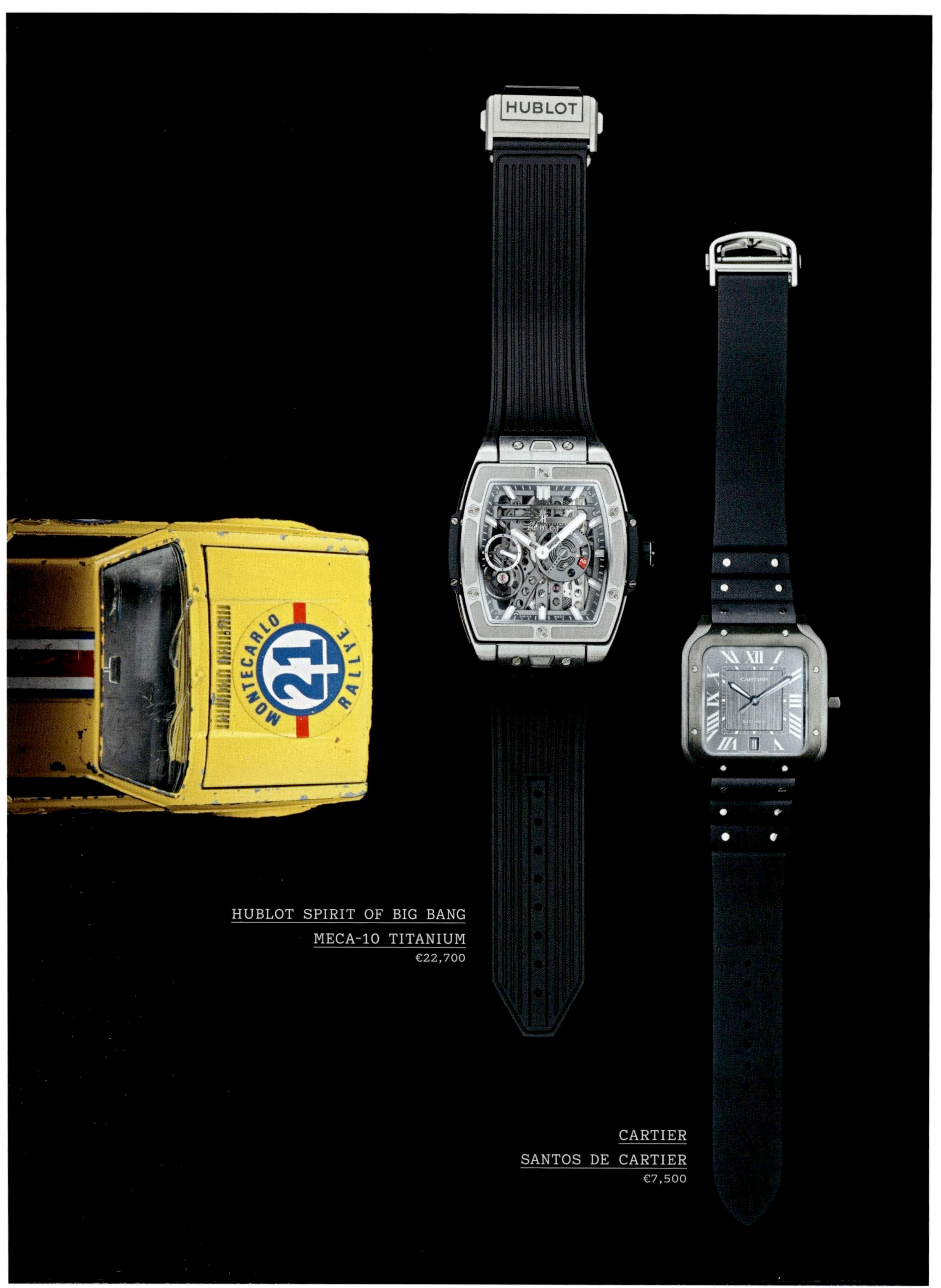

HUBLOT SPIRIT OF BIG BANG
MECA-10 TITANIUM
€22,700

CARTIER
SANTOS DE CARTIER
€7,500

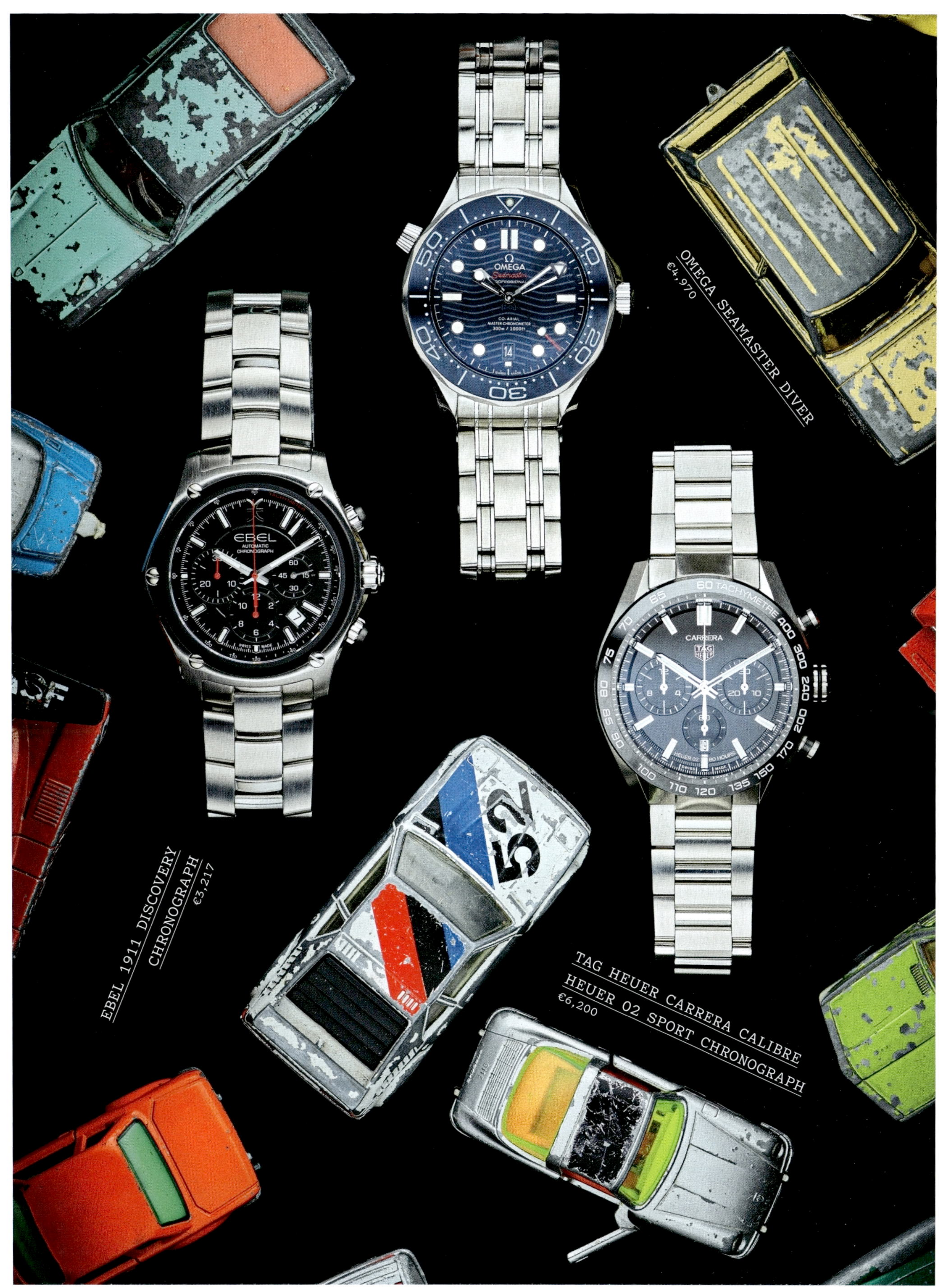

OMEGA SEAMASTER DIVER
€4,970

EBEL 1911 DISCOVERY CHRONOGRAPH
€3,217

TAG HEUER CARRERA CALIBRE HEUER 02 SPORT CHRONOGRAPH
€6,200

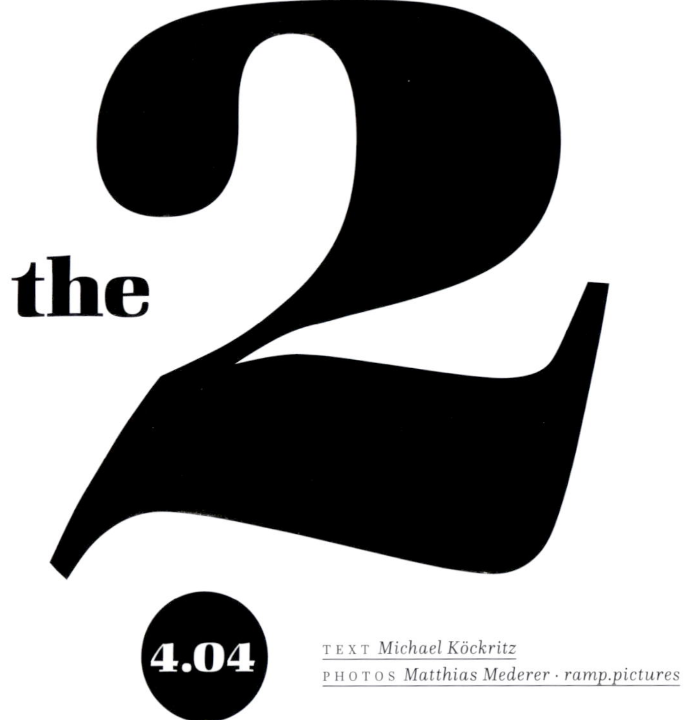

TEXT *Michael Köckritz*
PHOTOS *Matthias Mederer · ramp.pictures*

THERE ARE CARS THAT MAKE YOU STOP THINKING IN CATEGORIES.

WHERE REASON AND EMOTION NOD TO EACH OTHER AND SAY: YOUR TURN TODAY.

JUST A BRIEF WARM-UP TO A LOVE LETTER DEDICATED TO TWO VERY SPECIAL SPORTS CARS.

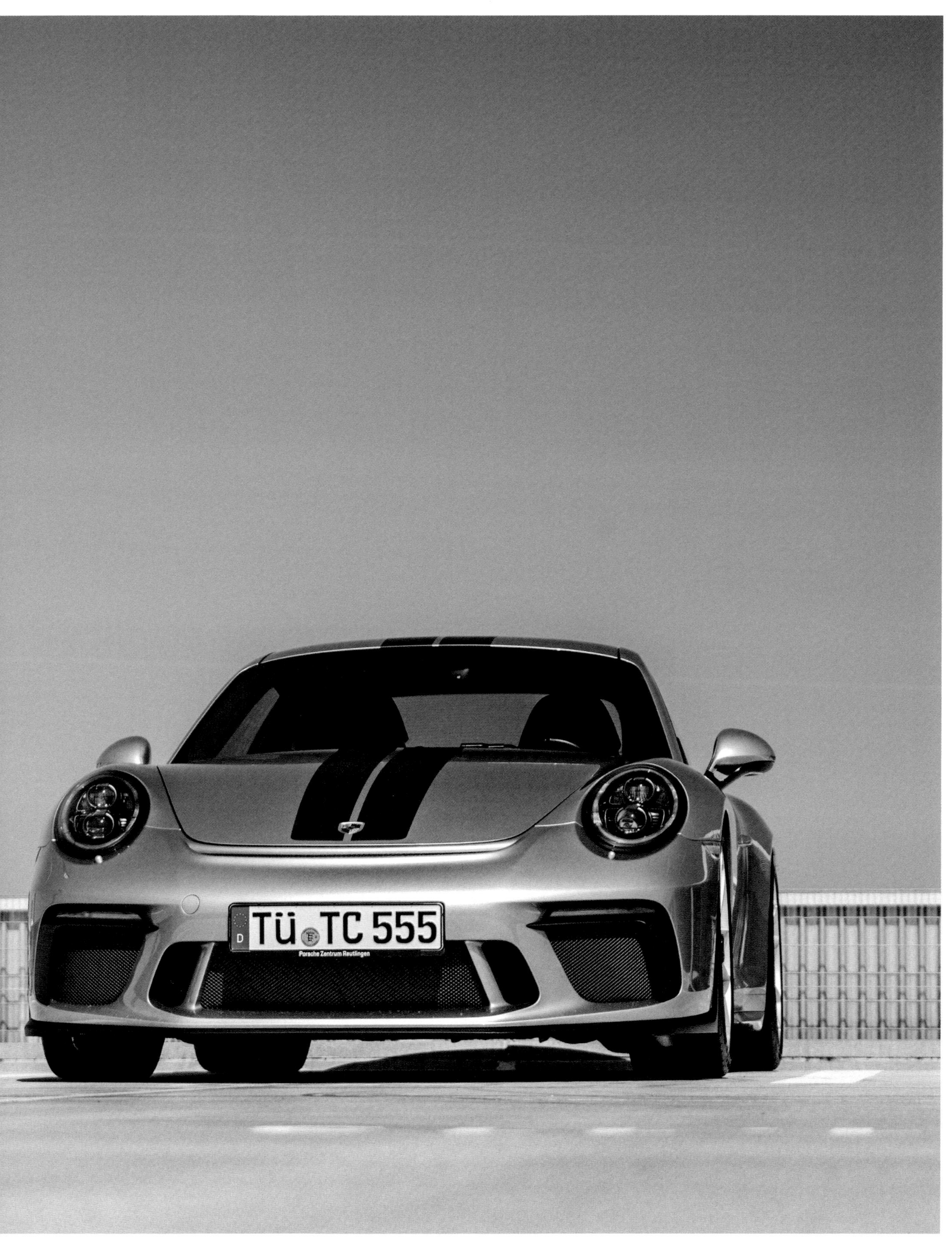
Tü TC 555
Porsche Zentrum Reutlingen

Their names: Porsche 911 Turbo S and Porsche 911 GT3 Touring. Both 991.2. Both, in their own way, pure and uncompromising interpretations of what a 911 can be – neither in need of constant evolutionary updates to validate the idea. The 991.2 here serves as the perfect modern base: more compact, lighter, more direct than its successor, the 992. Less digitalized, less "locked in" by technology and algorithms. It allows more freedom, more play, more connection. And both are so different that they reflect each other – like two sides of the same truth. Two ways, in short, to be real. But let's take it step by step.

THE PORSCHE TURBO S – THE EASE OF SUPREMACY

You can show power – or simply have it. The Turbo S has it, and smiles. It's the leader, not the loud one. The grand seigneur of sports cars – charming, fast, effortless. A sports car that never insists on attention yet is always there when you need it. It has nothing to prove, and that's its strongest argument. You get in, and everything feels . . . right. The seat as an extension of your body, the leather not an accessory but a mood. Start the engine, and the world falls into place. Not loud, not rushed.

More like a deep breath.

The Turbo S lives its supercar status with understatement. It wears its power like a tailored suit – perfectly cut, never showy, never strained. Its all-wheel drive glues the road to your consciousness, its dual-clutch transmission thinks faster than you can feel.

And yet it remains a pure 911: powerful, compact, raw.

Some cars scream when they're fast. The Turbo S whispers, hoarsely. The 580 hp aren't an attack, but a quiet promise between friends. One push of the pedal and the world contracts. The Turbo S accelerates as if careful not to disturb itself. Zero to 100 km/h in 2.9 seconds – but numbers don't tell you how effortlessly that feels. How cultivated. The pulse stays polite. Serenity at 330 km/h.

That's not coldness. That's cool. That's style. And it sets the standard. It's the automotive equivalent of someone at a dinner party who knows all the best stories but doesn't tell them. Because he doesn't have to. The Turbo S is triumph over noise. A car you don't choose to impress others, but to find your own peace. Composure, speed, perfection – all wrapped in refined design. A sports car that doesn't demand, but understands. And, after a long drive, leaves you feeling that life isn't about speed – it's about balance.

Some cars scream when they're fast. The Turbo S whispers, hoarsely. The 580 hp aren't an attack, but a quiet promise between friends.

THE GT3 TOURING – THE GRAVITY OF PASSION

If the Turbo S is the gentleman, the GT3 Touring is the romantic. Someone who's not afraid to get his hands dirty. Who knows that passion doesn't work when it's filtered. Anyone who drives the GT3 Touring knows: true passion doesn't need wings.

It's the opposite of show. It's substance.

You slip inside and instantly know: nothing here is superfluous. No all-wheel

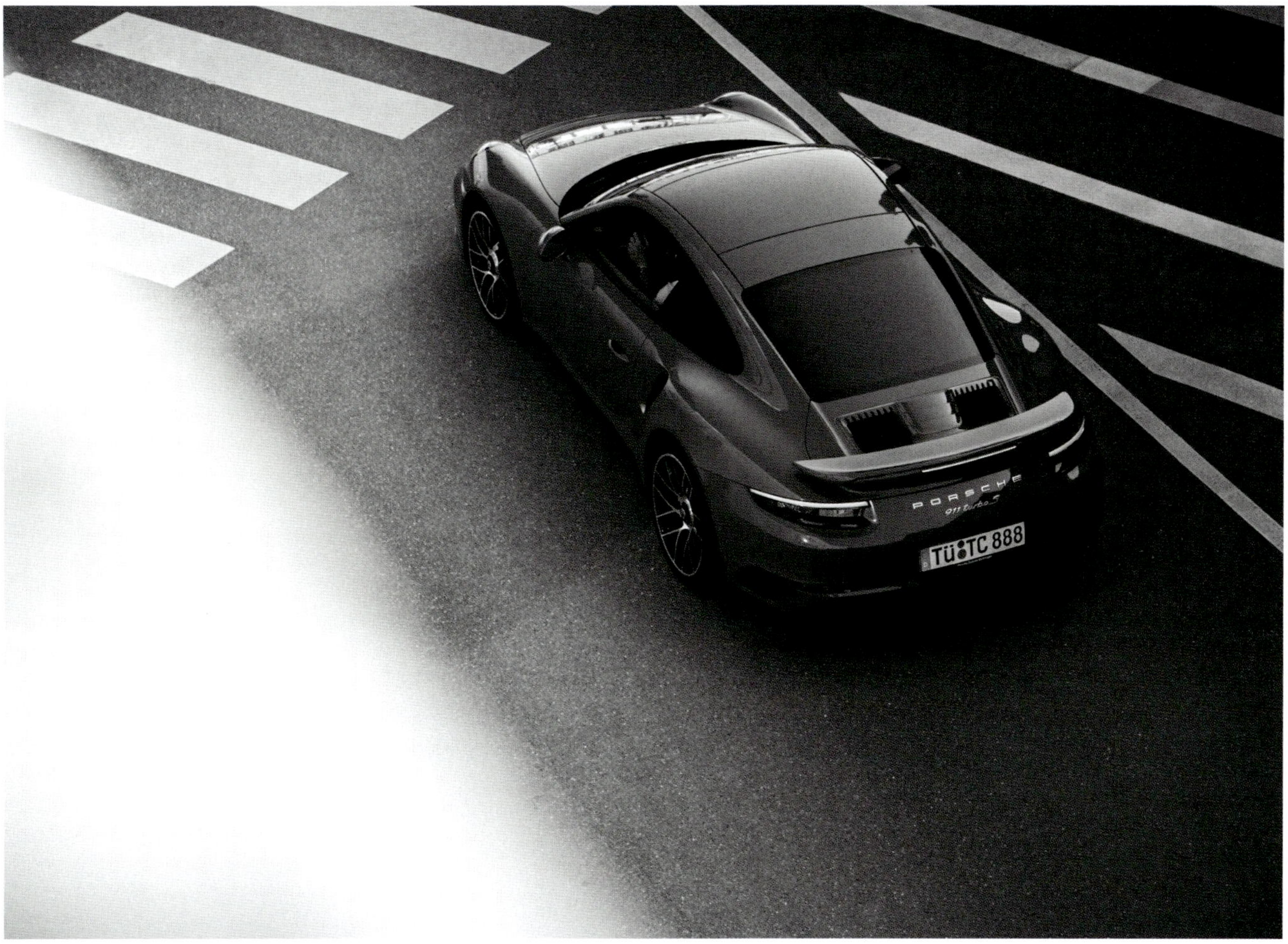

Start the engine, and the world falls into place. Not loud, not rushed. More like a deep breath.

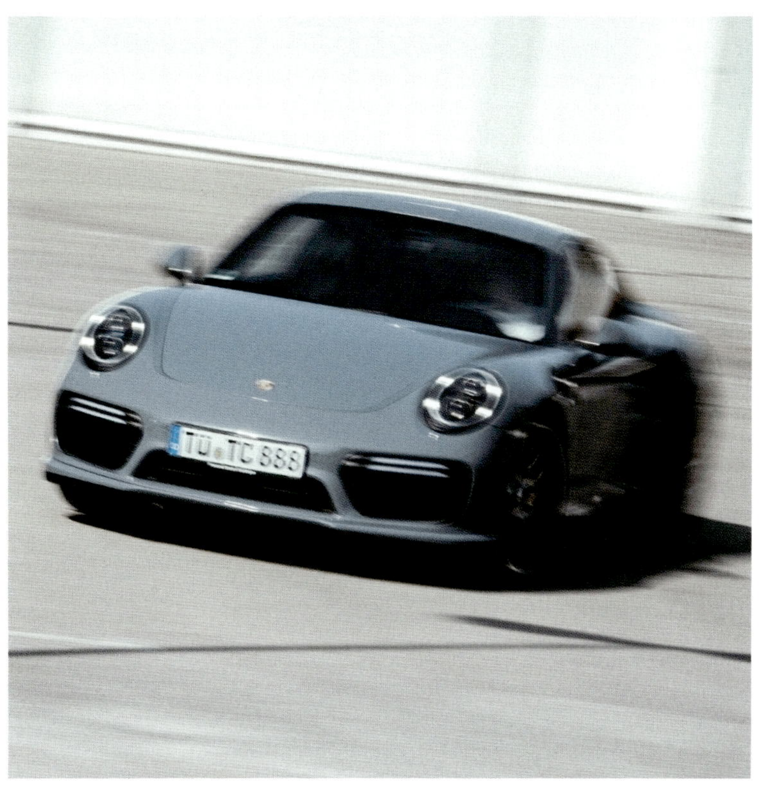

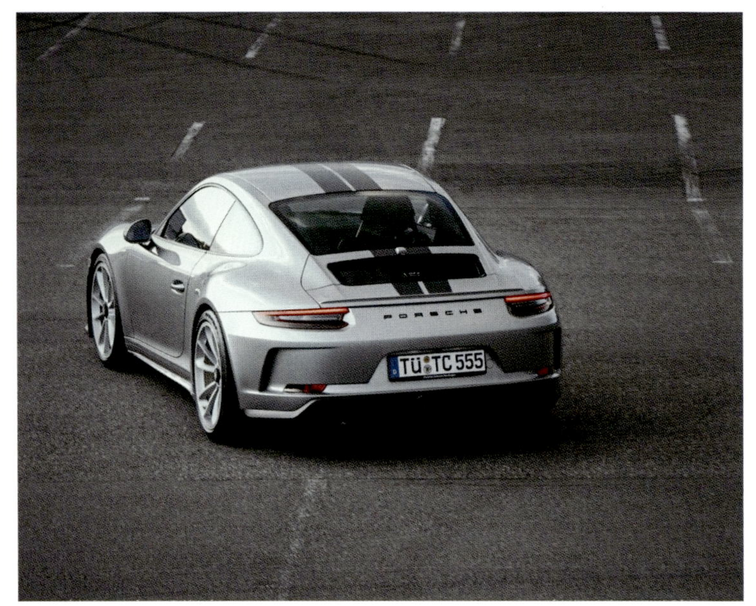
PORSCHE
TÜ TC 555

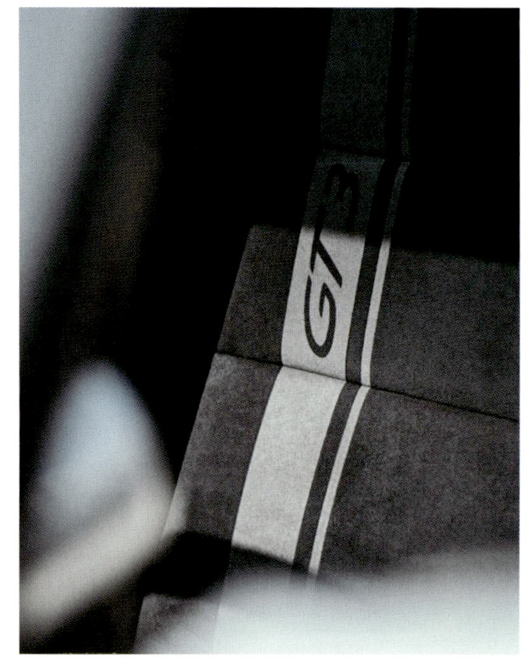
GT3

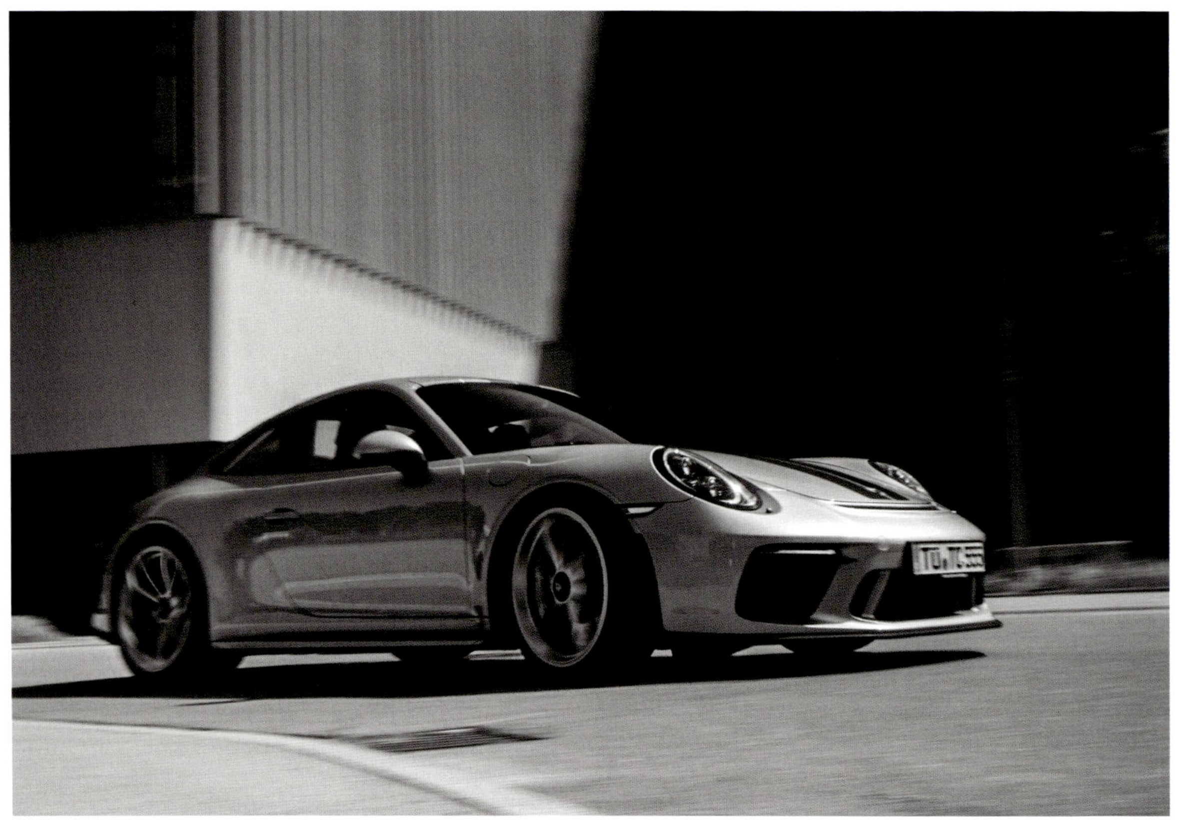

tricks, no turbo, no flash. Just a naturally aspirated flat-six that howls at 9,000 rpm like an opera house on speed after midnight. A clutch pedal that signals the seriousness of the occasion, a manual gearbox that clicks like a perfectly timed punchline – this is the most analog Porsche you can buy today. The GT3 Touring isn't a car for chasing seconds – it's for living moments. The steering wheel trembles slightly, the road speaks. And you respond – with feeling, not force. Nothing about it is synthetic. Everything is in tune. Every reaction direct. A car that doesn't just drive, but communicates. It smells of asphalt, not algorithms. It resonates – with the road, with yourself.

The GT3 Touring is the opposite of comfortable. It's pure. Direct. Intimate. It rewards those who understand it – and punishes multitasking. Because driving here isn't consumption. It's conversation. An intense dialogue between man and machine, full of trust, tension, tenderness. Always on point. Always. The GT3 Touring is conviction on wheels. A return to essence: driving as language, not as a numbers game.

It's what remains when you strip away everything unnecessary – and thus have everything. A sports car that doesn't aim to impress but to move you. Perhaps that's the greatest irony: the GT3 Touring is ascetic – yet pure sensuality. It's gloriously loud, never annoyingly noisy. Honest, because it promises nothing it can't deliver. It reminds us that joy in driving is serious business – and beautiful for exactly that reason.

CONCLUSION – TWO SIDES OF ONE TRUTH

You shouldn't play them off against each other. The cultivated Turbo S, sounding like an aria on velvet. The authentic GT3 Touring, turning every mile into a front-row hard rock concert. Two extreme interpretations of the same idea. The one: a perfect all-rounder that can do everything and needs nothing. The other: a purist that forgives nothing and gives it everything. The Turbo S, the philosophical comment on modernity: acceleration, control, mastery. The GT3 Touring, its psychological counterpoint: experience, immediacy, dialogue. Both are etched deeply into pop culture – as symbols of an attitude, a freedom, an idea beyond engineering.

Both – the Turbo S and the GT3 Touring – are more than just cars. They're manifestations of desire. A canvas on which we project power, youth, beauty, freedom and defiance. Icons that show what happens when you turn the unnecessary into the essential. Both are highly entertaining proof that perfection speaks many languages – and sounds best when it's called Porsche. Because in the end, it's not about faster or prettier. It's about the deeply personal feeling behind it all. About what feels real to you. And the most honest answer to which one to choose is probably: both.

No all-wheel tricks, no turbo, no flash. Just a naturally aspirated flat-six that howls at 9,000 rpm like an opera house on speed.

And besides:

The best car is a fast one. And the best argument for a sports car is that it doesn't need one.

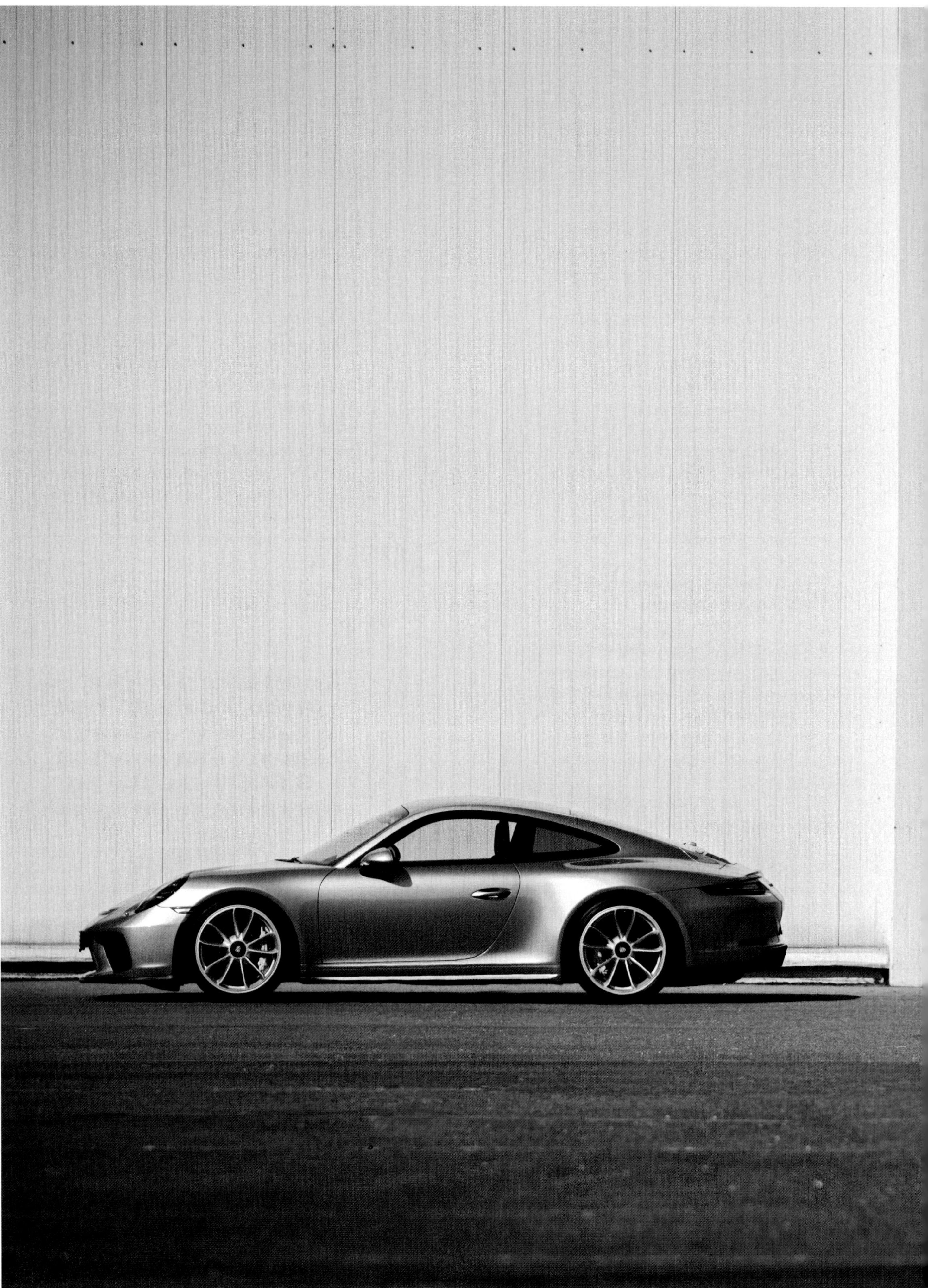

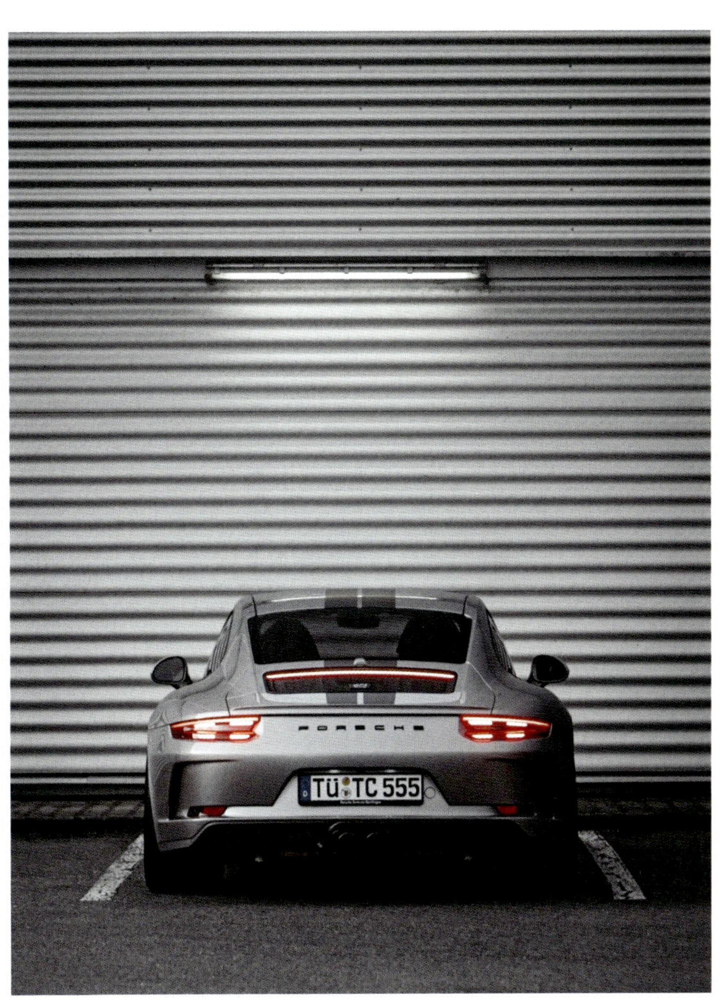

Porsche 911 GT3 Touring (991.2)

ENGINE	naturally aspirated flat-six boxer
DISPLACEMENT	3,996 cc
POWER	500 hp (368 kW) at 8,250 rpm
TORQUE	460 Nm at 6,000 rpm
WEIGHT	1,505 kg
0-100 KM/H	3.9 s
TOP SPEED	316 km/h

Porsche 911 Turbo S (991.2)

ENGINE	twin-turbocharged flat-six boxer
DISPLACEMENT	3,800 cc
POWER	580 hp (427 kW) at 6,750 rpm
TORQUE	700 Nm at 2,100-4,250 rpm
WEIGHT	1,675 kg
0-100 KM/H	2.9 s
TOP SPEED	330 km/h

Admiration apparently consists of surprise associated with some pleasure and a sense of approval.

*To err is human.
For a real disaster, you need a computer.*

SOMEONE ACTUALLY ASKS ME, "WAITING FOR THE ELEVATOR?"

So I say, "No, I'm waiting for the fourth floor to come down."

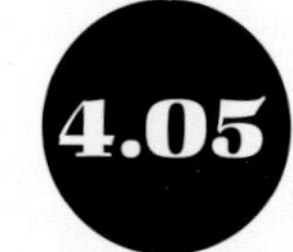

It's no drama if the project doesn't go according to plan. It's a drama if the project manager doesn't know about it.

PETER HOBBS, AUTHOR OF A BOOK ON PROJECT MANAGEMENT

***Panda: "I'd like a passport photo, please."
Photographer: "Black and white, or in color?"
Panda: "In the face, or upside the head?"***

**AS A CHILD:
"YOU'RE GROUNDED!"
AS AN ADULT:
"YOUR PACKAGE WILL ARRIVE SOMETIME BETWEEN 8 A.M. AND 6 P.M."**

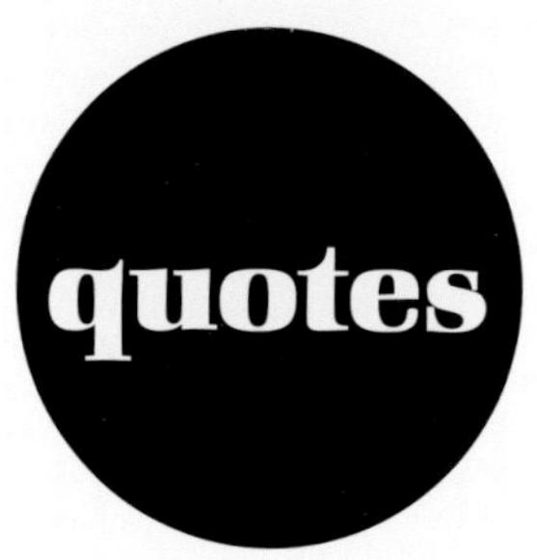

*Female friendship:
"I'm fat!"
"No way, girl, you're sexy!"
Male friendship:
"I'm fat!"
"Yeah, and ugly to boot!"*

***"Is this the seminar for subtle insults?"
"That's right, just grab two chairs and sit with us."***

Life is full of plot twists. Everything goes differently than expected and in the end you're surprised at how things turned out.

"I'M WORKING OUT NOW TOO. MEET MY NEW TRAINER."
"THAT'S A SOFA!"
"CORRECTION: PERSONAL COUCH."

FRIENDS ARE PEOPLE WHO KNOW YOU REALLY WELL AND LIKE YOU ANYWAY.

"THE PROBLEM IS NOT THE PROBLEM. THE PROBLEM IS YOUR ATTITUDE ABOUT THE PROBLEM."

CAPTAIN JACK SPARROW IN *PIRATES OF THE CARIBBEAN*

The biggest difference between men and women is the meaning of the phrase "What an ass!"

"Have you got one of those stepcounters too?"
"I'm starting slow. I have a motion detector."

THE MORE HUMAN BEINGS PROCEED BY PLAN, THE MORE EFFECTIVELY THEY MAY BE HIT BY ACCIDENT.

FRIEDRICH DÜRRENMATT

AT THE JOB INTERVIEW: "HOW WOULD YOU DESCRIBE YOURSELF?" "VERBALLY, BUT I'VE ALSO PREPARED A DANCE."

A woman comes out of the dressing room crying, "It's too small!"
Her husband says, "The shirt or the dressing room?"
Death was instantaneous.

I have noticed that even those who assert that everything is predestined and that we can change nothing about it still look both ways before they cross the street.

STEPHEN HAWKING

4.06

hard facts

EVERYTHING YOU SHOULD MORE OR LESS KNOW

Koi No Yokan

Let's leave good old Freud out of this completely. It's complicated enough as it is. We're talking about love. When it comes to the Japanese concept of *koi no yokan*, however, things are a bit different. Unfortunately, the phrase has no direct English translation, but what *koi no yokan* describes is a kind of premonition, the sense that upon first meeting someone that you will inevitably fall in love with them. Even before

A Premonition of Love

Japanese (n.)
[ko-ee no yo-kan]

the first feeling of infatuation sets in, even before love at first sight. And because it is such a wonderful thing, it needs no translation and can just stand on its own.

But as always with Asian characters, caution is advised if you're thinking about getting the phrase tattooed somewhere on your body. So, to be on the safe side, here's the correct spelling:

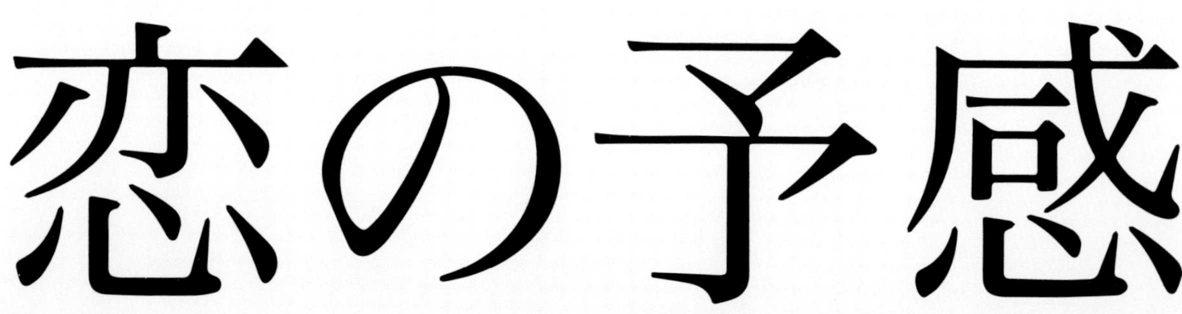

YOU MUST REMEMBER THIS

How exactly are memories formed? A significant role, according to the latest research, is played by so-called head direction cells, neurons found in our brain that enable us to create an image of the direction in which our head is facing. This "inner compass" apparently also plays a key role in the formation of memories.

Brain researchers at the University of Tübingen found that the head direction cells in the thalamus play an important role in the reception and subsequent transmission of sensory information, states of attention, and arousal to the episodic memory system. This is where memories of past events are stored.

Further research is currently underway to determine whether these insights can be used for therapeutic purposes, for example by learning how to better form and recall memories in a targeted manner.

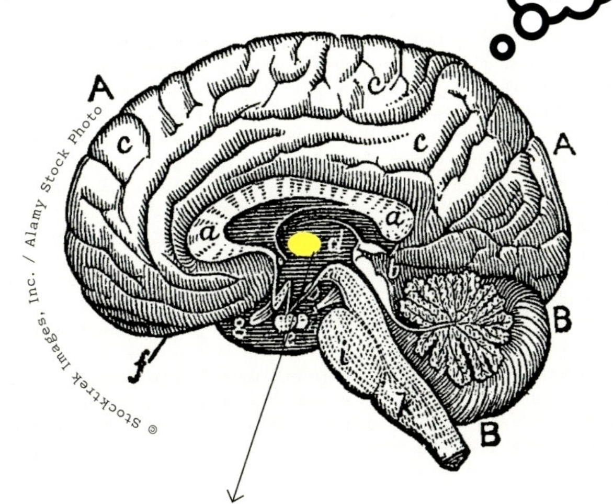

The Thalamus

This large mass of gray matter is also known as the "gateway to consciousness" because this is where all sensory impressions are collected and passed on to the cerebral cortex.

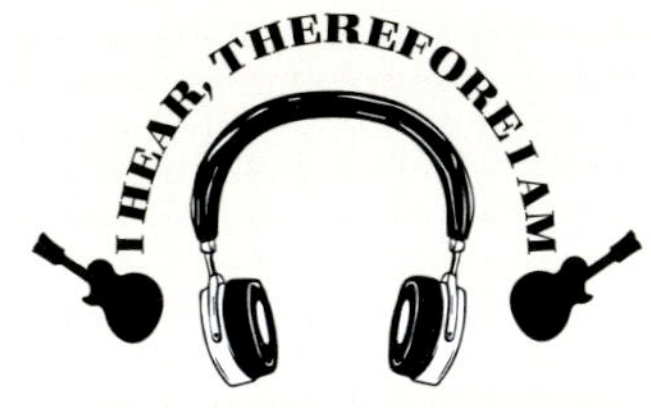

GREG GONZALEZ AND CIGARETTES AFTER SEX RECOMMENDS:

DOIGTS
Françoise Hardy

*

BY YOUR SIDE
Sade

*

YOU'RE LOST LITTLE GIRL
The Doors

*

NO DIGAS NADA
Pic-Nic

Smells Like Teen Spirit

How we rate our favorite songs based on when the song came out

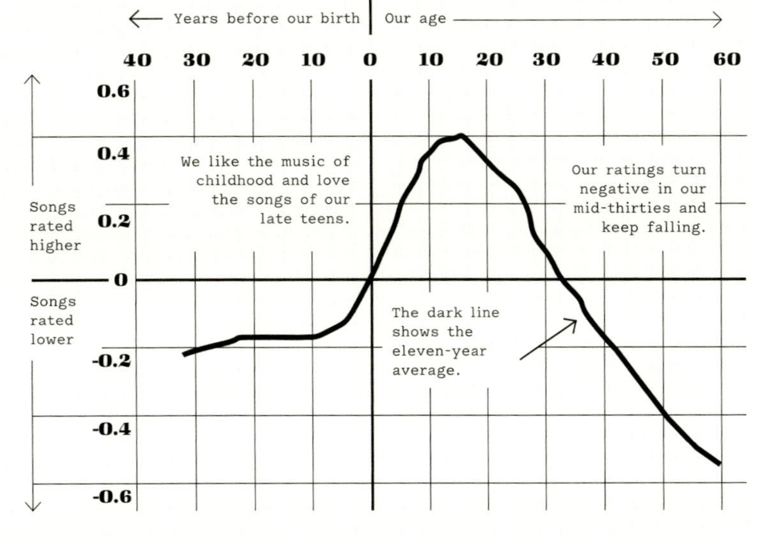

EMOTIONAL CARTOGRAPHY

Happiness Love Surprise Fear Sadness Depression

Emotions are all in your head? Nonsense! When something moves us emotionally, whether it's anger, a surprise or great joy, we feel it physically from our head to the tips of our toes. In an experiment involving 761 people, neuroscientist Lauri Nummenmaa and his team at Aalto University in Finland produced a map showing where emotions are experienced in the body.

Increased activity Decreased activity  Neutral

WOW, WHO WOULDA THUNK IT?

Research shows: being surprised can help you learn. The more surprised someone is about the difference between what they've learned and their own expectations, the greater the learning effect. In other words: if you have no assumptions about something, you won't remember anything.

Feeling stressed? Calm yourself down with the 4-7-8 breathing technique*

1. Position your tongue towards the roof of your mouth, with the tip of the tongue touching the back of your two front teeth.
2. Breathe out deeply until your lungs are completely empty.
3. Now inhale slowly through your nose for **4 seconds**.
4. Hold your breath for **7 seconds**, staying calm and relaxed.
5. Exhale forcefully and noisily through your mouth for **8 seconds** with your lips slightly pursed around your tongue.

Repeat three more times.

* This exercise has its roots in the ancient yogic practice of pranayama. The aim of 4-7-8 breathing is to bring our mind in harmony with the body by focusing on regulating our breath. This can activate our parasympathetic nervous system, which is responsible for the body's "rest and digest" functions. The technique can also help when you're having trouble falling asleep.

The Center of Fear

You've probably heard of the amygdala before, a pair of almond-shaped clusters at the center of our brain that plays a role in fear conditioning. More specifically, whenever fear, anxiety or aggression are involved, the amygdala is there.

Using animal models, researchers have shown that a missing amygdala results in a complete loss of fear and aggression (but also increased sexual activity). More recent experiments have demonstrated that the amygdala also plays a role in facial recognition. In one experiment, a monkey with a missing amygdala withdrew socially, possibly because it could no longer distinguish between friendly and unfriendly expressions on the other monkeys' faces.

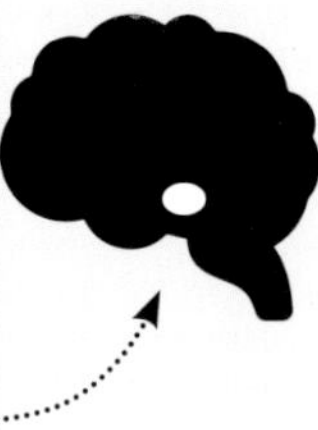

What I do when I don't understand what someone said

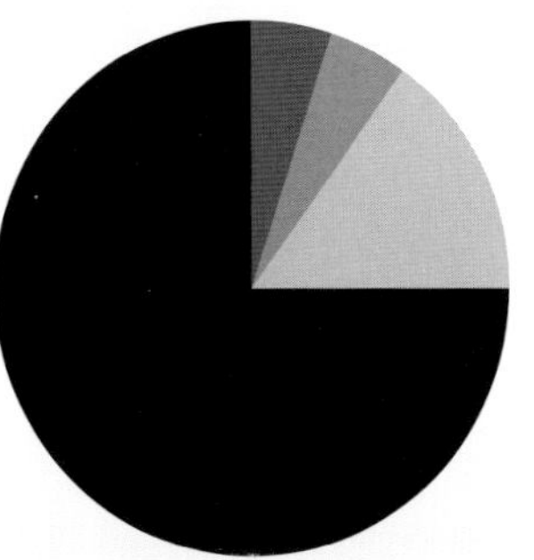

Coffee to know

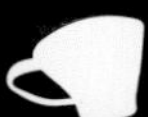

Drinking coffee after studying boosts memory retention, as a group of researchers led by Michael Yassa from Johns Hopkins University in Baltimore has found. But before you start running off to your espresso machine, there's something you should know: the effect cannot be increased indefinitely.

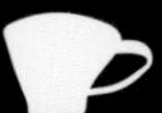

Methusalem macchiato

Coffee can prolong your life. A study conducted by the Harvard School of Public Health evaluated the health data of more than 200,000 people collected over the course of thirty years. The results show that coffee drinkers live longer than people who don't drink any coffee at all.

Caffeine kick

According to a study published in *The New England Journal of Medicine*, coffee drinkers move more. On the other hand, they also sleep less.

Coffee in, coffee out

Contrary to popular opinion, coffee actually doesn't dehydrate you. In fact, because coffee contains water, it may even be as hydrating as water or tea. The glass of water that is often served with your coffee is a nice gesture, but not necessary.

Stimulating substitutes

A study published in 2023 in *Frontiers in Behavioral Neuroscience* shows that the placebo effect involved in drinking coffee is greater than previously suspected. In other words, if it looks like coffee and smells like coffee, it will have a stimulating effect.

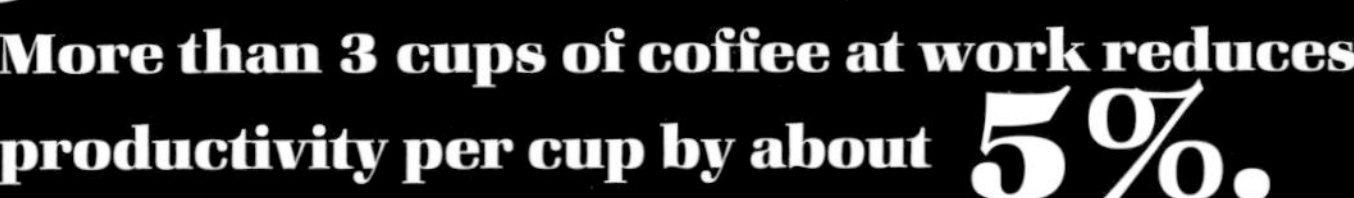

More than 3 cups of coffee at work reduces productivity per cup by about 5%.

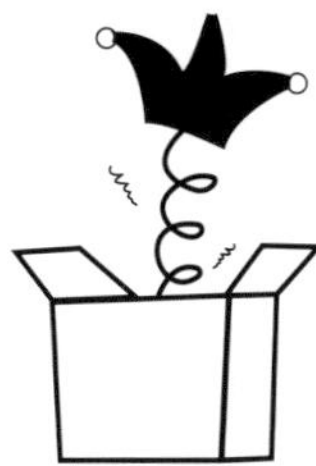

Jack-in-the-Box

Though tame by modern standards, the jack-in-the-box is the origin of the jump scare. For centuries, the figure of a jester popping out of a toy music box triggered in people the sort of surprise reaction that we usually experience while watching a horror movie alone at home.

Surprise Gifts

Women prefer to be surprised more than men. In a recent survey, **47%** of **women** said they would rather be surprised by a gift than receive something they had asked for.

Surprise Cake

If you've ever wanted to jump out of a cake for someone's birthday, you can **rent** one. Cost: around €180.

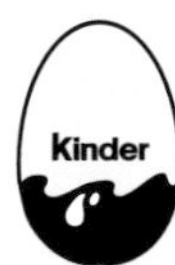

No Kinder Surprise

Kinder Surprise, the milk chocolate egg with a little toy inside, are illegal in the United States. That's because the Federal Food, Drug, and Cosmetic Act of 1938 prohibits confectionery products that contain a "non-nutritive object". As a result, Kinder Surprise eggs are extremely popular on the black market.

PUBLISHER
Michael Köckritz

EDITOR-IN-CHIEF/CREATIVE DIRECTOR
Michael Köckritz

COO/HEAD OF RAMP MEDIA HOUSE
Cedric Pfaus

DEPUTY CREATIVE DIRECTOR/ ART DIRECTOR
Philipp Gentner

GRAPHIC DESIGN
Carolin Watzlawik

PICTURE EDITOR
Antonietta Procopio

PROJECT MANAGEMENT
Julia Kamm

MANAGING EDITOR
Mario Puksec

CHIEF COPY EDITOR
Wiebke Brauer

EDITORIAL STAFF
Wiebke Brauer, Lutz Fügener, Bernd Haase, Marko Knab, Ulf Lippitz, Matthias Mederer, Kurt Molzer, David Staretz, Philipp Tingler, Martin Trockner, Burkhard Maria Zimmermann

TRANSLATION & LINGUISTIC REVIEW
Christoph von Pohl

MEDIA HOUSE
ramp.space GmbH & Co. KG
Obere Wässere 5
72764 Reutlingen
Team Assistant
Andrea von der Ruhr
T +49 7121 433 04 - 700
info@ramp-space.com
→ www.ramp.space

PRODUCTION, PRINTING AND BINDING
Production: bookwise GmbH, Munich
Printing: Lanarepro, Lana

ISBN 978-3-948046-30-9

gpsr@ramp-space.com

Cover: © Image courtesy of M+B and John Grannis

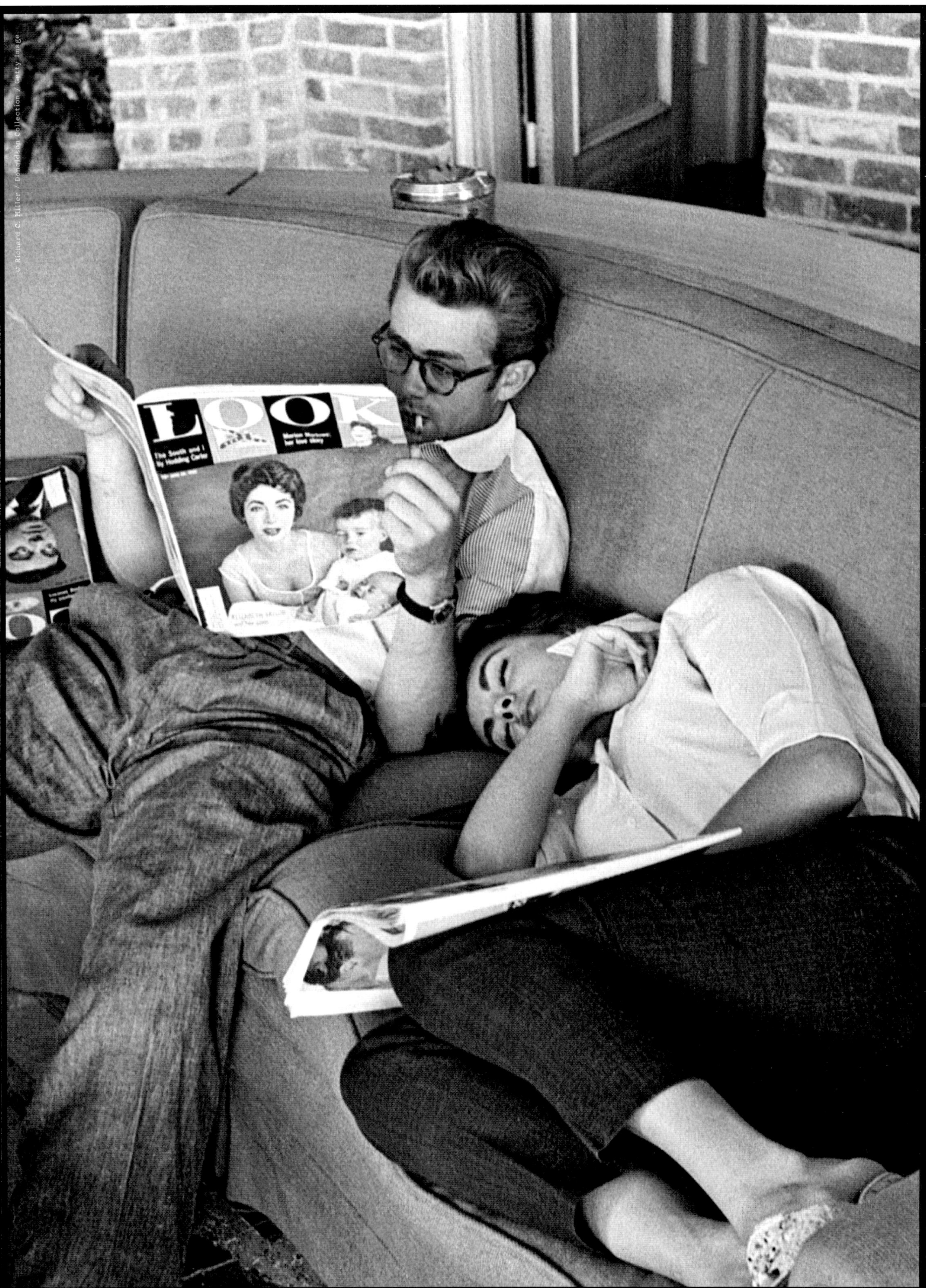
LOOK
The South and I
By Hodding Carter
Marilyn Monroe:
her love story

“When some-one tells me I can’t do some-thing, I do it even more.”

NICOLAS CAGE